MW00412286

Holocaust Film

Holocaust Film
The Political Aesthetics of Ideology

By

Terri Ginsberg

CAMBRIDGE SCHOLARS PUBLISHING

Holocaust Film: The Political Aesthetics of Ideology, by Terri Ginsberg

This book first published 2007 by

Cambridge Scholars Publishing

15 Angerton Gardens, Newcastle, NE5 2JA, UK

British Library Cataloguing in Publication Data
A catalogue record for this book is available from the British Library

Copyright © 2007 by Terri Ginsberg

All rights for this book reserved. No part of this book may be reproduced, stored in a retrieval system, or transmitted, in any form or by any means, electronic, mechanical, photocopying, recording or otherwise, without the prior permission of the copyright owner.

ISBN 1-84718-263-1; ISBN 13: 9781847182630

In memory of Sam and Lucille Fine

[F]ilm offers the possibility that some of this world can be explained, in the hope that no one will be forced to understand—to experience—such conditions again.

—Judith E. Doneson

TABLE OF CONTENTS

LIST OF IMAGES

ACKNOWLEDGMENTS

This book has been a long time in the making and could not have been completed without the help of friends and colleagues. Several of you took substantial time and effort to offer invaluable critical commentary and editorial suggestions at various stages and incarnations of this project: David Slocum, Joanna Zylinska, Dorota Glowacka, Marcia England, Gabriele Griffin, Esther Rothblum, Henry Giroux, Irene Kacandes, Marianne Hirsch, Larry Wilcox, Roy Grundmann, Alisa Lebow, Francis Guerin, Renata Jackson, David Lugowski, Seth Farber, Robert Stam, William G. Simon, Zmira Heizner, Jessica Rechtschaffer, and Lisa Rofel. This project likewise could not have been completed without artistic and technical support from Elle Flanders, Ann Harris, David Bloom, Carol Koulikourdi and Amanda Millar, and without institutional support enabled by colleagues at Rutgers University, Dartmouth College, Florida Atlantic University, Brooklyn College, College of Staten Island, and the United States Holocaust Memorial Museum, not least of whom include John Belton, Sandy Flitterman-Lewis, Alexandra Keller, Susannah Heschel, Farshad Araghi, Paula Massood, David Gerstner, the late George Custen, and Thomas Doherty. I would also like to express deep gratitude and appreciation to Norton Mezvinsky, Hamid Dabashi, B. Ruby Rich, Dennis Broe, Richard Porton, Bertell Ollman, Benjamin Beit-Hallahmi, Ranjani Mazumdar, Kirsten Moana Thompson, Imke Lode, Nirit Ben-Ari, Gloria Bletter, Kristen Fitzpatrick, Merrick Wolfe, Riva Sura, and Pudden Pÿe. Although I am fully and solely responsible for what is written herein, each of you has helped me along the way toward disenchanting the future as much as the present of Holocaust film.

A very different version of Chapter One was published as "Holocaust Film Criticism and the Politics of Judeo-Christian Phenomenology," in *Violence and American Cinema*, 271-95, edited by J. David Slocum ©2001 by Routledge, Inc. Chapter Two is an expanded and revised version of "St *Korczak* of Warsaw," which was published in *Imaginary Neighbors: Polish–Jewish Relations after the Shoah,* edited by Dorota Glowacka and Joanna Zylinska and is reprinted here by permission of the University of Nebraska Press ©2006 by the Board of Regents of the University of Nebraska. Chapter Four is a revision of "*Entre Nous,* Female Eroticism, and the Narrative of Jewish Erasure," which was published in *Journal of Lesbian Studies* 4, no. 2 (2000): 34-63, edited by Gabriele Griffin ©2000 by The Haworth Press, Inc., Binghamton, New York. (Article copies are available from The Haworth Document Delivery Service: 1-800-HAWORTH;

e-mail address: docdelivery@haworthpress.com.) Chapter Five is an expanded and revised version of *"Balagan* and the Politics of Israeli/Palestinian 'Identity'," which was published in *disClosure: a journal of social theory* 14 (2005): 62-93, special issue on "Incarnations: Religion and Identity," edited by Marcia England ©2005 by *disClosure* and the Committee on Social Theory.

Terri Ginsberg
May 2007

CHAPTER ONE

TOWARDS A CRITIQUE
OF HOLOCAUST CINEMATIC CULTURE

> Regenerative anti–Semitism [...] is the clue to the uniqueness of
> National Socialism [...] But it would be a mistake to deduce
> from this that those historical circumstances had isolated
> Germany from the West and had set it on a separate "special
> path" [...] The massacres of the imperialist conquests and the
> Final Solution are linked by more than "phenomenological
> affinities" and distant analogies. Between them runs a historical
> continuity that makes liberal Europe the laboratory of the
> violence of the twentieth century, and Auschwitz the authentic
> product of Western civilization.
> —Enzo Traverso, *The Origins of Nazi Violence*

It is a commonly accepted fact that the first images of the Holocaust
transmitted to the European and North American publics took the form of short
documentaries and newsreels containing select footage of concentration camp
atrocities either expropriated from Nazi archives or filmed first-hand by Allied
liberating forces.[1] It is a commonly accepted opinion that the footage contained
in these newsreels comprises some of the most gruesome, horrific, violent
images ever to have been recorded on film. Indeed, this footage turns precisely
on the sight of mounds of naked corpses numbering in the thousands, droves of
skeletal prisoners crammed three to a single wooden bunk or wandering
aimlessly after their liberations, scraping rubbish piles for a morsel to eat, and
trainloads of displaced and uprooted persons, exhausted from countless days of
journey without food or water after months or perhaps years of having been
lined up for selection either to be worked or gassed to death. These are the
images to which historians, critics, philosophers and theologians alike have
referred when designating the Holocaust—the systematic, industrialized mass
murder of approximately twelve million people, including Jews (who comprised
a disproportionately large percentage of victims), Gypsies (Sinto and Lalleri
"Roma"), Soviet prisoners of war, lesbians and gays ("glbtqs"), political
resistors (communists, socialists, trade-unionists, and Freemasons), dissident

religious groups (Jehovah's Witnesses, Jesuits), Slavs (Poles, Czechs, Ukrainians), and the mentally and physically infirm and disabled, under the auspices of the German National Socialist Party ("Nazis") during the Second World War. They are also the images that have helped accord the Holocaust the problematical, if undeniable status as one of the most heinous, atrocious, unspeakable, unimaginable, incomprehensible, unrepresentable genocides of all time.

Against this backdrop, however, Holocaust cinematic culture has proliferated and expanded in scope. According to Norman Finkelstein, the Hollywood industry alone has produced at least one hundred seventy-five films on the topic since 1989,[2] but what Finkelstein might call the "Holocaust film industry" began much earlier, most notably with the highly abstract poetic documentary, *Night and Fog* [*Nuit et brouillard*] (Alain Resnais, France, 1954). This culture then moved into Hollywood melodramas[3] which aped formally and ideologically some of the very earliest, pre- and immediate post–liberation films on the subject[4] and which soon after were accompanied by U.S. network television interviews with survivors and traditional, explicative documentaries about the concentration camp structure and experience.[5] It then passed into the post–realist, "retro-style" and high art films of the European auteurs,[6] which eventually also were appropriated into a "New Hollywoodian" aesthetic format,[7] most notably and paradigmatically by *Schindler's List* (Stephen Spielberg, U.S.A., 1994), but also earlier, by *Sophie's Choice* (Alan J. Pakula, U.S.A., 1982), and later, by *Jacob the Liar* (Peter Kassovitz, U.S.A./France/Hungary, 1999), *Train de vie* ["Train of Life"] (Radu Mihaileanu, Romania/France/Belgium/Netherlands/Israel, 1998), *The Grey Zone* (Tim Blake Nelson, U.S.A., 2001), *The Pianist* (Roman Polañski, Poland/Germany/U.K./France, 2002), *Sophie Scholl–The Last Days* [*Sophie Scholl–Die Letzten Tage*] (Marc Rothemund, Germany, 2005), and *Zwartboek* ["The Black Book"] (Paul Verhoeven, Netherlands/Belgium/U.K./Germany, 2007). Finally, and after a spate of popular melodramatic docudramas and theatrical re-runs aired over Hollywood network television,[8] Holocaust cinematic culture has moved into today's veritable multimedia museum spectacular-extravaganza.[9]

Not widely discussed, however, is the fact that this cinematic cultural proliferation and expansion has been accompanied by a converse movement in cultural theory. That movement relies on a general consensus—fostered and encouraged by both popular and scholarly criticism as well as by many of the films themselves—of the proverbial assignation of the Holocaust as beyond intelligibility or cultural representation. Ideologically speaking, the basis of this consensus is a philosophical problematic for which the Holocaust was so monumental, so horrific, so unique, so phenomenologically *sublime* as to be capable neither of adequate aesthetic reproduction nor definitive historical and epistemological explanation.[10] Associated with the post–Holocaust writings of Theodor W. Adorno, this consensus consolidates an unspoken taboo against the formal academic study of Holocaust and film, the idea being that such study is tantamount to indulging in obscenity. The range of practices deterred by this consensus varies, furthermore, and includes historical and critical analyses of Holocaust film culture's proliferation and expansion, the institutional sponsorship of such study, curricular development of Holocaust film courses, the funding of Holocaust film research and its publication, and the analysis of film and media installations at Holocaust memorials and museums. Indeed, to date, and contrasting the voluminous character of Holocaust historical, sociological, and philosophical studies, one is struck by the relative dearth of Holocaust film criticism, not to mention courses, in the contemporary academy, where Holocaust cinema studies finds its structural origin and center.[11] This contrasts the popular print media's preponderant, often vibrantly contestational focus on the subject both in North America and parts of Europe, which strikes one as ironic in that one of the most canonical, widely read and discussed, and not coincidentally controversial Cinema Studies texts, Kracauer's *From Caligari to Hitler*, articulates its critique of Weimar cinema in terms of pervasive discursive affiliation with the Third Reich and the Holocaust.[12] Moreover, where criticism of Holocaust film does exist, the interpretive paradigms to which it adheres are not generally those established from within Cinema Studies but from within fields largely unassociated with the study of moving-image culture such as Sociology, History, Religion, Philosophy, and Language Studies. In these discursive contexts, Holocaust film is more often than not confined to an informational or illustrative function rather than presented as an occasion for analysis in its own right: Holocaust documentaries are lent scholarly priority, whereas Holocaust narrative and experimental films are marginalized or ignored, as are critical analyses concerned with the specifically cinematic aspects of Holocaust representation, including especially their rhetorical implication in the ideologics of Holocaust reproducibility itself. The result is a series of conventional thematic and stylistic readings or, in an opposite—yet at times complementary—sense, a congeries of mystical and theosophical speculation for which the Holocaust emblematizes a category of *belief* rather than marks a node for its critical theorization.

As an entry point into this issue, the present book poses the following question: Is there some underlying or extenuating rationale for the apparent contradiction between an expansive array of Holocaust film production, on the one hand, and a disproportionately minimal amount of serious Holocaust film scholarship, on the other? After all, whether one agrees or not with the ostensibly Adornian paradigm, Holocaust films do often lend themselves to the literal definition of obscenity. Newsreel documentaries and documentaries containing newsreel footage, with their pathetic depictions of naked corpses and barely clad concentration and death camp prisoners, do meet the cultural, if not legal, criteria of "obscenity." This condition, which cultural theorist Peter Michelson has defined lucidly and candidly as "the Greek sense of bringing onstage what is customarily kept offstage in western culture," entails a presumably necessary aestheticization of the so-called un(re)presentable, "a perceptual alteration whereby the obscene, a species of the ugly, is reconstituted to a function akin to that of the beautiful."[13] "Obscenity" is a condition that consequently adopts and tries to domesticate qualities simultaneously of the culturally offensive, perversely pleasurable, and socially threatening.[14] More figuratively and complexly, the Adornian taboo, as it is commonly interpreted, presupposes the Holocaust as a socially enabled occasioning of death so horrible, unprecedented, and historically paradigmatic that its representative artistic rendering is conceivable only as a mimesis of Nazi ideology itself. In other words, the representation of the Holocaust is considered an aesthetic reformulation of an historical phenomenon considered always already generative of mass destruction, and henceforth as *essentially* obscene, in both structure and spectatorial effects.[15]

This perspective, widely attributed to Adorno, is in fact prototypical of Michelson. The latter's literal definition of "obscenity" is undergirded by a structuralist understanding of the philosophical dialectic on the sublime, for which the cultural reconstitution of what is traditionally forbidden from appearing "onstage" is an effect of "the modern and especially contemporary assertiveness of [...] materialism." In this sense, Michelson's "obscenity" is reminiscent of the Freudian "uncanny," which, accessing aesthetic-idealist philosopher Friedrich W. J. v. Schelling, refers to everything "that ought to have remained hidden and yet comes to light."[16] Yet Michelson sees the "obscene" not as some romantic or idealist notion of a profound, uncannily alluring truth of nature, but as those global conditions and practices of capitalism, including the technological development it fosters, that are sublimated, suppressed, dissimulated, or diverted from view. To be clear, Michelson ultimately understands such conditions and practices along Heideggerian lines, as fundamental and irrepressible, even while recognizing their quite visible perpetuation of social misery.[17] On his apologetic view, these conditions and practices can and must be relegated to "obscenity" for the threat of violence widespread knowledge of them is thought capable of posing to the status quo.

Michelson's apologeticism is likewise discernible in the ontological analogy he draws between this structural-materialist dialectic (which he affirms as a necessary existential context for techno-capitalist development) and the post–romantic Freudian libido (which he upholds as a referential axis of naturalized corporeal experience). By marked contrast, Adorno's analysis of the Holocaust cultural problematic is more theoretical and decidedly politicized. Accessing and incorporating critiques of ontology by Max Horkheimer, Walter Benjamin, and György Lukács reading Karl Marx and Friedrich Engels,[18] Adorno foregrounds what he sees as the social institutional parameters of the "obscene."[19] In so doing, he critically reorients the traditional discursive mediation and dissimulation—*reification*—of "obscenity" by relocating aesthetic concerns away from the ontological onto the class-political and -conceptual planes. From this social-relational—*praxological*—perspective, by and large ignored by Holocaust film critics but increasingly apparent in Adorno's subsequent attempts to qualify his original statement,[20] no strict ontological affinity obtains between or amongst the material and the libidinal registers of Holocaust cultural production: attempts to represent the Holocaust are viewed politically rather than poetically. Holocaust representation is always in the first instance an economic question of conceptual division and selection—*exploitation*—framed historically by aesthetic ideologies, especially those associated with romantic tradition, themselves overdetermined within the asymmetrical social relations of capitalist reproduction as they extend, most pertinently, into Africa, Asia, and the Middle East.[21] The phenomenon of libidinal attraction to the sublime is itself likewise always preconditioned—at the level of technocultural form as well as referential content—and linked ideologically to the aesthetic philosophical series; again, especially problematic, nay, "obscene," is the (post–)romantic tendency to thematize the material register across, or otherwise reduce it to, a libidinal-cultural nexus.[22]

* * * * *

As the relative dearth of serious Holocaust film scholarship over the years suggests, the purported Adornian taboo against comprehending the Holocaust through romanticized, rhetorically abstract lenses has been greatly misunderstood. The consistent scholarly tendency has been to interpret the Holocaust according to a perspective more akin to that of Michelson, for whom the "obscene" is conceived phenomenologically, almost mystically, as an event that can never really be comprehended, much less known conceptually. This tendency conveniently rapproches iconoclastic claims dependent upon the proverbial, oft-misunderstood Judaic proscription against fideistic imagery,[23] which lend religious credence to that tendency while in fact further mystifying attempts to visually represent the Holocaust. The consequence for Cinema Studies is that the Holocaust can never really be represented, much less understood, beyond those romantic, aesthetic-philosophical, techno-libidinal parameters misidentified with Adorno. Apropos of this misidentification,

Holocaust film criticism, when practiced with at least a semblance of disciplinary seriousness, has consistently conformed to the basic discursive parameters of phenomenology and, by historical extension, the ideology of Christian moral philosophy.[24] With remarkably few exceptions, all of them important and valuable but finally phenomenological in approach,[25] most texts of Holocaust film criticism have presented analyses or reviews of Holocaust films which devise an irreducibly opaque epistemological relationship across the historical, philosophical, and formal-textual registers of those films. On this tack, the only guiding question permitted is methodological: how best to ascertain, or at least to approximate, the relationship between representation and event. What this allows, however, is little more than the management and containment of any real knowledge one might acquire about that relationship, including its purported aesthetic foundations and the instability and volatility attributed to them. In short, Holocaust film criticism has disallowed *radical* connection between the historical generation, industrial production, technological construction, and subjective interpellation of Holocaust cinematicity itself. In an uncanny rehearsal of Christian medieval scholasticism, which disassociated historical and epistemological relationships from their empirical or existential axes and rearticulated them to ostensibly inaccessible, sensual or highly privatized states, most of this criticism limits itself instead to a skilled hermeneutic decoding of complicated, often esoteric rhetorical forms, an elite practice compelling critics to approach those ostensibly inaccessible states as though, in so doing, they will manifest protection against the perceived chaos or evil of what comes in turn to stand as the material, quotidian—"Jewish"— world.[26]

Even as Holocaust film criticism has moved from its earlier, existential-ontological articulations to the hermeneutic modalities informing contemporary postmodern scholarship, it has continued to uphold basic phenomenological postulates that are in line with the Christian moral foundations of aesthetic philosophy.[27] One of these postulates is that objects, including objects of culture, can and should be known only approximately, by cognitive inspection of their apparent forms. Another is that the binding analogy of these forms is an intentional, normative, synthetic, self-correcting, ever-excessive "elsewhere" or "other," the introjection and displacement of which by the community of critics is thought to render it universally valid by virtue of its imbrication within a social logics of imminent but unknowable necessity.[28] A third is that the meaning and significance of this consensual analogy between object and form— this structuring absence—may itself only be approximated; this approximation can at best be pursued, furthermore, by comparative analysis of plural, uncanny variations as these are perceived to manifest self-evidently in the very object of analysis, the (un)intended, sacralized "thing-in-itself" (*die Sache*).[29] This is to say, more plainly, that Holocaust film criticism has enacted a paradigm shift from high philosophical to more conventional aesthetics, by which it has been able to re-articulate theological premises to a quotidian, ecumenical framework known commonly as the "Judeo-Christian."[30] From this perspective, the "other" of traditional aesthetics—the "Jew" of Christian moralism—is assimilated onto a post–philosophical, immanent, anthropological plane, where its distinguishing cultural markers are relinquished and its social stigmatization is ameliorated, but where its "otherness" is nonetheless retained. An abiding example is the persistent Wandering Jew myth, with its connotations of inherent or unavoidable sinfulness and deserved, eternal suffering,[31] in discourses on modern Jewish tribulation and catastrophe, including those of Holocaust film criticism. These essentially christo-phenomenological—*christological*—foundations, contextualizing a modern-day, at times secular, revision of christic nature and redemption, profoundly contradict the Holocaust film criticism that on its face purports to theorize its critical difference on, inter alia, Judaically informed principles.

Suffice it here to say that the effect of this persisting christological approach has been the propagation of a relatively circumscribed perspective on Holocaust film culture, the judgmental lapses and misprisions of which have become excusable on private (legally protected) grounds of religious propriety. A telling characteristic of this perspective is that a refusal to merely approximate the purported, designated "other," whether conceived on Christian or "Judeo-Christian" grounds, becomes tantamount to hubris, to the promotion of critical modalities deemed intellectually violent or "totalizing."[32] Holocaust film criticism has, in effect, by and large preempted critical epistemological theorization by implicitly adopting the conciliatory, Christian moral belief in the material world as an essentially fallen, inherently destructive, teleologically motivated "acceptance-phenomenon."[33] In this context, the *radical* materialist kernel of the Adornian taboo, which would facilitate rearticulating the opacity at the core of the phenomenological function to the systemic structures of social relations and institutional practices that comprise its historical-objective crux, is denied. Indeed, what for Adorno is etched indelibly at the barbaric core of Western civilization—of global capitalism and its ideological ethos—as an occurrence incomprehensible without sustained consideration of its social-institutional and especially political-economic determinants, becomes instead for Holocaust film criticism an index of human fallibility. That fallibility, moreover, lies beyond the conceptual horizon where questions can be posed without provoking the same sorts of barbarity against which human society has historically been compelled to struggle and to seek "redemption." On the christological reading, Holocaust film criticism presents the Holocaust as but a necessary irruption and reenactment of this presumed essential human fallibility, the social significance of which is reduced to the proverbial moral lesson: Jewish victims of the Holocaust—*Judeocide* victims[34]—like Jesus "Christ" before them, are raised—resurrected—to the status of that event's defining, (self-)sacrificial "other." By extension, the question of the Holocaust's *other* victims—not to mention the victims of additional prior, concurrent, and subsequent genocides and ethnic cleansings—and the question of the social determinants of all these events, are effectively ignored or transposed and played out in terms of christic sacrifice, via the standardized dialectic of the Holocaust.[35]

One might usefully invoke in this regard the philosopher Emmanuel Levinas, whose secular Jewish-phenomenological critique of ontological formulations has itself been justifiably critiqued for its contradictory reinscription of conceptual opacities ("Infinity," "the Other") that have been considered symptomatic of his equivocal position on Zionism as well as of his patriarchal bias.[36] At his most interesting, Levinas warns emphatically against the adoption of christo-anthropocentric notions, that is, of the mythicized phenomenological groundings which he sees dangerously precluding sustained interrogation of the means of forestalling genocidal violence and catastrophe.[37] To Levinas, the invocation of notions such as these leads to an elision of the very different Judaic concept of sacrifice, which entails an interrogative and entirely worldly adherence to a critical, anti–authoritarian, radically differential—proto–Adornian—Judaic social covenant of mending the universe [*tikkun ha-olam*].[38] Indeed as Levinas recognizes, the Judaic conceptualization of sacrifice is largely unconcerned with the appropriative re(an)nunciation or regenerative (re)assumption of an "other," whether anthropologically or ideally conceived. This is by no means to suggest that certain prevailing notions of "otherness" do not figure within Judaic textual tradition and extenuating social practices, as Jewish anti–Zionist scholars Israel Shahak and Norton Mezvinsky powerfully remind.[39] It is to clarify, however, that when "otherness" is invoked in Jewish philosophy, it figures not an ideal allegory of suffering and exclusion—the universal *epōkhe* (bracketing) of the phenomenological reduction—but marks the praxology itself of social materiality which affects differentially—and therefore does not necessitate teleologically—the historical framing and development of so-called objective reality and the functioning of human subjects in relation thereto.

At the hermeneutical register, this critical praxis may be expressed in terms of *le-didakh*, a Judaic analytic technique which involves extending a hypothetical, second-person perspective a sometimes indefinite concession in an initial, if eventually relinquished effort to render possible a primary postulate or contention. The Eastern Aramaic phrase, *le-didakh*, is a dialectical concept deployed most recently by Judaic scholar Yosef Hayim Yerushalmi,[40] which occurs in the Babylonian Talmud approximately eighty-seven times. It means "according to that (opinion) which is yours," that is, "according to your opinion." Its Hebrew equivalent is *le-daatkha*, and its definition is similar to that of the Hebrew phrase, *u-le-ta'amekh*, meaning "according to your reasoning." According to Talmudic scholar Louis Jacobs, whose position in this regard is implicitly supported by Yerushalmi, *u-le-ta'amekh* is but one of three types of comparative or differential Talmudic argumentative methods, the other two being *ve-tisbera* ["and even according to your theory"], which entails exposing flaws in an opponent's position, and *ka-saleka da'atekh* ["you might have supposed"], which entails forwarding an argument with the intention of rejecting it.[41] On the further view of another Talmudic scholar, Adin Steinsaltz, *u-le-ta'amekh* (or, what we shall refer to in our text as *le-didakh* for the sake of linguistic ease and expedience as well as in deference to the popular-mass significance of the Aramaic) is distinguished by its tactic of *shinuya* ["argument by alternative demonstration"], which entails both the question, posed by a *makshan* [questioner], *Ve-dilma ipkha?* ["And perhaps the opposite is true?"], and the hypothetical reply, offered by the *tartzan* [respondent], *Ipkha mistbra* ["The opposite holds"].[42]

Importantly, the "other" in a "le-didakhic" encounter refers to neither the hypothetical second person nor his/her perspective, whose designations as such would only serve to reify them vis-à-vis the first person and, by the same token, lend sovereign authority to the latter: *le-didakh* is fundamentally obverse to the techniques of opportunism and cooptation.[43] More and other than sophistical rhetoric (although it can and does devolve into that, as I shall discuss in Chapter Three), *le-didakh* refers instead to a conditional dialectic which overdetermines any such perspective and whose asymmetrically attuned, ultimately social grounding signals a seeming paradox that is nonetheless historical and, as such, subject to concrete—really contested—knowledgeability and change: it hails both the "not-yet" and the "might-have-been."[44] Serious engagement with the praxis of *le-didakh* can therefore contribute to effecting radical paradigm shifts in prevailing understandings of the social conditions in which it may be possible to approach and (come to) know the second person, the "other" and his/her perspective.

A phenomenologist, Levinas will in the end only *perform* any such intellectual shift; his imperative is to achieve "ethical rapport with the face of the other."[45] Indeed Jewish phenomenology does not finally reject the moral comprehensibility of its Christian counterpart but supplements it with a Judaic bracketing of the ontological register on iconoclastic grounds that to name or otherwise thematize it, as Christianity does via the figure of Christ, is to hypostasize it and thereby to collapse it onto an existential realm whose infinite limits confine metonymically the dialectics of social reparation to the telos of regenerative sacrifice.[46] This metaphysical limitation notwithstanding,[47] Levinas' anti–philosophical thematization of *le-didakh*, that is, of Judaic sacrificial hermeneutics, renders the horizons of his ethical imperative and its performance structurally inseparable from the critical epistemology, familiar to Adornian critical theory and contemporary derivatives such as cultural materialism and structuralist Marxism, that works to resituate and resolve the social contradictions underlying historical and cultural dramas of differentiation while refusing nonetheless to discount different narratives and modes of response to them, whether these derive from the recognized past or arise concurrent with those dramas. Jewish philosophical "otherness" thus refers to the possibility of an a-theological—in effect, atheistic—field of social organization entailing a self-consciously problematical view to institutions and other systemic structures of social division and intelligibility such as class, gender, sexuality, ethnicity, and creed. It involves, in effect, a simultaneously *ideological* and *interrogative* praxis subtending the asymmetrical historical rift Jew–Gentile, which the albeit marginalized "Jewish" is obligated to help repair, or mend—not by figuring a false and premature assimilation of one pole of the binarism into the other, but by cleaving to, while critically destabilizing, the deep structures of their differentiation.

This historical rift, it must also be recognized, is sometimes thought so deeply ingrained in the social imaginary that a protracted, seemingly unresolvable, often mutually exacerbated struggle has been considered necessary for its reparation actually to occur.[48] "Judeo-Christian" opponents of social reparation have often exploited this assertion in reactionary terms to affirm a penultimate sense of perpetual trial and tribulation that justifies continued propagation of eschatological and certain messianic modes of "Otherness." On these assertions, the "Jewish" emblematizes an eternal or at least divinely ordained crusade against the West's presumed mortal enemies, including especially Palestinians, Arabs, and Muslims, but also Blacks, indigenous peoples, people of the Left, glbtqs, and feminists.[49] It is this development which symptomatizes the metaphysical, reificatory, even christological horizon of Jewish phenomenological ambivalence, both through and against which the present book will work via the critical theoretical analysis if offers of Holocaust cinematic culture.

* * * * *

However the "obscene" quality of Holocaust cultural representation may be conceived and dealt with, the dedicated Holocaust film scholar must inevitably struggle with these overriding aesthetico-moral contentions. Recalling Hannah Arendt's perception of incisive intellectual practice as, following Camus, both "*solidaire et solitaire,*"[50] these contentions position the critic as both an exemplar of "redemptive" Holo-sacrifice and a "perverse" purveyor of a cultural practice notable, even laudable, for marking what Horkheimer and Adorno might have called an "embarrassment beyond intelligibility"[51] with the extreme horror and violence it undeniably depicts and displays. Keeping this in mind, I shall endeavor in the present book to pursue a serious analysis of Holocaust film culture. In view of the phenomenological character of much Holocaust film criticism, I will supply an analysis of specific Holocaust film critical texts which saliently exemplify this character and its ideological implications. Aiming toward a socially grounded, historically attuned, theoretically oriented approach, this intellectual analysis will not be limited to a comparative description (explication or mimesis) of films or critical texts. Rather, it will work epistemologically to elucidate, interrogate, and critically resituate reasons they offer critics for resisting a sustained critique of Holocaust film onto the material institutional register that Adorno believed so crucial to an anti–genocidal—if not entirely comfortable or reassuring—Holocaust cultural analysis.

Before doing this, however, it behooves me to acknowledge briefly that the development of Holocaust film culture has in fact been approached in decidedly political, if not always materialist ways both outside the academy and mostly in fields other than Cinema Studies. Most prominent in this regard are popular print media reviews of, and ensuing public debates over, various Holocaust films as well as significant scholarly publications on, and likewise ensuing public debates over, the relationship of the Holocaust to the contemporary study of history, social science, philosophy, and law. For instance, following the onset of Holocaust historiography debates in France and Germany during the late 1970s and early 1980s,[52] themselves responding in part to the politically provocative Hollywood tele-films, *Holocaust* and *Playing for Time*, and to controversial developments in the scholarly critical sphere (deconstruction, cultural studies, new historicism, critical legal theory), a wave of book-length texts on contemporary Holocaust culture and society began to be published. The primary source materials for these texts were print media reviews of and debates over Holocaust (film) culture and other public occasions of Holocaust discourse such as those involving Holocaust denial and revisionism. The underlying if not always explicit contentions of these otherwise widely divergent texts supported the liberal notion that, for better or worse, Holocaust culture, discourse and representation were irrevocably political—especially national-political—in both context and orientation. Moreover, attempts to argue otherwise, despite or even because of the Holocaust's irrefutable horror and violence, were themselves implicated in dubious ideological agendas. These texts displayed and in some instances argued for a broad, interdisciplinary approach to the subject of the Holocaust, even when the scope of that subject's articulations became

necessarily limited by particular methodologies and the critical, often
ideological, tendencies associated with them.

    In *The Holocaust and American Film*, for example, Judith Doneson, a
Jewish Studies scholar trained largely in Israel, insists upon the situation of
Holocaust film culture within a specific national-political context. Although
conceding with her contemporary, film scholar Annette Insdorf (*Indelible
Shadows*), the legitimacy of the aesthetic-philosophical problematic, Doneson
lends priority to the historiographic question of Holocaust cinema's public
presence and concern in the postwar U.S. Acknowledging with Kracauer, whose
later writings on cinema have been a central reference point in contemporary
film phenomenology,[53] a lurid shock-effect of violent Holocaust imagery,
Doneson is more interested in how Holocaust films—especially Hollywood
productions—have helped to "assimilate the Holocaust into the popular
consciousness," such that the Holocaust has become a paradigm of the U.S.
"immigrant" experience: "thematizing" current events, "catalyzing" the
European Holocaust historiography debates, and adopting a "specific
Jewishness" while also becoming "a universal message for mankind."[54]
Doneson's perspective is supported in its critical effect by *Denying the
Holocaust*, in which historian Deborah Lipstadt critiques North American
Holocaust historiography debates for their imbrication with the postmodern
literary theory known as deconstruction and associated most prominently in the
Anglo-American academy with literary theorists Jacques Derrida and Paul de
Man. Extending and honing the historicism necessary to Doneson's
formulations, Lipstadt argues for a return to a more empirical scholarly practice
that, by its requisite collection and specification of data, can, on her view, offer
a corrective to postmodern antifoundationalism and the "relativism" with which,
again on her view, it has served Holocaust denial and right-revisionism.[55]
Doneson's implicit reading is that such postmodern theories have served to
undermine the positive ideology-effects she associates with North American
Holocaust films. Her decidedly culturalist focus is, however, less specifically
concerned with Holocaust historiography than with Hollywood's uncertain
ability to offer a "balanced" negotiation of the Holocaust's "universal and
particular" significance, which Holocaust historiography debates have on her
view neglected: she contends that to ensure such a balance, Hollywood
filmmaking must affirm a "Jewish particularity" of the Holocaust, then
"triangulate" that assumed particularity with the larger role she believes its
cinematic rendering plays in justifying the existence of Israel, its political stance
and military actions, to the U.S. general public. Indeed for Doneson, this Zionist
triangulation—"America at the top with Israel and the Holocaust at the base"—
is inseparable from and "forms the foundation of [a globally significant]
American Jewish identification" that she considers necessary to "[our]

vigilan[ce] in defense of freedom."[56]

More sophisticated theoretically in its approach is *Screening the Holocaust*, in which Israeli literary and cultural scholar Ilan Avisar applies the conservative methodology, New Criticism,[57] to a close textual analysis of Holocaust film noticeably absent from the thematic and generic approaches of Doneson and of Insdorf.[58] Despite and because of its methodological and disciplinary difference, however, *Screening the Holocaust* remains ideologically consonant with the critical aims of its predecessors. Indeed Avisar's relatively traditional interpretive methodology flatly disregards deconstruction as a possible mode of Holocaust analysis. It respects the same aesthetic moralism, for which Holocaust imagery is essentially obscene (hence the book's subtitle, "Cinema's Images of the Unimaginable"), and it recommends that Holocaust filmmaking exercise "artistic restraint" lest spectators become dangerously "saturated" with Holocaust films' admittedly difficult imagery. Echoing feminist cultural theorist Julia Kristeva, whose *Powers of Horror* makes no secret of its christo-romantic underpinnings, and literary theorist Saul Friedländer, whose *Reflections of Nazism* marks the seminal designation of Holocaust imagery as pornographic,[59] Avisar is concerned that such a saturation will, by its apparent sensuality, arouse extreme visceral reactions in spectators that may promote a fascist resurgence accompanied by antisemitic violence.[60] Although Avisar refers to these reactions as "emotional, mindless, and even convulsive (e.g., nervous laughter, or even perverse pleasure),"[61] his ideas about the social and historical conditions which might provoke them are politically limited and lacking in scholarly credibility. The military occupation and protracted war that may be linked to Doneson's U.S.–Israel triangulation and the Jewish particularism thought necessary to it, for instance, both of which have been considered responsible for a contemporary blowback that has ironically fomented and renewed "real" antisemitism in the contemporary social arena,[62] go unremarked. Avisar instead focuses on condemning the "nihilistic irony and pessimistic vision" of modernist Holocaust films, which he accuses of "decadence" and associates prejudicially with their depiction of non-normative sexualities.[63] For him, cinematic displays of homosexuality, understood in reactionary terms as a flagship of social decay, is a forboding omen of future holocausts and our inability to forestall them. After a mystical fashion that recalls Michelson but overlooks his (and Kracauer's) materialism, Avisar quotes Jewish cultural historian Irving Howe in contending that this socially dangerous potential of Holocaust imagery is "absolute[ly] revelatory": it is an organic effect of mysterious compulsion originating beyond social proprieties and cultural constraints, and oriented past the competing nationalisms allegorized but not, on Avisar's view, overcome by the inherent polysemy which a New Critical approach attributes to (film) textuality.[64] As a corrective, Avisar quotes structuralist literary critic Tzvetan Todorov in calling for a Holocaust film criticism that can screen out these purported dangers through a clarifying technique of descriptive demonstration, and that can thereby resist the Holocaust's so-called obscenity while retaining for it Doneson's sacral, singularly Jewish significance.[65]

Likewise clearly political and interdisciplinary in its approach to the problematics of Holocaust cultural and historical intelligibility is Dominick LaCapra's *Representing the Holocaust*. LaCapra's work is a sustained analysis of Holocaust cultural and historiographical critique for which deconstruction is also a questionable mode of Holocaust analysis; it posits historical specificity, empirical factuality, and textual clarity as less crucial to a serious understanding of the Holocaust and its socio-cultural effects, however, than a controlled, psychoanalytically based exposure and rehearsal of Holocaust discourse itself. A socially meaningful Holocaust cultural practice entails for LaCapra an allegorical performance, a controlled reflection of traumatic, Holocaust-rooted (I shall call these *holocaustal*) symptoms from their perceived manifestations in cultural and behavioral forms back onto the discursive conditions thought possibly to enable them. LaCapra's idea is that such symptoms not be understood primarily as threats to a national-political or ethno-religious order, as would seem the case for Lipstadt and for Avisar, but on a transnational-political scale more akin to the culturalist perspective of a likewise ethnocentric Doneson. In his view, holocaustal symptoms are occasions for a transferential, dialogic "exchange" between contestatory, even formerly ideologically opposed interlocutors, namely Jews and Gentiles, interested in "mediating" and "modulating"—but, importantly, never in closing off—their perspectival differences. LaCapra believes that this "Judeo-Christian" exchange, this ethical reenactment of holocaustal feelings between assumed victims and assumed perpetrators, marks the essential, irreducible instability of Holocaust symptomaticity; its causal or epistemological explanations, including analysis of their applicability to global politics, not least as symptomatized by the conflict in Israel/Palestine, would by contrast, on his view, spell a recipe for repeated disaster.[66]

The explicit attention lent by these well-known, oft-cited works in Holocaust studies to the (trans)national politicality and cross-disciplinarity of Holocaust critical and cultural discourse is not only crucial to their respective arguments but intersects the tendency of earlier, politically progressive, though persistently controversial Holocaust studies texts. *Eichmann in Jerusalem, Anti–Semite and Jew, Faschismus, Rassenwahn, Judenvervolgung, Fascism and Dictatorship*, and *Why Did the Heavens Not Darken?* are among texts in which Holocaust knowledgeability is determined and comprehended socio-historically before aesthetically.[67] It is therefore all the more unfortunate that, unlike their predecessors, the more recent, film critical efforts take explicitly conservative positions vis-à-vis their subject matter by accessing and employing the phenomenologically structured, christologically oriented paradigm in order to dissimulate the very knowledge they would appear interested in exploring.

Both Doneson and Lipstadt belie their ostensible political progressivism with qualifications consonant with a neoliberal agenda. For Doneson, this entails designating Holocaust film culture a viable means of projecting and universalizing the North American ideology of a manifestly destined, redemptive melting pot—an ideology well known to critics of the film western, *film noir*, and science fiction film[68]—to a global audience, and hence of its advocating North American "democratization" (socio-economic expansion) abroad, especially in the Middle East. Such an assertion, furthermore, has an ontotheological layer, which Doneson attempts tenaciously to legitimize by reference to the writings of Talmudic scholar Jacob Neusner:[69] she holds that the Holocaust, as the domain of the christological "Jew," is best represented as an allegory of universal human sin, suffering, and salvation:

> [T]he Holocaust functions as a model, a paradigm, or a framework for understanding history. It is a metaphor that teaches a lesson [...] The more visible the event becomes, the greater are its chances of being internalized by the American psyche [which] brings with it a tendency toward Americanization. [In this way] the Holocaust becomes part of the American tradition [...] one of the principle components of the civil religion of American Jews [a redemptive modality which] defies despair [...] and connotes the idea of integrating into the myth of liberty and equality. (Doneson, *Holocaust in American Film*, 9–10, 91, 146, 161, 201)

Celebrating the Holocaust as "Holocaust," as a concept allegorizable to North American manifest destiny, Doneson rehearses the tendency of much non-Holocaust film genre criticism to exculpate cinematic depictions of extreme violence against marginalities and "others" such as Native Americans (the western), women (*film noir*), and "aliens" (science-fiction) as part of a larger project of regenerating and universalizing the "American" national mythos.[70] Her references to a "triangulated" U.S. "vigilance" and support for Israeli "political and military actions" in the name of a bolstered "Jewish identity" must therefore be read as transcribing that tendency toward violence so emphatically into a discourse on redemptive civil religiosity that what may at first have appeared a principled historiographic critique of Hollywoodian constructions of the Holocaust is revealed as nothing less than their dubious affirmation.

Although less blatant, Lipstadt likewise upholds the Holocaust and, by extension, the "Jews," as exemplars of North American manifest destiny, as she rehearses a theologically rooted transcription of that discourse onto contemporary U.S. foreign policy practices.[71] Ironically appropriating the very deconstructionism she has ostensibly rejected, Lipstadt, in an opposite yet complementary tack to that of Avisar, selectively abandons empiricism for rationalist abstraction, thereby downplaying the centrality of the actual genocides of Native Americans and African-American slaves to North American "destiny." In the process, she dislocates the support she more explicitly offers the deregulatory economic policies of Reagan and Bush from concomitant criticisms, such as those advanced by Doneson, of Reagan's 1986 visit to the S.S. cemetery at Bitburg.[72] The glaring contradictory quality of these tacks is not resolved by a subsequent reference to Genesis: "God's presence can be found in many different places and made manifest in a variety of ways."[73]

Avisar's stated belief in the Jewish specificity of the Holocaust likewise symptomatizes a dubious if more sectarian politics. Like Doneson, Avisar purports to ground his analytic rationalism in empirical practice and historical specificity, as he advises Holocaust filmmakers to uphold "respect for fact," "truthful referentiality," and "historical allegiance."[74] On his view, only Holocaust survivors may be excused for "excessive" fictionalizing, and that is because their accounts are based ostensibly on "direct personal experience."[75] But whereas Doneson and Insdorf may refuse the application of "Holocaust" to what they otherwise clearly recognize was the Nazi targeting of Roma, glbtqs, Freemasons, leftists, and other dissenters, Avisar entirely and unabashedly denies the well-documented victimhood of these groups.[76] On his finally ahistorical view (typical of many Zionist and most official Israeli narratives of the Holocaust), it is simply antisemitic to designate as Holocaust victims non-Jews persecuted by the Nazis; this can only contribute to the "fostering of Christian ideology on the back of the Jews and their tragedy." For Avisar, such an approach in fact "dominates the cinematic treatment of the Holocaust."[77] Notwithstanding these pronouncements, Avisar concurs with the similarly self-contradictory Doneson that the Holocaust furnishes universal ethical dimensions that may be safely represented in careful deference to Christian sensibilities. Hence his ironic reference to Christian existentialist philosopher Søren Kierkegaard in the course of imploring Holocaust filmmakers to take a "leap into unfaith" while "imagining" how best to depict the Holocaust.[78]

The liberal Insdorf (until more recently the only professional film scholar of the group), likewise does not refute the Christian view, entailed by Avisar's Jewish particularist critique, that Jews are especially vulnerable to social violence for their perceived unique character as perpetually homeless and wandering. On this view, Jews threaten "national consciousness" and trigger a Western "suicidal impulse" that marks theologically the conditions for a voluntary "second Fall."[79] As a preventative antidote to this apocalyptic scenario, Insdorf quotes right-libertarian ideologue Bernard Henri-Lévy, conservative literary critic George Steiner, and renowned Holocaust survivor Elie Wiesel in advocating for an elevation of Holocaust imagery beyond commodification. By this she does not mean to oppose Holocaust representation to the system of capitalism per se or indeed to the Western democracies that comprise its global hegemon. Insdorf in fact confuses commodification with mythification: in view of the latter, which in this instance entails rehearsing a morally buttressed, intrinsic linkage between capitalism and Judaism, Insdorf finds highly suspect much popular, mass-culture Holocaust film. For her as for Avisar, "Holocaust" is not a commoditizable concept but an "ontological phenomenon" dangerously allegorized by mythical, usually Christian accounts.[80] This suspicion of Holocaust commodification is certainly not unjustifiable in light of historical findings which reveal how the "Jew" did come to figure a paradigmatic, ideological agent and barter-ball—indeed a supra-commodity—in the racialized destruction of peoples and places that since the Holocaust has come to emblematize the post–European reorganization of global capitalism of which German fascism was a political symptom and facilitator. That figuring may indeed have enabled the sort of philosemitic recasting of Jewish subjectivity in the postwar era which Doneson implicitly promotes, but does not name, as an ideological means by which Western capitalist nations, including Israel, may seek and receive moral compensation for the violence they continue to commit in the "humanitarian" names of democracy, peace and freedom. Insdorf's and Avisar's understandings, however, of the theoretical relation, commodification–mythification, sidesteps this crucial point, turning instead upon a category error which collapses the register of social-systemic praxis (the relations of capitalist reproduction) onto that of cultural-structural organization (the ideological institutionalization of myth), and in this way obscures important functional differences between the two registers that are only explained away by deference—positive or negative—to the "Jewish." It does not seem to occur to either Insdorf or Avisar that a call for the elevation of the Holocaust, or any historical event, "beyond commodification" is impossible because already intrinsic to that very system, for which the idea or product divested of exchange value marks precisely the horizon of universal value against which all other, lesser values are gauged[81]—and which, in the contemporary global arena, configures the direction and scope of U.S. foreign policy, including its "special alliance" with Israel. By overlooking this systemic function, these critics actually alienate the Judeocide within a socially disengaged framework of Holocaust analysis eerily compatible with the Christian narratives they reject.[82] Avisar's positioning of the Holocaust beyond competing nationalisms and social propriety, then, like Insdorf's elevation of the Holocaust beyond commodification, is not merely ahistorical; it is nothing less than reificatory, serving disingenuously to dissimulate the violent, exploitative *epōkhe*, the rationalist reductivism at the core of both New Criticism and the U.S.–Israeli alliance supported implicitly by Avisar's and Doneson's particularist characterizations of the Holocaust as specifically "Jewish."

Even more problematic in this series of key examples is LaCapra, for it is his methodological recommendation which marks an increasingly predominant discursive tendency within an already problematic Holocaust cinema studies. Like Doneson, LaCapra supports the global dissemination of "Americanism," to which he refers at different points as "pragmatism," "ethicopolitics," "creative modes of consumption," "secular sacrifice," and, most tellingly, "wizened evangelicism."[83] Like Lipstadt and Avisar, he appropriates into this overtly "Judeo-Christian" ideologic the politically more progressive writings of earlier Holocaust theorists whose respective critiques of particular modalities of Holocaust intelligibility he at once rejects and co-opts.[84] Unlike these contemporaries, however, and in a move that is cannily attractive to contemporary film scholarship, LaCapra's methodological grounding in post–Lacanian psychoanalysis lends his "Judeo-Christian" appropriation of earlier Holocaust theory a decidedly *neo*phenomenological character. That is to say, LaCapra incorporates the poststructuralist psychotherapeutic concept of perpetual dialogic exchange and (counter)transference associated with object-relations theory and rearticulated most recently in film studies via the postmarxist writings of Gilles Deleuze.[85] As a result, LaCapra's call for a renewed Holocaust studies remains as dependent as Insdorf and Avisar upon aesthetically mediated and theologically oriented discourses and thereby serves to preempt a sustained social-institutional interrogation of Holocaust theory and culture. Instead of basing his claims simply upon either a political-economic project (Doneson) or a rationalized empiricism (Lipstadt), that is, LaCapra actually revises the very aesthetic register along which any such preemption may occur. This revision entails a relocating of the aesthetic register from the idealist and rationalist planes on which it has traditionally been situated onto a plane of quotidian experience, wherein the operative agency of its interpretability shifts from the ethereal realm of moral feeling to the tangible activity of the human body.

In order to accomplish this, LaCapra refines a concept, the *differend*, inaugurated within contemporary literary theory by postmodern philosopher Jean-François Lyotard. For Lyotard, a performative enactment of inaudibility, rather than any reasoned discursive enunciation, is seen as the last remaining mode of authentic post–Holocaust representation. In Lyotard's view, the Adornian contention that the history and culture of the Holocaust may be ascertained and subjected to critical analysis, even judgment, through a socio-historically reflexive philosophical praxis, is no longer relevant to/in the postmodern era. He argues, instead, that the rhetorical structures necessary to such a praxis have been detached or deflected ineluctably from any discernible, reliable conceptual axis that might otherwise authorize them and henceforth legitimize truth claims about the Holocaust.[86]

For LaCapra, who likewise calls for a mode of Holocaust knowledgeability synchronous with the postmodern notion of a self-evident real, however, the liminal inaudibility signified by the performative *differend* circumnavigates an "extreme theoreticism"[87]: the *differend* disallows the dialogics of witnessing and confession so central to the "Judeo-Christian" ethos he believes pervades and demarcates the Holocaust and its psychotherapeutic rehearsal as "Holocaust." So as to retain the "extreme" core of the Lyotardian view, LaCapra supplements *"differend"* with a notion of "anthropological sacrifice" he gleans carefully and selectively from René Girard.[88] This unmistakably christological interpolation of Judaic notions of sacrifice[89] presupposes a "primitive" economics of social determination; the repeatedly violent, often murderous, frequently celebrated displacement and projection of meaning onto designated and particular (groups of) subjects is deemed by Girard the central and necessary defining praxis of cultural identity and communal survival. For LaCapra, this veritably organic-racialist theory of social foundation and regeneration, which he himself initially concedes may offer little more than a nostalgic, pseudoscientific rationale for universal social destruction, can nonetheless be culled strategically to ground and thereby ameliorate the elusiveness of the Lyotardian *differend*. The capacity to speak or to represent vis-à-vis "others" supplies the means by which to reinscribe the *differend*'s liminality into a recognizable as well as prescriptive cultural form—namely, into a myth allegorizable to the Girardian paradigm, a myth perennially familiar to Western culture, but to which LaCapra does not refer outright as the Christian mystery play.[90]

On this line, what previously was considered the *differend*'s speculative significance, incapable by its presumed contingency of serious review, may now claim legitimacy and accountability as an accessible, realizable, *speakable* manifestation of an essential and eternal *human* condition.[91] This claim is made, more precisely, through an allegorical rearticulation of the dominant, ever prevailing, christo-sacrificial myth. With respect to Holocaust theory, this (onto)mythological reinscription allows what Lyotard presupposes, and LaCapra does not dispute: the liminal character of holocaustal horror and violence undergoes a reenactment whose ensuing viability of expression and enunciation becomes proof both of "Holocaust"'s human pervasiveness and the persisting ontological necessity of its repetition for the survival of human community.

LaCapra underscores this remythologization by likewise granting to the human condition an epistemologically diffuse temporality, a "lived experience" of time's passage bound immanently within an eternally recurring, intersubjective cycle. LaCapra posits an irruptive quality to this recurrent passage, which may displace discursive and rhetorical structures of speech, and in this way compel historical transformation, from an asymptotic position inascertainble to theory but subject to normative regulation within an "ethicopolitical" space of ritual interaction.[92] Citing both Kierkegaard and social theorist Jürgen Habermas, LaCapra clarifies that, for all its opacity, this impulse to historical transformation is not impossible but will impart primarily by virtue of a "conversionlike experiential choice" to which members of the ritually bound human community may consent vis-à-vis its presumed unintelligible because ambiguous horizon of "repetitive temporality"—in fact, its *differend*.[93] The existential-phenomenological sense of temporal alterity and its perceptual cognition undergirding this formulation contrasts an *historical* sense for which the experience of time is construed socially, in accordance with class, gender, and racial positioning within the material relations of production and exchange, and for which qualitatively different experiences of temporality and change, and the strategic decisions made possible in relation to them, are therefore fundamentally political, not merely existential.[94] Apparently inconsequential to LaCapra is the fact that, through this naturalizing, mythologizing conceptualization of temporal passage and social interaction and cohesion, the erroneous but persistent formulation of Jewish history as intrinsically (self-) sacrificial and beyond reasoned intelligibility remains implicitly unchallenged. In effect LaCapra precludes awareness and critique of that formulation's material historical conditions: the christological discourse framing LaCapra's anthropological turn ramifies on/to an otherwise post–hermeneutic, post–theological scholarly terrain. Meanwhile the familiar phenomenological notion of the Holocaust is upheld, as is, by association, the notion of the proverbial suffering Jew as ineffable—nay, obscene—and as an index of transhistorical truth.[95]

LaCapra in this way implicitly disregards the Levinasian admonition against christo-anthropological modalities, and henceforth redeploys a decidedly Christian notion of "Otherness"—the universal and eternal recurrence of pathetic human suffering—as the fulcrum of Holocaust intelligibility.[96] He thus lends credibility to the holocaustal fears of Jewish particularists like Avisar and Doneson, as he belies the ameliorative function of "dialogic exchange" while mollifying its real divisiveness through patronizing gestures of communal incorporation. He in turn disallows what otherwise might have helped enable more thoroughgoing, substantive kinds of Holocaust, not to mention Judaic and Christian, knowledgeabilities. This would have had the effect of opening the question so crucial within Cinema Studies, and raised variously within certain strands of liberation theology,[97] of the relevance of "Holocaust" to contemporary global culture. As such, the broad interdisciplinary scope of LaCapra's post–Holocaust therapeutic must finally be seen as an elite-populist, christo-ecumenical gesture not dissociated from the legacy of European racialism. This gesture not only demotes prevention of future holocausts to the status of pipe-dream; it also rejects such efforts at prevention as negative examples of hubristic (read: "Hebraistic") obstinacy in the face of a presumably natural, universally manifest social-economic system that in fact entails U.S. military-industrial expansion into the Middle East assisted by Israeli exceptionalism and served by the "Judeo-Christian" ideologic of anthropological sacrifice.

* * * * *

The preceding foray into the viable contradictions of four paradigmatic Holocaust studies texts not only illustrates some pervasive ideological tendencies within Holocaust scholarship but also indicates the challenge facing critics interested in something other than the simple, comparative, even performative appreciation of Holocaust film. As suggested earlier, the charge of hubris(/"Hebraism") has served effectively to squelch the formulation and articulation of both a non-(neo)phenomenological, non-christological Holocaust film theory and a sustained Holocaust film studies curriculum. Indeed, little significant analysis of Holocaust films has emerged which does not comprehend and understand the violence and horror—the so-called obscenity—of their subject-matter in fatalistic terms, as "luminous emanations" of the "ontological reduction of the cinema," or as "inaccessible" *figuren* of "a vanished interiority,"[98] and which therefore does not consider the theorizing of that "obscenity" off-limits to critical—political—intelligibility.

Within Cinema Studies proper, this overall absenting of a critical Holocaust intelligibility has often borne the particular mark of a twofold neglect. The first aspect of this neglect is an apparent obstinacy toward focusing on Holocaust films that either have never achieved popular acclaim or have at one time or another become subject to serious, even vociferous public contestation and debate. The second of these aspects comprises an apparent inability, if not refusal, to question prevailing criteria for what counts as a Holocaust film and, in turn, what sort of genocide may be described as at least comparable to the Holocaust and, moreover, the Judeocide. From the writings of Friedländer to Doneson, Insdorf to Avisar, and Colombat to Hirsch (two scholars whose work I shall presently analyze), one is hard-pressed to locate Holocaust film scholarship which focuses on films *other* than *Schindler's List*, *Shoah* (Claude Lanzmann, France, 1986), *Night and Fog*, *Life Is Beautiful* [*La Vita È Bella*] (Roberto Benigni, Italy, 1998), and a few additional European art cinema and Hollywood productions. Largely missing from the limited scholarship on the topic are sustained analyses of films such as *Camp de Thiaroye* (Ousmane

Sembène and Thierno Faty Sow, Tunisia/Algeria/Senegal, 1987), *Memories of Prison* (Nelson Pereira dos Santos, Brazil, 1984), *Come See the Paradise* (Alan Parker, U.S.A., 1990), *Still Life* (Cynthia Madansky, U.S.A., 2004), and *Route 181: Fragments of Journey in Palestine/Israel* (Michel Khleifi and Eyal Sivan, Palestine/Israel/France/Italy/Germany, 2004), whose categorizations as Holocaust films would be considered debatable in most circles because of the broader applicability this would propose of the term "Holocaust." Sustained analysis of films such as *Jakob der Lügner* ["Jacob the Liar"] (Frank Beyer, East Germany/Czechoslovakia, 1975), *Balagan* (Andres Veiel, Germany/Israel, 1994), *Entre Nous [Coup de foudre]* (Diane Kurys, France, 1983), *Bent* (Sean Mathias, U.K., 1997) and *The Sorrow and the Pity* (Marcel Ophuls, France, 1970), which have been subject to varying degrees of censure and suppression in both the academic and popular spheres for their overt problematizations of prevailing understandings of the Judeocide, are likewise lacking if not entirely missing. Few if any Holocaust film critical texts, furthermore, ever place their analyses of Holocaust films into the sort of discursive relation to the institutionalized field of Cinema Studies or to the public debates over Holocaust historiography so widely engaged in other fields. References to cultural criticism are regularly confined to the fields of art and literature, while discussions of film theory and historiography, most notably the phenomenological approaches of Béla Balázs and Kracauer, are almost completely absent.

This is especially surprising in the instance of Gertrud Koch, one of the most prolific and respected philosophers of Holocaust and film, who does in fact write on both Balázs and Kracauer as well as frequently references Sartre. These writings have involved repeated insistence upon the experiential self-evidence of the sort of heightened imagery often projected in Holocaust film, without so much as a nod to its socio-political significance. Indeed in her two published reviews of *Shoah*, this phenomenological vein translates merely into a general claim, adducible to an unreferenced combination of Balázs and the later Kracauer, that, through heightened and recurrent depictions of "gesture, mien and mimicry," *Shoah*'s imaging of the Holocaust transcends the empirical and conscious to "grasp the [unconscious] somatic impact of traumatic shock," and thereby figurally "proves" the Holocaust by "becom[ing] the phenomenological physiognomy of [its] fact[icity]."[99]

But even when attempts have been made toward more epistemologically attuned, politically oriented analysis, as in André Pierre Colombat's *The Holocaust in French Film*, a resounding, overriding call to "Judeo-Christian" ecumenicism works to contain the historical contradictions and philosophical inconsistencies thereby accessed. Despite referencing film history and theory and in turn engaging in a wholehearted, explicit contextualization of Holocaust film criticism in public debates over Holocaust historiography, Colombat prematurely resolves the social issues raised by his analysis into an unmistakably Christian allegory. This is most demonstrable in his apparent unwillingness to concede the applicability of "Holocaust" to any but the Jewish and Roma genocides (the genocides of "wandering" peoples); it is also clear in his understanding of those genocides as occasions for gleaning moral lessons about rescue (read: "salvific") efforts undertaken by/within Nazi-occupied France during the Second World War and for reversing contemporary historiographic attempts to distinguish anti–Zionism from antisemitism. Colombat indeed asserts that such attempts are part and parcel of a "lie […] that has continued to prosper since 1933" in the form of "new antisemitic" efforts to compare Jewish with Palestinian suffering and to inculpate Jewish elites who chose to collaborate with the Nazis allegedly for the sake of "Israel's survival."[100]

The Holocaust in French Film does not balk at extended analyses of controversial productions such as The Sorrow and the Pity and The Memory of Justice (Marcel Ophuls, U.S.A., 1976), which, respectively, expose and critique the contradictions and hypocrisy of the French Résistance and the Nuremburg trials. However, its ostensibly critical narrative culminates in an appreciative affirmation of the widely acclaimed film, Weapons of the Spirit (Pierre Sauvage, U.S.A., 1988), a historical documentary about members of the Huguenot community of Le Chambon-sur-Ligne who selflessly and on solely religious grounds aided hundreds of Jews wishing to flee the Nazi Occupation. Rather than delve critically into urgent political questions about anti–Nazi rescue and resistance raised by the Le Chambon phenomenon (not to mention The Sorrow and the Pity), or excavate and elaborate upon the film's political allegorical significance (as has been attempted with Night and Fog vis-à-vis the Algerian anti–colonialist struggle),[101] Colombat facilely resuscitates the christological notion of the Holocaust. He refers consistently to its persecuted and victimized Jews as "the 'others'" and affirms a moral imperative to convey their suffering as an expression of "religious faith," "Lazarean heroism," and "feminine love."[102] By extension, he rearticulates Holocaust rescue and resistance as a locus of personal sacrifice, such that the community of Le Chambon portrayed in Weapons of the Spirit can be interpreted and subsequently valorized as a convocation of Christian sainthood. In so doing, Colombat implicitly characterizes the Holocaust perpetrated against Jews and Roma alike as a reenactment of the christic sacrifice and, in turn, ironically reinscribes a necessity onto that event eerily reminiscent of Girard. Recalling Koch, that necessity is lent philosophical credibility by reference to phenomenological theories of Sartre, Edmund Husserl, Heidegger, Freud, and film semiologist Christian Metz, which authorizes Colombat's assigning an "affective intentionality" to Holocaust imagery.[103] Instead of elaborating the political questions raised by *The Sorrow and the Pity* and *Night and Fog*, which might consider how the imperative to rescue Jewish "others" ramifies so-called humanitarian ventures within the contemporary global arena (not to mention the political revisioning of French Protestantism), this culminative analysis has the counterpolitical effect of collapsing any *critical* notion of the Holocaust—including its conception as an event overdetermined by *an ideology of sacrifice*[104]—onto the christological notion of the Holocaust *as sacrifice*. Such a category error makes it nearly impossible to deploy "Holocaust" in ways that can both acknowledge and critique its religious, including *Jewish* messianic, contextualizations—as has recently been attempted by the celebrated Agamben[105]—for this rhetorical collapse dissolves the historical factuality and residing political significance of the Le Chambon phenomenon into that to which Colombat actually refers as an obscurantist allegory of "disorienting mystery."[106]

In effect, and pace the paradigm undergirding LaCapra's position as well as the imperative outlined by Lipstadt to remain truthful to the empirical facts of Holocaust history, texts of Holocaust film criticism have remained fixated upon the aesthetic problematics of representation. On the one hand, they aspire to uphold the priority of historical *experience* in the analysis of Holocaust culture. On the other hand, they neglect the social and conceptual *overdetermination* of any such experience, thus serving to transpose its material significance onto a privatized, esoteric register that comprehends Holocaust culture in mystical terms—as at once an intangible mnemonic analogue of the actual Holocaust and a literal exemplification of that event's primarily "Judeo-Christian" interpretability. Even subsequent, secondary literature in this area, invigorated by the dismantlement and liberalization of the former Soviet bloc, understands the Holocaust as both empirically self-evident and (onto)theologically predetermined. Much of this criticism relies on and recycles an ambiguous, if familiar, anthropological structure of redeemed sacrificial alterity; within this structure, the Holocaust becomes, in the context of the classic, allegorical "lost object" retrieved from potential oblivion, the proverbial "other planet" of concentration camp memoirs.[107] Briefly put, these texts of Holocaust film criticism refashion the event into a broadly, if not universally, palatable commodity that befits, apropos of critiques by Peter Novick and Norman Finkelstein, prevailing tastes and presumed ideological needs.

In line with the liberal populism of Doneson, however, this latest series of texts articulates markedly different terms than did the philosophically informed, discursively challenging excurses of LaCapra, Colombat, and others. Indeed, a distinctly mainstream, at times journalistic modality characterizes many of these texts; the glib subjectivism of this modality assumes certain knowledge or its acceptance on the part of their readerships[108] and, as with Lipstadt, seeks to achieve legitimacy by approximating empirical accuracy.[109] This is the case even when these texts refer, atypically for Holocaust cinema studies, to contemporary and topical issues such as pornography, propaganda, humor, sexuality, popular memory, Third World struggles, and the conflict in Israel/Palestine. Despite their ostensible novelty, these texts display an inability or refusal to break with the phenomenological paradigm. Exemplary are the concluding words of the introduction to the premier Holocaust film studies anthology, *Spielberg's Holocaust*, which insist that questions about the Holocaust are "not easily answered" and are therefore best contextualized within "an ongoing, provocative debate."[110] As if recalling LaCapra's subtle analogy of Holocaust discourse to "creative modes of consumption," these words bespeak an understandable refusal to supply easy answers to urgent questions while also running the risk of privileging Holocaust studies approaches that not only acknowledge but affirm ambivalence. While perhaps unintentionally, these works also finally condone efforts to keep the issue a lucrative one.[111]

This subtle alignment of Holocaust critical ambivalence with cultural commodification finds a blatant Christian analogue in Miriam Hansen's contribution to *Spielberg's Holocaust*, "*Schindler's List* Is Not *Shoah*." To its credit, this text is much more theoretically sophisticated than its contemporaries; however, it lends an imperialist twist to the problematics of critical ambivalence by conceiving Holocaust films as affirmative allegories of transnationalism that make a case "for a capitalist aesthetics and culture which is at once modernist and popular, which would be capable of reflecting upon the shocks and scars inflicted by modernity on people's lives in a generally accessible, public horizon."[112] Hansen is committed to formulating and ascribing to this pragmatic, populist, and capitalist aesthetics despite the potentially destructive, even holocaustal ramifications of the accommodation it proposes to contemporary neoliberalism. On her view, failing to do so would mean "missing a chance to understand the significance of the Shoah in the present [...] as a kind of screen allegory behind/through which the nation is struggling to find a proper mode of memorializing traumata close to home."[113]

On the other hand, filmmaker and journalist Haim Bresheeth's contribution to the same anthology would appear to contradict Hansen's (trans)nationalist overtones by offering an unfailing critique of the relationship between Holocaust cinematic representation and the global politics of the conflict in Israel/Palestine. In implicit contradistinction to her and to Doneson, he states,

> The Holocaust has been used stereotypically for a long period, supplying *post factum* justification not just for the existence of Israel but for its defensive (and offensive) military stance. This is where the reevaluation of Holocaust memories

leads to a resultant reevaluation of that stance [...] Is the world possibly now more safe for Israeli Jews, or will they continue to represent every act against the state of Israel as a prelude or an echo of a new Holocaust? [...] The debate clearly represents an important stage in moving from forms of Holocaust remembrance controlled by the state and, to some extent, delaying a political solution to a new phase where popular understanding of the Holocaust may assist in bringing about such a solution. (Bresheeth, "The Great Taboo Broken," 209–10)

The unprecedented political candor of Bresheeth's analysis is nonetheless devoid of Hansen's film theoretical engagement. It focuses strictly on the Israeli public reception of *Schindler's List*, reverting to the historicism and culturalist phenomenology familiar in fact to readers of Doneson and of Avisar. This neglect bespeaks ambivalence in what would appear a self-consciously positioned argument. Upon encountering it, one is unsure whether Bresheeth's call for "popular understandings of the Holocaust" is grounded in support for Palestinian civil and political equality, which would at the very least entail an end to the Israeli military occupation of the Palestinian Territories, or whether it instead represents a plea for Israel/Palestine's full-scale, political and economic delinkage from U.S./European patronage, which could entail the formation of one multicultural state fully integrated into the region—or both.[114] This reading holds even in hindsight of Bresheeth's more recent emigration from Israel to England along with *Spielberg's Holocaust*'s editor, Yosefa Loshitzky, and their ensuing public renunciation of their Israeli citizenship. How might a *cinematic* critique of *Schindler's List* help supply answers to questions such as these? In effect, it remains unclear that Bresheeth's libertarian populist position on Holocaust cultural appropriation is qualitatively different from that of the elite christological Hansen.[115]

Boding poorly for the current direction of Holocaust cinema studies is the fact that these questions and issues are entirely neglected by both *Popular Culture and the Shaping of Holocaust Memory in America*, by Alan Mintz, and *Afterimage*, by Joshua Hirsch, the only two book-length scholarly monographs on Holocaust and film to have been published in English since Colombat—and the U.S. presidency of George W. Bush. This apparent academic reticence toward the political implications of Holocaust film is not surprising in the case of Mintz, a Hebrew literary scholar who unabashedly refuses to engage the film theory which might have made it more difficult for him to sidestep political analysis: "I have not set myself to work within the canons of film studies, film history, and film criticism. [This book contains] studies in reception, which means they examine how critics and audiences responded to the films and how they understood them."[116] Setting aside for a moment the long tradition of reception theoretical inquiry in Cinema Studies,[117] examples of which are Bresheeth and Ewout Van der Knaap, one is hard-pressed to locate sustained evidence in Mintz's analysis of the "responses" he claims to explore. Mintz meagerly explains reception studies methodology, omitting reference to important figures such as Paul Ricoeur, Wolfgang Iser, and Hans Robert Jauss,[118] phenomenologists all, the last of whom was scandalized during the late 1980s by public revelations concerning his wartime participation in Nazi Wehrmacht mobile killing units. In lieu of theory, the salient feature of Mintz's analysis is an unremarked reversal of Bresheeth's political position on cultural reception and the challenges it opens to prevailing discourse on Holocaust film. Recalling Doneson, whom Mintz cites occasionally for support, Mintz asserts the existence of a U.S. Jewish consensus affirmed in commitment to "the Zionist enterprise" by the fact of the Holocaust and its "hovering specter" (vis-à-vis which we might elicit how the latter may be exemplified by figs. 1-1 and 1-2); and he insists that Holocaust film underscores this commitment by producing "awareness that the state of Israel had been born 'out of the ashes' of the Holocaust."[119] Again Mintz supplies no sustained evidence to support his claims, which are patently false: significant numbers of Jews in both North America and Israel, not to mention Europe and elsewhere, share views closer to those of Bresheeth regarding Zionism and the conflict in Israel/Palestine;[120] moreover, contemporary historiographic research not only reminds us that Zionism predates the Holocaust but proves that narratives which assume a subsequent redemptive function for Israel are insupportable.[121] The presumptuous Mintz is apparently unfazed by these contradictions, which he largely evades as he shamelessly dedicates his book to Baruch Goldstein, a Jewish-American member of the right-wing Zionist Kach Party who, on February 25, 1994, was fatally apprehended by military police after he massacred in cold blood twenty-nine innocent Palestinians who were praying peacefully in a Hebron mosque.[122] Mintz refers to this extremist mass-murderer as a "Tzaddik Bedoratov"—one of the righteous of his generation. The scandalousness of this maneuver is not ameliorated by Mintz's numerous deferrals to the moral platitudes of Jewish exceptionalist Holocaust survivor Elie Wiesel.

In striking contrast is Joshua Hirsch's *Afterimage*, which earns distinction, nearly sixty years after the liberation of Auschwitz, as the first published monograph on Holocaust film ever to have been authored by a doctor of Film Studies. Like Koch, Hansen, and Colombat, Hirsch is theoretically informed and well-versed in film language. Unlike his predecessors, he devotes significant space to what he calls "cross-cultural" cinema, that is, to films which depict holocaustal events and experiences other than those of the Judeocide. His is also the first monograph to offer extensive focus on Eastern European Holocaust films, namely, the cinematic *oeuvre* of Hungarian auteur István Szabó.

For all its theoretical acumen and academic innovativeness, however,

Fig. 1-1 – "Expelled Again?" (Brian Vander Brug, *Los Angeles Times*, August 17, 2005)
– Gaza withdrawal protestors holding poster containing Holocaust-era photo

Fig. 1-2 – Gaza withdrawal protestor wearing concentration camp uniform

Hirsch's analysis does not break with the phenomenological paradigm or its political implications. In fact, that paradigm is reinforced by the book's critical positioning firmly within the context of trauma theory and its fashionable discourses of witnessing and memory.[123] Hirsch in this aspect continues LaCapra's project, but his analysis also differs in important respects. First, Hirsch resists LaCapra's christological naturalization of an endless working-through—what Freud might have referred to as melancholia—by positing the symbolic rehearsal of trauma as an eventually conclusive, if protracted, component of genuine mourning-work. Accordingly, Hirsch proposes a Holocaust film criticism that can "undo the [...] enforced historical isolation" of both Holocaust victims and spectators by offering both kinds of "witness" a "safe space" for mutual encounter and therapeutic transmission of holocaustal experience. Hirsh seems in this way to be positing a Judaic hermeneutic alternative to LaCapra's self-sacrificial scene of perpetual ritual interaction: culling from Marianne Hirsch's theory of "postmemory,"[124] Hirsch suggests that "cinematic knowledge of a traumatic past might not lead to the containment of that past, but rather to its *continued disturbance* of the present" (my emphasis).[125] On his view:

> Trauma, even before being transmitted, is already utterly bound up with the realm of representation. It is, to be more precise, a crisis of representation. An extreme event is perceived as radically out of joint with one's mental representation of the world, which is itself partly derived from the set of representations of the world that one receives from one's family and culture. The mind goes into shock, becomes incapable of translating the impressions of the event into a coherent mental representation. The impressions remain in the mind, intact and unassimilated [...] Its significance [...] transcends the literal referencing of any particular experience of trauma or vicarious trauma [...] and lies, rather, in the staking out, in the languages of various media, of a discursive space pertinent to all these experiences. (Hirsch, *Afterimage: Film, Trauma, and the Holocaust* [Philadelphia: Temple University Press], 15–18)

While writing from a theory of cognitive dissonance that differs from Marianne Hirsch's psychoanalytic approach (indeed Hirsch never cites his interdisciplinary namesake), Joshua Hirsch joins her in understanding Holocaust representation in a Jewish phenomenological sense that positions holocaustal experience not as an allegorical node of conciliation and consolation but as a paradigmatic vector of historical movement and change: at once unique and universal, the feelings which holocaustal experience may transmit culturally are understood to extend past their historical specificity, and thereby to disrupt and potentially to reorient—not just to regulate—social complacency in the face of new and ongoing traumas. Although clearly aestheticist in its transcendental framing of representational "shock" (it in fact recalls but simplifies Benjamin's similar notion),[126] this Jewish allegorical conception of Holocaust representation complicates and to some extent redirects both Hansen's and Doneson's hegemonic conceptions of its social function by illuminating the power relations mediating the global exchange of Holocaust cultural forms, hence tempering the preponderant tendency to appropriate ritually evoked "shared feelings" of holocaustal trauma on behalf of imperialist advance.

The Judaically informed quality of Hirsch's theory remains implicit, however, and he proceeds to excuse Holocaust films that he believes "repress" the Judeocide for nonetheless introducing a variety of useful cinematic techniques for conveying the traumatic experiences of the event:

> At the level of content, [*Night and Fog*] both combated the repression of the memory of the camps and contributed to the repression of the memory of the Jewish genocide. But at the same time, it contributed a new discourse of historical trauma through the content of its form. (Hirsch, *Afterimage*, 31)

Hirsch argues for a Holocaust film practice that, like Avisar's textualism, can (re)contain the experience of Holocaust trauma within its rhetorical interstices. In so doing, though, he proffers an apparently supersessionist claim against traditional realist depictions, which he considers "authoritarian," "forensic," and "moralistic," and which techniques of empirical transparency he decries, mistakenly, as "epistemological."[127] Here again Hirsch differs from LaCapra, for while both critics are rightfully suspicious of self-evident visual designations (even Bazin would concur), Hirsch's rejection of explicative Holocaust documentary is founded within a cognitivist belief that holocaustal experience is transmissible *mnemonically* rather than *subliminally*: the Holocaust is ineffable because it has been lost to memory, not because it transcends the ontos essentially. Hirsch's hope for Holocaust film is that it can retrieve this lost memory behavioristically, through practiced invocation of the mental impressions trapped within preconscious spectatorial states. As in a kabbalistic interpolation of *tikkun ha-olam*, for which remembering entails gathering concertedly the fragments of a shattered cosmos in an effort to reunite them and thereby to rectify existence, Hirsch's project is actually less supersessionist than gnostic; it assumes a relatively direct accessibility of experience to consciousness, a condition which Hirsch believes realist modalities tend to intercept and reduce but that experimental, non-realist modalities are able to harness and transport across identitarian borders, beyond but never past the "original," *Jewish* Holocaust.

It is in this mystical context that Hirsch advances his premier theory of a non-ethnocentric Holocaust cinema: *posttraumatic cinema*. "Posttraumatic cinema" is a film practice at once non-realist and variously resistant to the metonymization of holocaustal experience found in LaCapra's and Colombat's postmodern approaches. Posttraumatic cinema is not interested in sublimating the social-conceptual and ideological underpinnings of temporal passage, dialogic interaction, and textual layering of Holocaust film into serial oblivion. Instead it foregrounds the conflictuality of those formal-aesthetic and narrative-compositional structures, presenting them as intellectually variegated hermeneutic effects of "the structural relation between shots," not "the ontology of the photographic image"—that is, by way of metaphor.[128] Hirsch draws from Sergei Eisenstein's theory of montage to blast the canonical Holocaust studies proscription against metaphorizing the event, a tack understood by Jewish particularist critics Elie Wiesel, Alan Rosenfeld, and Lawrence Langer as precisely that unwanted means for broaching interpretations which may render the Judeocide comparable with other genocides.[129] In an uncanny rapprochement with LaCapra, Hirsch nonetheless dislocates his ostensibly daring notion of Holocaust cinematic metaphoricity from the differential logics of material social relations, recognized by Eisenstein as well as by Balázs and Kracauer as the systemic structures in critical relation to which a film's interpretive layering may be dehierarchized and democratized most effectively, and refastens its critical function to that of an anthropomorphic camera which may purvey the "existential point of view" of a "wandering consciousness" and project a "hyper–realistic representation of [that] consciousness, of the way in which the world is given meaning by the mind."[130] Hirsch in effect translates the textual-political leveling function of cinematic metaphor into a metaphysical operation of personified *technē*, thereby fetishizing the institution of cinema signified by the industrially produced device of the camera/projector and its planned orchestrations and reinstituting a reductive limit around the "universal" knowledgeability he claims for the apparatus in that respect. This *neoformalist* phenomenology of Holocaust film is compatible with postmodern approaches that disarm rhetorically the ideologics of cinematicity[131] and derogate epistemology, the potentially political study of systems of intelligibility—what Foucault famously calls *epistēmēs*[132]—to the status of "los[t] confidence." In turn this nostalgic approach travesties the Jewish allegorical ethic of Holocaust "witnessing," in which the asymmetricality—the exploitability—of spectatorship is recognized and taken into critical account, into an obsessive, cognitive-reflexive "listening to another's wound."[133]

Although proffering a "cross-cultural" exchange of holocaustal experiences via "posttraumatic" cinematic spectatorship, then, Hirsch betrays a conservative populist sense of the Holocaust's "uniqueness," for which the Judeocide is finally incomparable because knowable only experientially. That he discusses little if any of the political, historical, and economic conditions or significance of Holocaust filmmaking—not least in communist Hungary—is not surprising given this abstract angle. An "autobiographical" approach to Szabó substitutes for that, and as for the relationship of Holocaust film to Israeli culture and the conflict in Israel/Palestine, Hirsch claims ignorance of any but Avisar's secondary writing on the subject, likewise ignoring Bresheeth, the later Loshitzky, not to mention respected Israeli anti–Zionist film scholar Ella Shohat.[134] By these evasive means, Hirsch implicitly occludes the important thesis advanced by Jewish Marxist critical theorist Enzo Traverso, for whom the Holocaust is *historically* unique because it was "a genocide conceived on an exclusively 'racial' basis" within the context of a capitalist ideologics and/of secular religiosity, the understanding of whose distinctiveness as such does not require, as it finally seems to for Hirsch, "setting up a hierarchy," or "confer[ring] any particular aura on its victims or any privilege on its martyrdom [and] does not exclude other kinds of uniqueness"—all of which would reaffirm that genocidal context and its pseudo-scientific effects.[135] Unlike Hirsch, Traverso conceives the Holocaust historicopolitically and is therefore able to reconceive its dominant cultural interpretability as an index of perpetually devastating semiosis into "a tool with which to develop a [radical] hermeneutics of twentieth-century barbarism."[136]

What would it mean for Holocaust cinema studies to interpret Holocaust films along the lines set up by Traverso? Put another way, is a critical analysis of Holocaust film ever anything but obscene if it does not grapple seriously with the questions Traverso and others like him compel?

* * * * *

As I have argued, a dearth is demonstrable in both substantive scholarly criticism of Holocaust cinematic culture and in criticism of that culture which could break the intellectually, politically, and economically obfuscatory pattern of christology and derivative, including Jewish, phenomenologies. An apparently habitual scholarly academic neglect persists to examine 1) how the history of the Holocaust and its varied explanations are projected formally and discursively across the hermeneutic (interpretive) layers of Holocaust films, 2) how, why, and what kinds of public controversies, print media debates, and scholarly reactions have emerged in relation to certain of these films, and 3) what political consequences and ideological implications may be discerned at the critical intersections of these films' cultural articulations (their inscriptions of race, ethnicity, gender, sexuality, nationality, class, and religious creed) and their global social extensions. Still missing, then, is a sustained criticism of Holocaust culture's phenomenological interpolation which could resist and, potentially, work critically to transform the enabling conditions of anti–Judaism, Eurocentric racism, and pragmatic populism in Cinema Studies and beyond.

But from what position could one articulate and enact such a resistant and transformative Holocaust film criticism? Could one indeed initiate a Holocaust film theory that, while necessarily breaking the taboo against its formulation, does not also carry with it the stigma(ta) of hubris, mere speculation, or immanent (self-)destruction? Is it possible, that is, for traditionally sacral theologies bound up even with secular Holocaust film theory to be reconceived, on *radically* secular grounds, as nothing more than discourses among others and, as such, as subjectable to the same sorts of interrogations and critiques as are any phenomenological or epistemological discourses now familiar to film and cultural studies? Is it furthermore conceivable that such a veritable profanation would not take the form of a reinscribed christology or related mysticism, as is common in formalist avant-garde "materialism,"[137] and thus merely replicate the naturalization and normalization of sacrificial othering on the quotidian plane? Would it be possible, instead, to develop a Judaically informed mode of materialist film analysis that would enable a distinctive, potentially radical Holocaust film criticism? And, finally, if so, what would characterize such a *radically secular Judaic analytic*?

My aim in the present book is to reverse the general trend away from any such possibility by foregrounding the issues which the trend neglects in light of four Holocaust films released during the historical period spanning the early Reagan era through the early Clinton era and reaching its apex between the time of the Soviet dissolution and the fall of the Berlin Wall. This period of global interregnum is highlighted by, inter alia, the first contemporary Palestinian *intifada* (1987–1993) and the first U.S.-led military invasion of Iraq (1991). The period is characterized within the humanities by a general yet diversified (re)turn to phenomenology, a concomitant resistance to Marxism and left critical theory, and a historiographic revisioning of the twentieth century, including the Holocaust, from ideological perspectives locatable to a nexus of neoliberal and neoconservative tendencies which extend hegemonically and violently into the Middle East. The four films examined closely are: *Korczak* (Andrzej Wajda, Poland/Germany/U.K., 1990); *The Quarrel* (Eli Cohen, Canada/U.S.A., 1990); *Entre Nous* [*Coup de foudre*] (Diane Kurys, France, 1983); and *Balagan* (Andres Veiel, Germany/Israel, 1994). Of these films, *Korczak* and *Entre Nous* received international financing and distribution, international acclaim, and significant popular attention, while *The Quarrel*, although broadcast on both Canadian and U.S. public television and later featured at numerous film festivals and screening series in North America and abroad, was either ignored or dismissed by most film critics. All four films were distributed theatrically on the art cinema circuit and were received with some modicum of controversy, although only *Balagan*'s unconventional structure and irreverent content place it thoroughly outside the mainstream. Each film in its way pushes the limits of traditional cinematic realism; none depicts the Holocaust through explicative or naturalistic modes, and all to some extent engage the problematics of Holocaust uniqueness and Jewish particularism in ways that critically inflect the films' aesthetic ideological functions and affect the public and academic debates which have arisen over and around them.

My analysis of these films is especially concerned with the meaning and significance of these controversies and debates, and as such it partakes of reception theory as understood by Mintz and Bresheeth: it questions the effects of Holocaust film on received understandings of the Holocaust circulating within popular culture and academia. As Doneson and Hansen well know, such understandings bespeak political and ideological concerns pertinent to a film's conditions of production and distribution, whereupon analysis of emergent debates can prompt critical discussion about the political significance of Holocaust films in general. My analysis differs from this limited view of reception theory, however. I am indeed interested in proffering a serious, deep structural understanding of international Holocaust film, but the conceptual framework I henceforth utilize to help ascertain a film's social significance does not rest on phenomenological grounds. Like Hansen, it repositions the hermeneutic function of cinema—the possibility that spectators locate and make real sense of cinematic signifiers—in critical relation to a film's formal-aesthetic and narrative-compositional structures, not simply its image and story content, authorship, generic modality, or the affective moods and generalized opinions it may elicit. In contrast, however, to New Critical and historicist methods and their postmodern derivatives, my analysis recognizes formal-aesthetic and narrative-compositional structures *not* as ethereal or corporeal manifestations of an ideal or existential ontos, but as differentially mediated, layered and arranged articulations of situated, if fragmented, positions and perspectives within an asymmetrical social system that implicates the historical contradictions of Holocaust films, critics, and spectators ineluctably. On this critical historiographic grounding, I advance a Holocaust film theory that can recognize the politically motivated parameters of debate over and around Holocaust films, and that can intervene into ideological formations which compel extant Holocaust films and film theories to adhere more or less unquestioningly to those parameters. My analysis in this respect serves also to destabilize both orthodox Marxist and some left postmodern theories of cinematic culture, by upholding the Brechtian notion they often fail for which film is both an artistic and pedagogical medium.

More concretely, I shall consider the four selected films as paradigmatic examples of a claim that elisions and limitations within Holocaust cinematic culture, including Holocaust film theory and criticism, are symptomatic dissimulations of political and economic developments of the contemporary social arena. This consideration holds that critical understandings of these elisions and limitations are incomplete insofar as their function as exploitation-effects—as symptoms of and political interventions into the capitalist class struggle at the register of cultural practice—remains unrecognized and unaccounted for. In the spirit of Enzo Traverso reading Benjamin reading Marx,[138] Holocaust film criticism must not refuse inquiry into the hermeneutical, especially religious-utopian configurations of such developments and struggles in Holocaust films if it is to offer a socially meaningful, that is, truly anti–genocidal analysis of this compelling cultural phenomenon. The logic of my analysis is therefore at once theoretical and historiographic: it is allegorical. It entails locating and explicating the hermeneutic patterns and layering of the four respective films as each infers a particular modality of Holocaust discourse pervasive during the general period highlighted by the book and within the particular periods marked out by the films themselves. For *Korczak*, this means entering Jewish–Christian debates over ethnic and religious "ownership" of the Holocaust, and gauging their ramifications for renewed national consciousness and cultural appropriation of the event. For *The Quarrel*, it means resituating the orthodox Jewish argument that the Holocaust was brought about as a result of abandoned faith resulting from modern secular attachment to nationalism, including but not limited to Zionism. For *Entre Nous*, it involves revisiting the problematics of Holocaust cultural "obscenity" from perspectives of feminism and glbtq liberation struggles. And for *Balagan*, it necessitates sustained engagement with the still taboo question of how "Holocaust" functions within the context of anti–colonial and anti–racist struggles in Israel/Palestine. The orchestration of this logic traces contemporaneous developments within film and cultural studies, upon whose applicability the films' interpretability has often respectively turned: shifts and overlaps between classical phenomenology and photographic realism, structuralist semiotics and narrative deconstruction, psychoanalytic semiotics and poststructuralist historiography, and postmodern aesthetics and performance theory—whereby discussion of the films becomes also a discussion of the critical discourses around and about them and their social enabling conditions. In this way the relevance of the films to contemporary politics, especially U.S. and Israeli policy in the Middle East, can be clarified.

My methodology draws upon Marxian critiques of metaphysics and ontology that have long been at issue in Holocaust studies, namely those staged by the "culture industry" criticism associated with the Frankfurt School[139] as it encounters, and may be enlisted to challenge, postmodern theoretical developments (deconstruction, new historiography, performance theory, postcolonial and queer theories), which I have noted are often deployed against serious readings of Holocaust film. My methodology also draws upon by-now classic materialist theories of film movements and cinematic practices such as those forwarded by Noël Burch, David James, and Jonathan Crary, as they contend with and critically resist Cinema Studies' domination by psychoanalytic-semiotics, aesthetic ontology, cognitive theory, and authorship and genre studies—which together have facilitated the reintroduction of anti–theoretical and depoliticizing modalities into the field. Whereas I recognize a structural compatibility between those historically distinct frameworks, which I reformulate here into a generally resisted, critical cultural epistemology of Holocaust film, my analysis proceeds from a conceptual position politically distinct from positions marking the theme/genre/auteur approaches of most non-film studies-based Holocaust cultural analyses[140] as well as from the neoformalist criticism associated with film scholar David Bordwell, and from the aesthetic phenomenologies of Balázs and the later Kracauer, whose early works have enjoyed interdisciplinary renewal in the context of their engagement within Holocaust film. In effect, I analyze Holocaust film in strict terms neither of aesthetic philosophy nor conventional historicism, but—recalling works of the early Birmingham School and of the Screen Education group[141]—insofar as it may at once provoke and sustain incisive questions about how spectatorial subjectivities are themselves more or less imbricated within traditional, if not always dominant, understandings and explanations of the Holocaust as these are projected across and propagated by Holocaust films in particular and persist in turn as topics of debate within an increasingly neoconservative public sphere.

By extension, the methodology I adopt alters the problematics of Holocaust film criticism by engaging the crucial Judaic analytic technique, *le-didakh*. My engagement of *le-didakh*, which is defined and exemplified most saliently in Chapter Three, is meant not as a parochial or sectarian gesture—the technique is practiced variously within many religious orientations and their diverse secular rearticulations—but as a theoretical means for facilitating a paradigm shift in Holocaust film studies by prompting an opening in the field onto a differential reunderstanding of the "Jewish" as it has functioned historically in Holocaust film and film criticism. This reunderstanding entails repositioning the Judaic as philosophically prior within the criticism of Holocaust film, recognizing it as historically having both preceded and derived from, but as having neither ontologically founded nor ideologically determined, the christological. This differential reunderstanding is meant to help re-envision the Judaic and its "Jewish" intelligibility within Holocaust cinema studies not as the familiarly ideal "other" of, but as a philosophical system at once *other than* and *radical to*, that of the "Judeo-Christian." By this technique of radical supplementation, my analysis subjects Holocaust film culture to a sorely needed and thoroughgoing critique, exposing and delineating formal-aesthetic and narrative-compositional layers of Holocaust film as they become associable to non-cinematic fields of public contestation, (inter)national affiliation, and economic determination.

With due respect to Adorno, this methodology offers a radically reflexive reorientation of the social conditions that constitute and enable Holocaust films. It works not to reduce, divide, and redeploy its objects of analysis; rather, in the critical theoretical traditional of *immanent critique*, it relocates Holocaust films intellectually, engaging and interrogating the textual contradictions and aporias which symptomatize the ideological reduction of cinematic layers into apparent coherence and viability, and which preclude re-envisioning those contradictions and aporias, apropos of Marx, as reified principles of historical movement and change.[142] This relocation aims to pose the critical question of how *and why* these films might be theorized, produced, and received other than through reductive, phenomenological approaches that assimilate them, their means of conception and dissemination, into christological orientations.[143]

In effect, by at once foregrounding the dialectical character of the contrasting, often varied frameworks and perspectives through which the Holocaust has been understood by film culture at particular historical moments and within particular social arenas, the inquiry in which the present book engages directs critical focus on what Holocaust cinematic culture has tended repeatedly to leave out, even while it performs a certain appreciation of that culture's abiding achievements—its symptomatic kernels of emancipatory truth. Put another way, the critical method of this book resists reifying the Holocaust. Through its radical epistemological engagement, the Holocaust is transcribed into "Holocaust," an ideological concept the meaning and significance of which is reunderstood as a site of historical *mis*recognition whose entailments and ramifications have yet to be comprehended in terms of the commodity-function they really serve.[144] While never disavowing a secular project of worldly orientation and inclusiveness, then, the present book focuses reader attention upon the structuring absences of Holocaust cinematic culture, inviting the location and inspection of its social, political, and economic elisions from a "le-didakhically" grounded "inside."

Unfortunately, as it stands, the field of Cinema Studies has yet to see an actual and sustained critical theorization and materialist application of *le-didakh*, and a current wave of anti–theoretical scholarship threatens further to deter any such pursuit.[145] This includes postmodern Marxist works by Deleuze and Felix Guattari, and by Antonio Negri and Michael Hardt, which, in contrast to the economically more concrete works of Ellen Meiksins Wood,[146] likewise mystify the material grounding of contemporary social struggles in an explicitly undialectical, neo-ontological fashion. It is as though the supposition offered by Holocaust historian, John Weiss, were true, as he, a professed Christian, remarks, in another context,

> Even today in the most liberal of nations, such truly free expression is far too strong for most, for Christians would be forced to confront powerful arguments

against the idea that Jesus was the Messiah of the Jews, and this from a
community well represented by learned biblical scholars who best know the
original languages and texts. "Jews for Jesus" is one thing; Jews against Jesus
would be quite another. (Weiss, *Ideology of Death: Why the Holocaust
Happened in Germany* [Chicago: I. R. Dee, 1996], 43)

Some might question whether Weiss' remarks are applicable here—that is,
whether the persistent phenomenological occlusion of serious, Judaically
informed materialist discourse from Holocaust film criticism is merely a defense
against critiques, Judaic or otherwise, of Christianity per se rather than an
ideological effort, advanced by Jews and Christians and their secular
counterparts, to justify the pragmatic (re)generation of competing nationalisms
under the rubric of neoliberal capitalism that supports an exclusivist "Jewish"
state formation and a related agenda of U.S.-backed violence against Muslims
and Arabs in the Middle East and beyond. It nevertheless would be difficult to
deny a general, political-historical connection between the outright anti–Judaism
John Weiss believes prevalent within contemporary society and the more subtle,
philosemitic "Judeo-Christian" discourse that interpolates the Eurocentric
problematics of Holocaust film theory and culture and evidently requires for its
continued legitimacy the marginalization of the Judaic as well as the Judaically
informed.[147] On the other hand, it is the express purpose of this book to urge the
encouragement and support of a radical *le-didakhic* film theory—and to suggest
that failure in this respect occurs only as a symptom of a much larger dissolution
and collapse.

---

[1] E.g., *Death Mills* [*Die Todesmühlen*] (U.S. War Department/Hanuš Burger,
U.S.A./Germany, 1945); and *Les Camps de la mort* (Actualités Françaises, France,
1948). See K. R. M. Short and Stephen Dolezel, *Hitler's Fall: The Newsreel Witness*
(London: Croon Helm, 1988).
[2] Norman G. Finkelstein, *Beyond Chutzpah: On the Misuse of Anti–Semitism and the
Abuse of History* (Berkeley and Los Angeles: University of California Press), 83.
[3] *The Diary of Anne Frank* (George Stevens, U.S.A., 1959); *Exodus* (Otto Preminger,
U.S.A., 1960); *Judgment at Nuremberg* (Stanley Kramer, U.S.A., 1961).
[4] In addition to *Death Mills* and *Les Camps de la mort* are: *Long Is the Road* (Herbert B.
Fredershof and Marek Goldstein, U.S.-Occupied Germany, 1945); *The Last Chance* [*Die
Letzte Chance*] (Leopold Lindtberg, Switzerland, 1945); *Murderers Are Among Us* [*Die
Mörder sind unter uns*] (Wolfgang Staudte, East Germany, 1946); *Somewhere in Europe*
[*Valahol Európában*] (Géza von Radványi, Hungary, 1947); *The Last Stop* [*Ostatni etap*]
(Wanda Jakubowska, Poland, 1948); *The Blum Affair* (Erich Engel, East Germany,
1948); and *Border Street* [*Ulice Graniczna*] (Aleksander Ford, Poland, 1949).
[5] *Fighters of the Ghetto* (Mira Hamermesh, Israel, 1968); *The Warsaw Ghetto* (BBC-TV,
U.K., 1968); *Genocide* (Michael Darlow, Thames-TV, U.K., 1975); *The Eighty-First
Blow* (Haim Gouri, David Bergman, Jacquo Erlich, Israel, 1975). Regarding U.S.
network television talk-show appearances by Holocaust survivors, see Jeffrey Shandler,

While America Watches: Televising the Holocaust (New York: Oxford University Press, 1999).

[6] "Retro-style" films include: *Love Camp Seven* (R. L. Frost, U.S.A., 1968); *The Seven Beauties* [*Pasqualino Settebelezzi*] (Lina Wertmüller, Italy/U.S.A., 1975); *The Serpent's Egg* (Ingmar Bergman, U.S.A./West Germany, 1977); *Lacombe Lucien* (Louis Malle, France/West Germany/Italy, 1974); *The Night Porter* [*Il portiere di notte*] (Liliana Cavani, Italy, 1974); *The Last Métro* (François Truffaut, France, 1980); *Das Boot* ["The Boat"] (Wolfgang Petersen, West Germany, 1981); and *Lili Marleen* (Rainer Werner Fassbinder, West Germany, 1981).

Among the "European art film" category, under which the preceding films also may be listed, I include additionally: *The Garden of the Finzi-Continis* [*Il Giardino dei Finzi-Contini*] (Vittorio De Sica, Italy/West Germany, 1970); *Mr. Klein* [*Monsieur Klein*] (Joseph Losey, France/Italy, 1976); *Mephisto* (István Szabó, West Germany/Hungary/Austria, 1981); and *The Assault* [*De Aanslag*] (Fons Rademakers, Netherlands, 1986).

For an overview of the "retro" genre, see Robert C. Reimer and Carol J. Reimer, *Nazi-Retro Film: How German Narrative Cinema Remembers the Past* (New York: Twayne, 1992). See also Kriss Ravetto, *The Unmaking of Fascist Aesthetics* (Minneapolis and London: University of Minnesota Press, 2001). For a critical perspective, esp. as regards the French cultural scene, see Pascal Bonitzer and Serge Toubiana, "'Anti–Rétro': Entretien avec Michel Foucault," *Cahiers du Cinéma* 251–52 (1974): 5–17. Also belonging to this list are films and books which project this "retro" vision into a science-fictional or demonic-conspiratorial future: Tim Burris, *Genocide: The Anthology* (Stamford, CT: Knights Press, 1988); Alan Cantwell, Jr., *Queer Blood: The Secret AIDS Genocide Plot* (Los Angeles: Aries Rising, 1993); and in a subtle way, the film *Contact* (Robert Zemeckis, U.S.A., 1997).

[7] See Jon Lewis, ed., *The New American Cinema* (Durham, NC and London: Duke University Press, 1998).

[8] *Holocaust* (Marvin Chomsky, NBC-TV, U.S.A., 1978); *Playing for Time* (Daniel Mann, CBS-TV, U.S.A., 1980); *Skokie* (Herbert Wise, CBS-TV, U.S.A., 1981). A more recent example of the Holocaust tele-film is *Auschwitz: The Nazis and the "Final Solution"* (Laurence Rees, BBC-TV, U.K., 2005), which was broadcast in the U.S. on PBS.

[9] E.g., U.S. Holocaust Memorial Museum, Washington, D.C. (beside the Smithsonian); Simon Wiesenthal Center Beit Hashoah Museum of Tolerance, Los Angeles (near West Hollywood); A Living Memorial to the Holocaust—Museum of Jewish Heritage in Battery Park, New York City (in view of the Statue of Liberty); New England Holocaust Memorial, Boston (along the Freedom Trail); Holocaust Museum and Learning Center, St. Louis (a city known as the "Gateway to the West"); Miami Beach Holocaust Memorial (ninety miles from Cuba); The Holocaust Memorial Resource and Education Center of Central Florida, Orlando (in the vicinity of Disney World); and Museum to the Black Holocaust, Detroit (focusing on American slavery).

[10] For salient examples of the argument that the Holocaust is "unique," see: Nathan Rotenstreich, "The Holocaust as a Unique Historical Event," *Patterns of Prejudice* 22, no. 1 (1988): 14–20; and John K. Roth and Michael Berenbaum, eds., *Holocaust: Religious and Philosophical Implications* (New York: Paragon, 1989); esp. idem., "What

if the Holocaust Is Unique?" (1–8); André Neher, "The Silence of Auschwitz" (9–15); and Berenbaum, "The Uniqueness and Universality of the Holocaust" (82–97). For a counter-argument, see David E. Stannard, *American Holocaust: Columbus and the Conquest of the New World* (New York: Oxford University Press, 2001). My usage of "sublime" here is in reference to its formulation by Immanuel Kant, *Observations on the Feeling of the Beautiful and Sublime*, trans. John T. Goldthwait (1764; repr., Berkeley and Los Angeles: University of California Press, 1966). I shall elaborate the significance of this usage presently.

[11] For the extant book-length texts and notable short articles, see this volume's Selected Bibliography. The reader will note that the majority of these texts have been published only within the past ten to fifteen years. The length of the Selected Bibliography might be contrasted with that of the bibliography published quarterly in the important Holocaust studies journal, *Holocaust and Genocide Studies*, few of which listings ever concern film or other moving-image culture. By the same token, books on Holocaust pedagogy that reference Holocaust film are disproportionately prolific. Examples include: Gideon Shimoni, ed., *The Holocaust in University Teaching* (Oxford: Pergamon, 1991); Zev Garber, ed., *Methodology in the Academic Teaching of the Holocaust* (New York: University Presses of America, 1988); Rochelle L. Millen et al., eds., *New Perspectives on The Holocaust: A Guide for Teachers* (New York and London: New York University Press, 1996); Fred Davies, *Film, History and the Holocaust* (Portland, OR: Vallentine-Mitchell, 2000); Samuel Totten and Stephen Feinberg, eds., *Teaching and Studying the Holocaust* (Boston: Allyn and Bacon, 2004); Samuel Totten et al., eds., *Teaching About the Holocaust: Essays by College and University Teachers* (Westport, CT: Praeger, 2001); Marianne Hirsch and Irene Kacandes, eds., *Teaching the Representation of the Holocaust* (New York: MLA, 2004); Robert Eaglestone and Barry Langford, *Teaching Holocaust Literature and Film* (London: Palgrave, 2006); and the journal, *Holocaust Studies*. Cf. Terri Ginsberg, "Towards a Critical Pedagogy of Holocaust and Film," *Review of Education, Pedagogy, and Cultural Studies* 26, no. 1 (2004): 47–59; and Franklin Littell, "The Credibility Crisis of the Modern University," in *The Holocaust: Ideology, Bureaucracy, and Genocide*, eds. Henry Friedlander and Sybil Milton (Millwood, NJ: Kraus International, 1980), 271–83.

[12] Siegfried Kracauer, *From Caligari to Hitler: A Psychological History of German Film* (Princeton, NJ: Princeton University Press, 1947).

[13] Peter Michelson, *Speaking the Unspeakable: A Poetics of Obscenity* (Albany: State University of New York Press, 1993), xi.

[14] Ibid.

[15] Adorno's statement in this regard is by now proverbial:

Cultural criticism finds itself faced with the final stage of the dialectic of culture and barbarism. To write poetry after Auschwitz is barbaric. And this corrodes even the knowledge of why it has become impossible to write poetry today. Absolute reification, which presupposed intellectual progress as one of its elements, is now preparing to absorb the mind entirely. Critical intelligence cannot be equal to this challenge as long as it confines itself to self-satisfied contemplation. (Theodor W. Adorno, *Prisms*, trans. Samuel and Shierry Weber Nicholson [1967; repr., Cambridge, MA: MIT Press, 1981], 81)

[16] Sigmund Freud, *The Standard Edition of the Complete Psychological Works of Sigmund Freud*, vol. 17: *The Uncanny*, trans. James Strachey (1919; repr., London: Hogarth, 1955–74), 241.

[17] Michelson, *Speaking the Unspeakable*, viii, xii. The relevant text is Martin Heidegger, *The Question Concerning Technology and Other Essays*, trans. William Lovitt (1954; repr., New York: Harper, 1977). In this framework, "obscenity" is understood as a secular analogue to the Christian view of the world as fallen or descended from divine unicity to a mundane realm of dread, anguish, uncertainty, anxiety, homelessness, and ultimate commitment—"resolution"—to the atavistically founded inner tensions between "illumination" and "concealment" of "authentic danger." The view reformulates on ontological phenomenological grounds the christological project of salvation by passive acceptance of and/or active consent to helping perpetuate, while never questioning epistemologically, the presumed organic imperfection and chaotic disorder of the *Lebenswelt*, which *otherwise* is being organized behind the scenes by a select few. For further explication, see David Stewart and Algis Mickunas, *Exploring Phenomenology: A Guide to the Field and Its Literature*, 2nd ed. (Athens: Ohio University Press, 1990), 64–65; and Herbert Spiegelberg, *Doing Phenomenology: Essays On and In Phenomenology* (The Hague: Martinus Nijhoff, 1975), xxv. Heideggerian philosophy has been criticized as a sophistical rationale for Nazism, a criticism to which Heidegger himself never fully or clearly responded, much less refuted, and which has become a topic of ongoing scholarly controversy. E.g., Richard Wolin, ed., *The Heidegger Controversy: A Critical Reader* (Cambridge, MA and London: MIT Press, 1993); Tom Rockmore and Joseph Margolis, ed., *The Heidegger Case: On Philosophy and Politics* (Philadelphia: Temple University Press, 1992); Victor Farías, *Heidegger and Nazism*, trans. Paul Burrell et al., eds. Joseph Margolis and Tom Rockmore (Philadelphia: Temple University Press, 1989); and *Critical Inquiry* 15, no. 2 (1989), special symposium on "Heidegger and Nazism."

[18] Max Horkheimer, *...Eclipse of Reason* (New York: Continuum, 1974); Walter Benjamin, "The Work of Art in the Age of Mechanical Reproduction," in *Illuminations*, trans. Harry Zohn, ed. Hannah Arendt (1939; repr., New York: Schocken, 1968); and György Lukács, *History and Class Consciousness*, trans. Rodney Livingstone (1923; repr., Cambridge: Cambridge University Press, 1971).

[19] Theodor W. Adorno, *Aesthetic Theory*, trans. and ed. Robert Hullot-Kentor (1970; repr., Minneapolis: University of Minnesota Press, 1997), 114–20, 127. See also idem., *The Jargon of Authenticity*, trans. Knut Tarnowski and Frederic Will (1964; repr., Evanston, IL: Northwestern University Press, 1973).

[20] The relevant quotations are:

> When genocide becomes part of the cultural heritage in the themes of committed literature, it becomes easier to continue to play along with the culture which gave birth to murder. There is one nearly invariable characteristic of such literature. It is that it implies, purposely or not, that even in the so-called extreme situations, indeed in them most of all, humanity flourishes. Sometimes this develops into a dismal metaphysic which does its best to work up to atrocities into "limiting situations" which it then accepts to the extent that they reveal authenticity in men. In such a homely existential atmosphere, the distinction between executioners and victims becomes blurred; both, after all,

are equally suspended above the possibility of nothingness, which of course is generally not quite so uncomfortable for the executioners (Theodor W. Adorno, "Commitment," trans. Francis McDonagh, in *The Essential Frankfurt School Reader*, eds. Andrew Arato and Eike Gebhardt [1962; repr., New York: Continuum, 1982], 313);

[S]ince, in a world whose law is universal individual profit, the individual has nothing but this self that has become indifferent, the performance of the old, familiar tendency is at the same time the most dreadful of things. There is no getting out of this, no more than out of the electrified barbed wire around the camps. Perennial suffering has as much right to expression as a tortured man has to scream; hence it may have been wrong to say that after Auschwitz you could no longer write poems. But it is not wrong to raise the less cultural question whether after Auschwitz you can go on living—especially whether one who escaped by accident, one who by rights should have been killed, may go on living [...] [W]hat must come to be known may resemble the down-to-earth more than it resembles the sublime [...] This, nothing else, is what compels us to philosophize (Adorno, *Negative Dialectics*, trans. E. B. Ashton [1966; repr., New York: Continuum, 1973], 362–64); and

Ever since Attic classicism, the real barbarism of antiquity—the slavery, genocide, and contempt for human life—left few traces in art; just how chaste it kept itself, even in "barbaric cultures," does not redound to its credit [...] In capitalism, what forces art against art into an alliance with the vulgar is not only a function of commercialism, which exploits a mutilated sexuality, but equally the dark side of Christian inwardness. (Adorno, *Aesthetic Theory*, 161)

[21] See Ernst Wolff, "From Phenomenology to Critical Theory: The Genesis of Adorno's Critical Theory from His Reading of Husserl," *Philosophy and Social Criticism* 32, no. 5 (2006): 555–72.

[22] For a complementary explication of how the forces and relations of capitalist (re)production may be positioned as overdetermining without resort to ontological reductivism, see Nick Dyer-Witheford, *Cyber-Marx: Cycles and Circuits of Struggle in High-Technology Capitalism* (Urbana: University of Illinois Press, 1999), 10. For related critiques of romanticism, see Mary A. Favret and Nicola J. Watson, eds., *At the Limits of Romanticism: Essays in Cultural, Feminist, and Materialist Criticism* (Bloomington and Indianapolis: Indiana University Press, 1994); also David Simpson, *Romanticism, Nationalism, and the Revolt against Theory* (Chicago and London: University of Chicago Press, 1993).

[23] For explications and analyses of the Judaic proscription, see Kalman P. Bland, *The Artless Jew: Medieval and Modern Affirmations and Denials of the Visual* (Princeton, NJ and Oxford: Princeton University Press, 2000); Anthony Julius, *Idolizing Pictures: Idolatry, Iconoclasm, and Jewish Art* (London: Thames and Hudson, 2000); and David Novack, "The Law of Idolatry," in *The Image of the Non-Jew in Judaism: An Historical and Constructive Study of the Noahide Laws* (New York: Edwin Mellen), 107–65.

[24] For informative books about phenomenology and its historical variations, see Herbert Spiegelberg, *The Phenomenological Movement: A Historical Introduction*, 3rd ed. (The Hague: Martinus Nijhoff, 1982); and William L. McBride and Calvin O. Schrag,

Phenomenology in a Pluralistic Context (Albany: State University of New York, 1983). For a relevant critique of the phenomenological aspects of mainline epistemology, see Dominique Lecourt, *Marxism and Epistemology: Bachelard, Canguilhem and Foucault,* trans. Ben Brewster (London: New Left Books / Atlantic Highlands, NJ: Humanities Press, 1975); and Theodor W. Adorno, *Against Epistemology: A Metacritique; Studies in Husserl and the Phenomenological Antinomies,* trans. Willis Domingo (1956; repr., Cambridge, MA: MIT Press, 1983). For the connection to Christian moral philosophy, see Joseph Dabney Bettis, "Religion as a Faculty," in *Phenomenology of Religion: Eight Modern Descriptions of the Essence of Religion* (New York: Harper and Row, 1969), 139–68. For connections to orthodox Marxism, see Trân Duc Thao, *Phenomenology and Dialectical Materialism,* trans. Daniel J. Herman and Donald J. Morano (Dordrecht: Reidel Publishing Company, 1986); and Bernard Waldenfels et al., eds., *Phenomenology and Marxism,* trans. J. Claude Evans, Jr. (London: Routledge and Kegan Paul, 1984).

[25] E.g., Max Silverman, "Horror and the Everyday in Post–Holocaust France: *Nuit et brouillard* and Concentrationary Art," *French Cultural Studies* 17, no. 1 (2006): 5–18; Michael Rothberg, "W. E. B. Dubois in Warsaw: Holocaust Memory and the Color Line, 1949–1952," *Yale Journal of Criticism* 14, no. 1 (2001): 169–89; Susan Rubin Suleiman, "History, Memory, and Moral Judgment in Documentary Film: On Marcel Ophul's *Hotel Terminus: The Life and Times of Klaus Barbie,*" *Critical Inquiry* 28 (2002): 509–41; Sandy Flitterman-Lewis, "Documenting the Ineffable: Terror and Memory in Alain Resnais' *Night and Fog,*" in *Documenting the Documentary,* eds. Barry Keith Grant and Jeannette Sloniowski (Detroit: Wayne State University Press, 1998), 204–21; Pól Ó Dochartaigh, "Americanizing the Holocaust: The Case of *Jakob the Liar,*" *Modern Language Review* 101, no. 1 (2006): 456–71; Benjamin Robinson, "*The Specialist* on the Eichmann Precedent: Morality, Law, and Military Sovereignty," *Critical Inquiry* 30 (2003): 63–97; Robin Wood, "Gays and the Holocaust: Two Documentaries," in *Image and Remembrance: Representation and the Holocaust,* Shelley Hornstein and Florence Jacobowitz, eds. (Bloomington and Indianapolis: Indiana University Press, 2003), 114–26; and Caroline Wiedmer, "*The Nasty Girl,*" in *The Claims of Memory: Representations of the Holocaust in Contemporary Germany and France* (Ithaca, NY and London: Cornell University Press, 1999), 87–103.

An exceedingly rare exception to this phenomenological tendency, not least in its location of an ideological relationship between one particular Holocaust film and the politics of Zionism, is Ingeborg Mayer O'Sickey and Annette Van, "*Europa Europa*: On the Borders of *Vergangenheitsverdrängung* and *Vergangenheitsbewältigung,*" in *Perspectives on German Cinema,* eds. Terri Ginsberg and Kirsten Moana Thompson (New York: G. K. Hall / London: Prentice Hall International, 1996), 231–50. I shall return to this general matter.

[26] Regarding medieval scholasticism, see Erika Rummel, *The Humanist-Scholastic Debate in the Renaissance and Reformation* (Cambridge, MA: and London: Harvard University Press, 1995); also Gary Remer, *Humanism and the Rhetoric of Tolerance* (University Park: Pennsylvania State University Press, 1996). Regarding the anti–Judaic aspect of this discourse, see Rosemary Radford Reuther, *Faith and Fratricide: The Theological Roots of Anti–Semitism* (New York: Seabury Press, 1974); and idem., "The *Adversus Judeos* Tradition in the Church Fathers: The Exegesis of Christian Anti–

Judaism," in *Aspects of Jewish Culture in the Middle Ages*, ed. Paul E. Szarmach (Albany: State University of New York Press, 1978).

[27] Classic philosophical texts of the interpretive shift from existential ontology to hermeneutics include: Paul Ricoeur, *Interpretation Theory: Discourse and the Surplus of Meaning* (Fort Worth: Texas Christian University, 1976); and Maurice Merleau-Ponty, *Phenomenology of Perception*, trans. Colin Smith (1945; repr., London: Routledge, 1995). Compare Jean-François Lyotard, "Europe, the Jews and the Book," trans. Thomas Cochran and Elizabeth Constable, *l'esprit créateur* 31, no. 1 (1991): 158–61.

[28] See Pierre Macherey, *A Theory of Literary Production*, trans. Geoffrey Wall (London: Routledge and Kegan Paul, 1978).

[29] J. N. Mohanty, "Transcendental Philosophy and the Hermeneutic Critique of Consciousness," in *Hermeneutics: Questions and Prospects*, eds. Gary Shapiro and Alan Sica (Amherst: University of Massachusetts Press, 1984), 102–12. The notion of structuring absence is elaborated and critiqued most famously by Fredric Jameson, *The Prison-House of Language: A Critical Account of Structuralism and Russian Formalism* (Princeton, NJ: Princeton University Press, 1972).

[30] For examples of this framework, see J. H. Hexter, *The Judaeo-Christian Tradition*, 2nd ed. (1966; repr., New Haven, CT and London: Yale University Press, 1995); William J. Courtenay, ed., *The Judeo-Christian Heritage* (New York: Holt, 1970); A. Roy Eckhardt, *Jews and Christians: The Contemporary Meeting* (Bloomington: Indiana University Press, 1986); and the rabidly right-wing Gary North, *The Judeo-Christian Tradition: A Guide for the Perplexed* (Tyler, TX: Institute for Christian Economics, 1990). For a trenchant critique of this secularized, "Judeo-Christian" philosophy, see Arthur A. Cohen, *The Myth of the Judeo-Christian Tradition* (New York: Harper and Row, 1970); and for a useful historicization, see Mark Silk, "Notes on the Judeo-Christian Tradition in America," *American Quarterly* 36 (1984): 65–85. For related criticism, see Benny Kraut, "A Wary Collaboration: Jews, Catholics, and the Protestant Goodwill Movement," in *Between the Times: The Travail of the Protestant Establishment in America, 1990–1960*, ed. William R. Hutchison (London: Cambridge University Press, 1989); Walda Katz Fishman, "Right-Wing Reaction and Violence: A Response to Capitalism's Crises," *Social Research* 48, no. 1 (1981): 157–82; David Lumsdaine, *Moral Vision in International Politics: The Foreign Aid Regime, 1949–1989* (Princeton, NJ: Princeton University Press, 1993); and Robert Boston, *Why the Religious Right Is Wrong about Separation of Church and State* (Buffalo, NY: Prometheus, 1993), 163–64.

[31] Galit Hasan-Roken and Alan Dundes, eds., *The Wandering Jew: Essays in the Interpretation of a Christian Legend* (Bloomington and Indianapolis: Indiana University Press, 1986), esp. Hyam Maccoby, "The Wandering Jew as Sacred Executioner," 236–60, and Paul Lawrence Rose, "Ahasverus and the Destruction of Judaism," 23–43; and, more generally, Jules Isaac, *The Teaching of Contempt: The Christian Roots of Anti–Semitism* (New York: Holt, 1964), originally published as *Jésus et Israël* (Paris: Fasquelle, 1959); and Joshua Trachtenberg, *The Devil and the Jews: The Medieval Concept of the Jew and Its Relation to Modern Anti–Semitism* (New Haven, CT: Yale University Press, 1943).

[32] See Calvin O. Schrag, *Experience and Being: Prolegomenon to a Future Ontology* (Evanston, IL: Northwestern University Press, 1969), 10–11.

[33] Mohanty, "Transcendental," 107. For additional connections between this belief and phenomenological practice, see Paul Ricoeur, *Fallible Man*, trans. Charles Kelbley (Chicago: Henry Regnery, 1965). See also the New Testament books of Corinthians and Galatians.

[34] For the inaugural theorization of "Judeocide," see Arno J. Mayer, *Why Did the Heavens Not Darken? The "Final Solution" in History*, rev. ed. (New York: Pantheon, 1990).

[35] Implicitly corroborating this evaluation implicitly is Jon Petrie, "On the Secular Word 'Holocaust': Scholarly Myths, History, and Twentieth Century Meanings," *Journal of Genocide Research* 2, no. 1 (2000): 31–63, where a transformation of *holocaust* into christo-sacrificial "Holocaust" is traced to Cold War-related mystification.

[36] The relevant text is Emmanuel Levinas, *Difficult Freedom: Essays on Judaism*, trans. Sean Hand (Athlone Press, 2000). Critiques include Jacques Derrida, "Violence and Metaphysics: An Essay on the Thought of Emmanuel Levinas," in *Writing and Difference*, trans. Alan Bass (Chicago: University of Chicago Press, 1978), 79–153; Susannah Heschel, "Emmanuel Lévinas in feministischer Perspektive," *Kirche und Israel*, 15, no. 1 (2002): 41–46; and Hamid Dabashi, "In the Absence of the Face," *Social Research* 67, no. 1 (2000): 127–85. Cf. Jacob Meskin, "The Other in Levinas and Derrida: Society, Philosophy, Judaism," in *The Other in Jewish Thought and History: Constructions of Jewish Culture and Identity*, eds. Laurence J. Silberstein and Robert L. Cohn (New York and London: University of Chicago Press, 1992), 402–23.

[37] Emmanual Levinas, "Reflections on the Philosophy of Hitlerism," trans. Seán Hand, *Critical Inquiry* 17, no. 1 (1990): 62–71. Extending Levinas' argument is Phillippe Lacoue-Labarthe and Jean-Luc Nancy, "The Nazi Myth," trans. Brian Holmes, *Critical Inquiry* 16 (1990): 291–312, in which the concept of "myth" as an explanatory tool vis-à-vis postmodernity is itself deconstructed. In his *Representing the Holocaust: History, Theory, Trauma* (Ithaca, NY and London: Cornell University Press, 1994), which I address below, Dominick LaCapra tellingly rejects Lacoue-Labarthe/Nancy shortly before appropriating Lyotard and another cultural phenomenologist, René Girard.

[38] Asher Horowitz, "An Ethical Orientation for Marxism: Geras and Levinas," *Rethinking Marxism* 15, no. 2 (2003): 181–95; Matthew Edgar, "On the Ambiguous Meaning of Otherness in Totality and Infinity," *Journal of the British Society for Phenomenology* 36, no. 1 (2005): 55–75; Michael L. Morgan, "Levinas, Suffering and the Holocaust," in *The Representation of the Holocaust in Literature and Film*, ed. Marc Lee Raphael (Williamsburg, VA: Dept. of Religion, College of William and Mary, 2003), 75-92; and Alexander Kozin, "The Sign of the Other: On the Semiotics of Emmanuel Levinas' Phenomenology," *Semiotica* 152, nos. 1–4 (2004): 235–49.

[39] Israel Shahak and Norton Mezvinsky, *Jewish Fundamentalism in Israel* (London: Pluto, 1999).

[40] Yosef Hayim Yerushalmi, *Freud's Moses: Judaism Terminable and Interminable* (New Haven, CT and London: Yale University Press, 1991).

[41] Louis Jacobs, *The Talmudic Argument: A Study in Talmudic Reasoning and Methodology* (Cambridge: Cambridge University Press, 1984), 14–15.

[42] Adin Steinsaltz, *The Essential Talmud*, trans. Chaya Galai (New York: Basic, 1976), 231–41, 270. See also Robert Goldenberg, "Talmud," in *Essential Papers on Talmud*

(New York and London: New York University Press, 1994), 24–51. The proverbial reference for this methodology is Rabbi Hillel, "Do not judge your fellow until you come to his place," from Talmudic tractate Avot 2:5–7, quoted in Jacob Neusner, *Judaism in the Beginning of Christianity* (Philadelphia: Fortress Press, 1984), 68. Cf. Emmanuel Levinas, *Nine Talmudic Readings*, trans. Annette Aronowicz (1968; repr., Bloomington and Indianapolis: Indiana University Press, 1994).

[43] E.g., it starkly contrasts Paul in 1 Corinthians:

> Although I am not bound to anyone, I made myself the slave of all so as to win over as many as possible. I became like a Jew to the Jews in order to win the Jews. To those bound by the law I became like one who is bound (although in fact I am not bound by it), that I might win those bound by the law. To those not subject to the law I became like one not subject to it (not that I am free from the law of God, for I am subject to the law of Christ), that I might win those not subject to the law. To the weak I became a weak person with a view to winning the weak. I have made myself all things to all men in order to save at least some of them. In fact, I do all that I do for the sake of the gospel in the hope of having a share in its blessing. (1 Cor. 9:19–23 [New American Bible])

Cf. Martin Goodman, "Proselytizing in Rabbinic Judaism," *Journal of Jewish Studies* 40 (1989): 175–85.

[44] Cf. Annette Insdorf, *Indelible Shadows: Film and the Holocaust*, 3rd ed. (1983 and 1989; repr. Cambridge: Cambridge University Press, 2003). Citations are to the 1989 edition. Georgio Agamben echoes an aspect of this praxis in reference to an "aporia of testimony [that] coincides with the aporia of messianism" (*Remnants of Auschwitz: The Witness and the Archive*, trans. Daniel Heller-Roazen [New York: Zone, 1999], 163), but he in turn reduces the praxis, pace Paul's Letter to the Romans, to an allegorical "caesura" that marks cyclically, if not inevitably, a salvific christological rebirth.

[45] Robert Brinkley and Steven Youra, "Tracing Shoah," *PMLA* 111, no. 1 (1996): 124–26. See also Morgan, "Levinas," 77.

[46] See Emmanuel Levinas, *Entre nous: essays sur le penser-à-l'autre* (Paris: Grasset, 1991); and idem., *Ethics and Infinity: Conversations with Philippe Nemo*, trans. Richard A. Cohen (Pittsburgh: Dusquene University Press, 1985). Cf. Martin Buber, *Eclipse of God: Studies in the Relationship between Religion and Philosophy* (New York: Harper, 1952), and *I and Thou*, 2nd ed., trans. Ronald Gregor Smith (New York: Scribner, 1958).

[47] Derrida, "Violence and Metaphysics," has even referred to this limitation as a theoretical impossibility.

[48] Eg., Abba Hillel Silver, *Where Judaism Differs: An Inquiry into the Distinctiveness of Judaism* (New York: Collier, 1989); and Cohen, *Myth*. Cf. Derrida, *Of Spirit: Heidegger and the Question*, trans. Geoffrey Bennington and Rachel Bowlby (Chicago: University of Chicago Press, 1989).

[49] See Stephen Sizer, *Christian Zionism: Road-map to Armageddon?* (Leicester: Inter-Varsity, 2004), 138; Fuad Sha'ban, *For Zion's Sake: The Judeo-Christian Tradition in American Culture* (London: Pluto, 2005), 119–209; and Chris Hedges, *American Fascists: The Christian Right and the War on America* (New York: Free Press, 2006), 142–46, 185–91. But even ostensible pro-reparationists have succumbed to this theory on phenomenological grounds. E.g., Jean-Paul Sartre's post–Kierkegaardian ethics of

freedom was conceived in terms of an existential realm so total that transcendence of subjective alienation within it became impossible, whereupon neither consolation nor traditional Christian hope for reconciliation with the "other" was thinkable. See Sartre, *Being and Nothingness: A Phenomenological Essay on Ontology*, trans. Hazel E. Barnes (1956; repr., New York: Washington Square Press, 1993); also Spiegelberg, *Phenomenological Movement*, 470–80, 516–25; Stewart and Mickunas, *Exploring Phenomenology*, 73; Eugene F. Kaelin, An *Existential Aesthetic: The Theories of Sartre and Merleau-Ponty* (Madison and London: University of Wisconsin Press, 1966); and Laura A. Bell, "Loser Wins: The Importance of Play in a Sartrean Ethics of Authenticity," in McBride and Schrag, *Phenomenology*, 5–13. For a contrasting, Marxist perspective, see Bertell Ollman, *Alienation: Marx's Conception of Man in Capitalist Society*, 2nd ed. (Cambridge: Cambridge University Press, 1976). As with ontological, eidetic, and constitutional phenomenological theories before it (respectively, Martin Heidegger, *Being and Time*, trans. John MacQuarrie and Edward Robinson [New York: Harper, 1962]; Edmund Husserl, *Ideas: General Introduction to Pure Phenomenology*, trans. W. R. Boyce Gibson [1928; repr., London: Collier Macmillan, 1962]; Georg Wilhelm Friedrich Hegel, *The Philosophy of History*, trans. J. Sibree [1900; repr., New York: Dover, 1956]; and Immanuel Kant, *Critique of Pure Reason*, trans. Norman Kemp Smith [1787; repr., New York: St. Martin's, 1965]), Sartre's post–Christian existentialism founded its ethics upon the notion of aesthetic feeling, ultimately thematizing their social and material grounding into oblivion. In Sartre's case, what was actually unthinkable was an end to the Cold War.

[50] Idith Zertal, *Israel's Holocaust and the Politics of Nationhood*, trans. Chaya Galai (Cambridge: Cambridge University Press, 2005), 158–59.

[51] Max Horkheimer and Theodor W. Adorno, *Dialectic of Enlightenment*, trans. John Cumming (1947; repr., New York: Continuum, 1989).

[52] These include the French "Quarrel," an attempt by a largely discredited, ultra- and paleoconservative postwar fringe to deny the actual occurrence of the Holocaust, and the German *Historikerstreit*, a "serious" scholarly, public intellectual debate over the historiographic revisioning of Holocaust knowledgeability (Pierre Vidal-Naquêt, *Assassins of Memory: Essays on the Denial of the Holocaust*, trans. Jeffrey Mehlman [New York: Columbia University Press, 1992], 124, 188 n.104). Key texts of the "Quarrel" are Paul Rassinier, *La Passage á la Ligne* (n.p., 1948); and idem., *Le Drame des juifs européens* (n.p., 1954). Key texts of the *Historikerstreit* are: James Knowlton and Truett Cates, eds., *Forever in the Shadow of Hitler: Original Documents of the "Historikerstreit," the Controversy Concerning the Singularity of the Holocaust* (Atlantic Highlands, NJ: Humanities Press, 1993); Hermann Graml and Klaus-Dieter Henke, eds., *Nach Hitler: Der Schwierige Umgang mit unserer Geschichte; Beträge von Martin Broszat* (Munich: R. Oldenbourg, 1987); Dan Diner, ed., *Ist der nationalsozialismus Geschichte? Zu Historisierung und Historikerstreit* (Frankfurt am Main: Fischer, 1993), largely reproduced in Peter Baldwin, ed., *Reworking the Past: Hitler, the Holocaust, and the Historians' Debate* (Boston: Beacon, 1990); Hans-Ulrich Wehler, *Entsorgung der deutschen Vergangenheit? Ein polemischer essay zum "Historikerstreit"* (Munich: C. H. Beck, 1988); Jürgen Habermas, *The New Conservatism: Cultural Criticism and the Historians' Debate*, trans. and ed. Shierry

Weber Nicholson (Cambridge: MIT Press, 1989); and idem., "A Kind of Settlement of Damages: Apologetic Tendencies in German Historical Writing," in Knowlton and Cates, *Forever*, 34–44; Uwe Backes et al., eds., *Die Schatten der Vergangenheit: Impulse zur Historisierung des Nationalsozialismus* (Frankfurt and Berlin: Proyläen, 1900); Gina Thomas, ed., *The Unresolved Past: A Debate in German History* (London: Weidenfeld and Nicolson, 1990); and Imanuel Geiss, *Der Hysterikerstreit: Ein unpolemischer Essay* (Bonn and Berlin: Bourier, 1992). See also Alfred D. Low, *The Third Reich and the Holocaust in German Historiography: Toward the "Historikerstreit" of the mid-1980s* (New York: Columbia University Press, 1994); Gill Seidel, *The Holocaust Denial: Antisemitism, Racism and the New Right* (Leeds: Beyond the Pale Collective, 1986); and Michael Burleigh, ed., *Historikerstreit: Confronting the Nazi Past; New Debates on Modern German History* (New York: St. Martin's, 1996). The "Quarrel" began as a reaction to U.S. imperialism and anti–colonialist struggles in Asia and Africa and was revived during the late 1970s with help from a slightly more credible U.S. paleoconservative network in the wake of political and socio-economic crises marked by protracted, international struggles against Western expansion that would result in the renewed Cold War of the 1980s. For critiques of that network, see Norman Cohn, *Warrant for Genocide: The Myth of the Jewish World-Conspiracy and the Protocols of the Elders of Zion* (Chico, CA: Scholars Press, 1980); Benjamin Wolf Segel, *A Lie and a Libel: The History of the Protocols of the Elders of Zion* (Lincoln: University of Nebraska Press, 1995); Richard Abanes, *American Militias: Rebellion, Racism and Religion* (Downers Grove, IL: InterVarsity Press, 1996), 131–68; Russ Bellant, *Old Nazis, The New Right and the Reagan Administration: The Role of Domestic Fascist Networks in the Republican Party and Their Effects on U.S. Cold War Politics*, 2nd ed. (Cambridge, MA: Political Research Associates, 1989); James Coates, *Armed and Dangerous: The Rise of the Survivalist Right* (New York: Noonday, 1987); and Boston, *Religious Right*. By contrast, the *Historikerstreit*, which began during the heightened Cold War years and continued through the dismantling of the Berlin Wall, lent unprecedented credibility to its subject matter due to the phenomenological as opposed to empty rhetorical approach it took to Holocaust history. It focused less on the sort of casuistry and verbal sparring necessary to a project of denial than on the telos and ethos of national identities necessary to manipulating public attention from the actual, right-wing affinities between the two approaches.

[53] E.g., Siegfried Kracauer, *Theory of Film: The Redemption of Physical Reality* (London: Oxford University Press, 1965). Contemporary studies influenced by Kracauer include Dudley Andrew, *The Major Film Theories: An Introduction* (Oxford: Oxford University Press, 1976); Vivian Sobchak, *The Address of the Eye: A Phenomenology of Film Experience* (Princeton, NJ: Princeton University Press, 1991); Allan Casebier, *Film and Phenomenology: Towards a Realist Theory of Cinematic Representation* (Cambridge: Cambridge University Press, 1991); Steven Shaviro, *The Cinematic Body* (Minneapolis and London: University of Minnesota Press, 1993); and Miriam Hansen, *Babel and Babylon: Spectatorship in American Silent Film* (Cambridge, MA and London: Harvard University Press, 1991).

[54] Judith E. Doneson, *The Holocaust in American Film*, 2nd ed. (Syracuse, NY: Syracuse University Press, 2002; Philadelphia: Jewish Publication Society, 1987), 7, 9, 11, 205.

Citations are to the Jewish Publication Society edition.

[55] Deborah Lipstadt, *Denying the Holocaust: The Growing Assault on Truth and Memory* (New York: Free Press, 1983), 17–26.

[56] Doneson, *Holocaust in American Film*, 146, 149, 200, 209.

[57] Classic texts of New Criticism include: I. A. Richards, *Principles of Literary Criticism* (London: Kegan Paul Trench Trubner, 1944); F. R. Leavis, *The Great Tradition: A Study of the English Novel* (New York: Doubleday, 1954); Cleanth Brooks, *The Well-Wrought Urn: Studies in the Structure of Poetry* (New York: Harvest, 1965); and Richard Hoggart, *The Uses of Literacy* (London: Pelican, 1958). Classic critiques include: Raymond Williams, *The Sociology of Culture* (New York: Schocken, 1981); and Terry Eagleton, *Literary Theory: An Introduction* (Minneapolis: University of Minnesota Press, 1983).

[58] Ilan Avisar, *Screening the Holocaust: Cinema's Images of the Unimaginable* (Bloomington and Indianapolis: Indiana University Press, 1988). Although a professional film scholar, Insdorf utilizes a minimum of film theory and critical methodology in all three editions of her book—hence inclusion of her mention in the present section. To be fair, I should remind that Doneson's book is now also in its second edition.

[59] Julia Kristeva, *Powers of Horror: An Essay on Abjection*, trans. Leon S. Roudiez (New York: Columbia University Press, 1982); and Saul Friedländer, *Reflections of Nazism: An Essay on Kitsch and Death*, trans. Thomas Weyr (New York: Harper, 1984).

[60] Avisar, *Screening the Holocaust*, 17–18, 182.

[61] Ibid., 17.

[62] As discussed in Stephen E. Bronner, *Blood in the Sand: Imperial Fantasies, Right-Wing Ambitions, and the Erosion of American Democracy* (Lexington: University of Kentucky Press, 2005), 76–81.

[63] Avisar, *Screening the Holocaust*, 89, 152–63, 170.

[64] Ibid., 180.

[65] Ibid., ix, 26, 182.

[66] LaCapra, *Representing the Holocaust*, 9, 37, 39 n.13, 93–94, 138, 174–75, 176 n.7, 193, 215, 220–21) Here LaCapra is critiquing Zygmunt Bauman, *Modernity and the Holocaust* (Ithaca, NY: Cornell University Press, 1989), Vidal-Naquêt, *Assassins of Memory*, and Mayer, *Why Did the Heavens Not Darken?* See also LaCapra, *History and Memory after Auschwitz* (Ithaca, NY and London: Cornell University Press, 1998), a follow-up to *Representing the Holocaust*.

[67] Hannah Arendt, *Eichmann in Jerusalem: A Report on the Banality of Evil* (New York: Viking, 1963); Jean-Paul Sartre, *Anti–Semite and Jew*, trans. George J. Becker (1943; repr., New York: Schocken, 1965); Kurt Pätzold, *Faschismus, Rassenwahn, Judenvervolgung: Eine Studie zur politischen Strategie und Taktik des faschistischen deutschen Imperialismus, 1933–1945* (East Berlin: Deutsche Verlag der Wissenschaften, 1975); Nicos Poulantzas, *Fascism and Dictatorship*; and Mayer, *Why Did the Heavens Not Darken?*

[68] E.g., Richard Slotkin, *Gunfighter Nation: The Myth of the Frontier in Twentieth Century America* (New York: Atheneum, 1992); James M. Mellard, "Lacan and the New Lacanians: Josephine Hart's *Damage*, Lacanian Tragedy, and the Ethics of *Jouissance*," *PMLA* 113, no. 3 (1998): 395–407; and Janice Hocker Rushing and Thomas S. Frentz,

Projecting the Shadow: The Cyborg Hero in American Film (Chicago: University of Chicago Press, 1995).

[69] Neusner, of course, would be very critical of such a designation.

[70] This is true even for the otherwise insightful Slotkin. See his *The Fatal Environment: The Myth of the Frontier in the Age of Industrialization, 1880–1890* (Middlebury, CT: Wesleyan University Press, 1985) for a more sustained example of my claim. For an interesting contrast, see Stannard, *American Holocaust*; and for a sharp contrast, see Ward Churchill, *A Little Matter of Genocide: Holocaust Denial in the Americas, 1492 to the Present* (San Francisco: City Lights, 1992).

[71] For sustained analyses of the relationship of manifest destinarianism to U.S. policy in the Middle East, see Lawrence Davidson, "Christian Zionism and American Foreign Policy: Paving the Road to Hell," *Logos* 4, no. 1 (2005), http://www.logosjournal.com/issue_4.1/davidson.htm; G. H. Jansen, *Zionism, Israel and Asian Nationalism* (Beirut: Institute for Palestine Studies, 1971), 83–89; Sha'ban, *For Zion's Sake*, 5; and Hilton Obenzinger, *American Palestine: Melville, Twain, and the Holy Land Mania* (Princeton, NJ: Princeton University Press, 1999).

[72] Lipstadt, *Denying the Holocaust*, 2, 154, 210; and Doneson, *Holocaust in American Film*, 201-2. Cf. Ilya Levkov, ed., *Bitburg and Beyond: Encounters in American, German and Jewish History* (New York: Shapolsky, 1987); and Geoffrey H. Hartman, *Bitburg in Moral and Political Perspective* (Bloomington and Indianapolis: Indiana University Press, 1986).

[73] Lipstadt, *Denying the Holocaust*, ix.

[74] Avisar, *Screening the Holocaust*, 181.

[75] Ibid., xi.

[76] Avisar, *Screening the Holocaust*, 89. See Angus Fraser, *The Gypsies*, 2nd ed. (Oxford: Blackwell, 1995); and Günter Grau, *Hidden Holocaust? Gay and Lesbian Persecution in Germany, 1933–45*, trans. Patrick Camiller (London: Cassell, 1995).

[77] Ibid., 131.

[78] Ibid. Here Avisar also references Jesus in what becomes an eclectic list of famous Jews that also includes Moses, Freud, Kafka, and Einstein.

[79] Insdorf, *Indelible Shadows*, xvii–xix, 169 quoted in George Steiner, *In Bluebeard's Castle: Notes toward the Redefinition of Culture* (New Haven, CT: Yale University Press, 1971), 45–46. The view is basically Hegelian: "On the whole, Jewish history exhibits grand features of character, but it is disfigured by *an exclusive bearing (sanctioned in its religion) towards the genius of other nations (the destruction of inhabitants of Canaan being commanded even)*—by want of culture generally and the superstition arising from the idea of the high value of their peculiar nationality" (Hegel, *Philosophy of History*, 196 [my emphasis]).

[80] Insdorf, *Indelible Shadows*, xi. This mythology is not, however, limited to traditional Christian moralism. For paradigmatic examples on the political Right, see Werner Sombart, *The Jews and Modern Capitalism*, trans. M. Epstein (New Brunswick, NJ: Transaction, 1982); and for an example on the Left, see Abram Leon, *The Jewish Question: A Marxist Interpretation* (New York: Pathfinder, 1970). Cf. the instructive Ilan Halevi, *A History of the Jews: Ancient and Modern*, trans. A. M. Berrett (London: Zed, 1987), for a relevant critique of these basically christological narratives. For specific

refutations, see Felice Yeskel, "Beyond the Taboo: Talking about Class," in Marla Brettschneider, ed., *The Narrow Bridge: Jewish Views on Multiculturalism* (New Brunswick, NJ: Rutgers University Press, 1996), 42–57; Naomi Levine and Martin Hochbaum, eds., *Poor Jews: An American Awakening* (New Brunswick, NJ: Transaction, 1974); T. J. Cottle, *Hidden Survivors: Portraits of Poor Jews in America* (Englewood Cliffs, NJ: Prentice-Hall, 1988); and E. Willis, "The Myth of the Powerful Jews," in *Beginning to See the Light: Pieces of a Decade* (New York: Knopf, 1982), 228–44.

[81] See Ollman, *Alienation*; Derek Sayer, *The Violence of Abstraction: The Analytic Foundation of Historical Materialism* (Oxford: Basil Blackwell, 1987); and Karl Marx, *Capital*, vol. 1: *A Critical Analysis of Capitalist Production*, trans. Samuel Moore and Edward Aveling, ed. Friedrich Engels (1867; repr., New York: International, 1967).

[82] For another example of this "oversight" in the area of Holocaust cultural criticism, see Tim Cole, *Selling the Holocaust: From Auschwitz to Schindler; How History Is Bought, Packaged, and Sold* (New York: Routledge, 1999). This tenor of discourse is also carried by the essays collected in Helene Flanzbaum, ed., *The Americanization of the Holocaust* (Baltimore: Johns Hopkins University Press, 1999).

[83] LaCapra, *Representing the Holocaust*, 7–8, 11, 14, 15 n.11, 37 n.7, 105, 172 n.4, 214–20.

[84] E.g., Habermas, "Settlement of Damages"; Mayer, *Why Did the Heavens Not Darken?*; Bauman, *Modernity and the Holocaust*; and Lacoue-Labarthe and Nancy, "Nazi Myth."

[85] LaCapra, *Representing the Holocaust*, 208–10. For pertinent examples of object-relations theory, see Juliet Mitchel, ed., *The Selected Melanie Klein* (London: Free Press, 1987); Jay R. Greenberg and Stephen A. Mitchell, *Object Relations in Psychoanalytic Theory* (Cambridge, MA and London: Harvard University Press, 1983); Jeffrey Seinfeld, Containing *Rage, Terror, and Despair: An Object Relations Approach to Psychotherapy* (Northvale, NJ: Jason Aronson, 1996); and C. Fred Alford, "Melanie Klein and the 'Oresteia Complex': Love, Hate, and the Tragic Worldview," *Cultural Critique* (1990): 167–89. For the classical psychoanalytic contrast, see Sigmund Freud, "The Economic Problem of Masochism," 1924, trans. Joan Riviere, in *On Metaphysics and the Theory of Psychoanalysis*, ed. Angela Richards (New York: Penguin, 1984), 411–26; and for a critical historiographical appropriation, see Janice Doane and Devon Hodges, *From Klein to Kristeva: Psychoanalytic Feminism and the Search for the "Good Enough" Mother* (Ann Arbor: University of Michigan Press, 1992).

Relevant texts of Gilles Deleuze include *Masochism*, trans. Jean McNeil (New York: Zone, 1991), *Cinema 1: The Movement-Image*, trans. Hugh Tomlinson and Barbara Habberjam (Minneapolis: University of Minnesota Press, 1986), and *Cinema 2: The Time-Image*, trans. Hugh Tomlinson and Robert Galeta (Minneapolis: University of Minnesota Press, 1989). See also David Toole, "Of Lingering Eyes and Talking Things: Adorno and Deleuze on Philosophy since Auschwitz," *Philosophy Today* 37, no. 3 (1993): 227–46; and Nick Nesbitt, "The Expulsion of the Negative: Deleuze, Adorno, and the Ethics of Internal Difference," *SubStance* 34, no. 2 (2005): 75–97.

[86] See Jean François Lyotard, *Heidegger and "the Jews"*, trans. Andreas Michel and Mark Roberts (Minneapolis: University of Minnesota Press, 1988); and idem., *The Differend: Phrases in Dispute*, trans. Georges Van Den Abbeele (Minneapolis: University of Minnesota Press, 1988). It should be noted to his credit that LaCapra

justifiably criticizes another postmodern theorist of Holocaust culture, Shoshana Felman, for analogizing pathetic silence to an authentic, if cryptic, mode of Holocaust explanation. Cf. Shoshana Felman and Dori Laub, *Testimony: Crisis of Witnessing in Literature, Psychoanalysis, and History* (New York: Routledge, 1992).

[87] LaCapra, *Representing the Holocaust*, 99.

[88] Girard's theories have been linked to a school of thought known as liminal anthropology with which Mary Douglas, *Purity and Danger: An Analysis of the Concepts of Pollution and Taboo* (London: Routledge, 1992) and Georges Bataille, *The Accursed Share: An Essay on General Economy*, vol. 1: *Consumption*, trans. Robert Hurley (New York: Zone, 1991) have also been associated. Cf. Sigmund Freud, *Totem and Taboo: Some Points of Agreement between the Lives of Savages and Neurotics*, trans. James Strachey (1913; repr., New York: Norton, 1952) and *Moses and Monotheism*, trans. Katherine Jones (New York: Vintage, 1939) for an analysis and critique, respectively, of notions of ritual sacrifice which differ significantly from the ultimately Jungian, implicitly anti–Judaic approaches to the subject from within the liminal anthropological school.

[89] For distinctions between Judaic and Christian notions of sacrifice, see Robert L. Cohen, "Sainthood on the Periphery: The Case of Judaism," in *Sainthood: Its Manifestations in World Religions*, ed. Richard K. Kieckhefer and George D. Bond (Berkeley: University of California Press, 1988), 43–68; Yoram Bilu, "Dreams and the Wishes of the Saint," in *Judaism Viewed from Within and from Without: Anthropological Studies*, ed. Harvey E. Goldberg (Albany: State University of New York Press, 1987), 285–313; Ivan G. Marcus, "From Politics to Martyrdom: Shifting Paradigms in the Hebrew Narratives of the 1096 Crusade Riots," in *Essential Papers on Judaism and Christianity in Crisis*, ed. Jeremy Cohen (New York: New York University Press, 1991), 469–83; Sidney Goldstein, *Suicide in Rabbinic Literature* (Hoboken, NJ: KTAV Publishing House, 1989); Lawrence Fine, "Purifying the Body in the Name of the Soul: The Problem of the Body in Sixteenth-Century Kabbalah," in *People of the Body: Jews and Judaism from an Embodied Perspective*, ed Howard Eilberg-Schwartz (Albany: State University of New York Press, 1992), 117–42; and Eugene Weiner and Anita Weiner, *The Martyr's Conviction: A Sociological Analysis* (Atlanta: Scholars Press, 1990).

[90] Here one might recall the historical proximity of the staging of mystery plays and the perpetration of anti–Jewish pogroms during the medieval period. For an overview of this phenomenon, see Léon Poliakov, *The History of Anti–Semitism*, vol. 2: *From Mohammed to the Marranos*, trans. Natalie Gerardi (New York: Vanguard, 1973). Regarding the specific genre of the mystery play, see Robert Speaight, *The Christian Theatre* (London: Burns and Oates, 1960), 9–36. But see also Norman Finkelstein, *The Holocaust Industry* (London: Verso, 2000) quoting Peter Novick, *The Holocaust in American Life* (Boston: Houghton Mifflin, 1999), for whom "Holocaust" has effectively become "a 'mystery' religion" (45).

[91] Lyotard himself encourages such a reinscription in his blatantly christological allegory "Europe, the Jews, and the Book." Cf. Jacobowitz, for whom postmodern "relativism" may be contained by a film's capacity to "register" the holocaustal event visually. Jacobowitz confuses visibility with a certain objectivity, as LaCapra seems to do with

speech (Hornstein and Jacobowitz, *Image and Remembrance*, 10–11).
[92] LaCapra, *Representing the Holocaust*, 177, 207–15. This of course recalls the constitutional phenomenology of Kant.
[93] Ibid., 54.
[94] See Louis Althusser and Etienne Balibar, *Reading Capital*, trans. Ben Brewster (London: New Left Books, 1970), 91–118; and Ammiel Alcalay, *After Jews and Arabs: Remaking Levantine Culture* (Minneapolis and London: University of Minnesota Press, 1993), 165–66.
[95] A more recent and very important example of this general problem is Agamben, *Remnants of Auschwitz.* Referencing Lyotard and Felman/Laub, Agamben compellingly insinuates an anti–Muslim/–Arab underside onto the christologically understood Holocaust via an allegorical reading of the ghostly, dead-alive concentrationary figure of the *Muselmann* [Muslim]. Unfortunately Agamben can do no more than reaffirm the *Muselmann*'s perceived pathos within mystified, performative horizons analogous to the *differend*. Reminiscent of Doneson, the result is a Eurocentric and transhistorical conflation of Jew and Muslim/Arab under a reinscribed rubric of imperialist triangulation. For additional critique of Agamben in this regard, see Robinson, *"The Specialist* on the Eichmann Precedent."
[96] This point is echoed in Robinson, *"The Specialist* on the Eichmann Precedent," 69 n.16, which briefly locates this problematic in LaCapra, *History and Memory*. Accordingly, LaCapra's "Holocaust" is its own limit case, a normative counterforce and corrective to its real repetition. See also LaCapra, "Lanzmann's *Shoah*: 'Here There Is No Why'," *Critical Inquiry* 23 (1997): 269.
[97] E.g., Marc Ellis, *Unholy Alliance: Religion and Atrocity in Our Time* (Minneapolis, MN: Fortress, 1997); and Naim Stifan Ateek, *Justice, and Only Justice: A Palestinian Theology of Liberation* (Maryknoll, NY: Orbis, 1997).
[98] Nicolas Losson, "Notes on the Images of the Camps," trans. Annette Michelson, *October* 90 (1999): 30–31.
[99] Gertrud Koch, "The Angel of Forgetfulness and the Black Box of Facticity: Trauma and Memory in Claude Lanzmann's *Shoah*," trans. Ora Wiskind, *History and Memory* 3, no. 1 (1991): 131. See also idem., "Rudolf Arnheim: The Materialist of Aesthetic Illusion—Gestalt Theory and Reviewer's Practice," *New German Critique* 51 (1990): 164–78; idem., "The Aesthetic Transformation of the Image of the Unimaginable: Notes on Claude Lanzmann's *Shoah*," trans. Jamie Owen Daniel and Miriam Hansen, *October* 48 (1989): 15–24; idem., "Transformations Esthétiques: Dans la représentation de l'inimaginable," trans. Catherine Weinzorn, in Bernard Cuau et al., *Au sujet de Shoah: le Film de Claude Lanzmann* (Paris: Editions Belin, 1990), 157–66; idem., "'Not Yet Accepted Anywhere': Exile, Memory, and Image in Kracauer's Conception of History," trans. Jeremy Gaines, New *German Critique* 54 (1991): 95–109; and idem., "Sartre's Screen Projection of Freud," *October* 57 (1991): 3–17.
[100] André Pierre Colombat, *The Holocaust in French Film* (Metuchen, NJ: Scarecrow, 1993), 115, 117, 235.
[101] Louisa Rice, "The Voice of Silence: Alain Resnais' *Night and Fog* and Collective Memory in Post–Holocaust France, 1944–1974," *Film and History* 32, no. 1 (2002): 22–29.

[102] Colombat, *Holocaust in French Film*, 22–23, 97, 121–22, 140.

[103] Ibid., 153–56.

[104] See Mayer, *Why Did the Heavens Not Darken?*

[105] Agamben, *Remnants of Auschwitz*, 31.

[106] Colombat, *Holocaust in French Film*, 325. As mentioned, Agamben also finally performs a similar collapse.

[107] The classic instance of this discourse is David Rousset, *The Other Kingdom*, trans. Ramon Guthrie (1947; repr., New York: Fertig, 1982), where the perpetration of the Holocaust is said to have taken place in an entirely "other" world, the *universe concentrationaire*.

[108] E.g., Rachel Leah Jablon, "Witnessing as *Shivah*; Memoir as *Yizkor*: The Formulation of Holocaust Survivor Literature as *Gemilut Khasadim*," *Journal of Popular Culture* 38, no. 2 (2004): 316, which presumes an "ever-expanding audience" for the Holocaust films it interprets through a moral-aesthetic lens. This essay won the 2004 William Brigman *Journal of Popular Culture* Award.

[109] E.g., *Film and History* 32, nos. 1–2 (2002), special double-issue on "The Holocaust on Film"; the published debate over *Life Is Beautiful* in *Yale Journal of Criticism* 14, no. 1 (2001), viz. Helene Flanzbaum, "'But Wasn't It Terrific?': A Defense of Liking *Life Is Beautiful*," 274–86; Ruth Ben-Ghiat, "The Secret Histories of Roberto Benigni's *Life Is Beautiful*," 253–66; and Sidra DeKoven Ezrahi, "After Such Knowledge, What Laughter?" 287–313. See also the slightly more sophisticated essay collections edited by Marc Lee Raphael, *Representation of the Holocaust in Literature and Film*; by Toby Haggith and Joanna Newman, *Holocaust and the Moving Image: Representations in Film and Television Since 1933* (London: Wallflower, 2005); and by Caroline Joan (Kay) S. Picart and David A. Frank, *Frames of Evil: The Holocaust as Horror in American Film*, foreword by Dominick LaCapra (Carbondale: Southern Illinois University Press, 2006); and the recent monograph by Lawrence Baron, *Projecting the Holocaust into the Present: The Changing Focus of Contemporary Holocaust Cinema* (New York: Pantheon, 2005).

[110] Yosefa Loshitzky, ed., *Spielberg's Holocaust: Critical Perspectives on "Schindler's List"* (Bloomington and Indianapolis: Indiana University Press, 1997), 13.

[111] Apropos of Insdorf's back-cover blurb, which reads, "How does one make a [Holocaust] movie that is both morally just and marketable?" Picart and Frank echo this sentiment, which references LaCapra: "An ethic of response and spectatorship calls for the use of blended and multiple frames [which] actively resists definitive answers and allows the issues raised by the Holocaust to remain open to further interrogation" (*Frames of Evil*, 145).

[112] Miriam Hansen, "*Schindler's List* Is Not *Shoah*: Second Commandment, Popular Modernism, and Public Memory," *Critical Inquiry* 22, no. 2 (1995): 292–312; repr. in Loshitzky, *Spielberg's Holocaust*, 97. Citations are to the Loshitzky edition.

[113] Ibid., 98–99.

[114] For positioned analyses of these varied solutions to the conflict, see Mazin B. Qumsiyeh, *Sharing the Land of Canaan: Human Rights and the Israeli–Palestinian Struggle* (London: Pluto, 2004); Ali Abunimah, *One Country: A Bold Proposal to End the Israeli–Palestinian Impasse* (New York: Metropolitan, 2006); and Rashid Khalidi,

The Iron Cage: The Story of the Palestinian Struggle for Statehood (Boston: Beacon, 2006).

[115] A similar, if more scientific approach is taken by the recent Ewout Van der Knaap, ed., *Uncovering the Holocaust: The International Reception of "Night and Fog"* (London: Wallflower, 2006), which utilizes applied sociological theory to ascertain and evaluate popular audience responses to *Night and Fog* within particular national contexts, including that of Israel.

[116] Alan Mintz, *Popular Culture and the Shaping of Holocaust Culture in America* (Seattle and London: University of Washington Press, 2001), xii.

[117] See Terri Ginsberg, review of *"Der Ewige Jude": Quellenkritische Analyse eines antisemitischen Propagandafilms*, by Stig Hornshøj-Møller (Göttingen: Institut für Wissenschaftlischen Film, 1995), *Holocaust and Genocide Studies* 13, no. 3 (1999): 484–88.

[118] Representative texts are: Paul Ricoeur, *Interpretation Theory*; Wolfgang Iser, *The Implied Reader: Patterns of Communication in Prose Fiction from Bunyan to Beckett* (Baltimore: Johns Hopkins University Press, 1974); and Hans Robert Jauss, *Toward an Aesthetic of Reception*, trans. Timothy Bahti (Minneapolis: University of Minnesota Press, 1982).

[119] Mintz, *Popular Culture*, 14–15, 26.

[120] Esther Kaplan, "The Jewish Divide on Israel: A Growing Grassroots Movement Has Challenged the Artificial AIPAC Consensus," *The Nation*, July 21, 2004: 20–23. Representative organizations include Tikkun (http://www.tikkun.org); Jewish Voice for Peace (http://www.jewishvoiceforpeace.org); Jews Against the Occupation (http://www.jatonyc.org); Brit Tzedek v'Shalom [Jewish Alliance for Justice and Peace] (http://www.btvshalom.org); Jews for Justice for Palestinians (http://www.jfjfp.org); International Jewish Solidarity Network (http://www.jewishsolidarity.info); Jews for a Free Palestine (http://www.jffp.org); and Gush Shalom [Front for Peace] (http://www.gush-shalom.org).

[121] E.g,. Yosef Grodzinsky, *In the Shadow of the Holocaust: The Struggle between Jews and Zionists in the Aftermath of World War II* (Monroe, ME: Common Courage, 2004); Idith Zertal, *From Catastrophe to Power: Holocaust Survivors and the Emergence of Israel* (Berkeley and London: University of California Press, 1998); Lenni Brenner, *Zionism in the Age of the Dictators* (Westport, CT: Lawrence Hill, 1983); and Tamar Katriel, "'From Shore to Shore': The Holocaust, Clandestine Immigration, and Israeli Heritage Museums," in *Visual Culture and the Holocaust*, ed. Barbie Zelizer (New Brunswick, NJ: Rutgers University Press, 2001), 198–211.

[122] For a critical discussion of the massacre, see Shahak and Mezvinsky, *Jewish Fundamentalism in Israel*, 96–112; also Janet L. Dolgin, *Jewish Identity and the JDL* (Princeton, NJ: Princeton University Press, 1977); and Ian S. Lustick, *For the Land and the Lord: Jewish Fundamentalism in Israel* (New York: Council on Foreign Relations, 1988).

[123] Cultural historian Kerwin Lee Klein refers to a Holocaust "memory industry" ("On the Emergence of Memory in Historical Discourse," *Representations* 69 [2000]: 127), and sociologist Frank Furedi, to a "trauma industry" for which the Holocaust has become "the icon of therapeutic history" following a contemporary reorientation of U.S. manifest

destinarianism away from future optimism towards a pre-occupation with past suffering (*Therapy Culture: Cultivating Vulnerability in an Uncertain Age* [London: Routledge, 2004], 99, 150). Noting the plethora of Holocaust studies texts on the subject, one might now also refer to a "witnessing industry." Examples include: Marianne Hirsch, *Family Frames: Photography, Narrative, and Postmemory* (Cambridge, MA and London: Harvard University Press, 1997); E. Ann Kaplan and Ban Wang eds., *Trauma and Cinema: Cross-Cultural Explorations* (Hong Kong: Hong Kong University Press, 2004); E. Ann Kaplan, *Trauma Culture: The Politics of Terror and Loss in Media and Literature* (New Brunswick, NJ: Rutgers University Press, 2005); Janet Walker, *Trauma Cinema: Documenting Incest and the Holocaust* (Berkeley and Los Angeles: University of California Press, 2005); Cathy Caruth, ed., *Trauma: Explorations in Memory* (Baltimore: Johns Hopkins University Press, 1995); Carrie A. Rentschler, "Witnessing U.S. Citizenship and the Vicarious Experience of Suffering," *Media, Culture and Society* 26, no. 2 (2004): 296–304; Kirby Farrell, *Post–traumatic Culture: Injury and Interpretation in the Nineties* (Baltimore and London: Johns Hopkins University Press, 1998); Michael Rothberg, *Traumatic Realism: The Demands of Holocaust Representation* (Minneapolis and London: University of Minnesota Press, 2000); Vivian M. Patraka, *Spectacular Suffering: Theatre, Fascism, and the Holocaust* (Bloomington and Indianapolis: Indiana University Press, 1999); Paul Eisenstein, *Traumatic Encounters: Holocaust Representation and the Hegelian Subject* (Albany: State University of New York Press, 2003); Dora Apel, *Memory Effects: The Holocaust and the Art of Secondary Witnessing* (New Brunswick, NJ and London: Rutgers University Press, 2002); Barbie Zelizer, *Remembering the Forget: Holocaust Memory through the Camera's Eye* (Chicago and London: University of Chicago Press, 1998); Andrea Liss, *Trespassing through Shadows: Memory, Photography and the Holocaust* (Minneapolis and London: University of Minnesota Press, 1998); Janina Struk, *Photographing the Holocaust: Interpretations of Evidence* (London: I. B. Tauris, 2004); Jenny Edkins, *Trauma and the Memory of Politics* (Cambridge: Cambridge University Press, 2003); Oren Baruch Stier, *Committed to Memory: Cultural Mediations of the Holocaust* (Amherst, MA and Boston: University of Massachusetts Press, 2003); Gary Weissman, *Fantasies of Witnessing: Postwar Efforts to Experience the Holocaust* (Ithaca, NY and London: Cornell University Press, 2004); James E. Young, *The Texture of Memory: Holocaust Memorials and Meaning* (New Haven, CT and London: Yale University Press, 1993), and *At Memory's Edge: After-Images of the Holocaust in Contemporary Art and Literature* (New Haven, CT: Yale University Press, 2000); and *Screen* 42, no. 2 (2001), special issue on "Trauma and Screen Studies." The work of Marianne Hirsch is of particular interest here for its seminal application of the Barthesian punctum as a *differend*-like marker of lost memory in relation to the Holocaust photographic image.

From an angle critical of this general turn, the political limitations of the Holocaust memory, trauma, and witnessing "industries" may be understood in terms of what historian Alan R. Taylor refers to as the infantilizing ideology-effects of Zionism on Jewish Israelis: "The Israeli is like a child whose parents dote on him to the point of stifling his identity while he is trying to find his way in a world which his parents reject because they see it as a recapitulation of old enemies and a threat to the image in which they wish to cast their offspring," (*The Zionist Mind: The Origins and Development of*

Zionist Thought [Beirut: Institute for Palestine Studies, 1974], 145).

[124] "Postmemory characterizes the experience of those who grow up dominated by narratives that preceded their lives, whose own belated stories are evacuated by the stories of the previous generation shaped by traumatic events that can be neither understood nor recreated. I have developed this notion in relation to children of Holocaust survivors, but I believe it may usefully describe other second-generation memories of cultural collective traumatic events or experiences," Marianne Hirsch, *Family Frames*, 22. Hirsch never explicitly names Israeli cultural memory in this regard.

[125] Hirsch, *Afterimage*, 61–62, 84.

[126] For Benjamin, shock is an effect of the development of the social means of production as played out in the realm of modern collective urban experience. See Benjamin, *The Arcades Project*, trans. Howard Eiland and Kevin McLaughlin, ed. Rolf Tiedemann (1927; repr., Cambridge, MA and London: Harvard University Press, 1999).

[127] Hirsch, *Afterimage*, 34; see also Andreas Huyssen, "Of Mice and Mimesis: Reading Spiegelman with Adorno," in Zelizer, *Visual Culture and the Holocaust*, 41 n.11.

[128] Hirsch, *Afterimage*, 39, 49, 52–53.

[129] See Naomi Seidman, "The Holocaust in Every Tongue," in Raphael, *Representation of the Holocaust in Literature and Film*, 109 n.22, which cites both Rosenfeld and Langer in context of favorably referencing Mintz.

[130] Hirsch, *Afterimage*, 37–43, 41–42, 52–53, 56.

[131] David E. James refers to the "idealist encomiums sustained by formalist hermeneutics," *Allegories of Cinema: American Film in the Sixties* (Princeton, NJ: Princeton University Press, 1989), 31. For a critical analysis of this development in film and media studies, see Terri Ginsberg, "'Dumbing Down' and the Politics of Neoliberalism in Film and/as Media Studies," *Review of Education, Pedagogy, and Cultural Studies* 25, no. 1 (2003): 21–22.

[132] Michel Foucault, *The Archaeology of Knowledge; and The Discourse on Language*, trans. Alan M. Sheridan Smith (New York: Pantheon, 1972).

[133] Hirsch, *Afterimage*, 162. Cf. Don Ihde, *Hermeneutic Phenomenology: The Philosophy of Paul Ricoeur* (Evanston, IL: Northwestern University Press, 1971), 21; Stewart and Mickunas, *Exploring Phenomenology*, 65; Maurizio Ferraris, *History of Hermeneutics*, trans. Luca Somigli (Atlantic Highlands, NJ: Humanities Press International, 1996), 274–81; and Paul Ricoeur, *The Rule of Metaphor: Multi-disciplinary Studies of the Creation of Meaning in Language*, trans. Robert Czerny et al. (Toronto and Buffalo, NY: University of Toronto Press, 1977). Michael Bernard-Donals and Richard Glejzer echo Hirsch by prioritizing postnarratological witnessing over testimony in the name of a "beyond of epistemology" ("Film and the Shoah: The Limits of Seeing," in *Between Witness and Testimony: The Holocaust and the Limits of Representation* [Albany: State University of New York Press, 2001], 120–23). See also Nelly Furman quoting trauma theorist Cathy Caruth, for whom the role of witnessing is to remind us that "we are implicated in each other's traumas" ("Called to Witness: Viewing Lanzmann's *Shoah*," in *Shaping Losses: Cultural Memory and the Holocaust*, ed. Julia Epstein and Lori Hope Lefkowitz [Urbana and Chicago: University of Illinois Press, 2001], 64). For a relevant critique of the contemporary resistance to Eisenstein, see Ann Kibbey, *A Theory of the Image* (Indianapolis: Indiana University Press, 2004), 160–64.

[134] Hirsch, *Afterimage*, 111–39, 164 n.3. See Yosefa Loshitzky, ed., *Identity Politics and the Israeli Screen* (Austin: University of Texas Press, 2001); and Ella Shohat, *Israeli Cinema: East/West and the Politics of Representation* (Austin: University of Texas Press, 1989).

[135] Enzo Traverso, *Understanding the Nazi Genocide: Marxism after Auschwitz*, trans. Peter Drucker (London: Verso 1999), 70.

[136] Ibid.

[137] E.g., P. Adams Sitney, *Visionary Film: The American Avant-Garde, 1943–1978*, 2nd ed. (Oxford and New York: Oxford University Press, 1979); and Peter Gidal, *Materialist Film* (London: Routledge, 1989).

[138] Enzo Traverso, *The Marxists and the Jewish Question: The History of a Debate, 1843–1943*, trans. Bernard Gibbons (Atlantic Highlands, NJ: Humanities Press, 1994); and T. J. Clark, "Should Benjamin Have Read Marx?" *Boundary 2* 30, no. 1 (2003): 131–49.

[139] E.g., Horkheimer and Adorno, *Dialectic of Enlightenment*; and Ernst Bloch, *Literary Essays*, trans. Andrew Joron et al. (Stanford, CA: Stanford University Press, 1998).

[140] The possibility of referring to Holocaust film as a cinematic genre was proffered and debated at a two-week workshop in which this author participated on the subject of Holocaust film at the U.S. Holocaust Memorial Museum's Center for Advanced Holocaust Studies, June 2000, Washington, D.C. (Delia M. Rios, "Holocaust Film Footage Defines Not Only the Event, But Our Relationship to It," *Newhouse News Service*, August 3, 2000, http://www.newhousenews.com/archive/story1a080300.html). Texts which categorize Holocaust cinematic culture generically include: Insdorf, *Indelible Shadows*; Picart and Frank, *Frames of Evil*; and, in the theatrical realm, Edward R. Isser, *Stages of Annihilation: Theatrical Representation of the Holocaust* (Teaneck, NJ: Fairleigh Dickenson University Press / London: Associated University Presses, 1997), 22–25.

[141] E.g., Michael Gurevitch et al., eds., *Culture, Society and the Media* (London: Methuen, 1982); George Bridges and Rosalind Brunt, eds., *Silver Linings, Some Strategies for the Eighties: Contributions to the Communist University of London* (London: Lawrence and Wishart, 1981); Rosalind Coward and John Ellis, *Language and Materialism: Developments in Semiology and the Theory of the Subject* (London: Routledge and Kegan Paul, 1977); Catherine Belsey, *Critical Practice* (London; Methuen, 1980); Tony Bennett, *Formalism and Marxism* (London: Methuen, 1979); Stephen Heath, *Signs and Meanings in the Cinema*, 3rd ed. (Bloomington: Indiana University Press, 1972); Terry Lovell, *Pictures of Reality: Aesthetics, Politics and Pleasure* (London: BFI, 1983); Colin MacCabe, *Tracking the Signifier: Theoretical Essays; Film, Linguistics, Literature* (Minneapolis: University of Minnesota Press, 1985); and Annette Kuhn, *The Power of the Image: Essays on Representation and Sexuality* (London: Routledge and Kegan Paul, 1979).

[142] For a sustained explication of immanent critique, see Robert J. Antonio, "Immanent Critique as the Core of Critical Theory: Its Origins and Development in Hegel, Marx and Contemporary Thought," *British Journal of Sociology* 32, no. 3 (1981): 333.

[143] With this theoretical possibility in mind, the contemporary film scholar may be reminded of the recent and ongoing debate in film historical circles of the role and

significance of Jews in the Hollywood studio era, in relation to which a critical deconstructive methodology akin to *le-didakh* has been deployed in efforts to comprehend and explain Jewish-American complicity in anti–Black racism. Notable instances of this deployment, which are in fact relevant to our discussion for their focus on a form of violent racist imagery, include Neil Gabler, *An Empire of Their Own: How the Jews Invented Hollywood* (New York: Crown, 1988); and Michael Rogin, *Black Face, White Noise: Jewish Immigrants in the Hollywood Melting Pot* (Berkeley and Los Angeles: University of California Press, 1996). In differing but related ways, these texts, written by Jewish Americans, rationalize the prevalence of racist images of African Americans in Hollywood cinema of the studio era as the effect of a masquerade, a displaced allegory-effect of suppressed, often repressed, Jewish anger and indignation over historical, including North American, antisemitism, which, on this view, continues to be necessary to the legitimation of the Hollywood studio system and the ideology of industrial capitalism in which that system was, and remains, based. This perspective, eerily reminiscent of Zionist ideology (which shall be explained more fully as we proceed), has been echoed subsequently pace the culturally more conservative Gabler in the film, *Hollywoodism* (Simcha Jacobovici, Canada, 1998). Important to our formulation of *le-didakh* as a Holocaust film analytic is the crucial difference it marks between the "Jewish" as the subject of an ethno-credal positionality and/or as descended (*herkunft*) from that subjectivity, and the "Judaic" as the intelligibility of an ideological creed staking a hermeneutic relationship to the world that is philosophically distinct from, while critically foundational to, that of the "Judeo-Christian" mainstream into which the majority of actual "Jews," studio moguls among them, along with Christians, Black and white, have been interpellated. On the basis of this marked difference, and while by no means denying the psychology of racism effectuated via the Holocaust and other watersheds in the history of antisemitism (*The Pawnbroker* [Sidney Lumet, U.S.A., 1965] is probably the best cinematic examination to date of this phenomenon), the allegorical methodology employed by Rogin and by Gabler is only cursorily le-didakhic; insofar as it collapses the philosophical layer of critical praxis onto an existential layer of untheorized social groupings, it not only implicitly occludes the crux of the Jewish–Christian differentiation I am otherwise here positing, but also subtly disallows the possibility that more thoroughgoing and sustained understandings be reached, and critiques be formulated, of Jewish-American racism.

[144] See Finkelstein, *Holocaust Industry*, 41.

[145] Beginning a decade ago with David Bordwell's conservative tract, *Making Meaning: Inference and Rhetoric in the Interpretation of Cinema* (Cambridge, MA: Harvard University Press, 1989), and taking hold later with ostensibly more critical collections such as Cynthia A. Freeland and Thomas E. Wartenberg, eds., *Philosophy and Film* (London: Routledge, 1995); and Irving Singer, *Reality Transformed: Film As Meaning and Technique* (Cambridge, MA and London: MIT Press, 1998). For a useful critique, see Robert Stam, *Film Theory: An Introduction* (London: Blackwell, 2000), 235–47.

[146] Ellen Meiksins Wood, *Empire of Capital* (London: Verso, 2004); and idem., *The Origin of Capitalism: A Longer View* (London: Verso, 2002).

[147] See Joseph Massad, "The Persistence of the Palestinian Question," *Cultural Critique* 59 (2005): 18.

CHAPTER TWO

ST. *KORCZAK*, MARTYR OF POLAND

> It is the inherent tendency of dialectical experience to dissipate
> the semblance of eternal sameness, and even of repetition, in
> history. Authentic political experience is absolutely free of this
> semblance.
>
> —Benjamin, "On the Theory of Knowledge,
> Theory of Progress," *The Arcades Project*

The following chapter is an analysis of an Eastern European Holocaust film, *Korczak*. *Korczak* was produced at a time during which Poland's historical relationship with the capitalist West was undergoing a fundamental political and economic transformation. At that watershed moment, public discourse in Poland about the Holocaust experienced an unprecedented resurgence fueled by international controversies over the so-called right to speak about the event and claim victim status with respect to it, that is, to "own" it. *Korczak* now forms part of a legacy of Polish art films that have transported, by their international orientation and distribution, an array of compelling perspectives on these controversies which has both challenged and reproduced the widespread tendency to commodify the Holocaust. In the spirit of *le-didakh*, the following analysis clarifies *Korczak*'s positioning within those controversies through a critical reading of the film's poetic realism, especially its allegorical quality and related epic temporality, as it recalls and intersects the discourse of deconstruction and the neoformalist approach of Joshua Hirsch. The analysis inquires through this effort whether *Korczak* does not in fact occasion a perspective on the question of Holocaust "ownership" that transcends the controversies' visible parameters for reasons the film's mostly Jewish critics chose to ignore on grounds remarkably similar to those of the film's ardent, Catholic supporters and of christological tendencies attributable to the film and its national authorship. Most notable among these critics is renowned filmmaker, Claude Lanzmann, a Zionist whose experimental Holocaust documentary, *Shoah*, was purportedly made in reaction to the "taboo" on Holocaust representation misidentified with Adorno.

* * * * *

Korczak is the more well-known of two extant cinematic attempts to trace the life and legacy of renowned Jewish-Polish teacher, pediatrician, and children's rights advocate, Janusz Korczak (b. Henryk Goldszmit), who perished in the gas chambers of Treblinka after a 1942 deportation there from the Warsaw Ghetto with two hundred orphans in his charge.[1] *Korczak* is a layered film with manifold significance. At the level of story, *Korczak* is a film about pedagogy, especially as it may be practiced with regard to the Holocaust. It is likewise concerned with defining the Judeocide for its non-Jewish Polish spectators. As an international co-production marketed as both an art film and a popular melodrama, released in the current of Soviet bloc dismantlement, furthermore,[2] *Korczak* is imbricated within, and to a certain extent symptomatizes, political and ideological conflicts cleaving Polish and Western European self-understandings at a watershed moment in global history. Such conflicts include those involving the end of the Cold War, the ascendance and suppression of Solidarity [*Solidarność*], and the re-envisioning of the paradigmatic Nazi death camp, Auschwitz, as a multinational Holocaust memorial. At the aesthetic theoretical register, *Korczak*'s conflictuality iterates an international controversy staged primarily in the French popular press and argued vociferously by filmmaker Claude Lanzmann and journalist Danièle Heymann, the crux of which was the film's apparent kitsch revisionism, but, in addition, its explicit christology.[3] For these critics, *Korczak* was another in a long series of incidents and occasions symptomatizing the postwar persistence of Polish antisemitism. Its specific articulations entailed: 1) a recuperation of the Jewish Holocaust victim, Janusz Korczak, as a Christian martyr whose death would be perceived as a redemptive allegory for the postwar founding of Israel; and 2) a right-revisionist representation of Polish wartime sympathy for and assistance to persecuted Jews.

For Lanzmann, known famously for his monumental Holocaust documentary, *Shoah*, *Korczak*'s docudramatic structure was the primary reason for its presumed failings. Whereas *Shoah* utilizes only contemporary footage and survivor testimonies so as not to break, in Lanzmann's view, Adorno's misunderstood taboo against Holocaust mythicization,[4] *Korczak* is a fictionalized re-enactment of Janusz Korczak's imprisonment in the Warsaw Ghetto. Recalling Wajda's prior, social realist docudramas, *Korczak* utilizes black and white stock and archival footage partly in an effort to lend credibility and authenticity to the re-enactment, including material that refers intertextually to the Nazi propaganda film, *The Eternal Jew* [*Der Ewige Jude*] (Fritz Hippler, Germany, 1940).[5] This utilization of black and white stock pre-dated its very different effectuality in the Hollywood melodrama, *Schindler's List*, which also makes intertextual reference to social realist Holocaust films including *Long Is the Road*. In Lanzmann's peculiar existentialist historiography, efforts such as these are redundant and, by extension, unacceptably revisionist: recalling various scholarly adaptations of trauma theory such as LaCapra and Joshua Hirsch, authentic Holocaust knowledge is, on Lanzmann's view, only ever fragmentary, its credibility dependant strictly upon proximity to memorial evocation by actual Holocaust survivors. On this phenomenological line, Lanzmann and Heymann were likewise able to criticize *Korczak*'s purely fictional scenes as Holocaust kitsch. Instead of depicting the fateful arrival of Korczak and his orphans at Treblinka, for instance, *Korczak* substitutes a pastoral scene derived from a well-known Polish postwar fantasy in which Korczak and his orphans survive their fateful trip to Treblinka when their train is diverted to safety by partisans.[6] *Korczak* portrays the diverted children disembarking in slow motion from the train into a hazy fog and rallying behind the orphanage banner, which on one side depicts the orphanage logo, a four-leaf clover, and on the other, a Star of David in emblematic context of what would soon after become the Israeli flag (fig. 2-1).

Fig. 2-1 – Postwar fantasy scene in *Korczak*

In addition to its romantic transhistoricity and, in relation, its conveyance of an albeit ambiguous narrative closure, the scene's allegorical reference to Israel, marked by the flag-like banner bearing the Star of David, led Heymann to criticize *Korczak* for propagating Christian (in apparent contrast to Jewish) Zionism. For Christian Zionism, a biblical imperative holds which correlates a large concentration of Jews in Israel with apocalyptic global conflagration. Called *Armageddon*, this fiery catastrophe, or literally, *holocaust*,[7] is conceived as divine retribution against non-believers in the christic redemption signified by Jesus—namely Jews but now, also, lapsed Christians—who are henceforth sacrificed so that believers, miraculously immune to the horrors of the holocaust, may prevail in a peaceful, bucolic aftermath.[8] By contrast, Jewish Zionism, which also calls for mass Jewish emigration to Israel, promises neither conflagration nor salvation but simply an antidote to antisemitism through modern restoration of a nostalgically envisaged, ancient Jewish homeland.[9] Although recent and ongoing archival research reveals that many official Zionist documents and tracts explicitly acknowledge the violence entailed by their admittedly colonialist project,[10] such violence is rarely expressed or understood in apocalyptic terms, nor are its results foreseen as necessarily peaceful. In fact, Christian Zionism was formulated and adopted by non-Jewish European and North American ideologues for the purpose of promoting colonialist enterprise in the Middle East and elsewhere.[11] While the Jewish Zionist reaction to antisemitism supplied such persons with an opportunity for political and economic expansion, proponents of Jewish Zionism have variously negotiated that opportunity to their own, ethno-nationalist advantage.

Although Heymann is not incorrect, then, to interpret *Korczak*'s ending as an allusion to *Armageddon*, her failure nonetheless to distinguish between what must be seen as mutually compatible because politically intereffective Zionisms is symptomatic of her and Lanzmann's dubious blind spots regarding the scene's broader significance, as I shall elucidate. Seeing merely the film's Christian Zionism, that is, Heymann can offer only unilateral dismissals of it. It must be remarked that this proclivity obtains not only vis-à-vis the film's final scene, but insofar as she and Lanzmann each criticize earlier scenes in which Polish Catholics, apparently imbued with Christian martyrial compunction, are portrayed yearning to suffer alongside their persecuted Jewish neighbors, as when the character Maria Falska [Teresa Budzisz-Kryżanowska], a headmistress at Warsaw's Christian orphanage, Our Home,[12] who will be instrumental in rescuing some of Korczak's children (residents of Warsaw's Jewish orphanage, the Children's Home), says auspiciously, "How awful not to be able to accompany them," while witnessing Korczak and his children being herded into the Warsaw Ghetto during a sequence that visually foreshadows the film's concluding redemption fantasy.

In effect, for Lanzmann, Heymann, and others, *Korczak* was an obscenity that proved *Shoah*'s polemical point.[13] The film's defenders, however, did not consider *Korczak* antisemitic, much less unacceptably revisionist. Simone Weil, David Lindenberg, Sylvie Kaufmann, and Alain Finkielkraut were among those in France for whom *Korczak* was undeserving of condemnation.[14] North

American reviews of the film took up likewise ambiguous or, at most, conciliatory positions, implicitly bowing to prevailing political pressure to "open up" to Poland.[15] And even those North American reviews critical of *Korczak* confined commentary to the film's formal techniques and left definitive interpretation to the religious Right.[16] Taken up primarily, although not exclusively, by North American orthodox Jews, such definitive interpretation tended ironically toward moral posturing that praised *Korczak* for its presumed spiritual uplift[17]—a view defended inter alia by literary theorist, Tzvetan Todorov, otherwise a liberal, who would assert, in debunking Lanzmann, that the debate over *Korczak*'s alleged antisemitism proved Jewish control of the media![18]

None of these rebuttals were inclined, however, to carry the *Korczak* debate past vying moral highgrounds onto the register of critical theory, which would have enabled interpretations of the film to transcend judgments based primarily upon varied codes of social propriety and taste by placing those interpretations into discursive context and analyzing the epistemology of their historical and conceptual differences. Instead the question remained simply, Which religious orientation can lay proper claim to Holocaust historiography and interpretation? Beneath this horizon, the Lanzmann/Heymann problematic became sublimated rather than effectively critiqued; key historical facts of Janusz Korczak's life and work were skewed, and the question of *Korczak*'s alleged antisemitism was merely deferred. In contrast to these moralizing positions, I propose that christology alone does not antisemitism make, and that fictionalized representation of the Holocaust does not necessarily imply kitschification, much less right-revisionism. As *Korczak*'s defenders remind us, Catholic Poles did in fact offer aid to persecuted Jews; in addition, the dialectical implication per se of documentary with fictive modes is no longer subject to debate in Cinema Studies. In contrast to the film's defenders, however, I must concede a phenomenological modality overdetermining the film's hermeneutic structure— a secular modality of abstract feeling linked inexorably here to Christian *martyrology*—which encourages an allegorical reception that may very well invoke antisemitism. That is to say, Lanzmann's and Heymann's arguments contain a kernel of truth worth pursuing. Despite themselves, these arguments highlight the fact that inaccuracies allegedly marking *Korczak*'s portrayal of Janusz Korczak are actually less damaging to either his memory or that of the Jewish Poles he would represent than are the ways in which such inaccuracies facilitate historical interpretations that favor the very perspectives they might also offend—interpretations often formulated by Jews themselves, particularists among them. In effect, I am proposing that, if *Korczak* is indeed interpretable as antisemitic, it is, again, not because of its Christian martyrological portrayal of Janusz Korczak—even though, as I shall elucidate, that portrayal is verifiable—

but because the film's formal-aesthetic structuring of that portrayal compels an interpretive transcendence, or, "ludic" allegorization,[19] of the political and economic foundations of modern antisemitism, foundations which happen to include Jewish as well as Christian Zionism, and which therefore are not opposed by *Korczak*'s most outspoken critics, for whom the Holocaust is essentially "Jewish."

As against either pole of the *Korczak* debate, then, I am proposing that *Korczak*'s phenomenological structuring, including what I shall describe is its visual metaphysic, is ideologically commensurate with *both* Lanzmann/Heymann *and* their ostensible detractors. *Korczak* neither strictly delineates nor subsumes the religious sectarian aspects of its eponymous persona, as is otherwise suggested within parameters of the debate, nor is Lanzmann's theoretical distinction of *Korczak* from *Shoah*—a distinction accepted on both sides of the *Korczak* debate—sustainable on either account. As I shall explain, *Korczak*'s formal-aesthetic structure serves rather to cleave sectarian differences between the film's Judaic and Christian aspects into a globalizing "Judeo-Christian" orientation that has been dissimulated by moralizing discourse on both sides of the debate as these implicitly designate the film, for better or worse, a passion play.[20]

In light of *Korczak*'s multinational production (Poland/Germany/U.K.), I shall in turn indicate that this dissimulation belies not only the humanitarian benevolence of the Polish anti–Nazi resistance depicted occasionally throughout the film. *Korczak* must also be seen for its positioning within the contemporary, post–Cold War film industry of which it is an undeniable product. Increasingly through deployment of religious discourse, that industry, still dominated by Hollywood, has developed new, hybrid modalities ("world cinema," "'indie' cinema") which converge aspects of the art film with those of popular melodrama. The result is creation of a global "market" for cinematic signifiers of neoliberal diversification, especially as these may re-envisage impoverished nations and regions of the global South and East as welcoming to Western/Hollywoodian culture and investment.[21] In this light, one may argue that a Judeo-Christian *Korczak*, however "liberal" or magnanimous may seem its portrayal of a Jewish Pole, belies complicity with the industry's verifiable right-hegemonic agenda—an agenda which, ironically, Wajda himself has tellingly opposed. Through my analysis of this and related ironies, I offer a means by which *Korczak*'s checkered public reception may be re-understood as one occasion among many in today's Holocaust-cultural sphere (cf. controversies over *Schindler's List*, *Life Is Beautiful*, and *Jacob the Liar* [Kassovitz]) on which the Holocaust and, by christological association, the "Jewish" are (re)positioned as ideological exemplars—often willing agents—in European and, especially, U.S. struggles for post–Cold War global dominance. I hold that the terms of this (re)positioning, reminiscent as they are of German right-revisionism, obstruct critical recognition of how the Judeocide is (re)made to articulate to neoliberal aims, not least as these would affect Jews, Catholics, and others engaged variously in socially transformative struggles.

* * * * *

Before proceeding, I should first like to clarify precisely how I will be using *allegory* in this analysis. Here "allegory" shall refer to a narrative-compositional nexus at which subjective and objective, literal and figurative, denotative and connotative registers of *Korczak* appear to meet asymptotically, and via this only apparently indeterminate encounter, trope the film's diegesis into a contemporaneous signifier. My usage of "allegory" differs from that of Paul de Man, which has enjoyed an albeit uneven academic prominence in Holocaust studies for its phenomenological designation of indeterminacy.[22] Prototypical of LaCapra's understanding of existential duration and of the Lyotardian *differend*, de Manian allegory understands rhetorical indeterminacy as an aesthetic index of transcendental time, whereupon the subjectively mediated claims of Holocaust survivor testimonies are verifiable only in view of their displaced, posttraumatic performances, and whereupon, moreover, the ludic facticity of testimony forms an inviolable intellectual horizon.[23] By contrast, my usage of "allegory" derives from that of Walter Benjamin, whose writing on German tragedy illustrates the material-historical basis of rhetorical indeterminacy, thereby enabling its consideration as ideologically rather than merely aesthetically overdetermined.[24] Whereas de Manian allegory pays lip-service to historical temporality, that is, rendering it but a quasi-sacral means for aesthetic doubling, Benjaminian allegory resituates historical passage within a critical framework for which rhetorical shifts become interpretable as ideology-effects and mystifications of political and economic struggles at the register of cultural practice.[25]

As with the distinction I have outlined between factual inaccuracy and structural functioning in *Korczak*, in other words, Benjaminian allegory is less a signifier of experiential multiplicity than a crisis-riven symptom of its structuring absences—what Benjamin refers to elsewhere as a *dialectical image*.[26] "Allegory" for Benjamin is therefore less a barometer of spiritual faith contested by vying moral perspectives, a reading which becomes possible on the de Manian view as it derives finally, with Kantian liberalism, from Christian hermeneutic tradition,[27] than a vehicle for the sort of layered critique of idealist temporality and tropology which such christo-phenomenological allegory necessitates. Indeed, in view of these distinctions, I shall consider at once christological and phenomenological any hermeneutic layer of *Korczak* in which the narrative-compositional nexus appears determined to appropriate, reduce, and universalize the historical Korczak's enlightened, secular (*haskalik*) teaching philosophy into a project of sheer, even gnostic faith.

An obvious example of *Korczak*'s Christian allegorical structuring is its fashioning as such of Janusz Korczak after Francis of Assisi, a medieval Christian ascetic canonized for his saintly deeds on behalf of the poor.[28] This resemblance was not lost on the film's critics, who nonetheless focused primarily on nuances of costuming and gesture. Wajda's Korczak [Wojciech Pszoniak] wears a frock-like coat, carries a sack over his shoulder and sports a balding, monk-like head, all of which foster a Franciscan likeness. In addition, however, are his numerous sartorial poses and practices that evoke the Franciscan mystique. For instance, he kneels in solitary prayer on the bare floor of his bedroom, as though residing in an austere, reclusive monastery. While watering plants on the orphanage windowsill, he is approached fearlessly by wild songbirds—a classic Franciscan motif. A known homosexual,[29] furthermore, Wajda's Korczak never expresses sexual desire but instead performs duties traditionally perceived as humiliating, such as scrubbing floors, emptying the orphanage slop bucket, and begging for alms from the ghetto elite. Depiction of pleasure in general is largely confined to scenes of cenobitical bonding between Korczak and other orphanage residents and workers. In effect, Wajda's Korczak is lent neoplatonic qualities of second-century Christian gnosticism[30]—charitable humility, spiritual inwardness, sexual abstinence, and pastoral communitarianism—with which the Franciscans have been associated more than any other mendicant Christian order save the Carmelites, a female order whose involvement in a recently resolved public controversy over the construction of a Catholic convent/mission at the site of the Auschwitz death camp henceforth resonates and reverberates across the Korczak persona.[31]

Here one might object that my reading of *Korczak* is too narrowly focused on its Christian aspects—and s/he would not be mistaken. The Judaic is not absent from the film's characterization of Korczak; crucially, however, it is inscribed partially and reductively. One may possibly interpret Korczak's monk-like qualities, for instance, in terms of Jewish gnosticism. Historically, Judaism has spawned numerous gnostic tendencies (Kabbalism, Essenism, Hasidism) as well as deriving partially from certain religious practices of ancient and medieval Palestinian societies ('Anavim, Chashaim, Zhenuim, Isawaites, Yudghanites, Karaites, Rechabites, Amorites, Canaanites, Edomites, Jebusites, Moabites, Ammonites, Perizzites, Hivites, Arameans, Nabateans, Philistines, Phoenicians, Hittites, Nazarites, and Habirus), many of which are known to have encouraged solitary prayer and contemplation, respect for nature and work, charity, sexual continence, social cohesion, and ethical priority—otherwise associated commonly with Christianity.[32] The analogy ends there, however:

Judaism has historically rejected prostrate worship, extended religious reclusion, sexual abstinence, and self-endangerment for its own sake (in excess of ethical interpolation), all practices nevertheless attributed to Wajda's Korczak.[33]

A similar reduction of the Jewish to the Christian inscribes the film's construction of Korczak as teacher, and the orphanage as teaching institution, that is, as site of ideological instruction and inculcation. While *Korczak* cannot deny the Jewish provenance of the Orphan's Home and remain credible, it can and does emphasize and elaborate those aspects which are easily associable to Christianity. This occurs, for instance, when the orphans are portrayed reciting prayers common to both religions (e.g., Psalm of David). Likewise the film entirely realigns aspects of the orphanage less recognizable to non-Jewish spectators into accordance with Christian practice. This includes misrepresenting Jewish prayer as strictly individual, subjective, and spontaneous, when in fact it is also collective, textually engaged, and time-bound; as well as refiguring Jewish intellection as confessionalism, whereas it refers in fact to the studied interrogation and practiced exercise of social and ethical imperatives and obligations, which lend priority to critical discipline over ritual tolerance.[34]

Thus detaching Jewish practices from their cultural foundations at the rudimentary representational level, *Korczak* prepares its Catholic-Polish spectator for upcoming depiction of holocaustal horrors with a familiarized, comforting Korczak whose eventual demise may as such be perceived as more unsettling and meaningful than that of many other Jewish characters in the film who are portrayed stereotypically (e.g., as exotic "Jewesses" and "parasitical" *Judenrat* leaders and operatives of the Jewish ghetto "mafia"). In this regard, it is easy to concur with Lanzmann and with Heymann, who otherwise, like the film's North American critics, subordinate a structural analysis of Korczak's characterology to the remarking of superficial detail. By the same token, one is compelled to interrogate their conceptual priorities in order that the explication of *Korczak*'s christological overdetermination resists devolving into a conservative multicultural rehearsal of Jewish identity politics, for which non-stereotyped image diversification is promoted at the expense of critiquing its potentially self-endangering material and ideological conditions, and therefore of reinscribing parochial and sectarian formations. For this is precisely the point: As hinted earlier, those priorities entail affirmation of *Korczak*'s martyrology. More egregious than the films' reductive representation of the Judaic, this critical affirmation entirely neglects the legacy of *Jewish martyrdom* as it also functions, however restrictively, in the film. Indeed at most, *Korczak*'s martyrological hermeneutic was deemed an unintended flaw attributable, ironically, to Wajda's "good intentions," such that criticisms against it were vilified as "misguided and trivial."[35] Yet while a christological Korczak, like the

Carmelite convent/mission project, is both historically tendentious and culturally offensive to Jews, the *spectral Judaism* to which that figure also, necessarily refers offers critics—Jewish or not—a crucial insight into what we may call the film's *allegorical elegy* to a *Polish national history* that is contemporaneous with *Eastern European Jewish development up to and including the Judeocide, the Cold War, the Zionist turn, Communist reaction, the ascendance of Solidarity and beyond*.[36] To his discredit, Lanzmann, a well-known Zionist whose *Shoah* is perceived by many as blanketly anti–Polish, was reluctant to acknowledge this crucial insight for reasons I shall surmise in due course.[37]

*   *   *   *   *

Although it is beside the point of this inquiry to elaborate the historical and theoretical differences between Jewish and Christian "martyrdom," much less to debate their relative merits, it is important for my argument that we at least understand one such difference. Christian martyrdom entails a project of emblematic self-sacrifice that is voluntary, transgressive, heroic, and eschatological.[38] It is staked upon the palpable image of a suffering individual whose pre-ordained, (self-)sacrificial death is meant to signify a universal end to human suffering—lest his death have occurred in vain.[39] Insofar as worldly suffering persists, however, vigilant proof is required of the martyr's divine significance or, in the Unitarian context, its persisting social import. Such proof takes the form of the sacrifice's ritual re-enactment, which may be actual (pogroms, crusades) or representational (passion and mystery plays) depending upon historical exigency. This salvific, transcendental notion of martyrdom starkly contrasts the Judaic notion, which obligates socially reparative deeds *on behalf of*, rather than merely *for the sake of*, the world.[40] Jewish martyrdom is staked in the knowledge that mundane deeds are ineluctably social; as with the Jewish phenomenological critique of ontology, it rejects as needlessly utopian, even diversionary, the worldly abdication necessary to the very conception of christo-martyrdom in favor of a project of *immanent* redemption.[41] Jewish martyrology as such rejects voluntary self-endangerment and high mortal risk, which it considers blasphemous [*chillul hashem*] for its idealist reduction of the relational crux of social organization, and instead promotes social participation for which sacrificial heroics are supposed only to be a product of self-defense.[42] In effect, Jewish martyrdom does not promise redemption christologically, for to do so would reintroduce the reactionary, medieval notion of Jewish mortal suffering as the quintessence of *Christian* sacrifice. That the contemporary Jewish cult of military martyrdom in Israel/Palestine, for one instance, has not adhered to this Jewish martyrological ethic is a matter I shall confront in due course. [43] Suffice it here to say that historically (and while undeniably carrying an albeit different series of problematic effects), *the Jewish martyr has adopted the christological notion parodically (Jewish gnostics) and pragmatically (Zionism) during times of perceived threat.*[44]

Korczak's veritable first Act symptomatizes a grand phenomenological reduction of Jewish to Christian martyrdom, which prefigures the film's controversial final sequence and thus ramifies allegorically to the mentioned social relationship that has developed between Jews and non-Jews in connection with historical Poland, what I shall now refer to as the Polish–Jewish nexus. The critical evasion of this nexus by Lanzmann and Heymann betrays their uneasiness regarding that relationship, suggesting perhaps an unconscious concern on their part that the film's spectral Judaism enables reference not merely to Christian but to *Jewish* martyrdom as *it* has *likewise* been reductively culled *by Jews* in the interests of neocolonialist policies in Israel/Palestine— policies that today verge on the genocidal.[45] The Act's reduction articulates at the film's narrative-compositional registers, thus hermeneutically extending and deepening the film's problematic Judeo-Christian characterology.

At the narratological register, for instance, it is the subjective perspective of Korczak as it projects onto and extends across the diegesis, not the objective action of a drama, which compels narrative movement. Recalling conventions of medieval chronicle and the New Testament after which these are modeled, Wajda's Korczak is a *hermeneutical* matrix whose evolving moral perspective serves as the film's motive force and interpretive cipher, its fulcrum for registering temporality and reference.[46] From an opening shot in which Korczak appears metaphysically inspired, through a series of quotidian events circumscribing the establishment of the Warsaw Ghetto, the Act traces a generalized, synoptic pattern by which characters move, points-of-view shift, and mise-en-scène reconfigures, as the narrative alternates from subjectivized interiors to objectivized exteriors and, finally, back again, with Korczak's often disembodied perspective the vehicle of transition, as though a *personalistic* locus orienting a transcendental cause. The result is an epiphanic vision punctuating the passage of a christic parable in which Korczak's actions manifest pure will, an ubiquitous coalescence of moral feeling structuring the narrative into a cohesion and coherence uncannily emblematized by one of Korczak's memorable diegetic proclamations: "The world doesn't need oranges [Zionism] or labor [Communism]. It needs a new faith!"[47]

The Act begins with an interior shot of Korczak in the recording booth of recently Aryanized radio station for which he hosts a weekly children's show. He is framed in medium close-up but positioned at a rear angle that obscures and alienates the shot's perspective. A resulting sense of subjective intimacy is underscored by low-key lighting and chiaroscuro. In an ensuing scene set in the station director's office, however, perspective is broadened. Korczak is fully lit and framed in medium shot at thirty degrees, and whereas he was initially shown speaking in monologue, he is now portrayed in dialogue with the station director via the somewhat more objective shot/reverse-shot format. An ensuing sequence continues this externalizing orientation. Korczak and his orphans are in weekend holiday at the orphanage summer camp at Włocławek, where they are portrayed outdoors at lakeside. Prefiguring the film's final scene, the sequence is brightly lit and framed via frequent long-shots and tableaux. It includes dialogues between characters exclusive of Korczak, and its point-of-view is largely omniscient.

At each point along the way, the apparently broadening narrative perspective is recontained, primarily by an intersection of moralizing discourse and triangulated conflict. Korczak's on-air monologue may be seen, for instance, as a homily sermonizing a travestied relationship between altruistic sacrifice and love. It subsequently evolves, however, into an angry tirade against the station manager, whom Korczak accuses of mocking human dignity for catering to Nazi orders that he be fired and his show cancelled. The pattern complexifies during the Włocławek sequence, as Korczakian morality plays out across three incipient sub-plots, each of which exemplifies what will develop into a thematized moral dilemma. At each axis of conflict, Korczak's perspective, when not actually embodied, remains an intuitive presence, as though aligned with the omniscient point-of-view generally framing the sequence. In this way, it serves to articulate the varying conflicts into an intelligible whole while itself not necessarily inhering to them.

While it facilitates this analogic hermeneutics, however, the narrative passage is also interpretable Judaically, at the Polish–Jewish nexus. During the Włocławek sequence, for instance, where Korczak calls for a new faith, central features of the proverbial "Jewish Question" play out across a love triangle between a Jewish boy, Yusek [Piotr Kozlowski], his Catholic girlfriend, Ewka [Agnieszka Kruk], and a Jewish girl, Natka [Karolina Czernicka], who is jealous of Ewka. These features figure explicitly as the Jewish-genealogical problem of intermarriage, the Jewish-political problem of internecine struggles (between Zionism, Bundism, and Haskalism), and the Jewish-cultural problem of sustaining communal structure and ritual practice under historically diasporic conditions. At the same time, and because the character conflicts representing these features involve encounters with non-Jews, these problems transfigure implicitly into allegories of Polish concern (national legitimation, political-economic instability, and the role of a national religion/ideology, respectively). Moreover Korczak's narratology recalls Polish literary tradition, not least *Dziady*. The result of this twofold significance in the film's narratological context is a dialectical tracing of the Polish–Jewish nexus which illuminates the historical fact that *the "Jewish Question" at once pre-exists and partially constitutes the Polish sovereignty from which Polish–Jewish culture will subsequently derive*. Only when this twofold significance registers is Korczak's fateful claim uttered; only then are we able to sense the depth of the scene's abiding, prewar despair.

This historiographic twist likewise marks the Act's penultimate scene, in which Korczak examines a live x-ray of a child's beating heart while teaching a course on medical ethics subsequent to being fired from the radio station, and prior to the film's depiction of the Nazi invasion of Poland (fig. 2-2). Here the x-ray image itself becomes a hermeneutical matrix of Korczak's moral project. At its syntagmatic register, the image marks the brink of a major narrative ellipsis between the period immediately prior to the invasion and the Nazi takeover itself, whereupon the image accrues pre-apocalyptic significance as a minor catharsis. At its paradigmatic register, the image marks the function of a *heliotrope*, a rhetorical figure connoting a quasi-sacral, hermeneutic near-collapse.[48] As seen heliotropically, the image accrues an uniqueness barely distinguishable from the x-ray machine used to represent it, thus appearing almost entirely self-referential. Exemplified by the visual disembodiment of the child's heart within the diegetic x-ray frame and, near the end of the scene, through a medium close-up by which that frame is aligned with the non-diegetic one of the filmic shot, forming a visual mise-en-abyme, the heliotropized heart is at once decontexualized, as though displaced from its vital, organic function, and reduced to the apparatus which reveals it, as though a *prima facie* phenomenon, an animating force, or *élan vital*, of the x-ray machine. Here the actual function of x-rays to enhance the capacity of human vision is not simply depicted but, moreover, mystified, directly contradicting the Judaic injunction against revering images.[49] Indeed as Korczak's pedagogical voice, now also disembodied, is projected over the image, the heart's detached function and apparent hyperreality become interchangeable with the workings of the x-ray apparatus, which in turn expands into Korczak's perspectival ubiquity as it elevates the image-technological complex, and the cinematic apparatus it extends, to the status of *sacre coeur* (GK *gnosis kardias*).

Yet again, the scene's transcendent tropology also signifies Judaically, at the Polish–Jewish nexus. At the figurative register, the x-ray machine, an apparatus of medical science, reminds easily of concurrent Nazi medical experiments, including the "euthanasia" program decreed officially by Hitler at the conclusion of the Polish campaign.[50] The fact that the x-ray model is a girl invokes the edenic innocence and occultism of German Romanticism as these were appropriated into the eugenic theory used to rationalize the Final Solution. As cultural theorist Imke Lode has demonstrated, German Romanticism is an ineluctably modern development, a reaction to industrial development that, as such, always bears uncannily, and thereby stands to perpetuate, the marks of its ostensible nemesis.[51] Extending this view, Romanticism's mystical discourse on "blood and soil," invoked partially during the Włocławek sequence, may be considered to prefigure as well as to obscure the pseudo-scientific character of Nazi eugenic practices.[52] The medical scientific milieu of the x-ray scene invokes the postwar Doctor's Plot, a counterrevolutionary witch hunt inversely mirroring McCarthyism and aimed almost exclusively at Jewish physicians falsely accused of anti–Soviet conspiracy.

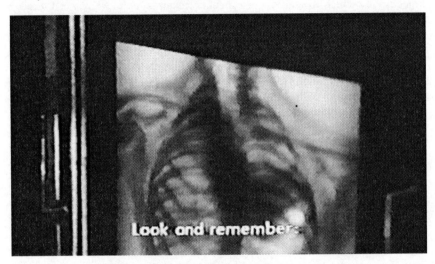

Fig. 2-2 – X-ray image of a child's beating heart in *Korczak*

At a literal register, furthermore, the fact that the x-ray is a *visual* technology suggests the critique of scientific looking staged vigorously in Cinema Studies by feminist film theory, for which spectatorship is linked problematically to fetishism and, by extension, reification.[53] In this respect, the scene prefigures the film's later incorporation of archival footage from the Warsaw and Łódź Ghettos, an historiographic gesture which, by the footage's intertextual citation of *The Eternal Jew*, returns images exploited by Nazi propaganda to their rightful context as well as compels critical interrogation of their function as visual (self-)evidence.[54] By this tack—a veritable secular rearticulation of the Judaic injunction against idolatry—*Korczak* evinces critical recognition of the relationship between cinema's aesthetic and ideological functions, a profoundly political move which by its likewise recognizable allegorical gesturing in turn implicates Polish cinema itself in a history of propaganda, whether produced under fascist, proletarian, or parliamentarian regimes.[55]

* * * * *

By the same token, the film's citation of *The Eternal Jew* also serves as a turning point in the narrative itself. Its recontextualization of images abstracted into a rhetorics of political violence effects an ironical redirection of narrative trajectory by which Korcak's transcendent orientation is now advanced through the occasioning of internalizing and introjective moments evocative of death. This hermeneutical inversion marks a crucial node in the film's allegoricality, whereupon Korczak's previous gnostic "ascent" is reoriented as infernal "descent" and, as such, as ostensibly punitive. As with Act One, this ensuing trajection follows a Judeo-Christian logic, its actions opening onto both Christian and Jewish interpretations within an overriding christo-phenomenology that reductively allegorizes the asymmetrical Polish–Jewish encounter. This latter is symptomatized most saliently by the film's theatricalization of its tendency to christic probativity, which hyperrealizes the "docudramatized" mise-en-scène, re-abstracting it from its historicized context, reifiying it so that it becomes an exceptional, almost microcosmic space in which Korczak himself may be judged a negative exemplar of Judeo-Christian "faith."

An important example of this phenomenon and its ideology-effects is the sub-plot involving Shlomo [Woyciech Klata], a street-smart young immigrant boy from the rural countryside whom the Orphans Home has adopted at his dying mother's request. Free-spirited Shlomo is resistant to orphanage life, with its daily regimen and enforced curfews: he never ceases to dodge scheduled activities in order to venture beyond the infamous ghetto wall, where he trades on the underground market that has become a primary means of survival for ghetto prisoners. During one such venture, Shlomo visits his mother, only to discover that she has died. Her untimely and unexpected death shocks Shlomo into abandoning his immediate goals; he returns to the despised because largely bourgeois orphanage, where he instigates a violent altercation with Yusek that ends in reconciliation with Korczak and the martyrial fate that will be elucidated for him as the sub-plot unfolds.

On the psychological view compelled by the sequence, Shlomo's actions following the discovery of his mother's death symptomatize a projection of maternal loss onto the orphanage resulting from his Oedipally-inflected incapacity to mourn her death. The narrative-compositional structuring of these actions broadens their interpretability, moreover, as it serves to thematize through ludic indeterminacy the exemplary function of Korczak across the

Polish–Jewish nexus. The operative spatio-temporal abstraction of this structuring figures at several key points during scenes which feature Shlomo. An example is the sequence beginning with Shlomo's discovery of his mother's corpse inside a dilapidated, makeshift hospital situated outside the orphanage— and interior placement of the Jewish corpse atypical for explicative Holocaust documentaries and newsreels, in which dead bodies are usually depicted lying exposed on ghetto streets. Rehearsing while altering the introjective and internalizing pattern characterizing *Korczak*'s narratological redirection and hermeneutical inversion, Shlomo's discovery here of monumental death is diegetically positioned to occur simultaneously inside and outside, within spaces that carry both interior and exterior signification. The destabilizing effect of this dual positioning, which recalls but significantly recasts the montage function of experimental Holocaust documentaries such as *Night and Fog* and *The Sorrow and the Pity*, is underscored and elaborated by a shot of Shlomo throwing a rock through a window from *outside* the hospital, followed by an elliptical cut to his return entry *into* the orphanage, by which his usually depicted homeward trek is absented. The scene's simulation of urgently, even mortally compressed time and overlapping senses of place is augmented when Shlomo confronts the older, economically more privileged Yusek in the orphanage mess hall which doubles as a theater. Their ensuing violent altercation entails noticeable visual disorientation constructed through 180-degree reverse-angle cutting, alternating long-shots, and sudden shifts in camera angle. These techniques and their theatrical mise-en-scène heighten the drama of confrontation; moreover, they condition an irruption of diegetic temporality that is barely contained by subjectivizing Korcak's ensuing perspectival interpolation of the conflict through simple reverse editing.

When the irruption is thusly contained, furthermore, its structured evocation of monumental death explicitly articulates Korczak, and the transcendent narrativity he subjectively (re)orients, to internalized anti–Jewish sentiment and confessional remorse. Yusek, bitterly realizing the impossibility of a future with Catholic-Polish Ewka, shouts at Korczak, "I don't want to be a Jew!" after which Shlomo, as though echoing the sentiment, confesses his guilt over his maternal projection to "father" Korczak. These articulations are explicitly christologized when Korczak hears Shlomo's confession: Korczak is portrayed extending an empathic gaze toward a saintly halo which has suddenly materialized above Shlomo's head (fig. 2-3). The exceptional moment, emphasized by melodramatic soundtrack and chiaroscuro, signals an epiphanic identification between the two interlocutors that is a hallmark of Christian encounter.

By way of these highly dramatized self-recriminations, which double as confessions to Korczak of social humiliation and (self-)degradation, the boys' extreme senses of alienation—as second-class Jewish Poles and unruly (in)dependent children—are reformulated for reabsorption into the narrative's christo-phenomenological perspective, thus facilitating an aesthetic (re)tracing of Korczak's ubiquitous subjectivity hypnagogically rather than anagogically, as deservedly sufficient for, and reconciled to, impending, catastrophic doom. Contrasting the apparently ideal orientation of the x-ray scene, that is, the transcendent narrativity which Korczak has come to figure now carries a specular "fallenness" characterized by the orphans' debasement in relation to significant female characters, itself overdetermined by a formal convolution of apparently progressive time that reveals itself always already anchored by an omnipresent Korczak who now serves at once as its identificatory matrix as well as its "descendental" locus. In effect, through their hyperreal (re)conditioning, the socio-historical determinants of Shlomo's maternal loss, Yusek's loss of his erstwhile girlfriend, and Korczak's imminent loss of the orphans are dissimulated christologically at the material core of the scene's allegory of "fallenness," as reified absence incorporated by "Jewish" Korczak at the mystical intersection of fatherhood, childhood, and sacral feminine passage.[56]

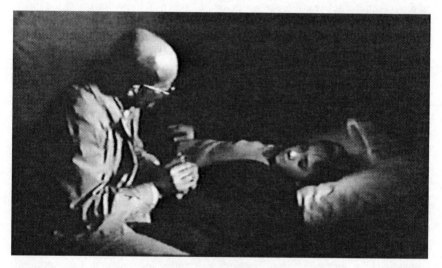

Fig. 2-3 – Halo above Shlomo's head in *Korczak*

Yet likewise recalling the x-ray scene is the fact that the ludic indeterminacy of the Shlomo sub-plot, and the trinitarian recontextualization it fosters of the Polish–Jewish nexus, also opens the sequence onto Jewish martyrological interpretability. Signifying this most saliently are frequent shots of the ghetto wall that Shlomo must scale or beneath which he must climb through secret tunnels in order to secure foodstuffs for himself and his mother and commodities to trade within the ghetto. Recalling the x-ray's hyperreal abstraction of the little girl's heart, the wall's diegetic positioning is rendered increasingly indefinite due to its multi-angled framing in narrative context. At times this visual metonymization of the wall additionally produces an uncertainty regarding Shlomo's diegetic location: it is often unclear whether Shlomo is emerging from inside or outside the ghetto, and he himself is often uncertain where best to transgress this arbitrary spatial boundary. The diegetically unhinged spatialization of the wall in these instances expresses the ghetto's Kafkaesque milieu; read hermeneutically, moreover, it figures a synecdoche of Jewish history, for which ghetto walls are commonplace, whether built by Christians to keep Jews out (medieval Europe), or by Jews to keep themselves in (the ultra-orthodox Tash in Canada and Netorei Karta in Israel/Palestine) and Gentiles out (Palestinians in contemporary Israel/Palestine). This historiographic tropology carries materialist implications for the Polish–Jewish nexus: the socio-economic conditioning of walls such as these have been clearly explicated by Jewish historian Ilan Halevi, for whom medieval Jewish negotiations over the ghettoization of European Jewish communities carry a class aspect ignored by most Jewish histories written after the Judeocide; hence, the temporal component marking *Korczak*'s wall synecdoche is imbricated within the asymmetrical political and economic structures of Jewish history.[57] Extending this reading, the ghetto wall signifies a double displacement: rural, uprooted Shlomo is a prisoner both of the Nazis and of the Jewish bourgeoisie which governs the ghetto and which trades internationally, via the Jewish lumpenbourgeois underground from which Korczak will refuse a passport to the U.S., in uneven collaboration with the Nazis and the Polish bourgeoisie, until the reversal of the anti–Soviet campaign (Operation Barbarossa) and U.S. preparation for entry into the war that in fact trigger implementation of the Final Solution, including liquidation of the Warsaw Ghetto.[58]

In effect, the metonymization of the ghetto wall collocates Shlomo and his "confessor," Korczak, into a dialectical image of *kashrut*, the Judaic problematic of ethical propriety for which spatial division or separation devolves readily into an ideological rationale for social class and ethnic division when its political and economic determinants, entailments and ramifications are obscured or misidentified. For Jewish history, this problematic has served variously to explain and to mystify racism, both within and outside Jewish communities, as well as the social exilic conditions of Jewish presence in Poland and other European countries up to, including, and *surpassing* the Second World War. It likewise overdetermines the self-sacrificial refusal—prototypical of Korczak— by the Jewish patriarch, Moses, to enter the mythical Promised Land following his forty-year desert hiatus. Indeed Shlomo's halo is interpretable Judaically, in reference to the halo that illuminates Moses when, in Exodus, he descends Mt. Sinai to deliver the Decalogue to his Hebrew followers, only to find them undeserving of the gift because, on his view, distracted by self-absorption.

It is telling in this regard that critics of *Korczak* failed to acknowledge another, lesser-known, Israeli film about Janusz Korczak, *Korczak und seine Kinder*. A German co-production, this film was released in the aftermath of the Yom Kippur War, when Jewish nationalism in Israel had begun to shift discursively from expressions of romantic heroism to those of postromantic martyrdom. The former disassociated a "salvific" Israeli present from its "vulnerable," holocaustal past, while the latter, still current, promoted a sense of "persistent" holocaustality considered crucial for reinstituting the ideology of besieged nationhood thought necessary to garnering continued international sympathy and support for Israeli policy.[59] *Korczak und seine Kinder* cast in its title role actor Leo Genn, who bears an uncanny facial resemblance to then Prime Minister of Israel, Golda Meier.[60] Its narrative convenes around Korczak's monumental decision to refuse a passport to Palestine in order to accompany his orphans to Treblinka. Through the film's narrative-compositional and generic structuring, a reading is encouraged that foregrounds the decision's Jewish martyriality: specifically, Korczak refuses to go to Palestine, because to do so would mean having to break the Judaic injunction against abandoning the children in one's midst to fear or death, regardless if that refusal forsakes others elsewhere.[61] Like the Judaic ethics of *le-didakh*, such a refusal betokens a profoundly anti–opportunistic gesture that is easily appropriated to opposite ends. For although this injunction applies literally to both Jewish and Gentile children and, by extension, to all human beings, its recognition in Israel/Palestine at the time of *Korczak und seine Kinder* would surely have registered still-simmering public debates over the class-based character of Jewish rescue efforts by the *Judenrat* in conjunction with the Zionist project that itself was hardly questioned by those involved at the time.[62] In this politicized context, the film's Jewish martyrology easily figures an *un*ethical ruse for Israeli "siege mentality," the post–heroic sense of perpetual self-sacrificial defensiveness which derives from but does not significantly alter the earlier romantic idealism that Israeli historian Idith Zertal has in fact attributed to Zionist, not Judaic ideology.[63]

Hence to have acknowledged *Korczak und seine Kinder* would have meant having had to engage the historical problematics and contradictions of Jewish martyrdom. The preceding analysis of *Korczak* invokes my earlier suggestion, however, that critics such as Lanzmann and Heymann evade *Korczak*'s Polish–Jewish nexus because to do otherwise would mean having had to confront their ideological implication—as propagators of Zionism—in the film's spectral referencing of Jewish martyrdom, which I have thus far illustrated figures dialectically, at manifold hermeneutic layers, as an allegorical elegy to a suppressed Polish history that is as tragically Jewish as it is triumphantly Christian. That theorists of *Shoah* such as Gertrud Koch, Elisabeth Huppert, and Shoshana Felman have confused that film's aesthetic with one of mainly christo-phenomenological import is in fact a telling indication of the tenor of this evasion.[64] Lanzmann films generally inscribe an immanentism which historical elusiveness belies an otherwise respectable refusal to forget the horrors of the Holocaust as a dubious equivocation on the ideological ramifications of that event's global appropriation in the name of those Jews today who are, at least for the moment, no longer the primary victims. Likewise Heymann's offense at *Korczak*'s "Christian Zionist" conclusion should be taken not as a literal call for more "authentic" Jewish Zionist representations, but as an obverse indicator of her support for a contemporary Western crusade mentality for which even the so-called involuntary, defensive heroics of Jewish martyrdom take on the mythical character of the pre-ordained. My point, again, is not to deny *Korczak*'s christological overdetermination; ironically, the film's Jewish interpretability actually opens articulation of Korczak's call for "a new faith" onto the longstanding anti–Zionist platform of Eastern Orthodoxy, also an irrevocable part of Polish history.[65] It is to insist that its undialectical interpretation dissimulates a similar overdetermination of that film's negative criticism which, considering its provenance, poses perhaps more of a danger than the liberal term, "hypocrisy," would imply.

One might concede on Lanzmann's and Heymann's behalf, of course, that during his chairship of the Polish Ministry of Culture under Solidarity, Wajda expressed publicly his enthusiasm for the sort of private Western (co-) sponsorship of popular Polish film production of which Lanzmann, a "high art" film director, was critical. Perhaps for that reason he was awarded an Honorary Oscar in 2000 by the Academy of Motion Picture Arts and Sciences.[66] Nevertheless, as Wajda's work on *Korczak* proceeded under that rubric, he found he could no longer sustain his initial openness: the international co-production, *Korczak*, at once popular melodrama and art film, had in one respect become a deterritorialized cultural product, a diversified commodity whose global circulation implicated it necessarily, along with Poland itself, in the posthistorical moment of capitalist development, with its neoliberal "world cinematic" manifestation travestying the Brechtian structures often otherwise inscribed across Wajda's political films.[67] Indeed, *Korczak*'s Judeo-Christian "merger" recalls the modern Polish practice of deploying sacrificial imagery to national-opportunistic ends—in view of which the film's synecdochal ghetto wall evokes the Berlin Wall that was still standing at the time of the film's release.[68] But Lanzmann, Heymann, and their critical supporters were oddly

silent on the matter of *Korczak*'s commoditizing effects, their condemnations
remaining detached from the *material* register at which aesthetic differences
find ideological common cause. My analysis suggests that *Korczak*'s repeated
deference to the Polish–Jewish nexus, despite and perhaps because of the
reductiveness of its means, rehearses this "uneasy commonality" to the point of
symptomatizing a radical social ambivalence regarding "What is to be done"
that is as common to Polish as to Jewish experiences of oppression and
exploitation in the modern epoch. Harkening to a pattern of compromise,
collaboration, and misplacement of blame, this ambivalence uncannily parallels
the ideology-effects of the proverbial *longue durée*,[69] in whose dialectical snare
Korczak and many contemporary international Holocaust films that grapple with
the Jewish-Polish legacy, not least those of Lanzmann, leave us to imagine but a
tragically redeemed utopia.

---

[1] The first film to be released about Janusz Korczak was Aleksander Ford's 1975
Israeli/West German co-production, *Sie Sind Frei, Doktor Korczak* ["You are Free, Dr.
Korczak"], also distributed as *Die Martyrer: Doktor Korczak und seine Kinder* ["The
Martyrs: Dr. Korczak and His Children"], *The Martyr*, and *Korczak Ve'Hayeladim*
["Korczak and His Children"]. I have been able to locate only one review of that film—
Vincent Canby, "'Martyr'—A Film about the Nazis and a Heroic Jew," *New York Times*,
June 17, 1976: 30—which represents the film in an unfavorable light, as overly
sentimental and emotive. I shall return to Canby's evaluation. A theatrical predecessor
and possible intertextual source of the Ford film, Erwin Sylvanus' *Korczak and His
Children* (trans. Eva Boehm-Jospe [New York: Samuel French, 1970]), premiered in
Germany in 1958, where it won the coveted Leo Baeck Prize awarded by Berlin's Jewish
community. See Robert Skloot, *The Darkness We Carry: The Drama of the Holocaust*
(Madison: University of Wisconsin Press, 1988), 95–99.
[2] France, Germany, and England all contributed financially to the film's production.
[3] Claude Lanzmann, interview by Catherine David and Nicole Leibowitz, "Un cinéaste
au-dessus du tout soupçon?" *Le Nouvel Observateur*, January 17–23, 1991: 71–73;
Danièle Heymann, "L'homme de rêve et l'homme de plomb," *Le Monde*, May 13–14,
1990: 10; Heymann, "Le dossier 'Korczak,'" *Le Monde*, June 19, 1990: 14; Heymann,
"Un homme exemplaire: Les faiblesses du film 'Korczak' n'empêchent pas son héros
d'être admirable," *Le Monde*, January 11, 1991: 13. Also participating in the debate was
A. Andreu in *L'Evenement du Jeudi*, n.d.
[4] See Lanzmann's relevant criticisms of *Schindler's List* in Lanzmann, "Holocauste, la
représentation impossible," *Le Monde*, March 3, 1994: 1.
[5] Wajda's rationale for utilizing archival footage is discussed in Andrzej Wajda, *Double
Visions: My Life in Film* (New York: Holt, 1989); Bolesław Michałek and Frank Turaj,
The Modern Cinema of Poland (Bloomington and Indianapolis: University of Indiana
Press, 1988); and Mira Liehm and Antonin J. Liehm, *The Most Important Art: Soviet and
Eastern European Film after 1945* (Berkeley and Los Angeles: University of California
Press, 1977). Ford's *Korczak und seine Kinder* also incorporates archival material, but in

the form of photographic stills rather than moving-image excerpts. Canby, "'Martyr,'" considered this the only memorable aspect of that film.

[6] Betty Jean Lifton, *The King of Children: A Biography of Janusz Korczak*, (New York: Farrar, 1988), 351.

[7] See Petrie, "On the Secular Word 'Holocaust'"; Uriel Tal, "Excursus on Hermeneutical Aspects of the Term *Sho'ah*," *Yad Vashem Studies* 13 (1976): 46–52; cf. Israel W. Charny, "Toward a Generic Definition of Genocide," in *Genocide: Conceptual and Historical Dimensions*, ed. George Andreopoulous (Philadelphia: University of Pennsylvania Press, 1994), 64–92.

[8] Regina S. Sharif, *Non-Jewish Zionism: Its Roots in Western History* (London: Zed, 1983), 17–19; also Sizer, *Christian Zionism*; Donald E. Wagner, "Marching to Zion: The Evangelical–Jewish Alliance," *Christian Century*, June 28, 2003): 20–24; Ruth W. Mouly, "Israel's Christian Comforters and Critics," in *Anti–Zionism: Analytical Reflections*, eds. Roselle Tekiner et al., (Brattleboro, VT: Amana, 1989), 257–79; Paul Charles Merkley, *The Politics of Christian Zionism, 1891–1948* (London: Frank Cass, 1998); and Timothy P. Weber, "How Evangelicals Became Israel's Best Friend," *Christianity Today*, October 5, 1998: 39–48.

[9] Mitchell Plitnik and Henry Picciotto, eds., *Reframing Anti–Semitism: Alternative Jewish Perspectives* (Oakland, CA: Jewish Voice for Peace, 2004); Michael Selzer, *The Aryanization of the Jewish State* (New York: Black Star, 1967); and Keith W. Whitelam, *The Invention of Ancient Israel: The Silencing of Palestinian History* (London: Routledge, 1996).

[10] Nur Masalha, *Expulsion of the Palestinians: The Concept of "Transfer" in Zionist Political Thought, 1882–1948* (Washington, D.C.: Institute for Palestine Studies, 1992), 5–28; and Edward W. Said, *The Question of Palestine* (New York: Vintage, 1979), 56–114.

[11] Sizer, *Christian Zionism*, 19, 55–60, 80; William Martin, "The Christian Right and American Foreign Policy," *Foreign Policy* (1999): 66–79; and Obenzinger, *American Palestine*.

[12] This name not only implies christocentrism (it designates an "our" [Catholic-Polish] vs. a "their" [Jewish] home); it also references the Polish resistance during the Second World War, Armia Krajowa (Home Army), as well as the political party formed by Solidarity, and the similarly pro-liberalization party to which belonged Russian premier Boris Yeltsin at the time of *Korczak*'s release. The name also currently references the extreme right-wing Israeli party, Yisrael Beiteinu (Israel Our Home), which advocates mass expulsion of Palestinians from Israel and the Occupied Territories.

[13] See Lanzmann, "The Obscenity of Understanding: An Evening with Claude Lanzmann," in Caruth, *Trauma*, 200–20.

[14] See, respectively, David Lindenberg, review in *Esprit*, February 1991: 141–42; Sylvie Kaufmann, "La nécessité selon Wajda," *Le Monde*, January 11, 1991: 1, 13; and Finkielkraut quoted in Eric Conan, "Qui a peur d'Andrzej Wajda?" *L'Express*, January 18, 1991: 42–44. For additional analysis of Simone Weil's perspective on the "Jewish Question," see Michael R. Marrus and Robert O. Paxton, *Vichy France and the Jews* (New York: Basic, 1981), 39, 190; and Richard I. Cohen, *The Burden of Conscience:*

French Jewish Leadership During the Holocaust (Bloomington and Indianapolis: Indiana University Press, 1987).

[15] Mary McElveen, "Washington Urges U.S. Firms to Invest in Poland," *Nation's Business*, May 1991: 10; Radek Sikorski, "A New Beginning?" *National Review* January 28, 1991: 49–50; and Leon Wieseltier, "The Milk Can," *The New Republic*, April 22, 1991: 47.

[16] Esp. Stanley Kauffmann, "Mazes," *The New Republic*, April 8, 1991: 26–27; also Vincent Canby, "Of a Saintly Jewish Doctor in Poland Who Died at Treblinka," *New York Times*, April 12, 1991: C8; J. Hoberman, "Poles Apart," *Village Voice*, April, 16 1991: 55, 66; "How It Was?" *The Economist*, February 9, 1991: 97–98; David Denby, "The Vanished," *New York*, April 22, 1991: 74–75; and M. Yung, review of *Korczak* in *Variety*, May 16, 1990: 25.

[17] Michael Fox, "Film Festival Screens Three Works from Noted Polish Auteur," *Northern California Jewish Bulletin*, July 16, 1993: 26, for which *Korczak* testified "to the moral power of a single person"; Michael Elkin, "Holocaust Hero As Child's Advocate," *Jewish Exponent*, January 17, 1992: 15x, which tacitly upholds this position.

[18] Tzvetan Todorov, "Parisian Themes: The Wajda Problem," trans. Robert Julian, *Salmagundi* 92 (1991): 35. Todorov subsequently published a phenomenology of concentration camp life, *Facing the Extreme: Moral Life in the Concentration Camp*, trans. Arthur Denner and Abigail Pollack (New York: Metropolitan, 1996). See also Rita Kempley, "*Korczak*: The Holocaust Healer," *Washington Post*, August 16, 1991: D1, 5; Kevin Thomas, "*Korczak* a Triumph of Dignity, Style," *Los Angeles Times*, June 26, 1991: F6–7; Julie Salamon, "Film: Children's Protector in Warsaw Ghetto," *Wall Street Journal*, April 11, 1991: A12; Hilary Mantel, "A Secular Sainthood," *The Spectator*, November 3, 1990: 53–54; and Edward Ball, "Citizen Wajda," *Village Voice*, April 23, 1991: 60.

[19] For a critical elaboration of the *ludic*, see Adorno, *Aesthetic Theory*, 318–19. Cf. Teresa Ebert, *Ludic Feminism and After* (Ann Arbor: University of Michigan Press, 1995), which, while offering a trenchant critique of this phenomenon of which my analysis is appreciative, oddly does not reference Adorno or his predecessors.

[20] For an explication of the "passion play," see Speaight, *Christian Theatre*, 9–36.

[21] Toby Miller, *Global Hollywood* (London, BFI, 2001).

[22] Paul de Man, *Allegories of Reading: Figural Language in Rousseau, Nietzsche, Rilke, and Proust* (New Haven, CT and London: Yale University Press, 1979). See Geoffrey Hartman, ed., *Holocaust Remembrance: The Shapes of Memory* (Oxford: Blackwell, 1994); and Saul Friedländer, ed., *Probing the Limits of Representation: Nazism and the Final Solution* (Cambridge, MA: Harvard University Press, 1992).

[23] As in Lyotard, *Differend*, 86–106; and Felman and Laub, *Testimony*. Cf. Angus John Stuart Fletcher, *Allegory, the Theory of a Symbolic Mode* (Ithaca, NY: Cornell University Press, 1964).

[24] Walter Benjamin, *The Origins of German Tragic Drama*, trans. John Osbourne (1928; repr., London: New Left Books, 1977).

[25] Jim Hansen, "Formalism and Its Malcontents: Benjamin and de Man on the Function of Allegory," *New Literary History* 35 (2005): 663–83; and Matthew Wilkens, "Toward

a Benjaminian Theory of Dialectical Allegory," *New Literary History* 27, no. 2 (2006): 285–98.

[26] Walter Benjamin, *The Arcades Project*, trans. Howard Eiland and Kevin McLaughlin, ed. Rolf Tiedemann (Cambridge, MA and London: Harvard University Press, 1999): 462. For critical analyses, see Michael Szekely, "Rethinking Benjamin: The Function of the Utopian Ideal," *Cultural Logic* 2006, http://clogic.eserver.org/2006/szekely.html; and Esther Leslie, "Space and West End Girls: Walter Benjamin versus Cultural Studies," *New Formations* 38 (1999): 110–24. For a comparison of Adorno's and Benjamin's theories in this respect, see Yvonne Sherratt, "Adorno's Aesthetic Concept of Aura," *Philosophy and Social Criticism* 33, no. 2 (2007): 155–77.

[27] See Mohanty, "Transcendental Philosophy"; Richard F. Brabau, "Kant's Proto–Phenomenology," in McBride and Schrag, *Phenomenology in a Pluralist Context*, 107–19; and George A. Schrader, Jr., "Kant and Phenomenology," in McBride and Schrag, 120–37. Cf. Roland Boer, "The Bowels of History, or The Perpetuation of Biblical Myth in Walter Benjamin," *Journal of Narrative Theory* 32, no. 3 (2002): 371–90.

[28] See Herbert Thurston and Donald Attwater, eds., *Butler's Lives of the Saints*, vol. 4 (New York: Kennedy and Sons, 1963), 23–32; and John R. H. Moorman, *St. Francis of Assisi* (London: SPCK Press, 1963).

[29] Lifton, *The King of Children*, 25; and Janusz Korczak, *The Warsaw Ghetto Memoirs of Janusz Korczak*, trans. E. P. Kulawiec (Washington, D.C.: University Press of America, 1979).

[30] See Robert A. Segal, ed., *The Allure of Gnosticism: The Gnostic Experience in Jungian Psychology and Contemporary Culture* (Chicago: Open Court, 1995); Michael Allen Williams, *Rethinking "Gnosticism": An Argument for Dismantling a Dubious Category* (Princeton, NJ: Princeton University Press, 1996); John MacQuarrie, "Gnosticism," in *Dictionary of Christian Ethics*, ed. MacQuarrie (Philadelphia: Westminster Press, 1968), 136; and William Barclay, "Stoicism," in MacQuarrie, *Dictionary*, 334. For an appreciative Cinema Studies approach to Christian gnosticism, see Tom Gunning, "In Your Face: Physiognomy, Photography, and the Gnostic Mission of Early Film," *Modernism/Modernity* 4, no. 1 (1997): 1–29.

[31] See Wladyslaw T. Bartoszewski, *The Convent at Auschwitz* (New York: George Braziller, 1991); Carol Rittner and Joel K. Roth, eds., *Memory Offended: The Auschwitz Convent Controversy* (New York: Praeger, 1991); and, more recently, Pam R. Jenoff, "Managing Memory: The Legal Status of Auschwitz-Birkenau and Resolution of Conflicts in the Post–Communist Era," *The Polish Review* 46, no. 2 (2001): 131–53. This convent/mission was planned by a Belgian faction of the Carmelite order, which foresaw construction on the site of an old theater used by Auschwitz administration to store the personal belongings of gas chamber victims. This storage shed was dubbed "Canada" by Auschwitz inmates. Orthodox Jews opposed the Carmelite plan, sometimes violently, on *halakhic* [Jewish legal] grounds which proscribe direct contact between a place of worship and a cemetery. As Maurice Lamm explains,

> Death is the crisis of life [not its dual opposite]. One may not deal with the dead as though he were living, as if he were merely sleeping. For those who thus ridicule the dead, the sages apply the phrase from Proverbs 17:5: "Whoso mocketh the poor, blasphemeth his maker" […] It is only by virtue of th[e]

acceptance of death as the just and inexorable terminus of life that life can be lived to its fullest [...] The consequence of this is a wide conceptual chasm between the faith which affirms life and also expects immortality beyond the grave, and the faith which denies the value of life as it seeks and strives for the beyond with all its power. (Lamm, *The Jewish Way in Death and Mourning* [New York: Jonathan David, 1969], xi, 28, 130, 157, 211; see also 196–97) For Talmudic references to this proscription, see *The Tractate of "Mourning" (Semachot): Regulations Relating to Death, Burial, and Mourning*, trans. Dov Zlotnick (New Haven, CT and London: Yale University Press, 1996), 6:1. And apropos of Levinas writing against Heidegger (in *Existence and Existents*, trans. Alphonso Lingis [Dordrecht: Kluwer, 1988]), to thusly ontologize death is to reify its determination, thereby facilitating the transference of its absoluteness into romanticism and tragico-history. Cf. Fredrick S. Paxton, *Christianizing Death: The Creation of a Ritual Process in Early Medieval Europe* (Ithaca, NY and London: Cornell University Press, 1990); and Sharon Patricia Holland, *Raising the Dead: Readings of Death and (Black) Subjectivity* (Durham, NC: Duke University Press, 2000). The Carmelites were also involved at the time in a public controversy over the beatification of Edith Stein, a Jewish convert to that mendicant order who was subsequently murdered by the Nazis. Stein believed that the Judeocide was divine punishment for the Jewish rejection of Jesus as the messiah.

Protests by observant Jews notwithstanding, Zionist outspokenness concerning the proposed convent/mission suggests an ulterior aspect to the controversy which likewise resonates across the Korczak persona. E.g., Monty Noam Penkower, "Auschwitz, the Papacy, and Poland's 'Jewish Problem,'" in *The Holocaust and Israel Reborn: From Catastrophe to Sovereignty* (Urbana and Chicago: University of Illinois Press, 1994), 302–14. I shall revisit the implications of this issue in Chapter Three.

[32] Gilles Quispel and Gershom Scholem, *Jewish and Gnostic Man* (Dallas: Spring Publishers, 1973); Qumsiyeh, *Sharing the Land of Canaan*, 2, 3–14. Cf. E. R. Hardy, "Monasticism," in MacQuarrie, *Dictionary of Christian Ethics*, 116–17; and Whitelam, *Invention of Ancient Israel*, 45–46, 76. See also Matthew 6:5–6:

> When you are praying, do not behave like the hypocrites who love to stand and pray in synagogues or on street corners in order to be noticed. I give you my word, they are already repaid. Whenever you pray, go to your room, close your door, and pray to your Father in private. Then your Father, who sees what no man sees, will repay you. (NAB)

[33] See Lewis I. Newman, *The Hasidic Anthology: Tales and Teachings of the Hasidim* (Northvale, NJ: Jason Aronson, 1987), 131.

[34] For elaboration of these distinctions, see Albert H. Friedlander, *Leo Baeck: Teacher of Theresienstadt* (Woodstock, NY: Overlook, 1968). For a classic critique of confessional tolerance as re-articulated in George W. Bush's "compassionate conservatism," see Herbert Marcuse, "Repressive Tolerance," in Robert Paul Wolff et al., eds., *A Critique of Pure Tolerance*, (Boston: Beacon, 1969), 93–138. The classic historiographic analysis of religious confession as social institution is, of course, Michel Foucault, *The History of Sexuality*, vol. 1: *An Introduction*, trans. Robert Hurley (New York: Pantheon, 1978). Regarding Jewish confession, see Newman, *Hasidic Anthology*, 71–72, 519; and Gershom Scholem, *Kabbalah* (New York: Meridian, 1974).

[35] Canby, "Of a Saintly Jewish Doctor"; Stephen Engelberg, "Wajda's *Korczak* Sets Loose the Furies," *New York Times*, April 14, 1991: 15–18; and Fox, "Film Festival."
[36] Polish scholar Ewelina Nurczyńska-Fidelska says as much when she writes, "The plight of Polish Jews in Wajda's films is a part of Polish history without which the picture of Polish history would be incomplete" (quoted in Marek Haltof, *Polish National Cinema* [Oxford: Berghahn, 2002], 231). Indeed Jews were given Polish right of abode during the fourteenth century by King Kazimierz III the Great and became instrumental in the national development at several social and economic levels. Jewish right of abode was granted concomitantly with Western European pogroms instigated during the Crusades and with Polish national establishment, itself entailing religious acquiescence to the Holy Roman Empire. By the time of the Swedish invasion of 1655–60, known as the Deluge, Poland comprised a larger Jewish population than the rest of Europe combined.
    The political limits of Nurczyńska-Fidelska's argument are revealed, however, as she attributes "the accusations of Wajda's anti–Semitism which appeared in the world press in connection with *The Land of Promise* and *Korczak*" to "evidence of a curious ill-will." Not only does this comment mystify the role of Cold War and Zionist politics in modern Polish culture; it distracts from recollecting the related historical fact that Poland's medieval opening to Jewish immigration set the stage for King John Sobieski's defeat of the Turks in the 1683 siege of Vienna, which marked the end of Muslim expansion into Christian Europe. See Feliks Gross, "Comments on Ethnic Identity in a Polish-Jewish Context," *The Polish Review* 35, no. 2 (1990): 137–48.
[37] Lanzmann's Zionism is confirmed in his subsequent film, *Tsahal* (France 1994), a documentary that views Israeli militarism ambivalently, with noticeable tolerance.
[38] Hardy, "Asceticism," in MacQuarrie, *Dictionary of Christian Ethics*, 20–21. As rationalized famously in Mark 8:34–35, quoting Jesus: "If a man wishes to come after me, he must deny his very self, take up his cross, and follow in my steps. Whoever would preserve his life will lose it, but whoever loses his life for my sake and the gospel's will preserve it" (NAB).
[39] Peter Brown, *The Cult of the Saints: Its Rise and Function in Latin Christianity* (Chicago: University of Chicago Press, 1981); Eugene Weiner and Anita Weiner, *The Martyr's Conviction: A Sociological Analysis* (Atlanta: Scholars Press, 1990); Richard K. Kieckhefer, "Imitators of Christ: Sainthood in the Christian Tradition," in Kieckhefer and George D. Bond, eds., *Sainthood: Its Manifestations in World Religions* (Berkeley: University of California Press, 1988), 1–42; and Wayne A. Meeks, "The Bodies of the Martyrs," in *The Origins of Christian Morality: The First Two Centuries* (New Haven and London: Yale University Press, 1993), 145–47.
[40] Abraham Joshua Heschel, *Moral Grandeur and Spiritual Audacity: Essays*, ed. Susannah Heschel (New York: Farrar, 1996), 382. Cf. Patrick G. Henry and Donald K. Sweaver, *For the Sake of the World: The Spirit of Buddhist and Christian Monasticism* (Minneapolis, MN: Fortress Press / Collegeville, MN: The Liturgical Press, 1989).
[41] See Lamm, *Jewish Way*, 157, 211; also Bilu, "Dreams and the Wishes of the Saint." Bilu likens Judaic sainthood to the Islamic *baraka*, a lingering sensibility thought beneficial to the saint's survivors. *Baraka* is not to be confused with the Christian pantheistic notion of a hovering, partially resurrected soul who makes worldly

intervention in anticipation of, or in order to hasten, the Second Coming of Christ, at which time it is supposed to reunite with its fallow body and achieve christic gnosis. As Lamm elaborates, Judaic death does not involve a body–soul division, nor is Judaic resurrection conceived as occurring until after the messianic advent.

[42] See Talmudic tractate Shabbat 32a: "A person should never place himself in a dangerous situation with the expectation that Hashem will perform a miracle, for perhaps he will not make a miracle. And if there is a miracle, it will be deducted from one's merits." Hence official Israeli insistence that its reprisals against the Palestinian Intifada are merely a Jewish "defense" against "hostile Arabs"; and hence the name of the Israeli home army, the Israeli *Defense* Force [my emphasis]. See also Daniel Boyarin, "Between Intertextuality and History: The Martyrdom of Rabbi Akiva," in *Intertextuality and the Reading of Midrash* (Bloomington and Indiana: Indiana University Press, 1990), 117–29; Sidney Goldstein, *Suicide in Rabbinic Literature* (Hoboken, NJ: KTAV Publishing House, 1989); Ivan G. Marcus, "From Politics to Martyrdom: Shifting Paradigms in the Hebrew Narratives of the 1096 Crusade Riots," in *Essential Papers on Judaism and Christianity in Crisis*, ed. Jeremy Cohen (New York and London: New York University Press, 1991), 469–83; and Weiner and Weiner, *The Martyr's Conviction*.

[43] Bilu, "Dreams and the Wishes"; Joseph Leon Blau, *The Christian Interpretation of the Cabala in the Renaissance* (New York: Columbia University Press, 1944); Robert L. Cohen, "Sainthood on the Periphery: The Case of Judaism," in Kieckhefer and Bond, *Sainthood*, 43–68; Marcus, "From Politics to Martyrdom"; Yehuda Liebes, "Christian Influences on the Zohar," trans. Arnold Schwartz et al., *Studies in the Zohar* (Albany: SUNY Press, 1993), 139–61; and Walter K. Sokel, "Between Gnosticism and Jehovah: The Dilemma in Kafka's Religious Attitude," in Segal, *The Allure of Gnosticism*, 147–66.

[44] See Elmer Berger, "Zionist Ideology: Obstacle to Peace," in Tekiner, *Anti–Zionism*, 6, 30 n.4; Masalha, *Expulsion of the Palestinians*, 25, 24 n.79, 207; and Zertal, *Israel's Holocaust*.

[45] Ilan Pappe, *The Ethnic Cleansing of Palestine* (Oxford: Oneworld Publications, 2006).

[46] A supreme example of this modality in Polish literary tradition is the writing of Poland's foremost nineteenth-century Romantic poet, Adam Mickiewicz, especially his four-part verse play, *Dziady* ["Forefathers' Eve"], a patriotic anti–Russian drama which famously hails Poland as the Christ Among the Nations. Mickiewicz is known inter alia for his sympathetic portrayal of Jews and for his later interest in mysticism and theosophy. In 1999, Wajda directed a cinematic adaptation of Mickiewicz's Romantic classic, *Pan Tadeusz*. (Pan Tadeusz is also a popular brand of internationally marketed Polish vodka.) For a relevant discussion of Christian subjectivism, see Herbert Waddams, who writes, "[A]ccording to Christian teaching, belief, faith and commitment precede their results in the form of behavior" ("Ascetical Theology," in MacQuarrie, *Dictionary of Christian Ethics*, 18).

[47] This remark would be echoed six years later in North America by the rhetoric of Christian Coalition leader Ralph Reed: "At heart, what America needs is not political revolution but spiritual renewal," *Newsweek*, May 13, 1996: 29.

[48] Derrida, "Violence and Metaphysics," 113, and "White Mythology: Metaphor in the Text of Philosophy," in *Margins of Philosophy*, trans. Alan Bass (Chicago: University of

Chicago Press, 1982), 245–47. In the Derridean thought representative of heliotrope theory, the quintessential heliotrope is, following the term's etymology, the sun, whose apparent autochthony and generic self-containment would prompt Hitler to compare it favorably to the imperialist aspiration of the "Aryan race." Not irrelevant to my usage of "heliotrope" is the fact that postmodern philosophy subverts the concept into a post–philosophical idea, for which a total collapse is effected of the literal onto the figurative layer of signification (e.g., Jean Baudrillard, *For a Critique of the Political Economy of the Sign*, trans. Charles Levin [St. Louis: Telos Press, 1981]; and Georges Bataille, *Visions of Excess: Selected Writings, 1927–1939*, trans. Allan Stoekl, ed. Stoekl et al. [Minneapolis: University of Minnesota Press, 1985]). The history of photography itself underscores this effect, as when the photographic inventor Niepce referred to the process whereby a photographed image appeared on the plate as "heliography," or "sun-writing," a phenomenon which, for him, would naturally require decoding (Susan Sontag, *On Photography* [New York: Doubleday, 1977], 160). In classical social psychology, however, the notion of the heliotrope is prefigured by that of bourgeois wealth, which may become its own, conspicuous sign in an effort to efface its exploitative function. Harkening furthermore to Marx, this so-called conspicuous sign refers to nothing less than the supreme commodity, religion, "the illusory sun which revolves around man as long as he does not revolve around himself" (Thorstein Veblen, *The Theory of the Leisure Class* [New York: A. M. Kelley, 1975]). A useful critique of heliotropy along Marxist lines is offered by Donald Morton, "The Politics of Queer Theory in the (Post)Modern Moment," *Genders* 17 (1993): 121–50.

[49] Regarding this injunction, see Heschel, *Moral Grandeur*, 80–99.

[50] For a history of this program, see Leni Yahil, *The Holocaust: The Fate of European Jewry, 1932–1945*, trans. Ina Friedman and Haya Galai (New York and Oxford: Oxford University Press, 1990), 306–12; Enzo Traverso, *The Origins of Nazi Violence*, trans. Janet Lloyd (London: New Press, 2003), 121–28; Robert J. Lifton, *The Nazi Doctors: Medical Killing and the Psychology of Genocide* (New York: Basic, 1986); Eugon Kogon, *The Theory and Practice of Hell: The German Concentration Camps and the System Behind Them*, trans. Heinz Norden (1950; repr., New York: Berkeley Books, 1980), 153–74, 223–30; and Walter Poller, *Medical Block, Buchenwald: The Personal Testimony of Inmate 996, Block 96* (New York: Lyle Stuart, 1960). An earlier (1978) Wajda film is perhaps not coincidentally entitled *Without Anesthesia* [*Bez znieczulenia*].

[51] Imke Lode, "Between Body and Space: Modern Vision and the Premonition of the Cinematic in E. T. A. Hoffmann's *wirkliches Schaven*" (PhD diss., New York University, 2000).

[52] Nazi pseudo-science is discussed by Nicholas Goodrick-Clarke, *The Occult Roots of Nazism: Secret Aryan Cults and Their Influence on Nazi Ideology, 1890B1935* (New York: New York University Press, 1992); and Janet Biehl and Peter Staudenmaier, *Ecofascism: Lessons from the German Experience* (Edinburgh: AK Press, 1995). A relationship between Nazi pseudo-science and christology has been located by David Roberts, "Eugenic Theory and the Thematics of Sin," *Renaissance and Modern Studies* 37 (1994): 47–58, special issue on "Foucault and Beyond." For an empirical study of this relationship, see Roland Blaich, "Health Reform and Race Hygeine: Adventists and the Biomedical Vision of the Third Reich," *Church History* 65, no. 3 (1996): 425–40. For

contemporary correlatives, see Steve Chase, "Green Stormtroopers in the Streets of Berlin? Confronting the Eco-Fascist Tradition in the German Experience," *Z Magazine*, October 1999: 37–44; and Tamara Traubmann, "Do Not Have Children If They Won't Be Healthy!" *Haaretz*, June 11, 2004, http://www.haaretz.com/hasen/spages/437879.html.

[53] E.g., Mary Ann Doane, *The Desire to Desire: The Woman's Film of the 1940s* (Bloomington: Indiana University Press, 1987); Jacqueline Rose, *Sexuality in the Field of Vision* (London: Verso, 1986); Annette Kuhn, *The Power of the Image: Essays on Representation and Sexuality* (London: Routledge, 1979); Lisa Cartwright, *Tracing the Body: Screening Medicine's Visual Culture* (Minneapolis: University of Minnesota Press, 1995); and Kibbey, *A Theory of the Image*.

[54] See Ginsberg, review of *"Der Ewige Jude"*; cf. Haltof, *Polish National Cinema*. Haltof reads the sequence out of narrative context, in deference to the phenomenological debate over Holocaust representability in which he presupposes Wajda intended *Korczak* to participate. Haltof's reading ignores the possibility that the formal ambiguity which he himself attributes to the utilization of stock footage in *Korczak* might serve an opposite than intended function.

[55] Cf. Paul Coates, "Notes on Polish Cinema, Nationalism and Wajda's *Holy Week*," in *Cinema and Nation*, eds. Mette Hjort and Scott MacKenzie (London: Routledge, 2000), 189–201, for which *Korczak*'s citation of propaganda constitutes less a committed critique than a mournful apology.

[56] The fact that Korczak himself is possibly feminized by his non-sexual character and homosexual intertext, and that his veritable side-kick, orphanage headmistress, Madame Stefania ("Stefa") Wilczynska [Ewa Dalkowska], is also encoded as possibly homosexual, enhances this reading and initiates a critique of the film's heterosexism as it functions in relation to christo-phenomenology.

[57] For sustained analyses of this asymmetrical structuring, cf. Halevi, *A History of the Jews*; Israel Shahak, *Jewish History, Jewish Religion: The Weight of Three Thousand Years* (London: Pluto, 1994); Raul Hilberg, *The Destruction of the European Jews* (Chicago: Quadrangle, 1967); and Salo W. Baron, *A Social and Religious History of the Jews*, 2nd ed. (New York: Columbia University Press, 1952–).

[58] For elaborations of this history, see Arno J. Mayer, *Why Did the Heavens Not Darken?*; and Sarah Gordon, *Hitler, Germans, and the "Jewish Question"* (Princeton, NJ: Princeton University Press, 1984). The presidential Bush family was one such business involvement during this period. See G. Pascal Zachary, *Endless Frontier: Vannevar Bush, Engineer of the New American Century* (Cambridge, MA: MIT Press, 1999). For documentation and analysis of similar and related involvements by IBM, Ford, and General Motors, see Edwin Black, *IBM and the Holocaust: The Strategic Alliance between Nazi Germany and America's Most Powerful Corporation* (New York: Crown, 2001); and Reinhold Billstein et al., *Working for the Enemy: Ford, General Motors, and Forced Labor in Germany during the Second World War* (New York: Berghahn, 2000).

[59] Finkelstein, *Holocaust Industry*; Tom Segev, *The Seventh Million: The Israelis and the Holocaust*, trans. Haim Watzman (New York: Hill and Wang, 1993), 424; Young, *Texture of Memory*, 214, 240; and Bresheeth, "The Great Taboo Broken," 196. On the

English-language version of the Yad Vashem website (Yad Vashem is the major Holocaust memorial museum in Israel), the word "martyr" occurs only four times, in contrast to "hero," which occurs nineteen times. "Martyr" is also deployed in the *Yad Vashem Bulletin*'s definition of the museum's names project, Daf-Ed, which is meant "to perpetuate the memory of the millions of martyrs, whose graves are unknown and unmarked, by registering their names and other particulars in 'Memorial Pages' and awarding them 'memorial citizenship of the State of Israel'" (quoted in Young, *Texture of Memory*, 247). On the other hand, "martyr" is entirely absent from the Yad Vashem section of the Israeli tourist guide, *The Museums of Israel* (Nitza Rosovsky and Joy Ungerleider-Mayerson [New York: Harry N. Abrams, 1989], 75–78).

[60] Golda Meier is notorious for having asserted that Palestinians do not exist and that Jews of Arab and Near Eastern descent are like children in need of moral guidance from Jews of European descent. See Sabri Jiryis, *The Arabs in Israel*, trans. Inea Bushnaq (New York: Monthly Review Press, 1976); Jada N. Jiladi, *Discord in Zion: Conflict between Ashkenazi and Sephardi Jews in Israel*, trans. R. Harris (London: Scorpion, 1990); and Ella Shohat, "Sephardim in Israel: Zionism from the Standpoint of Its Jewish Victims," *Social Text* 19–20 (1988): 1–35.

[61] As French film critic Eric Conan ("Qui a peur d'Andrzej Wajda?") noted, *"La sainteté existe aussi dans le judaïsme [...] Il ne s'agit pas de racheter les enfants ni de racheter leur mort. Il s'agit de ne pas les abandoner dans la mort"* ["Sainthood also exists in Judaism (...) It is a question neither of bringing back the children nor of compensating for their death. It is a question of not abandoning them in death"] (44) [my translation]. Cf. Pesach Schindler, "Refusal of the Rebbe to Abandon His Community," *Hasidic Responses to the Holocaust in Light of Hasidic Thought* (Hoboken, NJ: KTAV Publishing House, 1990), 74–75.

[62] See Zertal, *Catastrophe to Power*, 79–90; Segev, *The Seventh Million*, 255–320; and Sizer, *Christian Zionism*, 243.

[63] Zertal, *Israel's Holocaust*.

[64] Koch, "The Aesthetic Transformation of the Image of the Unimaginable"; idem., "The Angel of Forgetfulness and the Black Box of Facticity"; idem., "Transformations Esthétiques"; Elisabeth Huppert, "Voir (Shoah)," in Cuau, *Au sujet de Shoah*, 150–56; and Shoshana Felman, "Á l'Age du témoinage: *Shoah* de Claude Lanzmann," trans. Claude Lanzmann and Judith Ertel, in the same volume, 55–145. See also Catherine Zimmer, "Consuming Fascism: The Holocaust Documentary as Genre," *Film and History* 2001–02 CD-ROM Annual (special section on "The Holocaust"), 12.

[65] See Sizer, *Christian Zionism*, 259.

[66] Emanuel Levy, *Oscar®Fever: The History and Politics of the Academy Awards* (New York: Continuum, 2001), 5. In an historical irony, Wajda's award was presented by post–radical actress and producer, Jane Fonda.

[67] See David Ost, "Letter from Poland," *The Nation*, November 25, 2002: 16–20. For the classic theory of deterritorialized commodification and posthistorical capitalism, see Karl Marx, *Grundrisse*, trans. Martin Nicolaus (New York: Random House, 1973), 408–9. Regarding the intersection of modern Polish and world cinemas, see Engelberg, "Wajda's *Korczak*," 17; Michałek and Frank Turaj, *Modern Cinema of Poland*, 148–50; Wajda, *Double Visions*; and Alexandra Sosnowski, "Polish Cinema Today: A New Order

in the Production, Distribution and Exhibition of Film," *The Polish Review* 40, no. 3 (1995): 315–29.

[68] See Bradley E. Fels, "Polish Messianism *Redivivus*: The Use of Sacrificial Imagery to Gain American Support for Poland during World War II," *The Polish Review* 46, no. 2 (2001): 195–207. Wajda films which are recognized as allegorizing Zionism to Polish nationalism include *Landscape after Battle* [*Krajabsazpo bitwie*] (Poland, 1970); *The Gates of Paradise* [*Bramy raju*] (Poland, 1967); *Pilate and Others* [*Pilate i Inni*] (Poland, 1972); *The Conductor* [*Drygent*] (Poland, 1980); *Land of Promise* [*Ziema obiecana*] (Poland/France, 1975); and *Rough Treatment* [*Bez znieczulenia*] (Poland, 1978). Wajda has responded tellingly to criticisms of his filmmaking in this respect: "What is a director like me afraid of? He is afraid to make a film without nationality," quoted in Engelberg, "Wajda's *Korczak*," 17. A. Burguière corroborates this reading by referring to *Korczak* as a barometer of Polish society ("*Au nom de la vérité*," *Le nouvel observateur*, January 17–23, 1991: 72–73).

[69] Ferdinand Braudel, *Civilization and Capitalism, 15th–18th Century* (New York: Harper and Row, 1981–84).

CHAPTER THREE

THE QUARREL IN/OVER QUÉBEC

> [T]he religious encroaches on the *political*, which it cannot deny
> if it is ever to cause the untruth in the world to wither away.
> —Kracauer, "The Bible in German," *The Mass Ornament*

The political and ideological blind-spots structuring debates over and
around *Korczak* find instructive counterpart in absences informing the intertext
of a superficially very different Holocaust film released in Canada the same
year: *The Quarrel*. In contrast to *Korczak*, little debate has arisen concerning
The Quarrel's theological orientation or national politics, or in turn its
"ownership" or commodification of the Holocaust. In fact the film was
recognized as indubitably "Jewish"—but for related reasons, it was also
misrecognized as uncinematic and therefore unworthy of critical attention.
Unlike *Korczak*, *The Quarrel* did not benefit from broad international
distribution, nor was the Canadian public sphere embroiled then in the same
degree of contestation and debate over Holocaust representation. Holocaust
debates in Canada at the time were limited to an extreme-right fringe of
Holocaust deniers, notwithstanding Deborah Lipstadt having made larger truck
of the matter in her book on the general topic. More central was Canada's
Anglo–Québécois conflict, which was being hotly negotiated when *The Quarrel*
was released. The results of those negotiations would serve eventually to
disqualify Québec nationalism as an acceptable means for breaking the reigns of
Anglophone domination of Francophone Canada at a moment also marked by
the U.S. inception and propagation of the North American Free Trade
Agreement ("NAFTA"). The following analysis positions *The Quarrel* in
relation to the Anglo–Québécois conflict through a critical reading of the film's
"uncinematic" quality: its Judaic textual hermeneutics and their signifying
effects. The reading reconceives allegorical tropology and its aesthetic
formulation from the perspective of a Judaically informed rearticulation of
postcolonial theory—a reconception I suggest is made readily available by the
film's unusual rhetorical structure. In so doing, my analysis argues for
reclaiming *The Quarrel* as artistically both laudable and relevant. In decided
contrast to approaches to Holocaust film taken by Avisar and Mintz, however,

my analysis resists affirming *The Quarrel*'s peculiar version of Judaic hermeneutics, which deviates from the ethics of *le-didakh*. It likewise refuses to blanketly ascribe the film's negative reception to antisemitism. Instead it registers the persisting critical reluctance to seriously engage *The Quarrel* with ideological conditions articulating the Anglo–Québécois conflict and its historical coordinates to another national conflict whose citation is barely contained by the film's ultimately mystical aesthetic, in relation to which a Judaic reformulation of the proverbial taboo against Holocaust representation adds critical dimension in ways as dependent upon the exigencies of global politics as the culture of Wajda's Poland—and of director Eli Cohen's Israel/Palestine.

* * * * *

The Quarrel is a little known, seldom discussed Holocaust film adapted from a play, *My Quarrel with Hersh Rasseyner*, by Joseph Telushkin that was itself adapted from a novella of the same name.[1] The film was produced independently with support from both Canadian and U.S. public television. It was distributed on the North American art cinema circuit and, later, on public television in both Canada and the U.S. While set and shot in Montreal and comprising an entirely Canadian cast, *The Quarrel* was directed by an Eastern European Jewish ("Ashkenazi") Israeli, Eli Cohen, who is famous in Israel/Palestine for directing and acting in critical anti–war films often released during particularly volatile political periods (e.g., *Ricochets* [*Shtay Etzba' Ot M'Tzidon*] [Israel, 1986]).[2] Unlike *Korczak*, which premiered at the Cannes Film Festival and garnered international attention, *The Quarrel* premiered at smaller, localized venues and, despite having won a prize and elicited some favorable reviews, received scant publicity and media coverage.[3] Controversies surrounding the film were limited to on-set disputes over its political references; these disputes received negligible public attention, although they involved issues typical to Cohen's known *oeuvre*, such as anti–Arab discrimination and the politics of occupation, which have been widely discussed in relation to Cohen's other films and were evidently seen by *The Quarrel*'s cast and crew as pertinent to the Canadian and Québécois social arenas.[4]

The Quarrel is a dialogue film that depicts a day in the life of two estranged Ashkenazi Poles, former best friends and study partners [*chavrutim*] at an ultra-orthodox [*haredi*] institute of Judaic learning [*yeshiva*] in Bialystok. Chaim Kovler [R. H. Thomson] and Hersh Rasseyner [Saul Rubinek] are both Holocaust survivors who have immigrated to North America unbeknownst to one another following the Second World War. While promenading through Parc Mont Royale on the morning of a late 1940s Rosh Hashanah, Chaim, who is in

Montreal on business, happens upon Hersh as he leads a prayer service on the shore of Lake Beaver. Recognizable by his long, dark coat, black hat, and full beard as the religiously more observant of the two men, Hersh now lives in Montreal, where he has established a thriving mussarist yeshiva.[5] By contrast, Chaim is dressed in a modern suit and tie, and in a prior scene is even portrayed eating bacon and eggs at a diner (pork is proscribed as unkosher, or *treyf* [unclean], in Judaism). This visibly secular, assimilated Jew now lives in New York City, where he has become a successful author of popular, Yiddish-language novels. *The Quarrel* proceeds from these two estranged Holocaust survivors' unforeseen reunion as it reignites a bitter prewar dispute that had compelled their mutual falling out and separation. Through its practiced and rather intricately narrativized staging of an extended dialogue between the reunited antagonists as they take an unplanned, labyrinthine walk through the park, the film figures a rearticulation of their still simmering dispute to the contemporary problematics of modern Jewish identity as it ramifies postwar understandings of antisemitism and the Holocaust.

The intellectually dense and specialized quality of *The Quarrel*'s focus on these issues led some reviewers to designate the film a failed adaptation of a "boring" philosophical dialogue. Stephen Holden of the *New York Times* derogated as "mush" the film's major catharsis, which depicts the *chavrutim*'s spiritual reunification in a wave of kabbalistic ecstasy. *Montreal Gazette* theater critic, Pat Donnelly, described the film as a project that never should have been undertaken because, on his view, it bears no interest to persons outside the film's presumed small circle of family and friends: "This one is strictly PBS material, for serious minds only." One of the film's few U.S. reviewers, the *Chicago Tribune*'s Johanna Steinmetz, asserted, "'The Quarrel' suffers at times from feeling more on the page than on the screen."[6] Others, however, found the film exemplary for its conveyance of diplomacy through characters who "agree to disagree," "hold two diametrically opposed ideas in [their] head[s] at the same time," "[view] friendship [as] more important than winning the argument," and uphold "God" and "faith" at the center of both catastrophe and strained friendship.[7]

Notwithstanding these favorable reviews, and setting aside for the moment either position's questionable political implications, not a single scholarly analysis of *The Quarrel* has appeared in Canadian cinema studies texts, nor has the film ever explicitly been designated "Canadian" in scholarly circles.[8] Perhaps that is because *The Quarrel* was directed by a non-Canadian, or because its production and distribution were bound up with non-Canadian networks. By the same token, I would argue that the unfamiliarity and critical difficulty of *The Quarrel*'s Judaic hermeneutic structure also may have played a role in the film's canonical exclusion and may furthermore explain the film's additional absence from U.S. and Israeli scholarship, thus warranting what I shall posit is the film's institutional "statelessness." The following analysis echoes my critique of *Korczak* by illustrating nonetheless the persistence and significance of the "Canadian" and, in particular, the "Québécois" for *The Quarrel* and its primary referential intertext, the Judeocide. Engaging film semiotics and narrative discourse theory in the context of postcolonial problematics, my analysis of *The Quarrel* lends insight into how extant histories of wartime Québec, which explicate that province's ambivalent support for Vichy,[9] are made available for scrutiny by the film, as it encourages allegorical readings of what finally are insufficient because mystical explanations of its "statelessness." Taking up the spirit of film theorist Noël Burch's insistence that "we should not deprecate a film simply because it is 'obscure' [...] for obscurity of meaning does not necessarily imply an 'illegible' structure,"[10] my analysis in effect shows that *The Quarrel* compels a much broader, more serious interpretation than has been previously engaged, one which bespeaks the film's significance as a paradigmatic instance of Jewish postnationalist culture regarding the Holocaust.

* * * * *

Because the social and theoretical problematics engaged by *The Quarrel* are complicated and not widely recognized, I shall first offer an extended digression in order to supply the reader with some background information that will also help with the task of grasping how *The Quarrel*'s Judaic hermeneutic figures a narrative-compositional structure conceivably interpretable as "uncinematic." I begin with the question of modern Jewish identity and its problematics of secularization and assimilation.

It is commonly assumed that Jews who were once confined to medieval European ghettoes and, similarly, to Eastern European shtetls chose upon their emancipation to leave the religious fold and enter the mainstreams of their respective societies as a result of having lost religious faith in the face of modernizing conditions. In fact, this choice bore no direct correlation to degrees of religious belief, whereas it was largely motivated by political and economic determinants.

During the years leading up to the establishment of a modern Jewish state in former British Mandate Palestine, for example, a need was recognized by Zionist ideologues to develop a new, secular definition of the "Jewish" to cohere and grow the colony's then primarily European, pre-Holocaust Jewish settler population as a demographic bulwark against widespread, if varied resistance to the state's establishment by both Western and Arab powers. That definition had to be credible and consistent enough to offset indigenous, Muslim and Christian Palestinian claims to full citizenship in an emergent Ashkenazi-run state, and to subvert concomitant Palestinian resistance, echoed in some European/American circles, to the Jewish theocratic structures retained by Zionism from its European experience as these demoted non-Jews to second-class status.[11] Mindful of that need, a newly established Israeli government declared Jews of various nationalities and varying degrees of religiosity ethnologically "spoken for," whether residing in Israel or not, and Jews who emigrated from Europe to "Eretz Yisrael" [the biblical Land of Israel] were encouraged to assimilate into secular Israeli society in accordance with the Zionist imperative, considered necessary to the state's European, non-Arab/Muslim—pro-Western—character, of "Jewish" demographic majority. According to Michael Selzer, "In Israel, [traditional] Jewishness recede[d] into the background as a factor for social cohesion (and this is observable even in the large minority which is Orthodox) and bec[ame] instead merely a secondary identification."[12]

In the face of this new, Zionist definition of the "Jewish," Jewish Israelis of Middle and Near Eastern descent ("Mizrachim"), including Jewish Palestinians, whose religious self-definitions are differently motivated and configured, were henceforth positioned socially and culturally in ways eerily reminiscent of premodern Ashkenazi experience, for which a similar dialectic of social identity had obtained throughout much of the medieval period, but for which the definition of the "Jewish" was inflected not by Zionism, but by its ideological precursor and progenitor, the "Jewish Question," a Christian concern about potential Jewish disloyalty to "host" nations.[13] Whereas initially a christological projection that likewise drew upon ethno-racial conceptions of socio-cultural difference,[14] the "Jewish Question" was eventually internalized by the Ashkenazim to the point that any emancipatory reconceptualization of it became unthinkable to many Jews whose political and economic interests had been well-served despite—because of—ghettoization and related citizenship restrictions.

In revolutionary France, for example, the leadership of the religiously observant, economically constrained Ashkenazim of Alsace-Lorraine are known to have refused an initial grant of citizenship from the Paris Commune in exchange for cultural assimilation, on grounds that it would incite insurrection and usurp the Jewish leadership's communal authority. These Ashkenazim were viewed with embarrassment by their wealthier, more acculturated Southern European ("Sephardi") co-religionists, whose experiences of extreme oppression (the various Inquisitions, especially in Spain and Portugal) were far less recent; and they were held with suspicion by the French authorities until, under Napoleon, they were forcibly compelled to accept French citizenship and its terms.[15]

Interestingly, the ethno-racial and class demographics of the Jewish-French community were later to undergo a reversal, as modern anti–Sephardi racism, triggered by French colonialism, produced conditions which strongly favored

Ashkenazi embourgeoisement—and facilitated, in an historical irony, the Vichy implementation of Nazi racial laws prior to the German occupation of France during the Second World War. The ensuing denigration of Sephardim has only been exacerbated since the postwar founding of Israel and the related immigration of North African Mizrachim ("Maghrebim") to France and Canada following decolonization. In the course of these developments, however, the dialectics of Jewish identity have not changed significantly, while their scope has in fact extended globally: a revised antisemitic canard citing Jewish "dual loyalty" has emerged for the first time in modern history outside the European arena. The postwar Jew might be economically emancipated and politically enfranchised, but s/he is now viewed with international apprehension, the Zionist revision and exploitation of modern Jewish subjectivity having served to deregulate previously more discernible understandings of how one might define and adhere to the "Jewish." The extenuating ambivalence, which facilitates a confusion of Zionist and Jewish identities, has today induced a nostalgic resurgence of Jewish (ultra-)orthodoxy alongside a rise in Jewish nationalist sentiment amongst Ashkenazim, Sephardim, and Mizrachim in Israel and beyond. That ambivalence has been deployed most recently by U.S. Zionist ideologues as an ironical locus for claiming the emergence of a "new antisemitism" perceived as universal, persistent, and incessant.[16]

The dispute depicted and narrativized in *The Quarrel* over the question of Jewish secularization and assimilation is not unrelated to this extended and complexified dialectic of Jewish identity, which in fact articulates to a particularly longstanding dialogue about the historical relationship of mussarist Hasidism to the call for Jewish social acculturation by many Enlightenment-era European countries, France being but one of them. Modern Hasidism formed in Eastern Europe as a rural, class-based reaction to that call as well as to the orthodox rigidities which Ashkenazi authorities themselves imposed upon their ghettoized, largely impoverished communities.[17] Hasidism's counter-Enlightenment orientation inspired a Judaic version of romantic populism, replete with the charismatic leadership and cultism common to the era and region. It developed a substantial following among class and ethnic elements opposed not only to Jewish assimilation but to political and economic projects of the modern Christian nation-states (colonialism, industrialization, emergent Zionism) which served the interests of recently acculturated, assimilated and often wealthy Jewish citizens, whether Sephardi or Ashkenazi.[18] In contrast to contemporary Hasidism, now dominated by the right-wing Lubavitcher sect, and modern Jewish orthodoxy, now affiliated with the Israeli right-wing settler movement, both of which profess Zionist views, early modern Hasidism and its *haredi* offshoots, including mussarism, aspired to remain permanently diasporic. To this day, the ultra-insular and violently defensive *haredi* sect, Neturei Karta, upholds Diaspora as the fundamental condition of Jewish redemption [*teshuvah*], which it conceives as a collective end to worldly suffering, and deems blasphemous the secular messianism of Zionism for "forcing the hand" of God in this respect. For the Neturei Karta and most other *haredi* sects, including the Tash of Canada, such "forcing the hand" stymies authentic messianic redemption, for which collective "holiness" is a phenomenon of Jewish ethical practice that entails strict adherence to Talmudic law [*halakhah*], knows no secular correlation, and must be engaged diligently by all Jews in order that its proper realization be ensured.[19]

To this end, modern orthodox and ultra-orthodox Jewish sects have established programs in secular outreach [*kiruv*] which stake popular appeals to "disaffected" Jews through cinema, television, and other deterritorialized media, often with the financial backing of the international umbrella organization of Jewish orthodoxy, Agudat Yisrael. This proselytic *haredi* offensive is obversely reminiscent of the *Maskalim*, who were among the first Ashkenazim to negotiate modern Jewish acculturation, in that it endorses a *dissimilationist*, even separatist politics. Unlike Reform Judaism, which evolved from the *Haskalah* and repositioned Jewish ethics into a philosophy, a *Weltanschauung* compatible with the aims and interests of Christianity and the European nation-states it has served, Hasidism has resisted alienating Judaism and Jewish culture from their pre-capitalist interpellative structures. In contradistinction to Reform, it blames assimilation for modern antisemitism and, in response, recommends retaining Judaism as a total way of life. Postwar *haredism* shares this nostalgic belief, but in an historical innovation it has placed the Holocaust at the center of debates over the purported dangers of secularization and assimilation and the extenuating problem of Jewish religious alienation.[20] Again unlike Reform (as well as Conservatism, modern Orthodoxy, and Reconstruction), *haredism* rejects the Zionist vision of a Jewish state as the necessary means for eradicating antisemitism and related social ills and for effectuating collective redemption.[21]

Important to my analysis of *The Quarrel* is the overriding neglect by these ultra-observant sects, despite their proclaimed anti–Zionism, to envisage approaches to the question of modern Jewish assimilation and secularization that might open analysis of Jewish subjectivity onto the sort of materialist understanding of antisemitism and the Holocaust which Enzo Traverso proposes in his Jewish Marxist analysis of Holocaust history and by his readings of critical theorists including Adorno and Benjamin. This neglect is locatable to the contradictory and inconsistent manner in which these sects tend to apply Judaic hermeneutics. In order to make sense of this tendency, we continue our background explication with a second question, What is meant precisely by a "Judaic hermeneutic structure"?

In the Ashkenazi context, which like much of Europe and the U.S.
appropriates indigenous cultural modes, the Judaic interpretive paradigm bears
comparison to the dominant interpretive paradigm of European culture:
Christianity. Christian hermeneutics shares with its Judaic counterpart the status
of an ideologically overdetermined mode of interpretation classically comprised
of a four-tiered analytic schema.[22] Christian hermeneutics traditionally
articulates to the narrative-compositional structure of the New Testament, while
both Roman Palestinian and modern Protestant denominations, which otherwise
differ significantly, find additional interpretive grounding in the Christian
revision of the Hebrew Bible [tanakh], the Old Testament. Commonly
associated with Talmudic tradition, the Judaic schema likewise articulates to
tanakh, the Talmud's critical matrix and orientation, but it also integrates
written and oral, frequently non-Judaic traditions which precede and inscribe
those sacred texts. Christian and Judaic modes of interpretation have each been
subject to alteration marked by changing social, cultural, and political-economic
conditions; likewise each has sustained general, philosophical differences that
symptomatize longstanding ideological divisions over how to make sense of
those conditions in light of divergent textual histories.[23] Often developing in
contestation with other interpretive modes, these divisions are marked by
overlap and intereffectuality, which often discloses their distinctions as
inessential but also underscores the socially reactive character of attempts to
naturalize the differing conditions they symptomatize as ontologically binding.
For contemporary Judaism, such divisions congeal around the question of
Zionism; for contemporary Christianity, around the issue of eschatology.[24] It is
possible given this mutual imbrication to speak of an exclusivist "Judeo-
Christian" formation that marginalizes other and alternative interpretive modes
such as those rooted in non-Jewish Palestine and in cultures indigenous to pre-
Christian Europe and North America that do not historically serve the needs of
Western hegemonic development.[25]

In this historiographically revised context, the distinction between Judaic
and Christian hermeneutics is one of historical cleaving and its occlusions.
Judaic hermeneutics entails a dialectical mapping of the four-tiered analytic
schema across a disquisitional narrative understood to conclude definitively
only after the enabling conditions of disquisition have been resolved.[26] More
specifically, Judaic analysis premises a rigorous subjection of prevailing
hermeneutical foundations, including Judaism's Mosaic genealogy of election
and manumission, to an epistemological inquiry into the very project and
possibility of logical resolution and its perceived analogue, the attainment of
social justice [tikkun ha-olam]. The four-tiered Judaic schema—peshat, remez,
drash, sod—supplements the literal-explicative, figural-expansive, moral-
expository, and anagogic-interpolative layers of Christian interpretability with

an analytic schema comprised, respectively, of narrative-historical, allegorical-homiletic, pedagogical-interrogative, and poetic-intersubjective layers. Its deployment enacts what in Judaic tradition is known as *pilpul*, a counter-critical method of interrogation by which is foregrounded the multivalence and polysemy of (scriptural) textuality, and by which an ethical need is demonstrated for recognizing and taking into account the socially and conceptually overdetermined, non- and extra-textual character of rhetorical diversification—the historical, economic, political, racial, ethnic, gendered, sexed, philosophical, cultural, and aesthetic registers of (inter)textual interpolation—before establishing an authoritative opinion [*halakhah*] about the meaning and significance of a text.[27]

One important effect of the distinction between Judaic and Christian hermeneutics is a counter-critical development within Judaism of theoretical resistance to the classical phenomenological reduction [*epōkhe*] associated with Christian interpretive tradition. As Christian theologians remind apropos of Christian New Testament scholarship, Christian hermeneutics is a means of distinguishing right from wrong and, in relation, of justifying interpretations accordingly, in deference to faith: "The Christian method is to introduce a number of parallel and analogous situations and by comparing them to bring to light the essentially relevant considerations and pin-point the precise area of difficulty or obscurity."[28] As Herbert Waddams insists, "The aim of the Christian life is not in the first place to achieve Christian behavior according to some discoverable pattern [laws]; its aim is union with God, from which true Christian behavior can alone derive."[29] To accomplish this, Christian hermeneutics establishes a dualist axiology along which difference, understood as the obscure telos of sameness, may be pared or selectively subsumed into a manifest unity thought to contain an inherent difficulty, a necessary tendency to variance and deviation over chronological time. Such moral casuistry contrasts the differential Judaic axiology, which both Levinas and Derrida have engaged philosophically to critique aspects of Western, ethno-nationalist violence and chauvinism. Judaic hermeneutics premises that the comparative, Christian method is tautological and self-serving, its *epokhē* a blueprint for perpetual exploitation and its disastrous ideologic, regenerative human sacrifice. The problem is illuminated by post–Christian cultural philosopher, Slavoj Žižek, who concedes, "Christian love is a violent passion to introduce a *difference*, a gap in the order of being, to privilege and elevate some object above others [...] as it tears an object out of its context and elevates it to the Thing."[30] In an effort to forestall and defuse this destructive potential, a properly Judaic hermeneutics works to deconstruct and resituate the ideological conditions of "difference," that is, the unilateral compulsion toward reductive unification, whereupon the general, deep-structural *problem* of (Jewish, Québécois, Palestinian) marginalization may be recognized and potentially resolved on more substantive, less rhetorical grounds.[31]

This is by no means to excuse or exonerate the flaws and blind spots of Judaic analysis. Not only is New Testament scholarship not the exclusive provenance of Christianity; having been written by Jews, The New Testament is interpretable in Judaic terms.[32] The Judaic *pilpul* may devolve into a puerile casuistry known as *hilukim*, a rhetorical strategy that encourages hair-splitting textual distinctions, willful misreadings, and specious equivocation, the aims of which are neither moral nor ethical instruction but, at best, academic sparring and, at worst, social divisiveness. At the scholastic core of *hilukim* lies a characteristic to which George Orwell would later refer in another context as "protective stupidity." This practice involves "holding two contradictory beliefs in one's mind simultaneously, and accepting both of them."[33] *Hilukim* has been the negative inspiration for false and overarching claims across the political spectrum about Jewish intellectualism, rationality, and competitiveness.[34] In fact, this rhetorical devolution of interpretative practice is not limited to Judaism; as Orwell indicates, it is common to oppressive ideological formations which exploit it to political ends.[35] Hilukic decisions have been canonized in the Talmud and in the seminal text of Jewish orthodoxy, the *Shulkhan Aruch*.[36] Hasidism has reacted to the practice's elitist function by emphasizing homiletic storytelling, or *drash*, a mode of Jewish allegory. By contrast, *haredi* particularists deploy *hilukim* when engaging non- and secular Jews: "[E]mbracing the other is not equal to recognizing the other's legitimacy."[37] Similarly Zionism, which like Hasidism emerged in Central and Eastern Europe under strained socio-economic conditions, exploits the interpretive multivalence of Jewish historical narratives with what Middle East correspondent Erskine Childers calls "wordless wishes," clever circumlocutions that travesty an authentic *pilpul* and mask disreputable political aims meant to dash Jewish and Palestinian hopes for a just and lasting peace.[38]

The sin qua non of this effect is the Judaic praxis of problematizing the existence of God.[39] This praxis is represented during one of The Quarrel's more acute moments, when Hersh tries to persuade Chaim that the Holocaust was the result of divine decree against Jewish religious disaffection. To drive home his point that the Holocaust was God's punishment for Jewish failure to uphold his holy commandments, Hersh qualifies his essentially authoritarian claim by paraphrasing the Judaic funeral prayer, *Tzidduk Ha'adin*, which prohibits questioning divine decree: "God's ways are very hard to understand";[40] and Chaim retorts, Job-like, "If I knew God, I'd put him on trial." To be sure, Chaim is less concerned with the apparent incomprehensibility of "God's ways" than with their social asymmetricality; he is confused as to why some people were able to survive the Holocaust and others were not. But like Hersh, he holds open for question the function and efficaciousness of divinity, by foregrounding a tenuous distinction between the possibility of making ontological claims, or passing judgment on the ways of the world ("knowing God"), on the one hand, and making ethical determinations, or offering critical explanations of their various effects ("God's ways"), on the other. As the dialogue proceeds, however, this distinction nearly collapses, as neither interlocutor actually denies the existence or knowability of God: whether understood ontologically or ethically, the problematical matrix remains theological, while the undisputed fact that Holocaust survivorship was more often a matter of political and class positioning than one of sheer luck is never considered. Thus the scene recalls the judicious admonition of Jewish theologian, Elmer Berger, concerning the moral authority of ontological judgment:

> To attempt to proscribe the struggle, the debates which accompany human efforts to reach the greatest possible justice and the nearest approach to truth in answer to [...] earthly problems by having some mortal assert he or she has the authority to seal any one, human design with the insignia of God is arrogance in the superlative degree and a profanation of any of mankind's great religions. Any who attempt to foreclose debate of such political questions by claiming divine sanction for *their* particular answers do, indeed, "take the name of the Lord in vain." (Berger, "Zionist Ideology," 7)

Berger, a U.S. Reform rabbi and self-proclaimed "anti–Zionist Jew," interprets the Judaic taboo against ontological claims—which is not unrelated to the taboo against divine imaging—less as a rejection of critical explanation and decision-making, which Adorno would call "a keystone of bourgeois ontology,"[41] and more as a means by which to obviate the sectarianism and particularism which he imputes to Zionism and other ill-conceived political movements. For Berger, the possibility of making truth-claims clearly bespeaks recognizing and naming oppressive social institutions and systemic functions with an aim to their effective transformation. The argument between Chaim and Hersh, by contrast, subsumes this reasoned, ethical injunction into a rhetorical simulacrum that diffuses systemic analysis of the Holocaust's social determinants and replaces it with an ontological copula—"God"—that favors identitarian prevarication (What is a "Jew"? Am I a "Jew"?) over serious criticism of the social totalities (patriarchy, ethnocentrism, racism, capitalism) responsible for holocausts and genocides and for the identitarian formations usually necessary to their implementation.

For all the moral authority it may assert, the Judaic proclivity toward *hilukim* does not necessarily contradict the aims and effects of the Christian *epōkhe*; in many instances, these historically differing analytic modes work in tandem, as evidenced by the modern collusion between Christian and Jewish Zionism and between the philosophies of *Haskalah* and emergent Zionism, to which Middle East cultural theorist Joseph Massad has referred as a Christianizing tendency.[42] Confounded alliances notwithstanding, these modes' historical differences persist as socially divergent perspectives on the composition and horizons of the "human." Recalling LaCapra reading Girard, whereas Christian hermeneutics prioritizes repetition over deconstruction as a founding gesture of human community, and whereas the content of that repetition—the Christian sacrificial ethos—is conceived in terms of transhistorical human suffering emblematized by the christic passion (dramatic rehearsals of which serve to "prove" its veracity, validity, and necessity), a properly Judaic hermeneutics aims to forestall and finally to end the conditions of any such repetition, by structuring a critical framework that makes it possible to explain the enduring *regime of sacrifice*, its prevalent meanings and sense, in relative terms of its dominant modality—that is, as a utopian travesty of Christianity's own professed vision of universal peace and harmony.

It is possible to claim, then, that Judaic hermeneutics offers a critical means for reasoned inquiry into the politics and ideologics of human solidarity and emancipatory hope. The interpretive resolution or synthesis it conceives may in turn be restated apropos of Benjamin, whose writings on German tragedy position that "fallen" allegorical mode as an occasion for critiquing precisely those cultural formations—fetishes, idols, icons, and ontological claims—which are usually merely performed by sublative, comparative readings.[43] Yet as Adorno reading Lukács makes clear, and as debates over Jewish ontology demonstrate, Benajmain's "materialism," like Hasidic "worldliness" and Levinasian "Otherness," hinges uncomfortably upon a phenomenological messianism that tends to reinforce the hilukic function and, through its detour, to return emancipatory hope—and the peoples who bear it—to the prison-house of regenerative sacrifice.[44]

* * * * *

This contradictory, ahistorical logic pervades *The Quarrel* at numerous registers. Given the film's generic positioning, not least of these is dialogue. An instructive example is a minor scene which occurs not long after Chaim and Hersh begin their film-length walk through the park. During the scene, Hersh, who has been attempting to convince Chaim to return to *haredism* and Talmudic study, submits him to an exemplary *hiluk* involving a parable he claims Chaim originally recited to him back in yeshiva about a brooding, indecisive Jew with a complex about his family: "It was about the son of a great rabbi from Warsaw who brooded all the time, and he was visited by the ghost of his father, who he believed was murdered by his uncle." As Hersh's *drash* unfolds, Chaim is given to realize that the parable's troubled, indecisive Jew is not Jewish at all but

Hamlet, Prince of Denmark. Hersh's sly misidentification of the story's coordinates and characterology tricks Chaim into misinterpreting *Hamlet*'s tragic line of probability ("Something's rotten in the state of Denmark") as a Jewish condition bearing Jewish consequences (e.g., "Something's rotten in the state of Israel") and a possibly very different, Jewish ending. Although Hersh neither helps elaborate this intended misinterpretation nor explicates his particular sense of what a Jewish ending or consequences might be, Chaim appears to grasp their implications by his succinct verbal affirmation—"You've made your point"—and his gestural acknowledgement of Hersh's methodological ploy—he grimaces, uncrosses his arms, stands, and exits the frame. This ploy, a mode of alterior culling akin to *le-didakh*,[45] enables Hersh to divest the classic Shakespearean tragedy of its non-Jewish authorship and recast it in light of its contemporary relevance to a Jew like Chaim who has become disaffected from orthodoxy and will shortly express his pride in (secular) Israeli nationhood. By this tack, known in Talmudic discourse as *shinuya*, Hersh can allude, and Chaim can come to recognize, that a Jewish *Hamlet* might conclude comically rather than tragically depending upon whether Hamlet's personal-political dilemma is conceived differently, along Judaic hermeneutic lines.

Insofar as Hersh's *drash* turns on an allusion, however, it also opens Chaim's encounter with it onto *mis*recognition and a somewhat more dubious affirmation. Upon realizing Hersh's ruse, Chaim may cease momentarily to engage with his former *chavruta*, but that only serves to underscore the hilukic function of Hersh's *drash*. Indeed by his curt dismissal of Hersh's homiletic invitation to debate the relative merits of commitment to ultra-orthodoxy, Chaim at once acknowledges Hersh's pedagogical acumen and expresses exasperation at his proselytic persistence. This simultaneously ambivalent and dismissive gesture avails "disaffected" Chaim of the need to clarify his misinterpretation of the parable while inadvertently registering his latent affinity with Hersh's *haredi* agenda. Framed in two-shot seated on the edge of an antique fountain beside Hersh, Chaim does not bother to call him on his Jewish particularism, which might have entailed correcting the historical record by offering a reminder that non-tragic narratives are not necessarily of Jewish origin but were often integrated into Jewish culture as it encountered and assimilated into pre- and non-Jewish African, Palestinian, and Near Eastern civilizations as well as Hellenism. Such a reminder would have rendered easily reinterpretable the implied aim of Hersh's *drash*—Chaim's recuperation into *haredism*—as an affirmation, not a rejection, of the latter's secular turn and of the non-Jewish origins of the Judaic hermeneutics with which Hersh has attempted to lure Chaim back into the ultra-orthodox fold—and which might have been deployed to imagine a *radically* alternative Jewish ending to *Hamlet*. Instead by his relative silence, Chaim aligns himself implicitly with Hersh's particularism, revealing his own professed secularism as at least deferential to its reputed sacral opposite, and confining that opposite to an unspoken affinity with the non-Jewishness it purportedly rejects. In this context, the *drash* itself accrues a fundamental ambivalence analogous to that of *hilukim* and Orwell's "protective stupidity": whatever may be "rotten" enough in the state of Denmark/Israel to produce a Jewish tragedy shall remain unremarked, its discussion delimited by a question at once opened for consideration and obstructed from analyses which could implicate ultra-orthodoxy in broader narratives of national tragedy that are ineluctably bound up with the pitfalls and dangers of ethno-religious particularism.

The hilukic effect is also evident at *The Quarrel*'s narrative-compositional register, where its elusiveness accrues an obscurity commensurate to that of Jewish messianism. The ostensible worldliness of this mystical quality sets up an expectation that the film will soon engage Jewish nationalism and particularism seriously; however, the effect of its "protective stupidity" is in fact to defer any such engagement, to both lure and compel the spectator into a tenuous relationship with the film's dialogical structure as it continually approaches and just as quickly dismisses what Berger calls, in another context, "*their* particular answers." Whereas *The Quarrel* is a dialogue film adapted from literary and theatrical sources, it is neither a book nor a stage play. Like another, famous dialogue film, *My Dinner with André* (Louis Malle, U.S.A., 1981), whose protagonist has also abandoned a prior way of life, *The Quarrel*'s narrative relies for visual dynamism on careful editing and mise-en-scène. *The Quarrel* also organizes an audio-visual semiotic for which montage and pro-filmic orchestration work to position a spectatorial subjectivity who will evasively negotiate—like Chaim vis-à-vis Hersh's *drash*—the ideological ambivalence constructed by the film's hilukic hermeneutic. As a dialogue film, *The Quarrel*'s image–word montage is key to this interpellative function and therefore bears significantly upon the film's problematical refraction of both the Anglo–Québécois and Israeli–Palestinian conflicts.

Useful for understanding this crucial function is Noël Burch's classic writing on the "structural use of sound" and "sound dialectic."[46] For Burch, film sound should not be employed simply to illustrate the pro-filmic and mise-en-scène. That "imitative" function, which domination of Hollywoodian filmmaking has given critics a voluble rationale for dismissing it and for ignoring the aesthetic potentials of film sound, is on Burch's view artistically inferior to the "graphic" function:

> The spoken word [...] is a narrative vehicle that *describes* all of the action that has already occurred or will (perhaps) occur. One of the film's basic structures, in fact, consists of dialectical interaction between spoken descriptions on the screen and the past or future actions to which they refer [...] [In such instances]

the *complete freedom of the camera is restored* [...] [T]he manner in which both
the camera and the actors move is equally stylized, with each of these two sets of
movements determining the possibilities of the other. (Burch, *Theory of Film
Practice*, 76–77)

Burch's theory of "graphic" or "plastic" sound, for which the relative autonomy
of the aural function complements and may redirect that of the cinematographic,
not only anticipates Christian Metz's semiotic phenomenology of film narrative,
with its dialectics of langue–parole and of story–discourse;[47] it aptly describes
the function of the soundtrack in *The Quarrel*, thereby enabling us, contrary to
the film's critics, to declare its cinematic quality. In *The Quarrel*, dialogue is
precisely that barometer and verbal stylo of temporal passage and reflection
which helps figure the film's image–word montage into a balletic orchestration
that not only illustrates the drama between Chaim and Hersh but illuminates its
problematical nature by critically performing one of cinema's basic aesthetic
relations, continuity–discontinuity.

While Burch generally conceives of plastic sound as an "empirical
organization" that is "complete" and "organic" (in this Burch is indebted to the
phenomenology of Balázs),[48] however, *The Quarrel* refigures image–word
montage Judaically, into what might be called a *semiotics of redemption*. By this
structural twist, the intellectual effectuality Burch associates, reading Eisenstein,
to word–image montage is recast historiographically: the dynamic and
conceptual metaphoricity made possible through cinematic juxtapositions and
accompanying camera and character movements within narratological contexts
orienting transcendental time (as in the christological *Korczak*) may now also
figure the projection of social struggles that compel conditional, not merely
revelatory, readings, and which may therefore signify an uneasy collocation of
radically different, *literally* asymmetrical temporal registers.

This is all to say that *The Quarrel*'s image–word montage facilitates a
narrative semiosis that turns on a trope of possibility, not necessity. The film's
dramatic development is dependent upon a structured retrieval of lost and
suppressed memory-concepts that, far from being culled into a progressive
chronology, or "theology of consciousness,"[49] are displaced across a series of
contiguous diegetic registers, heterotopic strata comprising differing,
"inorganic" discursive fragments with which the quarreling characters must
grapple and contend in their efforts to justify their choices along the way.[50]
Among other things, this radically immanentist, Jewish anamnestics offers both
a cinematic model of genuine mourning-work and forms a structural analogue to
The Quarrel's institutional "statelessness," dislocating the film both
aesthetically and situationally and finally distinguishing its structural analytic
from that of the conceptually narrower neoformalism applied in related contexts
by Joshua Hirsch.[51] By its mystificatory, ultimately phenomenological

allegorization of the social struggles and delimitations it projects, however, this immanentist modality inexplicably subordinates some memory-concepts to others, trumping mourning into melancholia by marginalizing those analyses of institutional "statelessness" not confined to Holocaust cinema studies' prevailing problematics of representation. As I shall now indicate, the modality obscures how allegorical displacements may warp or travesty Holocaust memory when they are mediated by the sorts of mystified national-political intertexts which happen to modulate Chaim's film-length quarrel with Hersh Rasseyner.

This problematic Jewish allegoricality is evident in an early sequence that takes place prior to Chaim and Hersh's unexpected reunion, where it manifests as a narrative deferral motivated by the foreclosure of a particularly resonant image–word juxtaposition [*smuchin*]. In the sequence's first scene, Chaim has just entered the hospital room of a dying Jewish man [Michael Sinelnikoff] on whose spiritual behalf Chaim was recruited into a prayer quorum [*minyan*] by a local orthodox congregant [Arthur Grosser] in charge of such matters [*shames*]. The critical intertextuality of Judaic hermeneutics is clear from the scene's onset; the readily recognizable hospital setting recalls, for instance, the notorious case of antisemitism against one Samuel Rabinovitch, a Jewish intern at Montreal's Hôtel Dieu [House of God] Hospital, who was expelled from his post during the Second World War under pressure from fellow interns resentful that his position was not held by a Christian.[52] An immediately preceding confrontation between Chaim and the *shames* over the latter's targeting of Chaim for recruitment into the *minyan* lends a prophetic tone to what will transpire at the hospital by making available an additional intertextual reference; in Hasidic thought, a *minyan* is a requirement for designating a city a diasporic center, which also makes it a worldly locus of messianic redemption:[53]

(Chaim) "Why me?"

(*Shames*) "Why not you?"

The sophistic openness of this dialogue renders Chaim's recruitment into the *minyan* no arbitrary act. Indeed only in this mysterious, multivalent context— not, incidentally, by his prejudicial indexing[54]—is Chaim identifiable as "Jewish" despite his secular appearance. It is moreover in this context that Chaim's historical identification with ultra-orthodoxy will be revealed through a verbal-compositional memory play that pushes him nearly to misrecognize postwar Québec as prewar Europe, and as such to re-envision the present as a portal for revisiting, because conditioned by, the past. In what appears a mystically preconditioned context, then, the scene sets up a Jewish allegorical reading by establishing a historiographic configuration in relation to which

Chaim, and the spectator with him, may begin to recognize his prewar choice to abandon *haredism* as something more and other than lack of faith.

During the hospital scene, this historiographic dialectic proceeds along a twofold axis that hinges upon an indeterminate representation of Chaim's subjective ruminations. This indeterminacy is constructed by an internal voice-over to the scene's visible actions and is crucial to the allegorical configuration of Chaim's dilemma. As Chaim is portrayed in prayer [davening] at the dying man's bedside, we are privy to his thoughts: "Why did I feel compelled to follow this man? Certainly not to join in prayers that I'd stopped believing in years ago, and not to perform a *mitzvah* [blessed deed] for a man who was beyond our help anyway." Chaim's internal, unvocalized question is initially projected over a shot of him and the *shames* davening, but via a cut, it also forms a sound-bridge to a second shot comprising the blurred image of a *haredi* rebbe entering the room, who we will later realize, in narrative hindsight, is Hersh. An internal voice-over, the question's projection over these shots positions them, along with Chaim's ruminations, into uncertain contiguity: since only the spectator, not the characters, can hear his question, its enunciative matrix and diegetic status are ambiguous. Insofar as this ambiguity extends narratologically, moreover, via the image–word *smuchin* marking the sound-bridge, the visual portrayal of Chaim and the *shames* is divested of temporal stability, becoming, with Chaim's internal thoughts, anachronous. The resulting referential destabilization encourages a reading that signifies historiographically as well as differentially, in relation to the scene's dramatic substance, the imminent death of a Jewish man. In this way, Chaim's internalized voice-over is lent a conditional urgency that recalls while deepening Burch's theory of graphic sound.

The scene's critical effectivity is borne out and elaborated by further analysis of its image–word *smuchin*. In a preliminary sense, the montage figures a word-to-image application that locates Chaim's subjectivity, the immediate source of his ruminations, in the diegetic present-tense, whereupon his question becomes interpretable as a moral judgment against an obsolete, because literally fading, ultra-orthodoxy ("beyond our help anyway"). On this metonymic angle, the figurative juxtaposition of present and past produces an almost supersessional movement forward, in relation to which Chaim's present situation becomes interpretable as having replaced that of his past. A Jewish allegorical reading repositions the same application anamnestically [*im zekher*],[55] however, in the non-discursive but nonetheless conceptually mediated context of narrative temporality, in order to suggest the obverse: Chaim's subjectivity marks an as-yet indeterminate, ethical relationship to the *haredi* past. Far from having replaced that past, Chaim's present situation differs markedly from it for reasons that remain unclear to him but which the *smuchin* has nonetheless managed to relocate, aesthetically, from past to present. In so doing, the film here exposes both dimensions to critical questioning.

This redemptive allegoricality not only contradicts a progressive metonymy but grounds the scene's metaphorical aspects by *literalizing* the *relevance* of Chaim's past and, by extension, the very disquisition over it that founds *The Quarrel*'s narrative and motivates its trajectory. Put another way, what might be called the *smuchin*'s conditional proairetic carries a critical, even catastrophic significance, for which Chaim's prewar past is rendered unevenly comparable to his postwar present. The technique recalls Benjamin's definition of "catastrophe" as a situation in which the status quo persists, as well as invokes Marx's theory of surplus production, the modern systemic practice in which human exploitation turns on labor's uneven variability, its "reserve" and "dead" positioning relative to "constant" capital.[56] The prayer service's allegorical convention of Holocaust survivors around a dying Jewish man becomes in this light quite literally interpretable as an unsettled political matter, an inscription of irretrievable loss as the morally questionable exploitation-effect of prevailing social practices.

As with Hersh's *drash*, however, *The Quarrel* only offers to settle the matter mystically. Indeed Hasidic ideology holds that "settling" a matter— including that of millennial "wandering"—is only possible upon the messianic advent; and even then, as Adorno rearticulates in secular terms, the act of mourning over an alienated past remains unfinished.[57] *The Quarrel* clarifies its support for this messianic line when it indirectly projects a comment uttered externally by the *shames* over a clearly focused shot of Chaim. Extolling the fortuitousness of his having successfully organized a *minyan* on Rosh Hashanah, the *shames* says, "It's a very good sign." This ironically unequivocal *smuchin* literalizes the dramatic development of Chaim's ideological ambivalence by defining his participation in the prayer service as an ideal semiotic indicator—a "sign"—of ultra-orthodoxy's postwar survival and persistence. As a Judaic instance, however, the very strength and composition of that "sign" carries differential, historiographic weight. First, because the term's utterance marks an enunciative shift in the scene from internal rumination to external speech, its projection over the shot of Chaim displaces the subjective indeterminacy he has come to represent onto an immanent field, in effect objectivizing it in narrative context. Second, because the *smuchin* positions Chaim as "sign"'s referent, it refigures his newly objectivized character into an existential vehicle of the memory play which the narrative has initiated and that soon will develop into the titular quarrel. Chaim is no longer, if ever simply a protagonist; he is a performative vector of the conflicting historical sentiments he is unable to communicate but which his subjective crisis indicates are at least available to critical thought. Heightened and perhaps performed by a musical soundtrack comprised of eerie, monochromatic violin music, this semiological interpolation of Chaim as uncanny bearer of historiographic enactment encourages a mystical reading, upon which his differential semiosis rapproches that of the Holocaust testimonials in Lanzmann's *Shoah* which trigger and reenact but never evaluate holocaustal horrors through sense memory and emotional recall. In light of *The Quarrel*'s Hasidic intertext, this uncanny effectivity also recalls the *shekhinah*, a kabbalistic manifestation believed to be endowed with the anamnestic power to impel *tikkun ha-olam*.[58]

The mystical character of this redemptive semiosis is reinforced by events in an ensuing scene. Following his departure from the *minyan*, Chaim comes to stand before a Second World War memorial in Parc Mont Royale, where the prior verbal-compositional memory play and its historiographical articulations are further concretized. Reading an inscription on the memorial, Chaim's voice is once again audible as internal voice-over narration: "We of different races must never war against one another." Then, straying, the same voice comments upon the inscription: "It brought back my own dark memories of Europe." Close scrutiny of the image–word *smuchin* prompts a differential series of questions: Does it figure a simple analogy between two referentially distinct utterances (the first being relatively objective, the second relatively subjective)? Or does it affirm rhetorically an unspecified, historical connection between fallen Québécois soldiers and Holocaust victims? The latter would seem probable, until, almost immediately, two orthodox Jews, possibly also from the *minyan*, pass behind Chaim as one says to the other, "Most Jews know that, but not everybody knows it."

This second image–word *smuchin* complicates the first by appearing, impossibly and arbitrarily, as a critical response to it and, in turn, by rendering incomplete, even uncertain, an implied historical association of Canadian military victimhood with the genocide of the European Jews. Again, whereas the second juxtaposition is arbitrary, Chaim, having just left the eerily mmenonic *minyan*, interprets it and the epistemological problematic to which it refers as a real and necessary response to his internal thoughts; yet the actual impossibility of that response—Chaim's internal utterances would not have been audible to the passersby—effects an utopic quality that ironically facilitates Chaim's entry into serious rumination over his dark European experiences and thereby inaugurates what subsequently will become his—and the film's—central disquisition: the quarrel with Hersh Rasseyner.

In effect, the second image–word *smuchin* compels Chaim to pose, and to pursue an answer to, the question of what "most Jews" supposedly "know" that "not everybody knows" about the Second World War. Extending the moment Judaically, we can say that it problematizes Chaim's Ashkenazi identity, since he would seem not to "know" what "most Jews know" about the Second World

War. In turn, the scene places into question the very meaning of "to know":
What are its grounds? Ethno-national? Religious? Historical? Metaphysical?
Can a Québécois "know" what a Jew "knows" about the Holocaust and the
Second World War? If not, can only a Jew "know" thusly? But if so, what
precisely may be "known" mutually by these historically distinct social groups?
What precisely comprises, in other words, the relationship between 1930s
Québec and Nazi-occupied Europe? Between wartime Canada and Nazi
Germany? Between postwar Canada and the modern State of Israel? Between
postwar Québec and the Occupied Palestinian Territories? And why, moreover,
is this series of implied questions of apparently persisting concern within the
context of a "stateless," postnational Holocaust film, which instances a
cinematic genre comprised of contemporary international films regarding the
modern phenomenon of genocide?

It is not my intention to supply immediate answers to these epistemological
questions but to indicate that *The Quarrel* not only suggests we pose them but
itself offers provisional, if ideological, answers which nonetheless signify,
through their Judaic structuring, a consistent anti–cathartic refusal to sacrifice to
some unexamined, prematurely harmonious imperative the possibility of
interrogating deeply cherished concepts and beliefs about Jewish history and the
Holocaust, including assertions that the Judeocide was unique, that supreme
knowledge is available concerning it, and that *tikkun ha-olam* is feasible in its
wake. I shall suggest, however, that it is precisely this technique—*The
Quarrel*'s sustained hilukic turning on intertextual references to Canadian
wartime history and official policies toward Québécois Jews—that enables the
film to project an irresolutely neocolonial, orientalist refraction of crisis-ridden
Québec notwithstanding its own "stateless" significance and Ashkenazi-Israeli
intertext. In this context, which recalls debates surrounding *Korczak*, I will show
that *The Quarrel*'s "Jewish" projection once again serves to allegorize national
crisis negatively, and that critical reactions to it, which played out as dismissals
on false aesthetic grounds, are ineluctably bound up with how readily that
projection now figures Jewish history's own modern national crisis, Zionism.

* * * * *

To this end, another digression, a brief explication of Canadian wartime
history, is in order. Histories of Canadian politics during the Second World War,
like those of Canadian cinema, have received significantly less attention
internationally than their U.S. and European counterparts. A British protectorate
(a "Dominion State"), Canada was an Allied power that facilitated and
ultimately assisted the U.S. with its hegemonic incursion into war-torn Europe.
For various contested reasons, Canada's wartime immigration policy was far

more austere than that of the U.S.: relatively few refugees from Nazi-occupied areas, not least Jews, were permitted Canadian asylum.[59] Contributing to this apparent anomaly was official Canadian policy toward its internal colony, Québec. Strongly influenced by the Papacy, and led from 1936–39 and from 1944–59 by the right-populist authoritarian, Maurice Duplessis, Québec forged favorable diplomatic ties with Loyalist Spain, Fascist Italy, and the Nazi-collaborationist French Vichy regime led by Marechal Henri-Philippe Pétain.[60] Depression-era and wartime Québec enforced oppressive policies against its majority Catholic, working-class citizenry while nursing an ongoing, tenuous relationship with a central Canadian administration that was largely Protestant and for which such policies were considered an effective means for strengthening federal control over the economically underdeveloped, secession-minded Francophone province.[61] Unlike Vichy, the nominally antisemitic Duplessis regime exercised an official, nationally promulgated tolerance toward its Jewish citizens by granting them a modicum of socio-economic liberty unprecedented in Canadian history—thus harkening in certain respects to tendencies within parts of post–medieval Europe while eerily presaging administrative practices in some Nazi-run ghettoes. Most Jews affected by these policies were Anglophone or Yiddish-speaking Ashkenazim who, although once disproportionately representative of socialist, communist, and anarchist movements, had attained a higher average social status than Francophone Sephardim, over whom the former held an ethno-racial advantage which enabled their embourgeoisement. These Anglophone Jews' ability to assimilate into Canadian society at greater rates than their Sephardi co-religionists led the central Anglo-Canadian government to view them opportunistically.[62] Being of Anglo-Saxon rather than Latin or North African descent, Ashkenazim became a socially acceptable demographic means by which the potentially sovereign, majority white Canada could play the Allied card; wanting neither absorption into the U.S. nor re-absorption into the British Empire from which it was trying to negotiate its independence, Canada empowered these Jews socio-economically while in turn developing a viable arms and munitions industry for British and U.S. patronage in exchange for the latter's hemispheric protection and for the sake of the former's North Atlantic colonial hegemony.[63] Similarly, the collaborationist Duplessis regime saw this relatively privileged caste of Jews as a convenient means by which a politically subjugated, largely isolationist Québec might adhere to Anglo-Canadian nationalist imperatives without jeopardizing its semi-autonomous provincial relationship with French industry and culture.[64]

While helping to ensure the continued enrichment of Canadian, including Québécois, elites,[65] Canada's official philosemitism fanned the flames of an already deep-seated, popular antisemitism (the existence of which, unlike the history of the Duplessis regime, has enjoyed no shortage of documentation).[66] Likewise, the Canadian Jewish community's internal class, ethnic, and racial contradictions, especially the longstanding divisions between Ashkenazim and Sephardim, grew more flagrant.[67] Such divisions persist to this day, as evidenced by the intersecting plethora of Jewish and Québec nationalist polemics, in which Ashkenazim tend to oppose an independent Québec while supporting Zionism, and Sephardim tend to support an independent Québec while opposing the Israeli occupation of Palestine.[68] Ashkenazi–Sephardi divisions exacerbated during the Second World War, as Canada continued to negotiate its gradual independence from Great Britain and reorient itself as a North American "middle power" subject to U.S. political and economic pressures. Notwithstanding a limited increase in antisemitic incidents and policies within wartime Canada, not least of which was a pre-empted lobby effort to rescue persecuted Jews from Nazi-occupied Europe, Ashkenazim and Sephardim have retained alternate and opposing interests. Here it must be emphasized that the Duplessis regime's pervasive ethno-religious chauvinism was never adopted as a majority platform by postwar Québec's left-wing secessionist movement, regardless of the latter's demographic composition. The Duplessis phenomenon was none other than a right-collaborationist tendency that took and maintained Québécois power in part by exploiting the province's often willing Ashkenazi citizens in order to broker support from both pro-war, moderately pro-U.S. constituencies in Anglophone Canada and their isolationist adversaries at home and abroad. The Duplessis regime engaged thusly in full recognition of the dire consequences for Jews of either background as well as for Québec's majority Catholic citizenry. As these consequences materialized, the Canadian central administration's own dubious opportunism vis-à-vis its powerful U.S. neighbor would become increasingly visible in the dark mirror of the erstwhile tolerant Francophone colony.[69]

* * * * *

The series of contradictions sustaining Canadian wartime history is strikingly exemplified by *The Quarrel*'s transcription of narrative disquisitionality from word–image *smuchin* to the cinematographic deconstruction of diegetic space. In a scene remarkable for its critical projection of Judaic hermeneutic problematics, this transcription is enabled by a *smuchin* that carefully orchestrates mise-en-scène, apropos of Burch, in conjunction with studied camera positioning, and that in turn constructs a shifting, multiperspectival, if finally hilukic cinematic gaze. This striking effect is accomplished in relation to a barely noticeable series of breaks in the 180-degree rule, a classical cinematic injunction against disorienting the spectator spatially vis-à-vis the cinematic screen, during a chance encounter between a swarthy *yeshiva bokher*, Yeshia [Robert Haiat], who is one of Hersh's more enthusiastic students, and our two disputational protagonists, Chaim and Hersh.

By the time of this encounter, the quarrel between Chaim and Hersh over Jewish secularization and assimilation and their relationship to the Holocaust has begun to address the ethnic chauvinism and nationalist militancy associated with Zionism. Although that address is, recalling Hersh's *drash*, never explicitly politicized—Hersh never openly attests to the *haredi* view that Jewish religious disaffection is responsible for the Holocaust or that the State of Israel is in any way related to either phenomenon—the perspective is alluded to at numerous registers, and it eventually comes to underscore the theocratic nature of Hersh's mussarist convictions and Chaim's secular collusion with them.[70] Throughout the film, this dogmatic perspective, which attributes to Zionism a "false messianic" character while ignoring—collaborating with—its political and economic determinants,[71] becomes increasingly vigorous, coercing the narrative into rhetorical divergence from the reputed flexibility of classical Judaic hermeneutics to the sophistical legalism of medieval orthodoxy. Literalizing a medieval, largely Ashkenazi belief in a divinely sanctioned Jewish separatism and distinctiveness, this narrative divergence not only upholds the classical proscription against Jewish nationalism but retains, in what is only an apparent contradiction, the medieval prohibition of "liberal" phenomena such as women's participation in the public sphere and the social acceptance of homosexuality, both of which *haredism* blames, in part, for the Judeocide.[72] Nearly a decade prior to the construction an Apartheid Wall in Israel/Palestine, *The Quarrel*'s rhetorical containment of Judaic disquisition erects a cinematic barricade against modernity's alleged sex-gender decadence, first by exposing its perceived symptoms, then by imputing their presumed catastrophic consequences to the mutually intereffective projects of Euroamerican imperialism and Zionist supranationalism, in the form of mystified Jewish allegory.

The disturbing effects of this rhetorical tack persist even though, in contestation with Hersh, Chaim appears to resist them. Apropos of dismissing Hersh's *drash*, Chaim's ostensible rejection of *haredism* prefigures a reactionary reconstruction of the prewar friendship into a politically occlusive cleaving of mutually exclusive alter-egos [*maggidim*].[73] As literary critic Sidra Ezrahi writes regarding the original novella, the "polarization of attitudes [between and amongst Chaim and Hersh], however trenchantly represented, still resides within one closed universe in which God and the Jewish people are the two poles of reference."[74] And as Hersh confesses to Chaim near film's end, "I was broken when you left! It took me years to regain my faith! Even in Częstochowa, I was struggling—with you! [...] It's not me, don't you see; it's always been you, always been you!" Indeed at film's end, the unreconciled former *chavrutim* will be portrayed in two-shot bidding one another adieu, then exiting at opposite sides of the frame. On the larger reading I shall elucidate, this apparently benign cleavage symptomatizes a prevailing misrecognition of the "Jewish," as it obscures the varied and uneven participation of Jewish people in the project of modernity that overdetermines *The Quarrel* itself. It thus marks a veiled apology, even a self-censorial gesture disguising a purportedly anti–modern *haredism*'s implication in modern development; and it propagates the nostalgic view, compatible with christology, that Jews are a people *essentially* separate and apart, at once beyond and radical to history while ideally disassociated from the everyday.[75]

The exemplary cinematographic figuration of this problematic has its precursor in a much earlier scene, when Chaim first sees and recognizes Hersh. There the uncanny sensibility accrued to Chaim during the preceding *minyan* scene is exceptionalized by a subjective camera that telescopes his vexed point-of-view across Lake Beaver to a group of *haredim* with whom Hersh is davening at lakeside (figs. 3-1, 3-2). The shot first focuses on the group of daveners, with Hersh standing center, then cuts to a deliberate tracking shot that portrays each davener in turn until stopping at Hersh, as if quoting the Pasolinian pan and the sacrality which some critics have attributed it.[76] As the camera tracks left, the ostensible sacrality it projects adopts a Judaic character; unlike the Germanic, Romance, and Slavic languages most familiar to Euroamericans, Hebrew, a Semitic language is written from right to left. A singular movement, moreover, the tracking shot tropes the *haredim* metonymically, rendering each davener a serial revision of the "ultimate" Hersh. It must be said that Saul Rubinek's costuming, an obviously false beard and eyebrows, resists a culminative designation; hence the shot's serial effect conjoins the *haredim* less into symbolic totality than into a simulacrum, an idealized grouping of the sort Chaim will be unable to criticize effectively, in response to Hersh's *drash*. In any event, the tracking shot's telescopic context doubles its tropic effect: its matrix is not simply Hersh and his cultic entourage, but Chaim's already problematized subjectivity. Put more plainly, Chaim's telescopic location and recognition of Hersh is also a conceptual *dis*location and *mis*recognition of the *shames*' leading question, "Why not you?" The abstract projection of Chaim's gaze across the lake onto a group of people associated literally and figuratively with his past serves a reflexive function that is at once empirical, self-referential, and anamnestic, and that as such helps open conceptual space in which serious answers to the *shames*' question might be sought. The function's obscurantist delimitation is effectively underscored, furthermore, when Hersh, spotting an approaching Chaim, recites the mystical Jewish prayer, the *Shehekhianu*, which offers divine thanks for life and sustenance.

Fig. 3-1 – Ultra-orthodox Jews praying at lakeside in *The Quarrel*
Fig. 3-2 – Ultra-orthodox Jews praying at lakeside in *The Quarrel*, telescoped

This cinematographic figuration of Jewish allegoricality is complemented by editing that ramifies *The Quarrel*'s questionable sex-gender politic. In the above scene, a secondary break in Chaim's telescopic gaze, a cutaway to some *haredot* [female ultra-orthodox] also davening at lakeside, visually divides the diegetic space along traditional gender lines. The shot's gender segregation is underscored by a rapidly ensuing cut to a shot comprising only men. In keeping with kabbalistic cosmology and Judaic laws of *kvod ha-tzibbur*, which dictate public etiquette between the sexes, this large-scale shot/reverse-shot figures Chaim's telescopic gaze as a veritable cinematic *mehitzah* [the physical barrier erected between the sexes in Jewish prayer settings], both separating the men from the women and visually attributing an irruptive potential to the act of looking exemplified by that very gaze.[77] Insofar as it has been characterized as eliciting urgent and perturbing questions, Chaim's gaze carries a mythical danger, which Hasidism affiliates with "unruly" (female, queer) sexualities and imputes to the "evil inclination" [*yetzer ha-ra*] it believes is triggered by the mere act of "wrongful" looking. To stave off that inclination, it is thought, wrongful looking must be contained. Hence the rapid reverse-shot from the *haredot* to their male counterparts, and the visual obstruction of women throughout the remainder of the scene.

Similar sex-gender differentiation occurs during a later scene, in which Chaim and Hersh encounter Freda [Ellen Cohen], Chaim's erstwhile lover. Freda is excluded from shots comprising Hersh and by scene's end will depart by walking into the shot's deep space while Chaim and Hersh exit, obliquely, at the lower right-hand side of the frame. In a subsequent scene, this proscribed rationalization of traditional sex-gender roles will be expanded historiographically, in direct reference to the Canadian intertext, as Chaim and Hersh encounter one Solomon Rosenberg [Ari Snyder], an amateur writer and admirer of Chaim's novels who bears and transmits a classically related set of stereotypical codes: homosexuality, fascism, and communism.[78] In this scene, Chaim and Hersh are not simply separated by editing from the "evil" Rosenberg, as though protected from him and/or assuring the spectator of their own heterosexuality. They are also connected to him by a qualified necessity educed by the Québécois intertext. Stark intercutting just prior to the encounter, which involves an insensitive mounted policeman whose horse frightens Hersh as he drinks from a public fountain, interjects a negative reference to the "Canadian." Analogized visually to the stereotypified Rosenberg, postwar Québec is at least institutionally oppressive, even antisemitic, and possibly perverse. In fact, Rosenberg expresses verbal disdain for the policeman as he rides off; a need for critical response is proposed by Chaim's inaction vis-à-vis the anamnestic shock symptomatized by Hersh's excessively fearful reaction to the horse. Rosenberg's ostensible heroics overdetermine a visual alignment with his erstwhile adversary, however. Framed in a two-shot that separates them spatially from Chaim and Hersh, Rosenberg and the policeman are conjoined into the "unruly" conceptual domain comprised previously only by women. Yet this male-only congregation is not so easily contained; in lieu of Chaim's powerful, telescopic gaze, the sexually and politically ambiguous Rosenberg himself supplies the intervention, thus becoming a *necessary* evil, a homosocial agent and barter-ball negotiating anti–modern *haredism*, on the one hand, and Québécois right-nationalism, on the other. Contrary to Freda and the *haredot*, Rosenberg tropes the mounted policeman, a synecdoche of the reactionary Duplessis regime, as consistently as he does the dogmatic religiosity of Hersh. He cannot simply be relegated to separate, ineffectual space; the need for his intervention entails his elective affinity with both sides of the dramatized conflict, even as they mutually exploit the marginality which relegates him to negotiator status.

As mentioned, the need for Rosenberg's intervention is evinced dramatically by Chaim's inaction. In narrative context, this is ironic, insofar as Hersh has accused Chaim of passivity and spiritual weakness during the Holocaust. Having escaped Nazi persecution through the Soviet Union and China, Chaim allegedly abandoned his people and his faith, thus relinquishing his *haredi* interpellation as *kiddush ha-shem* [a martyr to Judaism]. Notwithstanding the anti–communist subtext of Chaim's accusation, the "necessary evil" it elicits in the form of Rosenberg's tropological ambivalence introduces a key supplement to Chaim's ideological indeterminacy and the conditional proairetic it figures, at once affirming the socio-cultural breadth of Jewish allegoricality in *The Quarrel* and symptomatizing its political limitations. Indeed the kabbalistic rationalization of *yetzer ha-ra* is nearly indistinguishable from the christo-phenomenological *epōkhe* but for its historiographic layering, suggesting an incipient interfaith gesture that cannot, in its obscurantism, but misrecognize its socially necessary conditions, even as these are more broadly conceived than a Christian *epōkhe* would allow.[79] Speaking in terms of narrativity, the quarrel between Chaim and Hersh does not even broach resolution until characterological bearers of *yetzer ha-ra* are met with and set aside, yet these bearers are not eliminated through subl(im)ation: they are deferred to what Freda herself calls "another time." On the film's Hasidic intertext, this "time" is constituted aesthetically rather than politically, by a cinematic rendition of *kavannah*, a divinely impelled, messianic force supposed to trigger unsettled memories.[80] Once the memories have been triggered and the "time" reached, their purported danger is reinscribed as a performance of the time's own exposure and containment—in fact as dialectical imagery. Hence *The Quarrel* will not conclude with a cathartic debate over the role of Holocaust mystification in perpetuating the conflict in Israel/Palestine, or over the role of patriarchy in sustaining racist ethno-nationalism and the global neoliberal capitalism it supports. Instead piggy-backing on the art cinematic tradition of studied ambiguity that was anticipated by the film's public television and film festival distribution, the incipient kernel of any such debate is telescoped into an aesthetic shock-effect reminiscent of the scene involving Hersh and the horse, a messianic hook that sparks awareness but just as quickly recontains it. Recalling the ludicity of which Adorno is so critical in Benjamin, this containment marks the very, Jewish ethical tack which *haredism* deems necessary to messianic advent but which Adorno will rearticulate, from a radically secular perspective, to the as-yet "incomplete" project of capitalism.[81] For Adorno, the completion of capitalism, a barbaric system that both necessitates holocausts and conditions their eradication, entails a contrary, epistemological move in which critical hindsight is projected onto historically marginalized subjectivities in order to redeem them—not as dead and reserve labor values to be reinvested as commodities in the system, but as exploitation-effects to be repositioned ideologically as modalities of revolutionary praxis.

The Quarrel's messianic politics are nowhere more vividly exemplified than in the mentioned scene with Yeshia, the swarthy *yeshiva bokher*. Here, in the context of the film's most memorable debate, Adorno's radical project is displaced mystically onto the Anglo–Québécois conflict for the sake of a Jewish ethic now placed seriously into question. Alone with Hersh, deep in a wooded enclave, Chaim comments favorably upon the reputed strength of the pre-state Zionist military [Haganah], and Hersh, ever the anti–Zionist, reacts with subtle counterpoint. Suddenly a downpour compels the men to take shelter in a spacious recreation hall where some Québécois workers are mopping the floor and painting. Once inside, Chaim and Hersh encounter Yeshia, who quickly identifies Chaim as someone against whom Hersh has spoken vehemently for his having abandoned *haredism* and thus having forsaken his less fortunate brethren during the Holocaust. Chaim is initially willing to debate this accusation, but Yeshia, who lacks Hersh's rhetorical sophistication, cannot give Chaim the requisite *pilpul*. Instead, the fervent young zealot overpowers Chaim verbally and, repeating the accusation, asserts, "All Jews must help one another!" In return, Chaim becomes incensed, shouts Yeshia down, and abruptly exits the building, leaving Hersh to discipline his volatile, belligerent student.

Punctuating the altercation are shots of two Québécois workers standing high astride ladders in the scene's background, who gesture in annoyance or perhaps incomprehension at the quarreling Jews. The ambiguity of their gestures recasts very different gestures performed by Chaim and Hersh in a previous scene during which the debating *chavrutim* seek refuge from a prior downpour in an old tool shed. During that scene, Chaim and Hersh discuss their pre-Holocaust past, including their friend Goldstein who did not survive the Judeocide, while gesticulating in a kabbalistic fashion known as *tzimtzum*—the paradoxical mapping of infinity. As their hands and fingers intersect without touching, Chaim and Hersh delineate a digital *danse macabre* that will be re-enacted full-figure during the film's penultimate scene, when, having finally remembered their rebbe's *nigun* [mnemonic tune], they will be portrayed dancing, again without touching, in a close two-shot decontextualized by shallow focus and slow-motion shooting. On the film's Hasidic intertext, these "infinite dances" mark the achievement of *devekut* [spiritual resolution] and a state of *yichud* [spiritual enrapture] that is often analogized to the founding of Israel, a mutual "uniting in the diverse name [...] of one great melody," by which the past is subject to mourning through a communal performance of exultant, if fleeting joy.[82]

The Québécois workers' gestures are not nearly so profoundly laden; in fact, they are almost banal. As the altercation between Chaim and Yeshia intensifies, a series of intercuts to the workers adds suspense to their apparent displeasure, eliciting the antisemitic undercurrent signified earlier by the mounted policeman and prefiguring vexed reactions by local Québécois onlookers to Chaim and Hersh's enraptured dance. Following one such cut, a subtle break occurs in the 180-degree rule that significantly repositions Chaim in relation to Hersh and Yeshia. As Yeshia shouts, "All Jews must help one another!" Chaim, previously portrayed on the left-hand side of the frame, is now portrayed on the right; and Yeshia and Hersh, previously portrayed on the right-hand side of the frame, are now portrayed on the left (figs. 3-3, 3-4). In addition to punning visually on the ambivalence and political indeterminacy signified by these characters, the 180-degree break enunciates a scenic shift from an initially omniscient, authorial point-of-view to one localized and attributable to the Québécois workers. In effect, this classical cinematic transgression carves out a collective viewpoint for the spatially marginalized Francophone workers, which extends them perspectival authority over the quarreling Jews. As the scene progresses, however, that authority is strangely undermined. No sooner is Chaim, preparing to exit, portrayed moving logically from right to left, than another 180-degree break enunciates a return to the prior, omniscient point-of-view. Moreover the direction of Chaim's movement remains constant: he continues moving left! (fig. 3-5) As in a *camera obscura*, the mise-en-scène appears magically inverted: the Jews are still quarreling in the foreground, the Québécois are still working in the background, but the workers' perspective has literally been usurped in the visual context of a Hebraic orientation that relegates the momentary, workers' viewpoint to oblivion. Having initially figured a straightforward alternation in scenic viewpoints, the film now projects a *kavannah*-like intercalation of shots and character movements, by which the perspectival authority momentarily granted to the Québécois workers is recaptured cinematographically from a "left-leaning" viewpoint not entirely disassociatable from the authorial perspective of the reputedly liberal

Ashkenazi-Israeli director, Eli Cohen. As the viewpoint is recaptured, however, its passing perspective is literally written off.

Fig. 3-3 – Shot prior to 180-degree break in *The Quarrel*
Fig. 3-4 – Shot following 180-degree break in *The Quarrel*

Fig. 3-5 – Subsequent 180-degree break in *The Quarrel*

The moment recalls film theorist Jonathan Crary's epistemology of cinematic perspective. As against a perceived technological determinism in the spectatorship theory of Jean-Louis Baudry and Jean-Louis Comolli,[83] Crary understands cinematic perspective as a historiographic field in which resistance may be organized and projected against the bourgeois *quattrocento* generally ascribed to classical Hollywood filmmaking. The cinema is accordingly a painterly as well as a photographic medium, its epistemology not restricted to representational rubrics. On Crary's important theory, *The Quarrel*'s "magical" deployment of the 180-degree cut may be interpreted in terms of a political aesthetic which Crary reading Benjamin ascribes to perspectival clashes, and that are also operative in prior scenes involving the *haredot*, Freda, and Rosenberg. This political aesthetic suggests that differences in perspective made visible through cinematic technique may highlight reflexively the uneven and contradictory relationship between modes of observation and modes of ideological production:

> [O]ne must recognize how the making, the consumption, and the effectiveness of art is dependent upon an observer—and on an organization of the visible that vastly exceeds the domain conventionally examined by art history [...] The meanings and effects of any single image are always adjacent to this overload and plural sensory environment and to the observer who inhabits it. (Crary, *Techniques of the Observer* [Cambridge, MA; MIT Press, 1995], 23)

In the Yeshia scene, this political "anti–aesthetic" evinces what Crary reading
Nietzsche calls a "crisis of assimilation"; the perspectival instability projected
by the "magical" 180-degree cut at once potentiates an autonomous collective
vision for the Québécois workers and symptomatizes its process of containment,
or disciplining, by the privatized, neoliberal regime of observation, or
surveillance, during which *The Quarrel* was conceived and produced. This
regime restricts broad access to small-scale, independent filmmaking by
dissimulating as "public" their private dissemination at elite film festivals, on
corporately funded state and membership-driven television networks, and in
university classrooms. In the case of *The Quarrel*'s, such systemic-institutional
conditions would only compound the film's "statelessness," its literal non-
assimilation, by limiting its Canadian exposure and steering its distribution into
global home video markets, a deterritorialized field of audio-visual exchange
that dilutes national designations into multicultural simulacra.

The structural imprint on the Yeshia scene of these global
commodification-effects is remarkable. At the second 180-degree cut, the
Québécois workers' perspective is eclipsed by one that appears magical but is
actually authorial—private. In the hypertextual name of Cohen's
Israel/Palestine, the eclipse marks a duplicitous convergence of viewpoints that
leaves intact the workers' stereotypified banality while authorizing Ashkenazi-
Israeli privilege over it. The resulting irrelevance of the Québécois perspective
is underscored by the 180-degree cut's barely detectable implementation and the
unconscious disorientation it effects. In a hilukic travesty of Judaic
hermeneutics, a politically scrambled context is constructed in which the
Québécois workers' social marginality is literally co-opted into a perspective
that trades on myths about pervasive Québécois antisemitism and proclivities
toward fascism in order to evade its own, unstable and discriminatory
tendencies. The workers' ambiguous gestures easily reinforce the Anglo-
Canadian canard about rampant antisemitism in the Québec labor movement,
whereas the same might be said about the role of the Israeli Labor Party in
exploiting Mizrachim, and the role of Anglo-Canada in fomenting Ashkenazi–
Sephardi and other ethnic divisions. In fact these workers might very well be
situated on the political Left or identify as Sephardi; organized Québécois labor
has never acceded to the conservatism and philosemitism of its more powerful,
pro-Canadian leadership.[84] Such historical possibilities are disavowed as the
scene's sophistic structuring positions the swarthy, physiognomically Sephardi
or Mizrachi Yeshia center-stage in the altercation with Chaim, where he can
serve as a visual fulcrum for scene shifts and help orient [sic] the spectator
spatially while figuring a conceptual analogue to the co-opted, stereotypified
workers through his own extreme zealotry. By this tack, the scene displaces a
violent, authoritarian particularism onto the workers and, metonymically,

Sephardi and Mizrachi Jews that is largely discontinuous with their histories but is easily assumed from within the film's production and distribution contexts as a correct image of the Québécois Left and of Jews from non-European backgrounds.

The hilukic eclipse in this respect bears a kernel of truth worth explicating. Like mid-century North American Jews and many Ashkenazim during the *Haskalah*, Jewish Israelis of non-European backgrounds have moved to the political Right in recent years. Many have abandoned the secular, leftist, and pro-Palestinian positions fostered during the 1960s and 1970s by the radical *Mizrachi* movement and have instead joined forces with Ashkenazi-dominated, often militant orthodox factions (e.g., Gush Emunim) that support political parties to the right of the reactionary Likud (e.g., the Sephardi-dominated Shas).[85] By the same token, formerly left-leaning Ashkenazim have exaggerated and generalized the socio-economic successes of a minority of this "oriental" population, which otherwise comprises an overwhelmingly poor, working-class majority of Jewish Israelis. Through its "magical" eclipse, *The Quarrel* refracts these contradictory and patronizing, self-hating projections onto popular Québec. In so doing, it not only reenacts an antisemitic gesture that belies the socially reparative impulse of its ostensible Judaic hermeneutics. Displacing its post–Holocaust problematics onto a conflict only circumstantially related to Jewish persecution, *The Quarrel* upholds the phenomenological taboo against Holocaust representation, obscuring the politics associatable to that event by misidentifying them with tangentially related struggles. It is on this clever turn that *The Quarrel* is able to suggest, if only momentarily, that a Gentile and a Jew, a Québécois and an Anglo-Canadian, a Sephardi and an Ashkenazi *can* "know" similarly regarding the Holocaust! No sooner does the film flash that reconciliatory idea kabbalistically before us, though, a cinematic *hiluk* revises it into an orientalist conflation of Québécois workers, Québec nationalists, Québec right-collaborationists, Sephardim/Mizrachim, and by intertextual extension, Palestinians and Native Americans, in effect distracting attention from the specificity of those often diametrically opposed movements and identities by facilely associating them all with the politics of holocaustal oppression.

While *The Quarrel*'s Judaic hermeneutic differs overtly from a hypothetical Christian structure, then, its "magical," "utopic" aspect functions less as a provisional digression in the interests of worldly reparation than as a reified modality that approaches the Christian *epōkhe*, endorsing an Ashkenazi redemption at the continued expense, the postnational "sacrifice," of women, queers, workers, and non-Europeans, whether of North American, North African, or Near Eastern descent. The fact that Chaim angrily dismisses Yeshia during their altercation once again indicates the former's implicit collusion with these politics. After pacifying Yeshia, Hersh pursues Chaim and persuades him to resume the debate, confessing his own, personal failure to mourn his wartime losses in lieu of Chaim's creedal abandonment. A "stateless," unassimilated film, *The Quarrel* uneasily inserts itself into and reenacts, on borrowed Canadian ground, this failed Jewish response to the Holocaust as divine judgment against modern secularization and assimilation. As debates around *Korczak* testify, this reactionary response has historically dissimulated marginalized cultures and movements in the unremitting name of a Euroamerican imperialism that requires for its hegemony the protracted statelessness, even homelessness, of non-Western peoples. It is possible that, on some level, Eli Cohen knew this, which might explain, recalling the "spiritual Zionism" of Ahad Ha'am[86]—an award in whose name *The Quarrel* was granted by the Ha'amian Center for Jewish Culture and Creativity in Tel Aviv—his attraction to an albeit ideologically uncertain project by which it could be demonstrated, if only fleetingly, allegorically, that just as Zionism has not eradicated antisemitism (in fact it has exacerbated it), internecine struggles within Québec nationalism persist at the expense of the Francophone region's cultural and political emancipation.[87] In any event, one wonders how differently *The Quarrel* might have ended had it not upheld the phenomenological taboo and instead projected Elmer Berger's Jewish ethical admonition against moral authority.

* * * * *

The following chapter considers Jewish response to the Holocaust with respect to a film whose representation of the Judeocide was ignored by film criticism for many years. Whereas *Entre Nous* largely refrains from representing the historical Holocaust, its release sparked vociferous public debate over its ideological orientation in other respects. In a rare move for Holocaust filmmaking, *Entre Nous* extends a progressive sex-gender politic. The film was subsequently both lauded and criticized for its portrayal of ambiguous female eroticism, while the question was almost completely ignored of how that eroticism was linked cinematically to the Holocaust, the Vichy collaboration, and U.S. transnationalism and global hegemony. Chapter Four theorizes this critical ignoring by relocating *Entre Nous'* widely unremarked Holocaust discourse to its ambiguous female bond. It draws upon film feminism and queer theory while questioning their capacities to address the film in its historiographical fullness or to understand why most film critics in turn were unable or unwilling to do so. A French art film produced mainly for international distribution during the Reagan-Thatcher-Kohl-Mitterand period in a country known for discouraging sustained public critique of anti–Judaism, *Entre Nous* projects "Holocaust" in structural consonance with the political economy that ensures a film's global viability under emerging neoliberalism. For that reason, the film occasions an opportunity more conducive to radically rearticulating the sex-gender politic inflecting its understanding of the Holocaust than that which is offered by other Holocaust films of that period or since. Moving backwards in time from the early post–Soviet era that produced *Korczak* and *The Quarrel*, the chapter critiques *Entre Nous'* allegorization of contemporary political economy by analyzing the film's key narrative-compositional trope, a parabolic ellipsis, which justly characterizes what most critics have considered the film's exceptional cinematic beauty, and which I read in terms of the "Judeo-Christian" discourse likewise, if differently, projected across *Korczak* and *The Quarrel*. In contrast to prior approaches, however, my analysis of *Entre Nous* explains that film's critically overlooked imbrication of "Holocaust" with erotic female bonding in terms of the latter's ambiguity rather than by its positive clarification. The chapter thus illuminates "le-didakhically" a cinematic projection of "Holocaust" which, recalling LaCapra and Hansen, accesses and replays scenes of holocaustal trauma not to help spectators overcome it, but to distract them by inducing an anxious, excessive, even amorphous desire for modern holocaustal effects and the contemporary transnationalist conditions which reproduce and transmit them globally.

---

[1] Chaim Grade, *My Quarrel with Hersh Rasseyner*, trans. Herbert H. Paper (Cincinnati: Hebrew Union College, 1982).

[2] Shohat, *Israeli Cinema*, 256–60.

[3] *The Vancouver Sun* ("Canadian Movie Reels in Top Prize at Santa Barbara Film Festival," April 10, 1992: C2) reported that *The Quarrel* beat out over one hundred films screened at that small, regional festival. This in contrast to Cohen's prior film, *Summer of Aviya* [*Hakaytz Shel Aviya*] (Israel, 1988), which was globally successful and won a prize at the Berlin Film Festival (Amy Kronish, *World Cinema: Israel* [Wiltshire: Flick / Cranbury, NJ: Associated University Presses, 1996], 99–100). *The Quarrel* was, however, given a special honor at the Jerusalem Film Festival, as the only film there that Israeli President Chaim Herzog was willing to attend (Patrick Martin, "Canadian Film Wins Raves in Jerusalem," *Toronto Globe and Mail*, July 16, 1992: C1–2).

[4] See Jan Hoffman, "This 'Quarrel' Spans the Ages," *New York* Times, November 15, 1992: B21. Indeed one month prior to *The Quarrel*'s first PBS broadcast, allusion was made to official Canadian response to the nascent NAFTA by a *New York Times* headline which read, "Canada's Quarrel with NAFTA" (October 30, 1993: 20).

[5] Mussarism is a sect of post–Enlightenment Hasidism that practices a Christian-like asceticism and strict adherence to religious proscriptions while recommending pragmatic adjustment to modern conditions through a controlled combination of secular study with the traditional, isolationist regimen (N. Menes, "Yeshivas in Russia," in Jacob Frumkin et al., eds., *Russian Jewry [1860–1917]*, trans. Mirra Ginsburg [New York: Thomas Yoseloff, 1966], 382–407; and Raphael Mahler, *Hasidism and the Jewish Enlightenment: Their Confrontation in Galicia and Poland in the First Half of the Nineteenth Century*,

trans. Eugen Orenstein et al. [Philadelphia: Jewish Publication Society of America, 1985]). Mussarism has as such been compared to modern evangelical Christianity (Eric Gormly, "Evangelical Solidarity with the Jews: A Veiled Agenda? A Qualitative Content Analysis of Pat Robertson's 700 Club Program," *Review of Religious Research* 46, no. 3 [2005], 258). *Musar* means "moral admonishment" or "chastisement" as well as "instruction" or "discipline" (David Landau, *Piety and Power: The World of Jewish Fundamentalism* [New York: Hill and Wang, 1993]).

[6] Stephen Holden, "On Faith and Reason and the Holocaust," *New York Times*, November 4, 1993: C22; Pat Donnelly, "Montréal-made *Quarrel* Is Rough Going Despite an Excellent Cast," *Montreal Gazette*, April 4, 1992: H3; and Johanna Steinmetz, "In 'Quarrel' Conversation Dominates," *Chicago Tribune*, October 23, 1992: J.

[7] Ray Loynd, "*The Quarrel* Frames the Debate on the Holocaust," *Los Angeles Times*, November 29, 1993: F10; Hoffman, "This 'Quarrel' Spans the Ages"; Garth Wolkoff, "*The Quarrel*: A Film Whose Argument Is with God," *Northern California Jewish Bulletin*, August 27, 1993: 33; Belinda Greenberg, "Belief System," *Baltimore Jewish Times*, February 19, 1993: 83; Michael Wilmington, review of *The Quarrel*, *Los Angeles Times*, November 24, 1992: 1; Jerry Tallmer, review of *The Quarrel*, *New York Post*, November 4, 1992: 31; and "Cohen's *The Quarrel* Focuses on More Than a Fight," *The Jewish Advocate*, February 25, 1993: 12.

[8] Mention of *The Quarrel* is missing, for instance, from Joseph I. Donohoe, ed., *Essays on Quebec Cinema* (East Lansing: Michigan State University Press, 1991); George Melnyk, *One Hundred Years of Canadian Cinema* (Toronto: University of Toronto Press, 1994); Janis L. Pallister, *The Cinema of Quebec: Masters in Their Own House* (Teaneck, NJ and Madison, WI: Fairleigh Dickinson University Press / London: Associated University Press, 1995); Eugene P. Walz, ed., *Canada's Best Features: Critical Essays on 15 Canadian Films* (Amsterdam: Rodopi, 2002).

[9] See Conrad Black, *Duplessis* (Toronto: McClelland and Stewart, 1977); Pierre Laporte, *The True Face of Duplessis* (Montreal: Harvest House, 1960); and Cameron Nish, trans. and ed., *Québec in the Duplessis Era, 1935–1959: Dictatorship or Democracy?* (Toronto: Copp Clark, 1970).

[10] Noel Burch, *Theory of Film Practice*, 71–72.

[11] Tekiner, *Anti–Zionism*; Berger, "Zionist Ideology," 14–19.

[12] Selzer, *Aryanization of the Jewish State*, 54; see also Uri Davis, *Israel: An Apartheid State* (London: Zed, 1987).

[13] Henry Berkowitz et al., "A Statement to the Peace Conference," in Tekiner, *Anti–Zionism*, 341–49.

[14] See Christina von Braun, "*Blutschande*: From Incest Taboo to the Nuremberg Racial Laws," in *Encountering the Other(s): Studies in Literature, History, and Culture*, ed. Gisela Brinker-Gabler (Albany: State University of New York Press, 1995); and Benzion Netanyahu, *The Origins of the Inquisition in Fifteenth Century Spain* (New York: Random House, 1995). See also Christine Caldwell Ames, "Does Inquisition Belong to Religious History?" *The American Historical Review* 110, no. 1 (2005), http://www.historycooperative.org/journals/ahr/110.1/ames.html.

[15] Weiss, *Ideology of Death*, 44–46, 55–56; Lawrence D. Kritzman, ed., *Auschwitz and After: Race, Culture, and "the Jewish Question" in France* (London: Routledge, 1995);

Pierre Birnbaum, "Between Social and Political Assimilation: Remarks on the History of the Jews in France," in *Paths of Emancipation: Jews, States, and Citizenship*, eds. Birnbaum and Ira Katznelson (Princeton, NJ: Princeton University Press, 1995), 94–127; and Arthur Hertzberg, *The French Enlightenment and the Jews: The Origins of Modern Anti–Semitism* (New York: Schocken, 1970).

[16] The most egregious and inflammatory examples of this claim are Phyllis Chesler, *The New Anti–Semitism: The Current Crisis and What We Must Do about It* (San Francisco: Jossey-Bass, 2003); and Alan A. Dershowitz, *The Case for Israel* (Hoboken, NJ: John Wiley and Sons, 2003). Trenchant critiques include Finkelstein, *Beyond Chutzpah*; Michael Neumann, *The Case Against Israel* (Petrolia, CA: CounterPunch / Oakland, CA: AK Press, 2005); and Brian Klug, "The Myth of the New Anti–Semitism: Reflections on Anti–Semitism, Anti–Zionism, and the Importance of Making Distinctions," *The Nation*, February 2, 2004: 23–29.

[17] Leon Poliakov, *The History of Anti–Semitism*, vol. 2: *From Mohammed to the Marranos*, trans. Natalie Gerardi (New York: Vanguard, 1973); and Robert J. Brym, *The Jewish Intelligentsia and Russian Marxism: A Sociological Study of Radicalism and Ideological Divergence* (New York: Schocken, 1978).

[18] Cf. Gershom G. Scholem, *Major Trends in Jewish Mysticism* (New York: Schocken, 1971).

[19] Benjamin Beit-Hallahmi, *Original Sins: Reflections on the History of Zionism and Israel* (New York: Pantheon, 1987), 137–52; Seth Farber, *Radicals, Rabbis and Peacemakers: Conversations with Jewish Critics of Israel* (Monroe, ME: Common Courage, 2005), 194–212; and Jews Not Zionists Home Page, http://www.jewsnotzionists.org.

[20] E.g., Yaffa Eliach, *Hasidic Tales of the Holocaust* (New York: Vintage, 1982).

[21] Shahak and Mezvinsky, *Jewish Fundamentalism in Israel*, 23–54; William Shaffir, "Separation from the Mainstream in Canada: The Hassidic Community of Tash," in *The Jews in Canada*, eds. Robert J. Brym et al. (Toronto: Oxford University Press, 1993), 126–41; Ian S. Lustick, *For the Land and for the Lord*; and Jeremy Stolow, "Transnationalism and the New Religio-Politics: Reflections on a Jewish Orthodox Case," *Theory, Culture and Society* 21, no. 2 (2004): 112, 115–19, 121, 123, 127.

[22] Dov Schwartz, "The Quadrapartite Division of the Intellect in Medieval Jewish Thought," *The Jewish Quarterly Review* 84, nos. 1–2 (1993–94): 227–36; Abraham Cohen, *Everyman's Talmud* (New York: E. P. Dutton, 1949); Jacob Neusner, *Talmudic Thinking: Language, Logic, Law* (Columbia: University of South Carolina Press, 1992); and Peter Ochs, "From *Peshat* to *Derash* and Back Again: Talmud for the Modern Religious Jew," *Judaism* 46, no. 3 (1997): 271–92.

[23] For a historical mapping of this axiology, see Halevi, *A History of the Jews*; for analyses of the intereffectivity of Judaic and Islamic hermeneutics, see G. R. Hawting and Abdul-Kader A. Shareef, *Approaches to the Qur'ān* (London: Routledge, 1993); of Judaism and Hellenism, see Moses Hadas, *Hellenistic Culture: Fusion and Difference* (New York: W. W. Norton, 1959); and of Christian and Buddhist hermeneutics, see A. S. Cua, *Ethical Argumentation: A Study in Hsūn Tzu's Moral Epistemology* (Honolulu: University of Hawaii Press, 1985).

---

[24] E.g., Abba Hillel Silver, *Where Judaism Differs*; Cohen, *Myth*; and Lamm, *Jewish Way in Death and Mourning.*

[25] Whitelam, *Invention of Ancient Israel*, 28, 58–70; Ellis, *Unholy Alliance*; Boaz Evron, *Jewish State or Israeli Nation?* (Bloomington: Indiana University Press, 1995); Sha'ban, *For Zion's Sake*; and Michael Warschawski, "The Jews and the Global War," *News from Within* 23, no. 1 (2007): 23–24

[26] Louis Jacobs, *The Talmudic Argument: A Study in Talmudic Reasoning and Methodology* (Cambridge: Cambridge University Press, 1984); and Meir Sternberg, *The Poetics of Biblical Narration: Ideological Literature and the Drama of Reading* (Bloomington: Indiana University Press, 1985).

[27] In Hebrew one refers to *vedok* [to continue the matter], *teko* [a problem without a solution], and *kushia* [an argument threatening to resolve a controversy]. Not surprisingly, the literal meaning of *halakhah* is "walking"; and the conclusion of a Talmudic benediction is described as a *chatimah*, meaning "eulogy" (Steinsaltz, *Essential Talmud*, 248, 273; Lawrence Hoffman, *Beyond the Text* [Bloomington: Indiana University Press, 1987], 87).

[28] R. C. Mortimer, "Moral Theology," in MacQuarrie, *Dictionary of Christian Ethics*, 218; also R. M. Hare, "Ethics," in MacQuarrie op cit., 114–16.

[29] Waddams, "Ascetical Theology," in MacQuarrie, *Dictionary of Christian Ethics*, 18–19.

[30] Slajoj Žižek, "Revenge of Global Finance," *In These Times*, June 20, 2005: 33.

[31] See Steven D. Fraade, "Navigating the Anamalous: Non-Jews at the Intersection of Early Rabbinic Law and Narrative," in Silberstein and Cohen, *The Other in Jewish Thought and History*, 159–60 n.4; David Biale et al., eds., *Insider/Outsider: American Jews and Multiculturalism* (Berkeley: University of California Press, 1998). It is useful in this context to mention that *drash* means literally "search," "inquiry," or "investigation" (Susan A. Handelman, *The Slayer of Moses: The Emergence of Rabbnic Interpretation in Modern Literary Theory* [Albany: State University of New York Press, 1982], 44).

[32] Susannah Heschel, "Revolt of the Colonized: Abraham Geiger's *Wissenschaft des Judentums* as a Challenge to Christian Hegemony in the Academy," *New German Critique* 77 (1999): 61–85.

[33] George Orwell, *1984* (1949; repr., New York: Signet/Penguin, 1977), 35, 212, 214. Orwell used this phraseology famously in the context of describing the modality of *doublethink* known as *crimestop.*

[34] See Sander L. Gilman, *Smart Jews: The Construction of the Image of Jewish Superior Intelligence* (Lincoln: University of Nebraska Press, 1996). It is not surprising to discover this narrative on the Right, but it may also be found in Left-oriented texts such as Nafeez Mosaddeq Ahmed, *The War on Freedom: How and Why America Was Attacked, September 11th, 2001* (Joshua Tree, CA: Tree of Life, 2002), 370 n.701, 382; Lance Selfa, "Zionism: False Messiah," in *The Struggle for Palestine* (London: Haymarket, 2002), 2–19; and Leon, *The Jewish Question.* These texts of the Left rehearse an albeit secular christology that denies class, race, and gender divisions within historical Jewish communities, thus reaffirming a monolithic Jewish "otherness" of which intellectual acumen is a perceived common characteristic.

---

[35] See Stolow, "Transnationalism," 114–16, 126; also Wagner, "Marching to Zion"; Sizer, *Christian Zionism*; and Mouly, "Israel's Christian Comforters." Compare Tariq Ali, *The Clash of Fundamentalisms: Crusades, Jihads and Modernity* (London: Verso, 2002).

[36] Samuel H. Dresner, "Hasidism and Its Opponents," in *Great Schisms in Jewish History*, eds. Raphael Jospe and Stanley M. Wagner (Denver: Center for Judaic Studies / New York: KTAV Publishing House, 1981), 127; also Steinsaltz, *Essential Talmud*.

[37] Quoted in Stolow, "Transnationalism," 129.

[38] Erskine Childers, "The Wordless Wish: From Citizens to Refugees," in *The Transformation of Palestine: Essays on the Origin and Development of the Arab–Israeli Conflict*, ed. Ibrahim Abu-Lughod (Evanston, IL: Northwestern University Press, 1971), 166, 170–71; also Jansen, *Zionism, Israel and Asian Nationalism*, 133–41. Jansen refers to "the [Zionist] policy of flexible and opportunistic vagueness" (133).

[39] This should not to be confused with denying the existence of God, which in Judaism is a logical impossibility that is otherwise beside the point. As Rabbi Eliezer said, "'Repent one day before your death.' Whereupon his disciples asked: 'How does one know which day that is?' 'Exactly,' answered the Sage, 'for that reason we ought to live every day as though it were our last,'" quoted in Sidney S. Greenberg, *A Treasury of Comfort* (Hollywood, CA: Melvin Powers, 1954), 191.

[40] The relevant passage reads: "We know, O Lord, that Thy judgment is righteous: Thou art justified when Thou speaketh, and pure when Thou judgest, and it is not for us to murmur at Thy method of judging. Just are Thou, O Lord, and righteous are Thy judgments," quoted in Lamm, *Jewish Way in Death and Mourning*, 63. For Talmudic elaborations of the Jewish concept of "judgment," particularly regarding death, see tractates Sotah 22a and Ketubot 105a–6a.

[41] Adorno, *Aesthetic Theory*, 117.

[42] Regarding the collusion between Christian and Jewish Zionism, see Gormly, "Evangelical Solidarity with the Jews," 259 and passim. For the relationship between *Haskalah* philosophies and emergent Zionism, see Massad, "Persistence of the Palestinian Question," 3–4, 8, 20 n.23.

[43] Bram Mertens, "*The Arcades Project*: A Talmud for Our Times," *New Formations* 54 (2004–05): 64–65.

[44] Adorno, *Aesthetic Theory*, 116, 310–11; also Clark, "Should Benjamin Have Read Marx?" 42–43.

[45] See Neusner, *Judaism in the Matrix of Christianity* (Philadelphia: Fortress, 1986).

[46] Burch, *Theory of Film Practice*, 90–101.

[47] Christian Metz, *Film Language: A Semiotics of Cinema*, trans. Michael Taylor (Chicago: University of Chicago Press, 1974), also Metz, "Aural Objects," trans. Georgia Gurrieri, *Yale French Studies* 60 (1980): 24–32.

[48] Burch, *Theory of Film Practice*, 88.

[49] James, *Allegories of Cinema*, 31.

[50] Cf. Theodor W. Adorno and Hans Eisler, *Composing for the Films* (1947; repr., London: Athlone, 1994).

[51] See the autobiography of post–Spinozean Jewish philosopher, Salomon Maimon, perhaps the earliest philosopher of this vein of immanentism (*Salomon Maimon: An*

Autobiography, trans. J. Clark Murray [1973; repr., Urbana and Chicago: University of Illinois Press, 2001]). See also Siegfried Kracauer, *The Mass Ornament: Weimar Essays*, trans. and ed. Thomas Y. Levin (1963; repr., Cambridge, MA and London: Harvard University Press, 1995), 259–64 for an illustrative critique.

[52] David Chennels, *The Politics of Nationalism in Canada* (Toronto and London: University of Toronto Press, 2001), 166.

[53] Stolow, "Transnationalism," 125.

[54] See Kibbey, *Theory of the Image*, 149.

[55] See Hoffman, *Beyond the Text*, 108–9.

[56] Benjamin, *Arcades Project*, 473; Marx, *Capital*; and Sayer, *The Violence of Abstraction*.

[57] Adorno, *Aesthetic Theory*, 260–61) "To settle an argument" is one interpretation of the Hebrew word for Zionist settlement, *yishuv*, meaning literally "to settle" (Naseer H. Aruri, "Anti–Zionism: A Democratic Alternative," in Tekiner, *Anti–Zionism*, 35).

[58] See Yehuda Liebes, "Christian Influences on the *Zohar*," in *Studies in the Zohar*, trans. Arnold Schwartz et al. (Albany: State University of New York Press, 1993), 139–61; Moshe Idel, *Hasidism: Between Ecstasy and Magic* (Albany: State University of New York Press, 1995), 16; and K. Kogen, "The Meaning of the *Minyan*," in *Understanding Jewish Mysticism: A Source Reader; The Merkabah Tradition and the Zoharic Tradition*, ed. David R. Blumenthal (New York: KTAV Publishing House, 1978), 146–60. Cf. Jonathan Boyarin, "Death and the Minyan," in *Thinking in Jewish* (Chicago and London: University of Chicago Press, 1996), 63–86. As Judaic scholar Lawrence Fine reminds, the kabbalistic interpretation of quotidian paths to *tikkun ha-olam* is cosmic rather than materialist (Fine, "Purifying the Body in the Name of the Soul: The Problem of the Body in Sixteenth-Century Kabbalah," in *People of the Body: Jews and Judaism from an Embodied Perspective*, ed. Fine [Albany: State University of New York Press, 1992], 133–34). In the kabbalistic tradition, the *shekhinah* is a volatile, feminine force comprised of fideistic shards left over from an originary cosmic blast. This blast was supposedly caused when its theophanous vector, the "godhead," became disenchanted by the worldly imperfection [*sitra ha-ra*] it attributed to its own feminine aspect [*nuqba*] and its perceived evil inclination [*yetzer ha-ra*]. (*Nuqba* should not be confused with the etymologically related Arabic term, *nakba*, which means "disaster" and is used by Palestinians to refer to the ethnic cleansing of their lands by Zionist forces during the 1948 Israeli war of independence.) On this mystical view, man's [sic] ethical task is to separate the *shekhinah* from its *yetzer ha-ra*, thought responsible for "infirmities" such as infertility and effeminacy. This separation, a Jewish phenomenological *epōkhe*, can be accomplished by performing *mitzvot* and adhering to *halakhah*. In turn the *shekhinah* may be reconnected to the good inclination [*yetzer ha-tov*], believed inaccessible to women, whereupon the purified shards may be sewn into a state of divine restoration [*tiferet*]. In this context, the meaning of *tikkun ha-olam*, "the mending of the world," becomes salient. Understood thusly, *tiferet* is a homosocial condition: it is attainable only by men, but it is characterized by feminine qualities associated with the purified *nuqba*, such as beauty, tutelage, and soulicality. These qualities render its condition analogous to the Greek *agapē*, or brotherly love, whose female negation is considered obscene, degenerate, and deadly. See Adolphe Franck, *The Religious Philosophy of the Jews*,

trans. John C. Wilson (Secaucus, NJ: Citadel, 1967); Israel Gutwirth, *The Kabbalah and Jewish Mysticism* (New York: Philosophy Library, 1987); Scholem, *Kabbalah*, 16–19; Z'ev ben Shimon Halevi, *School of Kabbalah* (London: Gateway, 1985); Siegmund Hurwitz, *Lilith—The First Eve: Historical and Psychological Aspects of the Dark Feminine*, trans. Gela Jacobson (Einsiedeln: Daimon, 1992); Joseph Dan, "Samael, Lilith, and the Concept of Evil in Early Kabbalah," in *Essential Papers on Kabbalah*, ed. Lawrence Fine (New York and London: New York University Press, 1995), 172; Louis I. Newman, *The Hasidic Anthology: Tales and Teachings of the Hasidim* (London: Jason Aronson, 1987), 415; Lawrence A. Hoffman, *Covenant of Blood: Circumcision and Gender in Rabbinic Judaism* (Chicago and London: University of Chicago Press, 1996), 70; Elliot R. Wolfson, "Beautiful Maiden without Eyes: *Peshat* and *Sod* in Zoharic Hermeneutics," in *The Midrashic Imagination: Jewish Exegesis, Thought, and History*, ed. Michael Fishbane (Albany: State University of New York Press, 1993), 155–203; idem., *Circle in the Square: Studies in the Use of Gender in Kabbalistic Symbolism* (Albany: State University of New York Press, 1995); idem., "On Becoming Female: Crossing Gender Boundaries in Kabbalistic Ritual and Myth," in *Gender and Judaism: The Transformation of the Tradition*, ed. T. M. Rudovsky (New York and London: New York University Press, 1995), 209–28; Daniel Boyarin, "Lusting after Learning: The Torah as 'The Other Woman'," in *Carnal Israel: Reading Sex in Talmudic Culture* (Berkeley: University of California Press, 1993), 134–66; and Schindler, *Hasidic Responses*, 145 n.64. Not surprisingly, in the *haredi* worldview, *tiferet* is the condition of reconstituted Jewish "rabbinocentric" authority, the historically oppressive sex-gender politics of which, along with those of the *shekhinah*, I shall elucidate below (Stolow, "Transnationalism," 111, 120). For Jewish feminist critiques of this worldview, see Susannah Heschel, ed., *On Being a Jewish Feminist: A Reader* (New York: Schocken, 1995); Judith Hauptman, "Feminist Perspectives on Rabbinic Texts," in *Feminist Perspectives on Jewish Studies*, eds. Lynn Davidman and Shelly Tenenbaum (New Haven and London: Yale University Press, 1994), 40–61; and Daniel Boyarin, "Rabbinic Resistance to Male Domination: A Case in Talmudic Cultural Poetics," in *Interpreting Judaism in a Postmodern Age*, ed. Steven Kepnes (New York and London: New York University Press, 1996), 118–41.

[59] Irving Abella, *None Is Too Many: Canada and the Jews of Europe, 1933–38* (Toronto: Lester and Orpen Dennys, 1982); and Yahil, *The Holocaust*, 617.

[60] Black, *Duplessis*; also Serge Bernier, "French Canadians in the Canadian Armed Forces," in *The Second Quebec Conference Revisited: Waging War, Formulating Peace; Canada, Great Britain, and the United States, 1944–1945*, ed. David B. Woolner (New York: St. Martin's 1998), 198–99; and John Bartlet Brebner, *North Atlantic Triangle: The Interplay of Canada, They United States and Great Britain* (1945; repr., New York: Russell and Russell, 1970), 306, 312.

[61] Marilyn F. Nefsky, "The Shadow of Evil: Nazism and Canadian Protestantism," in *Antisemitism in Canada: History and Interpretation*, ed. Alan Davies (Waterloo, ON: Wilfred Laurier University Press, 1992), 197–225.

[62] Jacques Langlais and David Rome, *Jews and French Quebecers: Two Hundred Years of Shared History*, trans. Barbara Young (Waterloo, ON: Wilfred Laurier University Press, 1991).

[63] Brebner, *North Atlantic Triangle*, 279–80; W. A. B. Douglas and Brereton Greenhous, *Out of the Shadows: Canada and the Second World War* (Oxford: and Toronto: Oxford University Press, 1977), 38–58; and Galen Rogers Perras, *Franklin Roosevelt and the Origins of the Canadian-American Security Alliance, 1943–1945; Necessary but Not Necessary Enough* (Westport, CT: Praeger, 1998).

[64] Louis Rosenberg, *Canada's Jews: A Social and Economic Study of Jews in Canada* (1939; repr., Montreal and Kingston: McGill-Queens University Press,1993); Douglas and Greenhous, *Out of the Shadows*, 235; J. English, "Atlanticism at High Tide: The Québec Conference of 1944," in Woolner, *Second Quebec Conference Revisited*, 110; Chennels, *Politics of Nationalism in Canada*, 173, 175.

[65] Douglas and Greenhous, *Out of the Shadows*, 272–73.

[66] Chennels, *Politics of Nationalism in Canada*, 165–67; Michael Brown, *Jew or Juif? Jews, French and Anglo-Canadians, 1759–1914* (Philadelphia: Jewish Publication Society, 1986); Pierre Anctil, "Interlude of Hostility: Judeo-Christian Relations in Quebec in the Interwar Period," in Davies, *Antisemitism in Canada*, 135–65; and Brym, *The Jews in Canada*.

[67] Rebecca Posner, "Ashkenazi, Sephardi, Québécois: Jewish Politics in Multicultural Canada," in *The Narrow Bridge: Jewish Views on Multiculturalism* (New Brunswick, NJ: Rutgers University Press, 1996), 73–85; and Katherine O'Sullivan See, *First World Nationalisms: Class and Ethnic Politics in Northern Ireland and Québec* (Chicago and London: University of Chicago Press, 1986).

[68] Langlais and Rome, *Jews and French Quebecers*; and Posner, "Ashkenazi, Sephardi, Québécois."

[69] Laporte, *True Face of Duplessis*; and Nish, *Québec in the Duplessis Era*.

[70] See Gerson Weiler, *Jewish Theocracy* (Leiden: E. J. Brill, 1988).

[71] Cf. Nathan Weinstock, *Zionism: False Messiah*, trans. and ed. Alan Adler (London: Ink Links, 1979).

[72] Rachel Biale, *Women and Jewish Law: The Essential Texts, Their History, and Their Relevance for Today*, 2nd ed. (New York: Schocken, 1995); Judith Romney Wegner, *Chattel or Person? The Status of Women in the Mishnah* (New York: Oxford University Press, 1988); Daniel Boyarin, *Unheroic Conduct: The Rise of Heterosexuality and the Invention of the Jewish Man* (Berkeley and Los Angeles: University of California Press, 1996); Rebecca Alpert, *Like Bread on the Seder Plate: Jewish Lesbians and the Transformation of Tradition* (New York and London: Columbia University Press, 1997); and Judith Plaskow and Donna Berman, *The Coming of Lilith: Essays on Feminism, Judaism, and Sexual Ethics, 1972–2003* (Boston: Beacon, 2005).

[73] Cf. Edward Alexander, "A Dialogue of the Mind with Itself: Chaim Grade's Quarrel with Hersh Rasseyner," in *The Resonance of Dust: Essays on Holocaust and Literature* (Columbus: Ohio State University Press, 1979), 233–47. See also Martin Buber, *Tales of the Hasidim*, vol. 2, *The Later Masters* (New York: Schocken, 1948); idem., "Spinoza, Sabbatai Zevi, and the Baalshem," in *Hasidism*, trans. Gert Hort (New York: Philosophical Library, 1948), 95–116; idem., *I and Thou*, 2nd ed., trans. Ronald Gregor Smith (New York: Scribner, 1958); and L. S. Dembo, *The Monological Jew: A Literary Study* (Madison: University of Wisconsin Press, 1988).

[74] Sidra DeKoven Ezrahi, *By Words Alone: The Holocaust in Literature* (Chicago and London: University of Chicago Press, 1980), 111.

[75] E.g., Géza Vermès, *Jesus the Jew: A Historian's Reading of the Gospels* (London: William Collins, 1973); cf. Kracauer, *Mass Ornament*, 263–64. This essentializing dialectic obscures the historical fact that, among other things, patriarchal control of gender and sexuality is as much a phenomenon of secular Jewish nationalism as of *haredi* anti–nationalism, and that its determinants are not correctly ascribable to the "Jewish" per se. In fact Judaism is neither more nor less patriarchal than other religious creeds, and contemporary Jewish ultra-orthodoxy, like the racialist antisemitism that would reject it outright, is a decidedly, though not essentially, modern phenomenon. See Farber, *Radicals, Rabbis and Peacemakers*, 178–93; and Heschel, ed., *On Being a Jewish Feminist: A Reader* (New York: Schocken, 1995), xi–xxviii.

[76] Noa Steimatsky, "Pasolini on Terra Sancta: Towards A Theology of Film," *Yale Journal of Criticism* 11, no. 1 (1998): 239–59; and Sam Rhodie, *The Passion of Pier Paolo Pasolini* (Bloomington and Indianapolis: Indiana University Press, 1995 / London: BFI, 1995).

[77] Cf. Louis M. Epstein, *Sex Laws and Customs in Judaism* (New York: KTAV Publishing House, 1967), 78.

[78] See Sander L. Gilman, *The Jew's Body* (London: Routledge, 1991); also Andrew Hewitt, *Political Inversions: Homosexuality, Fascism, and the Modernist Imaginary* (Stanford, CA: Stanford University Press, 1996); Terri Ginsberg, "Nazis and Drifters: The Containment of (Radical) Sexual Knowledge in Two Italian Neorealist Films," *Journal of the History of Sexuality* 1, no. 2 (1990): 241–61 and "The Violent Lesbian as Fascist Crusade in *Monster*," *Genders* 43 (2006), http://www.genders.org/g43/g43_ginsberg.html. Cf. Klaus Theweleit, *Male Fantasies*, vol. 2: *Male Bodies: Psychoanalyzing White Terror*, trans. Stephen Conway et al. (Minneapolis: University of Minnesota Press, 1987); and Dagmar Herzog, *Sex After Fascism: Memory and Morality in Twentieth-Century Germany* (Princeton, NJ: Princeton University Press, 2005).

[79] See Shahak, *Jewish History, Jewish Religion*. It might be mentioned here that, prior to directing *The Quarrel*, Eli Cohen played the role of John the Baptist in *Jesus* (Peter Sykes and John Krish, U.S.A., 1979), a film produced by the right-wing Christian organization, Genesis Project, and promoted globally by the right-evangelical Protestant organization, Campus Crusade for Christ. In addition, *The Quarrel*'s screenwriter, Joseph Telushkin, is an orthodox rabbi affiliated with CLAL: The National Jewish Center for Jewish Learning and Leadership, an organization of mostly conservative Jewish theologians whose mission is to proselytize "lapsed" Jews. Like Agudat Yisrael and right-evangelical Christian groups, CLAL stakes a popular appeal. See http://www.clal.org. Telushkin also writes an advice column that propagates anti–feminist, anti–glbtq, and right-wing Zionist views.

[80] See Yehuda Liebes, "Myth and Symbol in the Zohar and Lurianic Kabbalah," in Fine, *Essential Papers on Kabbalah*, 228.

[81] Adorno, *Aesthetic Theory*, 318–19. Cf. Sherratt, "Adorno's Aesthetic Conception of Aura."

---

[82] Dresner, "Hasidism and Its Opponents," 133, 149; also Martin Buber, *Tales of the Hasidim*, vol. 1, *The Early Masters*, trans. Olga Marx (1948; repr., New York: Schocken, 1975), 231. A Judaic concept, *devekut* derives from an imperative "to seek the divine name as mimed in the intertext of human practices" (Mahler, *Hasidism and the Jewish Enlightenment*, 11). For a rabbinical source, see Moses Maimonides, *The Guide for the Perplexed*, 2nd ed., trans. M. Friedländer (1204; repr., New York: Dover, 1956), 89–95. For a Jewish mystical elaboration, see Liebes, "Myth and Symbol." Judaic naming as social intertext is exemplified by character names in *The Quarrel*. "Hersh," for instance, may signify any number of famous, often heretical Hasidic rabbis and radical Jewish activists of the eighteenth, nineteenth, even twentieth centuries who were either extremely ascetic, even fanatical, or whose religious or political enthusiasm placed them into danger. The most illustrious of these is Rebbe *Hersh* Eichenstein (Hersh of Zydaczów), who in 1822 was accused of collecting money for Jewish settlements in Palestine and arrested for smuggling Jewish books from Russia into Poland, and who in 1824 was accused by Josef Perl, leader of the *Maskalim*, of fanaticism. Like the fictional Hersh Rasseyner, Hersh Eichenstein was known to have an irrational fear of police and police surveillance and, while financially well-endowed, lived a simple, ascetic life with his religious cohorts. Also of possible intertextual significance are: Rebbe Zevi *Hersh* Mendel, "the Attendant" of Rymanów, who opposed the secularization of Jewish education and culture and, recalling *haredi* military exemption in Israel, fought against special taxes levied on Jews in Poland; Rebbe Zevi *Hirsh* of Zhydatchov, who, like Hersh Rasseyner, was known to valiantly defend his *yeshiva* students while opposing idolization of Torah and wise men [*zaddikim*]; Rebbe Moshe *Hirsch* of the anti–Zionist *haredi* sect, Netorei Karta; and radical political devotees such as *Hirsh* Lekert, head of the Polish-Lithuanian Jewish Bund who was assassinated by a Russian policeman in Bialystok, a major center of Bund activities and Hersh Rasseyner's home town; and *Hersh* Mendel, author of the post–Trotskyist *Memoirs of a Jewish Revolutionary*. One might also mention some similarly positioned but more mainstream figures such as Rabbi *Hirsch* Zvi Chayes of Zolkiew, who was subjected to discrimination despite having been one of only three rabbis to satisfy the requirements of the "New Jewry" ordinance of 1789, which entailed acquiring and teaching secular knowledges to Jews; and *Herz* Homberg, a Jewish supporter of forced Germanization. See Mahler, *Hasidism and the Jewish Enlightenment*; and Buber, *The Later Masters*. Hersh's surname, "Rasseyner," recalls another Hasidic rabbi who, like Hersh, was sustained in his religious enthusiasm by others of his persuasion and was resisted by the secular Jewish community; Rebbe Israel Shulimovich Friedman of *Ruzhin*, whose efforts at circumventing Russian restrictions upon Jewish travel and mobility were supported financially by the mentioned Hersh Eichenstein, and whose denunciation by Josef Perl and subsequent arrest and interment for having ordered the murder of two Jewish informants (the Ushitsa Affair) led to his placement under permanent police surveillance. See Mahler, op cit.; Buber, op cit.; and Schindler, *Hasidic Responses to the Holocaust*. In the spirit of Hersh's Talmudism, Rasseyner also suggests the French word, *renseigner*, which means "to inform," "to inquire," and "to re-teach"; and in view of his extreme socio-cultural conservatism, "Rasseyner" also evokes Paul *Rassinier*, the notorious Holocaust revisionist, and, literally, the English word, "resign."

"Chaim" easily signifies *Chaim* Grade, the Yiddish-language author on whose novella, *My Quarrel With Hersh Rasseyner*, *The Quarrel* is based; *Chaim* Potok, the famous Hasidic author of secular, English-language novels; Chofetz *Chaim*, a founder of *haredism*; *Chaim* Guri, an Israeli literary figure supportive of the right-wing settler movement; *Chaim* Herzog and *Chaim* Weizmann, both formerly presidents of Israel, the former of whom attended the Jerusalem Film Festival screening of *The Quarrel*, which he lauded (Martin, "Canadian Film"), and the latter of whom is still considered one of Israel's Founding Fathers; and *chaim*, the Hebrew word for "life," which Chaim's secular modernism may also signify. "Chaim" also evokes a conceptual dialectic involving the German word, *Heim*, which means "home," and its derivative, *unheimlich*, which means "strange" or "uncanny"—and as such is redolent of Chaim's post–Holocaust subjective alienation. "Kovler" recalls Abba *Kovner*, a Zionist literary figure who was also a Holocaust survivor, underground resistance and rescue operator, and propagandist for the Haganah.

"Freda" evokes the English word, "freedom," the French word *fredain*, which means "prank," and the German word, *Frieden*, which means "peace"—all of which have been associated with the function and significance of Woman in patriarchy. In that vein, it also evokes the well-known feminist, Betty *Friedan*.

"Solomon" and "Rosenberg" might each signify topics that, like Rosenberg's political and sex-gender encoding, transgress *halakhah*. "Solomon" recalls King *Solomon* of the Bible, which while not in itself transgressive, prefigures Hersh's ironic remark to Chaim, "You would accuse me of being king?" which evokes the paradox of leadership in Jewish history (see Whitelam, *Invention of Ancient Israel*, 135). "Rosenberg" evokes Julius and Ethel *Rosenberg*, who during the McCarthy Era were, along with glbtqs, judged collaborators with a foreign power; and Alfred *Rosenberg*, the notorious Nazi ideologue whose ostensibly Jewish surname resonates to the duplicity ascribed prejudicially to both Jews and homosexuals. "Yeshia" (a.k.a. "Isaiah"/"Joshua") recalls several extremist persons and organizations in Jewish history: the messianic Biblical prophet and the heroic Biblical warrior of precise namesakes; Yeshua, the Hebrew name for Jesus; Rabbi *Yeshayahu* Karelitz, a founder of Hasidism; Rabbi Abraham *Yehoshua* Heschel of Apt, a strict and judicious Hasid who, like Yeshia, is known to have idolized his rebbes (he is also known to have referred to Israel of Ruzhin, one of Hersh's namesakes, as a "king in Israel"); and the *Yesha* Council, a leading Jewish settler organization in Israel/Palestine. "Yeshia" also recalls *Yeshua* Haben, a late medieval Jewish custom of celebrating on the night preceding a circumcision, a Jewish ritual whose racialist significance is invoked by the Yeshia scene; as well as the Biblical references in Genesis 6:10 and Isaiah to *teshuvah* [return/repentance], with which the messianic Yeshia is also associated semiologically.

Even the film's title carries intertextual significance. Its first letter, "Q," is also the first letter of *Q*uébec, the film's setting, and of the word, "*q*uestion," its proairetic impetus.

Finally, two names referred to but not represented by actual characters also carry semiological weight: "Pesha," Hersh's late wife, recalls both *peshat*, the literal-explicative register of Judaic hermeneutics; and *Pzhysha*, a school of Hasidism (the "Yehudi") known for the unorthodox practices of its founder, Rebbe Yaakov Yitzhak, who, like Hersh vis-à-vis Chaim, was plagued by a quarrel with the leader (the "Seer") of another, less eccentric school of Judaic thought (the Lubliners), and who was so convinced of the imminence of the messianic advent that he resisted socially tolerant modes of Talmudic inquiry in favor of extreme *hilukim*; and "Goldstein," a prewar friend of Chaim and Hersh who died in the Holocaust and shares the surname of *The Quarrel*'s musical composer, Michael *Goldstein*, which also recalls Emmanuel *Goldstein*, the Trotsky prototype in *1984* who is assassinated for ideological "heresy" but whose writings are appropriated for their theory of social control (which the Party has adopted) while also yielding a lesson in emancipatory praxis (which the Party has suppressed).

[83] Jean-Louis Baudry, "Ideological Effects of the Basic Cinematographic Apparatus," trans. Alan Williams, *Film Quarterly* 28, no. 2 (1974–75): 39–47; and Jean-Louis Comolli, "Technique and Ideology: Camera, Perspective, Depth of Field," Pt. 1, *Film Reader* 2 (1977); and idem., Pts. 3–4, in *Narrative, Apparatus, Ideology*, ed. Philip Rosen, trans. Diana Matias et al. (New York: Columbia University Press, 1986), 421–33.

[84] Selzer, *Aryanization of the Jewish State*; and Shohat, "Sephardim in Israel." According to R. L. Barsh, Inuits and Crees ["Eskimos"] have become the primary ethnic "barterballs" of the contemporary Anglo–Québécois conflict ("Re-imagining Canada: Aboriginal Peoples and Québec Competing for Legitimacy as Emergent Nations," paper presented at the New York Institute for Law and Society, 1995). Regarding the ethnic politics of Québécoise labor, see Sheilagh Hodgkins Milner and Henry Milner, *The Decolonization of Québec: An Analysis of Left-Wing Nationalism* (Toronto: McLelland and Stewart, 1973); Brian Young and John Alexander Dickinson, *A Short History of Quebec: A Socio-Economic History*, 3rd ed. (Montreal: McGill-Queens University Press, 2003); and Jacques Rouillard, "Haro sur le fascisme: La foundation de la Fédération provinciale du travail du Québec, 1938," *Canadian Historical Review* 71, no. 3 (1990): 346–74.

[85] See Yehoshafat Harkabi, *Israel's Fateful Hour*, trans. Lenn Schramm (New York: Harper and Row, 1988); and Shahak and Mezvinsky, *Jewish Fundamentalism in Israel*.

[86] Jansen, *Zionism, Israel and Asian Nationalism*, 26, 30, 71–72; Taylor, *Zionist Mind*, 45–46.

[87] See Dominique Clift, *Québec Nationalism in Crisis* (Kingston and Montreal: McGill-Queens University Press, 1982); and Paul Piccone, "Secession or Reform: The Case of Canada," *Telos* 106 (1996): 15–63.

CHAPTER FOUR

ENTRE NOUS AND THE EROTICS
OF HISTORICAL ERASURE

> Even in a legendary better future, art could not disavow
> remembrance of accumulated horror; otherwise its form would
> be trivial.
>
> —Adorno, "Paralipomena," *Aesthetic Theory*

In 1983, *Entre Nous* opened to international acclaim across Europe and, a
year later, North America. Distributed first in France and other Western
Francophone regions such as Belgium and Québec under the title, *Coup de
foudre* (literally, "thunderbolt"; figuratively, "love at first sight"), and in the
U.K. as *At First Sight*, *Entre Nous* presented French director Diane Kurys'
cinematic rendition of the dissolution of her parents' marriage and her mother's
entry into an erotically charged, commercially lucrative bond with a woman
seven years after her parents' return to France from Italy, where, as Jews, they
had hidden from the Nazis and their Vichy collaborators under the Sephardic
name, Piperno, for two and one-half years. Unlike her previous film, Prix Louis
Delluc recipient *Diabolo Mentha* ["Peppermint Soda"] (France, 1977), which
was also autobiographical but which focused on the local, suburban, quasi-
provincial French schoolgirl milieu of Kurys' teenage years, *Entre Nous*
explored the more complex, globally extensive, generationally distanced milieu
of her parents' early adulthood, a milieu in which the Kuryses, following their
persecution in the Holocaust, were compelled to begin their lives anew,
eventually building a successful small business and starting a nuclear family in
the provincial city of Lyon. Due partially to this broadened scope, *Entre Nous*
garnered significant press coverage in the U.S. and Canada, where, echoing
French praise for its supposed exemplary aesthetic sensibility, it was lauded as
masterful, mature, accomplished, humane, civilized, enlightening, and
representative of a giant leap forward in French filmmaking. In France, *Entre
Nous* was highly celebrated, winning the 1984 Prix de l'Académie national du
cinéma, and in the U.S., it received a 1983 Academy Award nomination for Best
Foreign Language Film.[1] By way of these rewards, *Entre Nous* was catapulted
to critical heights unprecedented for a female-directed, woman-centered

European film, as it became one of the first of its kind to be recognized and formally rewarded by the Hollywood film industry.[2]

The fact of *Entre Nous'* popular and industry success did not shield it from widespread criticism and debate. At the same time that the film won accolades for its formal accomplishment, dramatic consistency, thematic coherence, and evocative aesthetics (all qualities considered meritorious and praiseworthy on the European/American art cinema circuit), *Entre Nous* sparked a lively and polemical press debate across the North American public sphere. The crux of the debate was the ethical question of whether or not the erotic female bond portrayed in the film represented a socially responsible alternative either to the traditional heterosexual or male homosocial bonding usually depicted in cinema, and whether or not the representation of that alternative, as ambiguous and non-physical, was ideologically consistent with the political agenda of lesbian feminism as this was then gaining acceptance as a topic of public discourse. This debate, which took place across the pages of mainstream North American newspapers and magazines, had a lasting effect on how *Entre Nous* came to be characterized and understood in cultural circles—as a female bonding film, the central problematic of which concerned the sexual orientation of its female relationship and, in turn, the question of what it meant to define such an orientation as "sexual," not to mention "lesbian," in regard to a film which consistently refused to portray that relationship as physically consummated.

Typifying the negative side of the debate was Carole Corbeil, film critic for the *Toronto Globe and Mail*, for whom *Entre Nous'* female bond epitomized the superficiality and elitism of European/American art cinema as well as its social evasiveness:

> There is nothing particularly endearing in having the beautiful Miou Miou and Hiss Huppert run around in beautiful and imaginative retro dresses while bemoaning the stupidity of their husbands. It all seems redundant, somehow, as if a pretty-pretty French art director had thrown a bell-jar over the proceedings. [The film] is unbearably coy, incidentally, on the subject of just how physical this friendship gets. In France, the movie was called *Coup de foudre*; *Entre Nous*, the title of the North American release, desexualizes the friendship [...] What could have been authentic—and there is no doubt in my mind that many spirited women used fashion in the fifties as a springboard to independence, becomes too self-consciously aesthetic. (Corbeil, "Star Quality Burdens *Entre Nous*," *Toronto Globe and Mail*, February 17, 1984: E9)

And while Pauline Kael's review appears sweeping, its frankness makes it the most explicitly political of *Entre Nous'* critiques:

> [*Entre Nous*] has a political commitment to women's friendship, and it comes very close to having a political commitment to lesbian sex [...] but Kurys doesn't develop that. She just keeps it lurking in the air, though the film's title in

France was *Coup de foudre*—love at first sight [...] Léna and Madeleine are what used to be called soul mates; *Entre Nous* is about spiritual lesbianism [...] sexual politics without sex. (Kael, "The Current Cinema," *The New Yorker*, May 3, 1984: 133–34)

The debate over *Entre Nous'* "sexual orientation" inspired a number of critical questions, including those inquiring into its concomitant class orientation and, more formalistically, its cinematic structuring.[3] Despite the intellectual space opened by these questions, an overwhelming discursive focus on the ambiguous figuration of the film's female bond has given the erroneous impression that the question of female relationships per se is central and primary to *Entre Nous*, and that extenuating, potentially more far-reaching questions must be sidelined of how the depiction of such relationships intersect with and come to signify with respect to the non-sexual, non-erotic issues with which the film is also heavily concerned and which compel its broader, more complex characterization as a *Holocaust film*.

This critical exclusion of political and historical questions has been more evident in scholarly than popular press reviews, where one is least likely to find even a mention of the historical-diegetic placement of *Entre Nous'* narrative in Holocaust or post–Holocaust contexts or into associated, political, economic and ideological problematics of (post–)Vichy France. This despite the fact that approximately one-quarter of *Entre Nous'* running time is dedicated to depicting significant events from both women's wartime experiences, which include vivid portrayals of one of the women, Hélène (Léna) Korski (née Weber) [Isabelle Huppert], interned at the Rivesaltes deportation camp, where she, a Jewish Belgian, is rescued from certain shipment to Auschwitz by agreeing to marry one Mordeha Isaac Simon ("Michel") Korski [Guy Marchand], a Jewish-French *légionnaire* not yet subject to Nazi racial decrees; and the other, Madeleine Segara (née Vernier) [Miou-Miou], caught in the midst of a violent shoot-out between *Résistance* fighters and pro-fascist *miliciens*, during which her newlywed husband, Raymond Klinger [Robin Renucci], is killed by a ricocheting bullet, and after which she suffers a debilitating mental breakdown that confines her to convalescence at her parents' country estate for the duration of the war. During this early portion of the film, parallel sequencing suggests a metonymic symmetry between the two women which is then provisionally sutured by their first meeting. Following this meeting, the film traces a narrativized working-through of the ostensibly analogous choices the women have been compelled to make during the war and which now have landed each woman in similarly dissatisfying, indeed stifling, circumstances to which the other seems to hold the crucial, liberatory, and—not insignificantly— entrepreneurial key.

Instead of acknowledging and elaborating these matters and concerns in ways that might at least have called into question the structured symmetry between the women's wartime experiences, not to mention the representation of the Holocaust, the Second World War, Jewish–Christian relations, and internecine Jewish relations, popular press reviews of *Entre Nous* generally provided only abbreviated reference to these matters, usually in the form of supplying background information to the film's plot.[4] Scholarly reviews have effectively replaced these albeit limited references with descriptive analyses and normative criticisms of the film's formal properties (the Kurys *oeuvre*).[5] Even Andrea Weiss' *Vampires and Violets: Lesbians in Film*, which discusses *Entre Nous* amply, oddly cites in relation to it only texts that focused primarily on films *other* than *Entre Nous*, and does so abstractly, as does film scholar Chris Straayer, in formalist terms of the gaze.[6] Any ethical, political, or ideological criticism concomitant with the recognition and critique of the inscription of *history* in the film has been relinquished to the designs of aesthetic and thematic appreciation, often in the form of little more than a patronizing nod.[7]

The progressive absenting by critics of the significance of the women's wartime choices and experiences for the development of their erotic relationship is perhaps as glaring and consistent as is *Entre Nous'* ambiguous sexualization of that relationship itself. In considering it, one comes inevitably to the question of why such an absenting has occurred, for whom, and to what purpose. How is it that a film with such explicit historical-diegetic contextualization of the Holocaust and the Second World War could be received with international acclaim and debated prolifically in the North American public sphere with hardly a mention of how that contextualization ramifies the film's narrative-compositional structure and the erotic female bond which is that structure's thematic locus? How it is, furthermore, that focus on the film's erotic female bond has taken an almost obfuscatory precedence over focus on its historical, including political and ideological aspects *during a period in which serious discussion of female eroticism and lesbianism themselves not only was still marginalized within the mainstream but in which the Holocaust and the Second World War increasingly had become topics of widespread interest and debate?*

Answers to these questions lie first and foremost in the particular way in which *Entre Nous* positions itself as a Holocaust film—that is, how it depicts the Holocaust/Second World War as an irruptive issue of erotic female bonding, and how its portrayal of the erotic female bond comes to figure as a primary and overdetermining signifier of both holocaustal catastrophe, or holocaustality, and a particularly dubious mode of liberation from it. First I must concede that the public debate which developed around *Entre Nous* attests to the fact that it is an atypical Holocaust film: considering its limited depiction of the Holocaust/Second World War in the film's first twenty minutes, it is not wrong to read that aspect as mere background to the film's more obvious portrayal of erotic female friendship, as does, for instance, Carrie Tarr.[8] Indeed only after the narrative shifts from the depiction of the wartime "past" to the postwar "present" does *Entre Nous* become classically dramatic: significant plot interaction between the Korski and Segara families occurs only after the shift, marked by the initial, erotically charged encounter between the women, at which point these women quickly begin to understand their predicaments and start engaging in certain questionable, even unethical practices (lying, cheating, stealing) (fig. 4-1) which soon carry their marriages into ruinous dissolution and their erotic relationship into an uncertain, if promising, even redemptive, entrepreneurial future.

Fig. 4-1 – Léna stealing from cash register in *Entre Nous*

Precisely because this shift and its ensuing emplotment are marked dramatologically by the introduction of an erotic female bond, however, neither its significance nor that of the bond itself can accurately or reasonably be theorized without also to some degree theorizing the historical-diegetic context—the Holocaust and Second World War—in which are situated the initiation of that shift and that bond and against which the latter develops into a simultaneously catastrophic and liberatory relationship. This chapter analyzes the initial encounter between Léna and Madeleine, in which the theoretical connection between their erotic bond and *Entre Nous'* historical discourse on the Holocaust and Second World War is drawn in a paradigmatic and revealing way. This will entail both a narrative-compositional analysis of that particular moment in the film and, in keeping with the theme of past–present relationality, a critical elaboration of the conceptual framework functioning across the film such that its development of erotic female bonding comes to represent and, moreover, epitomize the sort of structural discourse on lesbianism coined aptly but uncritically by Straayer as "hypothetical lesbian narrativity." This discourse ironically reproduces some of the very perspectives associated with the Holocaust and Second World War—antisemitism, economic imperialism, historical fatalism—which many of these critics, especially feminists and lesbian-feminists, would oppose. After all, such perspectives are thought generally to have contributed to the conception and perpetration of Nazi atrocities themselves, including the persecution and murder of lesbians.[9]

* * * * *

Before continuing, however, it is important to review the ways in which the question of *Entre Nous'* past–present thematic have in fact been integrated into the discourse surrounding the film—especially within the popular press debate over the sexual orientation of its erotic female bond. In keeping with a general, implicit recognition of the film's ambiguous figuration of that bond, many reviews of *Entre Nous* have insisted that its sense of the past, while not a central focus, is one of the film's persistent, underlying motifs, a theme that resonates synoptically across its narrative and textual layers and registers tropologically, through varying allegorical modalities, during the film's post–historical portion. As Andrea Weiss has suggested, "Madeleine's and Léna's stories are intercut in such a way as to offer shrewd insight into how the war so profoundly shaped their adult lives and later their relationship with one another."[10] Likewise Maureen Peterson noted that "[t]his tale of 'love at first sight' is inextricably linked to its time in history, the years from 1940–54 [...] In essence these women might well have chosen other mates in other times [...] That fact is important enough to take on an almost symbolic significance."[11] Furthermore Barbara Quart asserted that "wartime upheaval serves [as] easy shorthand, but surely not a necessary one, to explain mismarriage"[12]; and Leo Seligsohn argued, on the contrary, that "It is [...] out of postwar trauma and a need for security and domestic normality that both women wind up settling for the wrong men [...] And Kurys [...] has directed her film with a sensitive eye and ear for things past."[13] In numerous interviews from the time of *Entre Nous'* North American release, Kurys encouraged interpretations of her film which would take into account her parents' experience of the Holocaust. Her written memoir,

Coup de foudre: Le rêve des années 50, co-authored with Olivier Cohen and published shortly after the film's French release, implies that such readings are not to be detached from the ethno-religious and socio-economic aspects of her parents' characters and beliefs as portrayed in the film. In an interview Kurys gave in *Film Comment*, for instance, she refers explicitly to her book's preface, where the legacy of the Holocaust and its effect on her understanding of the "Jewish" are recounted: "Our ambitiousness [that of children of survivors and, generally, Wandering Jews] is a kind of revenge but also a kind of protection against ever becoming the victims our parents were."[14] These encouragements and insistences highlight the theoretical absenting performed by other critics with respect to the film's hermeneutic and philosophical registers, that is, those aspects of its Holocaust discourse, the recognition, acknowledgment, and rigorous analysis of which are crucial to an *anti*–holocaustal comprehension not only of the film but of the Holocaust and Second World War in general.

Indeed crucial to an understanding of *Entre Nous*, its holocaustality and its "hypothetical lesbian narrativity" is a recognition and acknowledgment of one of its outstanding hermeneutic layers, the Judeo-Christian allegorization of Jewish history. This theological layer, I shall argue, serves rather dubiously in the film to subsume the questions *Entre Nous* raises about the Holocaust and French wartime history into a politically disengaged problematic of sexual (non-)expression, the critical glossing of which is implicated in perpetuating the antisemitism associated with the Christian worldview and exploited during the Third Reich to genocidal ends.

The Judeo-Christian interpretation of Jewish history has traditionally lacked accuracy and rigor. Most notorious is its imposition of a teleological reading onto Jewish genealogy, which it maps selectively across the *tanakh* and thereby reduces sophistically to a mystical prefiguration and, in turn, epiphenomenal residue of the christology.[15] In the wake of the European Enlightenment, this Judeo-Christian misinterpretation confined the "Jewish" to theological esoterica and ethno-cultural idiosyncrasy—and, like *Entre Nous*' generalizing portrayal of Jews as Ashkenazim, restricted those designations to Eurocentric terms. As a result, Judaism was theoretically divested of the social-worldly ethic it had developed in the course of its long and varied history and was reinscribed as a faith-based locus of confession and gnosis. The Judeo-Christian misinterpretation mirrors superficially the dialectics of tanakhic narrativity (exile–return) while foreclosing prematurely its structural and performative critiques of moral insularity, social elitism, sacrificial violence, and essential abode. The paradigmatic figure of this dissimulation is the *juif errant*, or, Wandering Jew.[16] During the prior, medieval epoch, this Judeo-Christian myth of inherent Jewish indigence and moral decrepitude as both fated retribution for alleged Jewish culpability for the death of Jesus and fulcrum of redemptive wisdom accrued as a result, became one of the most prevalent and enduring means by which the social cleavage between Jews and Christians would be rationalized.[17] As far back as the post–biblical era, early Roman Christian appropriation of the subtly distinct tanakhic dialectic, derived largely from readings of Isaiah[18] and characterized *inter alia* by an iconic hypostatization of the Talmud's critical, if only provisional undecidability and its interrogative praxis of *le-didakh*, prompted James, reputed patriarch of Catholicism, to proselytize the Jews of Roman Jerusalem by reflexively allegorizing the christic martyrdom to the catastrophic prophecies of *tanakh*. As with later confinements of Judaism to esoterica, these attempts to reconstruct the "Jewish" as at once symmetrical to the "Christian" and transcendent of the material histories of either discourse came to position the "Jewish" as a signifier of perpetual suffering analogous to the (self-)sacrificial trials of Jesus. Ironically, many Jews, especially of lower class status living within oppressive Ashkenazi milieus, would come to adopt this "suffering servant" role in a manner that merely increased their isolation and communal insularity and further limited any collective impulse for social transformation to messianic yearnings and ritual practices (for example, kabbalism). Indeed Jewish history has produced numerous messianisms, including but not limited to christological varieties such as Hasidism and Zionism—all of which, to recall Marx, expressed in mystified form the class-conscious hopes of the oppressed ethno-religious communities.[19] This mystical, self-defeating orientation had an opposite, worldly aspect, however largely absent from Eurocentric histories: whereas the "suffering servant" allegory would eventually be seized upon and co-opted by the Church Fathers as an ideological lynch-pin of Roman imperialism, the Jews of Palestine would revolt against them under the aegis of conquering Persians and commit violent, anti–Christian massacres before once again being subordinated under Byzantine rule.[20] It would take the subsequent Islamic conquest of the Levant to liberate them along with other local oppressed groupings, after which they would live for many centuries in relatively peaceful co-existence and accommodation. Important to my analysis is the fact that, insofar as the Roman (and Byzantine) demonization of the Jews—local converts to Christianity among them including what today are known as the Melkite Christians of Palestine, who for centuries remained unrecognized by either the Catholic or Eastern Orthodox Churches[21]—entailed a reflexive reading practice heavily indebted to Judaic hermeneutics, the Christian allegorization bore the *appearance* of *Jewish* authorship and, in turn, a rhetorical compulsion to Jewish answerability in the form of patronizing tolerance and confessional conversion.[22]

In uncanny consonance with this mythology and its allegory-effects, *Entre Nous* is organized overtly—*precisely by way of its ambiguous female bond*—to affirm the moral reduction of the "Jewish" to a locus of Christian confession; and it is on this basis that the film reconstructs the post–Holocaust era which is its primary diegetic setting as a period of *post*–sacrificial, *post*–confessional, even post–*national* salvation for its Jewish and Christian characters, who henceforth are construed erroneously and, notwithstanding their various class and ethnic differences, as having sustained comparable treatment by the Nazis during the likewise christologically understood Holocaust. Importantly, this is not by any means to criticize *Entre Nous* for its commendable willingness to highlight and draw analogies between the horrific wartime experiences of Jews and Christians. It is only, and crucially, to suggest that, as I shall illustrate, the conceptual framework through which the film makes these analogies serves to distract critical attention from the differing political-ideological explanations of Holocaust history which continue to vie for dominance in many spheres, and in turn to leave insufficiently problematized the dire ideology-effects of those distractions on the primarily Ashkenazi Jews who came in turn to wreak similar havoc on Palestinians, Mizrachim, and other victims of Zionism.[23] In *Entre Nous*' veritable postmillennial construction, the Holocaust is relegated to sublimity, and by characters who, perceiving their respective wartime experiences as symmetrical or at least closely analogous, end up ceaselessly deferring the critical social and self-interrogation necessary to genuine historical mourning-work over those experiences. Instead they engage in the ironically uncritical, socially divisive, self-defeating economy of an erotically charged entrepreneurism—an economy associated less with the facilitation of female bonding than with the large-scale, patriarchal-corporate transnationalism that, at least since the release of *Entre Nous*, has implicated France alongside the U.S. in the implementation of numerous Third World holocausts, not least in cooperation with the "Jewish" State of Israel.[24]

At its most schematic, the film's christo-allegorical structuring may be broken down into the following pattern: 1) a spatio-temporal dislocation of the film's narrative present from its diegetic past; 2) a present-tense sublation of that diegetic past into a (dis)continuous, ambiguous and sometimes disorienting narrative-textual configuration which symptomatizes but does not repair this dislocated quality; and 3) an ideological *re*location of the narrative, thusly disfigured, to its diegetic past, such that any future rearticulation of that past appears only as a highly privatized, imaginal, aestheticized banality, a dissimulation of what ostensibly is meant to pass as its comparative and relative historicization.

The initial meeting between Léna and Madeleine is particularly significant for the narrative's christo-allegoricality, because of its overdetermined structure and the rhetorical function it serves in hyperbolizing the editorial segue between the film's historical-diegetic and present-tense portions, that is, between the

Holocaust and the post–Holocaust portions, or between what might also be called the Jewish-historical and the post–Judaic portions. The meeting therefore stands, especially in view of the latter portion's ambiguity and asymmetricality, not simply as a syntagmatic node of spatio-temporal transition but as a paradigmatic hapax of the erotic female bond's christo-redemptive potentiation.

Apropos of the narrative's complex layering, this paradigmatic quality is discernable at multiple registers. The first of these is the dramatological layer of plot. Several plot discoveries are elicited across the scene concerning what has transpired since the period of Léna's wartime exile in Italy and, concomitantly, Madeleine's "exile" at her parents' home during the period of her nervous breakdown. We learn, for instance, that Léna and Michel not only have survived their exile but have experienced a mildly successful, regenerated life in France. We see an fashionably well-dressed, embourgeoisified Léna, proud of the talents of her two young daughters, Florence [Patricia Champagne] and Sophie [Saga Blanchard], who are performing in a school play, and altruistic enough to oversee the child, René [Guillaume le Guellec], of a complete stranger (who turns out to be Madeleine's husband, Costa [Jean-Pierre Bacri]), although it costs her time. Her acts and deportment reveal no trace of her wartime travails; she is exceedingly gracious and ebullient. We then learn that Madeleine, too, has survived her wartime trauma and now, likewise, is married, but to a man clearly frustrated with her capriciousness and lack of traditional motherly instinct. She no longer dresses in the black mourning clothes she had worn during her "exile" but instead has gone to the opposite extreme, sporting bright colors and styles quite daring for the socially conservative, provincial Lyon (slacks, stockingless legs and feet). Unlike Léna, Madeleine shows little interest in her child while identifying with his shyness and melancholia vis-à-vis an impatient father/husband. She, like Léna, bears no visible scars from her wartime travails, seeming to have overcome them through immersion in a romantic passion for fortune telling and sensual-mystical practices. Still, the rather superficial flightiness she displays throughout the scene toward both René and Léna indicates her more difficult readjustment to postwar, posttraumatic life and elicits an intensity of longing or loss strangely absent from Léna.

As these plot discoveries are elicited, the spatio-temporal framework contextualizing them is destabilized in a manner I suggest is Judeo-Christian in orientation. This second, poetical register emphasizes the scene's paradigmatic quality by contextualizing both an incipient undermining and a prefigurative rationalization of the characterological features and relationship evinced between the women at the plot register, features and relationality which are hence re-organized such that their ostensible symmetry—the analogy they articulate between Léna's and Madeleine's wartime experiences—becomes at once, and in perfect Judeo-Christian fashion, a structural facilitator of the alterior-symbolic repetition of those experiences, and a dissimulation of the ensuing identity reversal which Léna and Madeleine will undergo and which is necessary to that repetition. The series of shots immediately preceding the scene and contextualizing it within the historical diegesis epitomizes, via the device of narrative ellipsis, this christological destabilization and rationale. For this reason, I shall now analyze its formal construction and effectuality before continuing to investigate its effect on the erotic representation of the two women as it develops across the scene into an ostensibly complementary, if asymmetrical trope of christic allegoresis.

At the commencement of this series, a frontal view is presented of the Lyon art academy where Madeleine studied painting and sculpture before the war and is now encountering her wartime lover, Roland Carlier [Patrick Bauchau], who has just been released from a Vichy prison where he was incarcerated for his activities in the *Résistance*. It is V.E.-Day, and rowdy U.S. soldiers dance and drink with locals to blaring Glenn Miller music (fig. 4-2). As the shot continues,

Fig. 4-2 – V.E.-Day celebration in *Entre Nous*

the camera, following the path of a helium balloon released into the air by one of the soldiers, moves parabolically and in a rightward direction into an extended overhead shot of the sky above the celebration (figs. 4-3, 4-4), and it does not regain perspectival equilibrium for several seconds, when it comes to

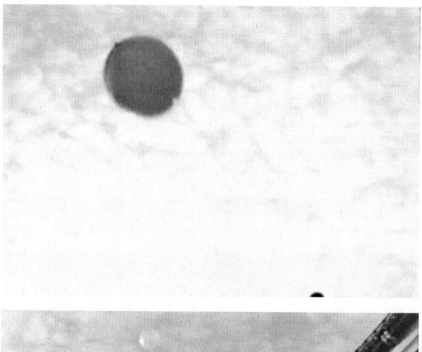

Fig. 4-3 – Parabolic ellipsis, pt. 1, in *Entre Nous*
Fig. 4-4 – Parabolic ellipsis, pt. 2, in *Entre Nous*

Fig. 4-5 – Parabolic ellipsis, pt. 3, in *Entre Nous*
Fig. 4-6 – Elementary school façade in *Entre Nous*

frame what soon is revealed as an elementary school almost identical in architectural structure to that of the art academy just depicted (figs. 4-5, 4-6). During the initial course of the shot, little if any indication is supplied of a spatio-temporal shift: clouds depicted via the vertical pan remain undistorted by any cut, and the sky's color remains constant. As equilibrium is regained, however, an alteration in both the soundtrack and the appearance of two signs, one diegetic, the other non-diegetic, inform us that, despite the initial semblance of continuity, a major contextual shift has occurred. As the camera comes to focus on the elementary school, for example, a sign appears carved into the façade which reads, "*Ecole de Filles*" ["Elementary School" (literally, "School for Girls")], thereby distinguishing the structure from that of the art academy. As the camera comes, after a brief cut, to focus more specifically on a window of the school, furthermore, the parodic singing voice of Maurice Chevalier replaces the celebratory Glenn Miller music, and an intertitle flashes up which reads "Lyon 1952," recalling but altering a much earlier, introductory intertitle, "Pyrenées 1942."

The christo-allegorical quality of this elliptical series becomes especially discernible in view of the peculiarly reflexive way in which it signifies temporal passage. Of course by the very definition of ellipsis, the shot is already imbricated within a certain chronological reflex: on the one hand, it facilitates temporal movement; on the other, it qualifies that movement as movement per se. This strictly formalist sense of the series' reflexivity is trivial, however, when compared to the larger sense associated with its iconographic and semiotic qualities. Only in their regard do the historical and ideological meanings of the temporal passage, necessary to the theological designation of its hermeneutic, become available.

In the first, iconographic instance, the series' unusual parabolic formation and prolonged duration have a noticeable effect on the plot. Dramatic tension is produced over both the fact that time has passed and the reason why such a passage has occurred. Questions are prompted about what actually has transpired since the Korskis' treacherous climb up the Madonna Pass and since Madeleine's mournful showing at the V.E.-Day celebration, and about why, moreover, it has even been necessary to ellipsize rather than depict the periods subsequent to those events. The result is the construction of an enigma, a narrative secret meant to produce suspense and hence suture the spectator more or less into the ensuing drama.

In the second, semiotic instance, the stark change in musical soundtrack and the uncanny similarity in the two intertitles affect potential solutions to the enigma. Foregrounding the mimetic layer of the drama, where particular events framing the ellipsis refer back to earlier ones, these devices make it possible to ascertain reasons for the particular mode and enactment of the temporal passage that are grounded less in dramatological pragma than in semiotic and discursive signification. The depiction of the elementary school's architectural façade partially repeats, via visual resemblance, the depiction of the pre-ellipsis art academy. This suggests that Madeleine's current, post–ellipsis situation, an effect of the horrific shooting that had occurred in the earlier locale, may at least partly be explained in terms of notions evoked by the later locale (education, childhood, and the "elementary"), which qualify those invoked by the earlier (romantic love, violent death, eros–thanatos). Likewise, as the intertitling over the first view of the elementary school partially repeats the intertitling over Léna's deportation camp-bound bus ride across the southern French landscape during the film's opening credits, a similar suggestion is made about the Korskis' post–exilic situation; namely, that it, too, is explainable via an intertextual cross-fertilization of notions—in this instance, of those just mentioned and others (fate, the pastoral, pragmatism) invoked by Léna's holocaustal internment. What's more, because the ellipsis itself occurs immediately after shots of an abject Madeleine, duly fallen from her prewar aristocratic security, juxtaposed with shots of a rowdy U.S. soldier, risen from the mass melting pot to the status of world conqueror ("That's for my mother in Jersey!"), the film seems also to suggest that what it thus far has evaded, and what perhaps now is being culled into its enigma, is explainable by reference to the notion of global politics invoked by the juxtaposition, which not only forms the matrix of the narrative jump to the present but is reconfirmed in its possible ideological significance by the hindsight afforded from within that present-tense—which marks a watershed in the history of U.S. hegemony on the European continent and beyond.[25]

In effect, through the typically allegorical mode of strategic intertextual, alterior repetition, each of these instances encourages a reflexive questioning not simply of the formal-aesthetic but also contential-contextual layers of the ellipsis and, by the extension, the narrative, a questioning that promotes the sort of alertness and attention to hermeneutical plurality that has frequently been considered characteristic of the Judeo-Christian appropriation of Judaic interpretive practice.[26]

* * * * *

That said, it cannot be denied that the characteristics just explicated are also interpretable from a primarily Judaic perspective, as constituting a Jewish allegorical inscription. This is true not least with respect to the way in which the historical relationship they undergird may be seen to invoke the hermeneutics of *tanakh*, that central text of Jewish mythology as explicated and interpreted by the Talmud and related commentaries. Differential textual devices predominate across the sequence, including semiographic patterning, syntactical repetition and hyperbole, and phonetic polysemy, which form a reflexive interpretative layering, familiar from Talmudic reading practice, that enables an extended series of potentially critical questions about the film.[27] The ostensible Judaic interpretability of *Entre Nous* is oriented, like that of the *tanakh*, toward a Jewish historiography, a genealogy that variously explicates an historical series of entanglements in, and recoveries from, social catastrophe, and that, from its inception, articulates those experiences intertextually vis-à-vis an assumed non-Jewish component which is never as such completely distinguishable from the Jewish self-same. In marking its diegetic shift from the narrative past to present, *Entre Nous* structures a cursory and schematic relationality between two women, one Jewish, the other Gentile, each of whom is "at first sight" portrayed undergoing parallel holocaustal experiences, then as coming together in their wake to form an interreligious, inter-ethnic bond, itself marked structurally by an allegorical ellipsis which would seem to invoke Judaic hermeneutics by its textual differentiality and its deferral of narrative resolution pending questions about its meaning and significance to the film as a whole, including the post–Holocaust context in which it emerges and is received.

But on this very line of reasoning, an ascription to the ellipsis of a primarily Judaic determination becomes difficult, if not impossible, to support. Indeed the differences between Judeo-Christian and Jewish allegory, especially as they inscribe respective interpretations—and narrative arrangements—of the Bible, mitigate against any such definitive ideological determination—and that is precisely the point: for whereas *there exists no Judaic determination that is not at once an historical collocation and critical refraction of the multifarious social collective comprising and inflecting Jewish experience and reality,*[28] *there is no Judeo-Christian determination that does not finally mystify this Jewish historiographical allegoricality, despite and perhaps because of Judaism's own mystificatory obfuscations, in the name of a transcendental unicity that travesties through dissimulation the material conditions of need and hope at the (dis)identificatory—Middle Eastern—matrix of **both** orientations.*[29]

To be sure, the Talmudically mediated interpretation of *tanakh* entails an understanding common to Judaism of textual layers as contradictory hermeneutical *extensions* rather than reductive *abstractions* of one another, as inscribing tropologically more broadly significant paths to social reparation [*tikkun ha-olam*] along an asymmetrical, historiographic axis. This interpretive practice involves inference by syntactical association or juxtaposition [*smuchin*], which finds its apogee in the contiguous lay-out of the Talmudic page;[30] apprehension and cross-narrative (dis)association of the phonetic properties of vowels [*al tikrei*], which traditionally are not included in Hebrew texts but, when inserted and altered by the reader, can significantly change the meaning of a passage (a well-known example of this practice is the intertextual reading of names); and apprehension and figurative association of the graphical form of Hebrew letters themselves [*gematria*, *notarikon*], which also propose intertextual, often numerical or acrostic-acronymic alternations in meaning.[31] Judeo-Christian interpretation of biblical narrative is basically respectful of these hermeneutic practices, yet in typical christological fashion, it contains their historiographical entailments and conceptual contradictions along the inversive and subsumptive lines pointed out during my general discussion above of Judeo-Christianity, rehearsed now in a modern, largely secularized milieu. This is true notwithstanding the teachings of modern Christian "Higher Criticism," which have placed into serious question the historical accuracy of biblical narrative, revealing it a collage written and compiled retrospectively in support of particular political agendas,[32] in turn adopting and critically elaborating ultra-orthodox Judaic understandings of redemption that hold "Zion" to mean a social promise independent and irrespective of ethno-nationalist claims. More specifically, the Judeo-Christian appropriation of tanakhic interpretability recognizes and acknowledges the latter's differential, polysemic, intertextual character and in some cases goes to great lengths to demonstrate this—for example the mistaken attribution of Protestant metonymics to Judaic textual tradition by literary theorist Susan Handelman.[33] In the end, however, it always manages to mystify that character by reasserting and substituting typically Christian truth claims and attendant qualifications: incessant, even essential ambiguity (asymptosis), figural iconicity, and moral reduction to christic etymologies and chronologies.[34]

It is perhaps out of concern, understandable in hindsight, that textualist readings of *tanakh* undertaken vis-à-vis such appropriation will be co-opted, or, on the obverse, that they will be taken antisemitically, as stereotypical Jewish poaching or corruption of presumed Christian insightfulness—and that they will therefore obviate Jewish particularism, in the first instance, and Jewish assimilationism, in the second—that modern Judaic exegesis deriving from European/American contexts and practiced by mainline Jewish denominations (Reform, Conservative, Orthodox), including some of Sephardic and Reconstructionist orientation, has until recently resisted Judaism's own vibrant history of historiographic, homiletic, interrogative, and intertextual interpretation in favor of logocentric readings bound up with source criticism and historicist apologetics.[35] The unfortunate result is that New Testament moralism, culturally dominant in the West while/because resistant to Judaically-grounded readings that are *neither* particularist *nor* assimilationist but that are nonetheless, unlike *haredism* or Zionism, *both* universalist *and* pluralist, has attained noticeable hegemony not only across the Third World, where it has served a colonial missionary function for centuries, but also in Judaic scholarship and its secular, including cinematic, articulations.[36]

* * * * *

Returning now to the parabolic ellipsis with these hermeneutical distinctions in mind, it is clear that the series of shots comprising the ellipsis cannot be designated strictly or primarily Judaic, but in fact supports a Judeo-Christian reading. While it does comprise a multilayered quality which promotes reflexive readings of the relationship between *Entre Nous'* historical and present-tense diegeses, this series also figures a metonymic structure that takes the graphical form precisely representative of the Judeo-Christian allegorical function: the asymptote. In addition, through its phonetic, semiotic, and intertextual associations back and forth across the narrative gap it tropes, the parabolic shot structure performs rhetorically a Judeo-Christian historicity. "History" as charted in this series of shots does not comprise, as it does in Talmud-*tanakh*, a temporal movement overdetermined variously by/in socio-historical struggles for material resources (land, water, oil, knowledge, institutions), notwithstanding the moment's diegetic contextualization in the Holocaust, an event brought about in relation to those very, ongoing struggles. "History" as charted here presumes christo-phenomenologically that temporal movement is an effect of mystical telos leading gradually, if unevenly, across the "debased," earthly realm toward apocalyptic or at least transcendental resolution. This would explain several aspects of the moment: its temporally prolonged depiction of the sky, as if to signify a "higher power"; its narrative elision of the Korskis' survival in favor of focus on Madeleine's, as if to underscore the asymmetricality of Jewish–Christian relations vis-à-vis that power; and its parabolic framing and propulsion of these aspects, which itself graphically figures an asymptote, as if to signify the formulaic iconicity itself of christo-allegorical projection.

The ensuing scene of Léna and Madeleine's first meeting serves furthermore to realize this teleological quality, as that meeting per se resolves anagogically the ethno-national and religious divide which previously had separated the women (and bound them to their men) in the historical-diegetic portion of the narrative. As mentioned, that divide was constructed through parallel editing, which collocated the women's respective wartime experiences on the basis of an intertextual overlap that rendered them so closely analogous as to have necessitated, even fated the women's meeting.

It is precisely this structural aspect of the women's relationship that was neglected by reviews which chose to focus their attentions on its erotic quality, its sexual indefinability and social irreverence—what in retrospect would be called its "queerness." This in turn contributed to their failure to view *Entre Nous* as both a Holocaust film and a film with dubious ideological overdetermination which, in contrast to the claims of a more recent reviewer, Lynn Higgins,[37] ultimately affirms performatively rather than simply describes the effects of the Holocaust and Second World War on postwar, economically liberalized France. Instead of extending critiques in this respect, which might have referred to French scholarly resistance to the "queer" in light of its appropriation against French political resistance to U.S.-led global free market reforms,[38] reviews by Andrea Weiss, Chris Straayer, and Hervé Wattelier, for instance, took the limited and facile position, now associated with mainstream queer theory, that the bond's sexual ambiguity is itself sufficient critical means. On their view, its undecidability signifies a subversive, erotico-aesthetic or onto-libidinal "excess" that renders the bond inherently resistant to containment or definition. In turn this incessant transgressive quality becomes the source for alternative, including lesbian responses to patriarchal control, in that it upsets, while not necessarily overturning, traditional gender and sexual hierarchies. As Weiss argues,

> [T]his reliance on feminine spectacle for male visual pleasure does not automatically preclude lesbian visual pleasure. [It] offers pleasure for women spectators in its inversion of the traditional hierarchy of cinematic images, while the shroud of ambiguity surrounding the exact nature of the women's relationship leaves space for the lesbian imagination. (Weiss, "Passionate Friends," 125)

And as Straayer writes,

> The focus on the two women together threatens to establish both asexuality and homosexuality, both of which are outside the heterosexual desire that drives mainstream film narrative. Therefore, simultaneous actions take place in the text to eroticize the women's interactions and to abort the resulting homoerotics. These very contradictions and opposing intentions cause the gaps and ambiguous figurations that allow lesbian readings. [Hence] rather than enforcing opposite meanings, the film [...] allows[s] for multiple readings which overlap. [The resulting lesbian aesthetic] neither replace[s] nor compromise[s] the heterosexual film event and text recognized and analyzed in prior feminist film theory, but rather offer[s] additions and alternatives to account for homosexual viewership and desire. (Straayer, "Hypothetical Lesbian Heroine," 9, 22)

Compatible with these views, although uninterested in lesbian spectatorship per se, is Wattelier:

> [*Entre Nous*] presents Madeleine's and Léna's dealings together as anomalous and thus dangerous—as outside the rationalized, socially justified system of norms based on their husbands' financial pursuits. The film insistently shows

that the women's bartering space is crowded with children when the women try
to take hold of their own desires. As mothers and wives, they must identify with
their children and husbands as well as with their own needs. In this way, by
constantly maintaining the characters within this specific kind of tension, the
film explicitly traces out the boundaries of a woman's discourse [...] Through
[this discourse,] gossip, the two women of *Entre Nous*, Léna and Madeleine, end
up creating a loose network of mutual support, a kinship which also proves far
superior to their husbands' ways of coping with emotional alienation. [In the
end] their economic dream takes form. It would let them go beyond their own
labor—love—and let them join socially as well as domestically. (Wattelier,
"*Entre Nous*: Gender Analyzed," 8, 32, 37)

Such attempts to explain the bond as reflexively resistant to and/or imminently
transcendent of patriarchal appropriation overlooks the long-established social
fact that patriarchy is more than simply a cultural or aesthetic phenomenon, and
that the confinement of its analysis to the formal and/or thematic register of
interpretation may merely reinscribe the very deep-structures of heterocentrism
which these otherwise feminist reviews would ostensibly oppose and in
contradistinction to which they attribute an emancipatory, subversive potential
to erotic female solidarity.

This is not by any means to deny claims forwarded by these and other
reviews concerning either the ambiguity or undecidability of that solidarity as
depicted in *Entre Nous*, or the possibility of its coming to serve any useful
function whatsoever for feminism or glbtq liberation. Despite, however, and
indeed because of those claims, *Entre Nous'* deployment of ambiguity and erotic
bonding lends little more than rhetorical lip-service to the problematics of
gender oppression and heterocentrism as articulated within feminism, film
theory, or the larger cultural arena. For just as the ambiguity of the women's
relationship and its narrative inscription affords a certain characterological
differentiation between Léna and Madeleine, such that their erotic bond is
prevented from signaling a totalizing drive toward irenic homogeneity, so
likewise does it leave untouched the deep-structural patterns and conventions,
not least those of ethno-religious and socio-economic history and orientation,
which condition each woman's gender positioning and, in turn, her
understanding that an economically lucrative, culturally daring friendship might
offer liberation from it. As put incisively, in another context, by French cultural
theorists Maria Klonaris and Katarina Thomadaki, this sort of unproblematized
understanding of sex-gender positioning "runs the risk of carrying some 'snob
value' or at best being part of a 'cult theory' more than that of a catalyzing
political idea. [It therefore] risks being assimilated into the politics of American
cultural exportation. For it is well known that the U.S. exports its dominant
culture with as much ardor as it exports its subcultures."[39]

Whereas sexuality and gender are destabilized throughout the film, for instance, the distinction between Léna and Madeleine as Ashkenazi-Belgian and Catholic-French, respectively, is cursorily emphasized to the point of its stereotypification. As the women's relationship tightens, each begins to adopt certain of the other's character traits, especially those which are gender based, with the effect that the traditional typology, Jew–Christian, is at once deconstructed and reaffirmed. Through her engagement with Madeleine, for instance, Léna's deportment alters drastically from conservatively clad and enculturated Jewish bourgeoise to fashionable neo-bohemian—an alteration made explicit by her adoption of a more strident, masculinized disposition than is evident prior to her encounter with Madeleine. As the friendship is realized economically, this disposition is further enhanced in its stereotypically Christianized aspect, as Léna, characterized previously as verbal-linguistic by her ability to compose letters, deploys visual-artistic knowledge gleaned from Madeleine in order to design and supervise the construction of a fashion boutique, Magdalena, to be co-managed by her and Madeleine. In this regard, Léna adopts a certain feminized aspect that both complements her newly acceded masculinity and increases its stridency. As for Madeleine, by contrast, the adoption of "Jewish" traits vis-à-vis Léna, while also stereotypically based and projected along the same gender axis, stops short of equitable reciprocity in the ethno-religious, socio-economic senses. From the moment of her traumatic "victimization" during the Second World War to her divorce from the inept and bungling Costa, any Judaization Madeleine undergoes presumes a Judeo-Christian understanding of both Jewishness and gender, one in fact prefigured by the initial, pre-marital, pre-exilic characterization of Léna. There, a dual construction of Léna is formulated that appropriates the axes of gender and ethno-religion toward what can only be described, as I shall qualify below, as an *anti*–feminist position.

Noting the masculine pole of the gender axis, numerous Lacanian critiques of *Entre Nous* have recognized the early construction of Léna in terms of the classic cinematic inscription of Woman. On this perspective, Léna is portrayed both as a subject of and beyond knowledge. On the one hand, her gaze often goes unreturned, so that she is positioned as subjectively stable or self-possessed; on the other hand, the objects of her gaze are frequently idyllic, pastoral scenes and scapes which, following the same tradition, suggests an alignment of her subjectivity and, in turn, her desire with that of an imaginal, even originary ineffability that cannot by its nature return a gaze and therefore cannot be known, for it neither exists nor functions on the same ontological plane. For Lacan, this sort of dualist construction bespeaks the very essence of Woman, which he designates *jouissance*, the silent, unattainable, unspeakable dynamic of phallic desire for both transgression of and conciliation to the primordial "Law of the Father," and which subsequently is identified with its ostensible opposite, the feminine absenting of desire, "aphanisis."[40] For *Entre Nous*' reputedly feminist reviews, this neoromantic theorization translates as the proverbial "desire that dare not speak its name"—lesbianism—which poses such a threat to patriarchy that it has to be idealized, and thereby defused, in the form of mystical, unknowable opacities such as *ekastasis, yichud, jouissance, jeu,* even divinity itself. In these reviews, the recognition and naming of lesbianism as an erotic, if not sexual, possibility for women—as well as a means for suspending and redirecting male sexuality and eroticism—is one of the first steps toward demystifying and overturning patriarchy. From their perspective, *Entre Nous*' construction of Léna as unknowing female subject—what Luce Irigaray has in another context referred to as an "awoman"[41]—is a first, clever, and effective means toward realizing that end.

While these critiques are prolific on the almost epitomical quality of Léna's engendering, however, they do not follow the Lacanian theory on which their analyses would seem to be based to the theological register which other, journalistic reviews have broached,[42] and which Lacan himself enters unabashedly, enabling him to liken the dualist dynamics of *jouissance* (the heteropatriarchal containment of lesbianism) to the phenomenology of *Christian trinitarian belief.*[43] For the latter reviews, the philosophical function of *jouissance* and/or Woman, like that of the Jew in traditional Christian theology[44]—and like the figure of Rosenberg in *The Quarrel*—is as an ethical exemplar, a model illustration of what is possible and what must be conceded, or confessed, with respect to the heteropatriarchal (or, in the case of the Ashkenazim, christological) status quo. Indeed for Lacan, who differs significantly from Freud in this respect,[45] acceptance of this exemplary function is key to psychological equilibrium in the face of existential provisionality and timelessness, which in turn are seen to necessitate, as if by automatic reflex, normative conventions of language and socialization (the "Symbolic"). On this basically Christian line, the realization and practice of lesbianism is tantamount to madness—to a hysterical suspension and uprooting of those conventions—and to a resulting divestment from the cognitive-discursive means by which one's intersubjective function is declared possible.

Entre Nous' elliptical, chronicle-like narrative, which figures discursive undecidability as well as a certain French feminist refusal to depict the women making decisions about their actions or desires,[46] is henceforth readable by the film's Lacanian critics largely in terms of sex-gender aesthetics at the expense of the film's concomitant, secular inscription of Judeo-Christian hermeneutics and any politically enhanced understandings that may be fostered about the film in its regard. Considering the Judeo-Christian reading of *tanakh* as anomic, endlessly interpretable and undecidable, the uncertainty *Entre Nous* projects about the sexual nature of the women's erotic bond would have to go without saying; to decide either way would connote a disambiguous, masculinist drive toward mastery and, ironically, a negative invocation of the very Judaism which the Judeo-Christian perspective, in its return to *tanakh*, would seem interested, at least cursorily, to emulate and support. Hence the narrative's persistent oscillation over the women's sexuality, their portrayal as indecisive, and even the depiction of their bond as both cathartic and salvific. All of this must be seen as a rhetorical means for resisting the post–Holocaust persistence of the "Jewish," for misrecognizing it as essentially masculinist,[47] and for tolerating it in the name of the financially controlling figure of the Jewish husband, Michel,[48] so that it might eventually benefit the postwar, restorative, Jewish–Christian business relationship, Léna–Madeleine—an observation lost on critics who see this resistance mainly through a Lacanian lens, as an arbitrary formal device for maintaining a "hypothetical" sex-gender distinction between the women and, in turn, a sense of sex-gender pluralism among the film's community of spectators that would be ideologically conducive to the U.S.-generated neoliberal culture which global augmentation, like that of Holocaust film production and even Cinema Studies itself (where Lacanian theory perhaps has been most strongly credited), marked the era of *Entre Nous*' release.

From the Lacanian-inflected perspective, that is, Madeleine's turn toward Léna's "Jewishness" can only be interpreted rhetorically, its Judeo-Christian quality deferred, like that of the early parallel between the women's wartime experiences, onto a patronizing celebration of sensually seductive subversiveness. Elided by this interpretation, moreover, is the fact that Madeleine's "subversive" turn thusly reinforces an asymmetrical, exploitative hermeneutic that, like modern Zionism, requires for its effectuality both antisemitism and an acknowledgement of its holocaustal effects.[49] Not surprisingly, for example, it is Madeleine, the narrative antagonist, who inspires, instigates, and provokes the actions which together culminate in both women's divorces and Madeleine's winning over of Léna. As mentioned, the women are at pains to make decisions; their choices are always undercut by either the enigmatic quality of ensuing behaviors or by their consequences for the development of the erotic bond. The possibility that they become successful entrepreneurs therefore arises only as a result of Madeleine's albeit inadvertent bungling of an adulterous affair she has with Roland, which Léna, the Jew, is compelled to repair with the boutique idea she brainstorms. Indeed the very idea of using a clothing boutique to gain financial, social and legal independence from their patriarchal confines occurs to the women *only after* Michel, jealously enamored of Madeleine, discovers her adulterous affair with Roland, thus sparking a potential family rift which threatens to keep the women apart indefinitely and undermine their liberatory aims. The actual contracting of

Magdalena, its financing and construction, also occurs at a "subversive" moment, following the newly divorced Madeleine's capricious announcement to Léna during their secret rendez-vous in Paris that she plans to leave Lyon for good, thus abandoning Léna to proceed with the store alone. Again it becomes the role of Jewish Léna to make good—in this case, to do all the legwork, finagle a start-up loan from Michel, and implement the designs suggested by Madeleine in order to make the boutique a reality. This economically mediated asymmetricality is itself anticipated by an earlier scene in which Madeleine, admittedly ignorant of monetary matters, must rely on Léna's apparently natural business savvy to prevent the gullible, money-lending [*aurifière*] Michel from discovering that Costa is unable to pay back a loan from him. Later, Léna's (undramatized) decision finally also to leave Lyon and abandon the boutique is prompted neither by arbitrary whim nor blind necessity associated with Michel's destructive violence, but through a "subversive" act by Madeleine, who, jealous and possibly resentful of him—her rival on all fronts—reveals to him her hidden presence one day at the boutique, knowing full well it will, understandably, provoke his volatile temper.

This *philosemitic* hermeneutic, which proffers a patronizing appreciation of the "industrious-but-suffering" Jew, symptomatizes a larger, ideological revision of the sex-gender and ethno-national oppressions which both Léna and Madeleine have endured in varying ways. The coordinates of this revisionism are visible at the very, formal-aesthetic register so insufficiently examined by *Entre Nous*' critics. A key moment of its projection is a superimposition which appears only seconds before Madeleine's entry into the school auditorium and only seconds after an impatient Costa has abandoned René to Léna, who is now trying to acquaint herself with her young charge. Just as Madeleine is about to enter, a shot occurs of a closing stage curtain taken from the perspective of Léna and René, who are subsequently shown in a superimposed reverse-shot taken from the perspective of the empty stage, seated alone in the now likewise empty auditorium. The immediate effect of this superimposition is—recalling the theatricalized altercation in *Korczak*—to destabilize the spatio-temporal integrity of the scene, but unlike an earlier, simple editorial alternation between stage and audience, which conveyed a similar, *transgressive* instability between Léna and her daughter, the Kurys prototype Sophie, the utter overlapping in this instance of spatial/existential and temporal/proairetic registers effects a *transcendence*, not merely a transgression, of those dimensions. Blending the "real" and "imaginary" fields of the auditorium and stage produces a hybrid image in which the two fields are at once distinct and interchangeable and thus together signify the very definition of transcendence.

Madeleine's arrival figures under the rubric of this superimposition, as she enters the auditorium toward its conclusion. As a result, that very arrival along with the desiring gaze she subsequently casts at Léna take on the character of this transcendence, this hybridity, so that they, too, are destabilized, and the erotic relationship they prefigure can accrue a qualitatively different meaning than was attributed previously to the purely filial bond between Léna and Sophie. Yet for all its apparent difference, the prescription of eroticism between Léna and Madeleine, occurring as it does on account of Madeleine's "transcendental" gaze, occurs also at the expense of the Jewish Léna's subjectivity, thereby performing an ideological limit to it and its structural context, which includes the mother-daughter bond, its ethno-religious significance, and its historico-political conditioning. Indeed Madeleine is not portrayed as the owner of her gaze but, instead, as its phenomenological agent. Through a series of reverse-angle two-shots framing the women seated beside one another within the same spatial plane, the typical Hollywoodian, masculine position supplied male characters in the film is disallowed her. Whereas this ordering might be welcomed as an opening of the gaze itself onto a broader than usual range of spectators, it also works to position this particular gaze into an originary matrix beyond the figure of Madeleine, within an "imaginary" field signified by the auditorium stage from which perspective her entrance is first depicted as well as by the extended screen-time during which she casts her gaze at Léna, prompting a romantic melody over the soundtrack. Seen thusly, it becomes apparent that a potential rendering ecumenical of the gaze in *Entre Nous* occurs at the expense of both the "awoman," Léna, and the ostensibly subjectivized Madeleine becoming subjects of their desiring gazes.

By the same token, those gazes and their projected desires are never rendered homologous; a certain differentiation persists. Only moments following their meeting in the auditorium, at which point Léna knows little more about Madeleine than that she is capricious and mystical, Léna is already relating to her the story of her holocaustal experiences, as though Madeleine's desiring gaze had established the requisite degree of trust for such personal sharing. Léna not only recounts but rehearses her concentrationary internment, as she momentarily adopts the character of her concentrationary friend—named, not incidentally, Sarah [Christine Pascal]—who had also related her troubles "at first sight," and whose advice about Michel's marriage proposal had been instrumental in what soon would become Léna's liberation from the camp. Léna's recounting and rehearsal may be read as a manifestation of *gilgul*, a kabbalistic term designating a consensual, erotically-tinged relationship based in the occasioning of metempsychosis, the passing of a dying person's soul into the body of one who still lives. In this case, Madeleine is positioned as the literal incorporation—not merely the allegory—of Sarah, and Léna, having adopted the latter's character, is positioned as Madeleine's figurative complement. Recalling the discourse of Jewish messianism, one might say that the relationship, its desiring gaze and verbal enunciation are *redemptive*, that they *instantiate* the Holocaust that is not represented directly in *Entre Nous* but, instead, by an indirect, textually mediated reference to the memory-concept, "Sarah." As such they perform the phenomenon of remembrance that would seem necessary to a Judaically conceived reparation [*tikkun*] of that event. The meeting between Madeleine and Léna is as much an occasion for mourning the loss of Sarah, or, metonymically, the dissemination of the Jewish(-Abrahamic) legacy up to and beyond the Holocaust, which includes the unfortunate tale of Hagar, the biblical Sarah's non-Hebrew (viz., Palestinian) rival/servant condemned for much of her adulthood to exile. Madeleine's desiring gaze is less autonomous than mnemonic, and Léna's misrecognition of it, signaled by her ensuing willingness to share a personal narrative of suffering, the means by which its allegorical referent, the pathos of the Holocaust, may be accessed and made available for mourning. As this is accomplished, the women suddenly awaken to the various ways in which they still have not shed the chains of the past and, as in a perfectly wrought prolepsis, intuit one another as the necessary tools with which to do so. It is not for nothing that Madeleine, for instance, will soon relate her "holocaustal" narrative to Léna, or that her illicit affair with Roland will take place in Léna's own bed.

The consensuality between Léna and Madeleine is so privatized, so historically dislocated, so resistant to symbolization, however, that its salvific manifestation as *gilgul*, like much else in *Entre Nous*, is finally more akin to that notion's christological interpretation as sacramental, thereby qualifying the relationship as Judeo-Christian rather than strictly Jewish. In the Christian reading of Kabbalah, metempsychosis involves a mystical emanation of force beyond and outside history and the social.[50] On this immanent-transcendental perspective, a metempsychosis that references holocaustal pathos would require for its realization the diversion [*détournement*] of that pathos into sheer *aesthesis*, a move which would entail a veritable denial of the Holocaust as an event, an occurrence with a political, economic, ideological and cultural *history*, and its re-envisaging as an ontotheological "happening," a gnostic, eschatological, catastrophic epiphany (a *shoah*). In such a case, the empathic experience required for genuine mourning-work would no longer signify a material, but rather ideal, referent, and the process of mourning itself, an incessant, universalizing, aphanisic struggle which neither broad investigation nor close analysis can forestall or bring to closure. Like a New Testament or, more recently, Zionist narrative,[51] holocaustal pathos is here, despite appearances, evoked and projected past the register on which *le-didakh* is possible, past the imperative of critical answerability (e.g., to the Arab descendents of mythological Hagar). Around this pathos is a hermeneutics of silence bespeaking reverence, transparency, and awe, a silence implying that the occasion of remembrance is not only devoid of answerability but, like the matrix of the female gaze throughout *Entre Nous*, emptied of discrete subjectivity: it is something sacred, untouchable, ineffable, omnipresent; something not locatable to any material particularity; something transparently applicable to a perversely inviting potpourri of traumatic personal experiences; something the perpetuation, not cessation, of which is key to liberation from its devastating effects.

This Judeo-Christian overdetermination of the nonetheless mystical moment would explain why Madeleine and Léna utter no words as they exchange erotic glances, not even ones inquiring into one another's name— something which otherwise marks the introduction of characters throughout the film, and which carries, as mentioned in Chapter Three, decidedly Judaic connotations.[52] It would also explain why, when Michel relates his Holocaust narrative to the Segaras over dinner (also during the acquaintanceship sequence), which recounts the Korskis' having had to use a false, very common Sephardic name, "Piperno," in order to evade the Italian fascists, he is dismissed, despite his socialist sympathies, as a petit-bourgeois bore, and the historico-political irony and implications of his tale are received in uncomprehending, disinterested silence. Apparently, interpellation into the Judaic covenant, along with the physical practice of sexuality and adherence to a living code of social ethics, all of which are overrepresented negatively in the film by the Jewish husband/father, socialist/capitalist Michel,[53] disqualify as ingredients for transcendence but do encourage a sustained positing of a fallen, cataclysmic, holocaustal world against which transcendence may be gauged. Such supersessionist positing is underscored by additional historical references, made ironically and performatively in the mystificatory context of the parabolic ellipsis and ensuing exchange of erotic female glances. These include Sophie, onstage at the elementary school, singing a Maurice Chevalier song, "Ma Pomme," and wearing a Chevalier mask: it is well-known that the famous entertainer was a Vichy sympathizer, for which he lost popularity in France while becoming an icon of Frenchness in the postwar U.S.;[54] René and his schoolmates wearing Native American costumes as René refuses to don a chief's headdress (fig. 4-7): Native Americans are victims of an ongoing genocide justified by the Judeo-Christian ideology of manifest destiny;[55] Léna's visible embourgeoisement having been facilitated by the postwar Marshall Plan synecdochized by the blaring Glenn Miller music: this economic redevelopment scheme constituted a U.S. imperialist gesture at the peak of that country's global power that is also allegorized by Michel owning a gasoline station that sells Shell Oil;[56] and the diegetic setting in Lyon recalling the initiation there of contemporary French Holocaust denial, even as that city boasts a strong history of feminism and political resistance.[57]

In light of this last example, the film's male characters and the varying histories they reference do not signify monolithically, as French cultural theorist

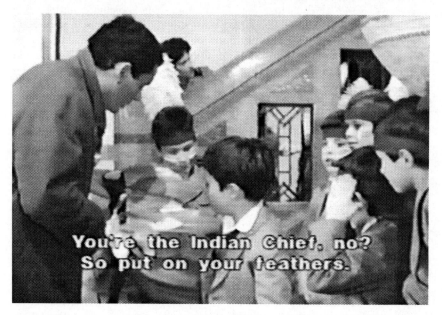

Fig. 4-7 – René in chief's headdress in *Entre Nous*

Lynn Higgins and film scholar Phil Powrie remind.[58] Through the film's narrative ambivalence, Michel's indignant perspective is finally reaffirmed as sympathetic and transferable to that of director Kurys, as in Kurys' original novel, where Léna's relationship with Madeleine clearly figures nostalgically as that of a mother-substitute, not as a rejection of Michel or even of men— something barely suggested in the film but asserted by Kurys herself in interviews about it.[59] Mother-bonding and paternal longing notwithstanding, insofar as readings such as Higgins and Powrie neglect to problematize the Judeo-Christian underpinnings of the triangulated relationship in which Michel, Léna, and Madeline find themselves entangled, that framework and its dubious ideological function are reinforced. For in the hyperreality of *Entre Nous*'s "hypothetical" structure, only an erotic, unnamable, antinomian bond is geared for transcendence, one based in an *entre*pre*neur*ial ethic of private, individual progress—what Straayer correctly but affirmatively refers to as "isolation," the "opportunity" of the film,[60] and that is nothing less than commodificatory. Tellingly, and pace the Benjaminian allegory which Roland Boer analyzes in another context ("[Baroque] allegory was primarily a method for theological institutional appropriation of foreign materials, whether pagan or Hebrew gods"),[61] this bond is viable only insofar as it contributes to the reification of a certain well-known typology of Jewish "difference" stubbornly resistant to the dominant, if secularized, Christian ethos, which since the Holocaust has ironically been re-enacted in the travestied name of a likewise secularized Jewish messianism in Israel/Palestine and beyond.

With this in mind, the rationale for critical silence around *Entre Nous'* Jewishness and holocaustality takes form. For although the three historically most attuned reviews of the film do at least acknowledge the inscription there of these and related discourses, none mentions that their hermeneneutic impetus is, in fact, the Judeocide, displaced as it is across the film, becoming the ecumenical matrix of a secular, "queer," Judeo-Christian call for Jews and Gentiles, gay and straight alike, to engage in the advancement of transnational capitalism, whatever personal-political sacrifices that might entail. Indeed whereas Seligsohn notes astutely that, "for all its fragile truths, *Entre Nous* has a tendency to wilt sometimes for a lack of light in some of its obscure corners," he is silent on the connection of that obscurity, which for him concerns the "Jewish," to the film's ideological displacement of the Judeocide.[62] Quart likewise fails to draw connections between this phenomenon and what she criticizes as *Entre Nous'* lack of "interest in what seems to be the wealth of Madeleine's background and Léna's having a maid and nouveau riche furs."[63] And David Denby, for all his insightfulness, confines an almost anomalous recognition of the film's displacement of the Judeocide to a commentary on personal ethics: "Kurys is not saying that Léna is wrong to leave [Michel], only that personal liberation can also be a form of murder."[64]

If critics remained silent on the broader issues, it is not simply for fear of opening the Pandora's box of "Jewish self-hatred," not least in light of Kurys' own history as a militant Zionist turned kibbutznik,[65] or because doing so would have delivered a blow to the expanding canon of woman-directed films and, in relation, the then-nascent fields of Women's Studies and lesbian/feminist theory, the proliferation of which was encouraged, if often only tolerated, during the neoliberal Reagan-era putsch. It is because recognizing and speaking to the film's structural, Judeo-Christian displacement of "Jewish Holocaust" onto an entrepreneurial trajectory would have meant having also to recognize and speak to something no film at that time, or for many years thereafter, was willing to confront: the philosemitic appropriation of the Holocaust as a rationale for a form of political-economic imperialism, transnationalism, which at once recruits the collaboration of women, homosexuals, and workers, whether Jewish or Gentile, currently or formerly oppressed, and—as *Entre Nous'* ambivalent performance suggests—denies them the very histories, intelligibility, and materiality which made it possible for them to have become so "victimized," and in turn so "redeemed," in the first place.

* * * * *

If critics of *Entre Nous* refrained from acknowledging that film's Holocaust discourse out of concern for political recrimination, no critic of *Balagan* could possibly do so and get away with it. Partly for this reason, *Balagan* has gone largely unremarked; of the Holocaust films analyzed or mentioned in the present book, it has enjoyed the fewest public screenings. Our next chapter offers an analysis of *Balagan* built upon a hypothesis concerning that film's critical as well as public ignoring. Unlike *Entre Nous'* "hypothetical" structure, however, my analysis is less interested in ensuring the widest audience availability at the expense of historiographical clarity, than in explaining why this most unusual Holocaust film, produced in the midst of the first contemporary Palestinian *intifada*, should be distributed and exhibited on a global scale. Like the films analyzed thus far, *Balagan* respects the phenomenological taboo against Holocaust representation. It is a postmodern documentary which incorporates neither archival footage nor dramatic reenactments of the Judeocide but instead tropes that event into a post–theological allegory that challenges the many commonplaces projected by much international Holocaust film before and since. Set in Israel/Palestine and directed by a German psychologist/filmmaker who trained with Wajda in Poland, *Balagan* knows and deploys christology *against* its predominant, often racist and antisemitic usages by the majority of Holocaust films which encourage acceptance of Zionism. As such it expressly critiques the persistence of holocaustality in Israel/Palestine and beyond. Put another way, *Balagan* performs the construction of a modern Zionist consciousness that identifies uncannily with the oppression supposed to justify it while producing a Palestinian national consciousness that on many levels rehearses Ashkenazi-Israeli ideology and outlook and the political economy which supports it. What follows draws upon postmodern performance, race and ethnicity theories to investigate the ideological limits of this *cinematic* performance with an aim to their appreciative resituation.

---

[1] One of its three running competitors was the Hungarian Holocaust film, *The Revolt of Job* (Imre Gyongyossi and Barna Kabay, 1983). The winner was *Fanny and Alexander* (Ingmar Bergman, Sweden, 1983). See Richard Shale, *The Academy Awards Index: The Complete Categorical and Chronological Review* (London and Westport, CT: Greenwood, 1993), 642; and Levy, *Oscar®Fever*.

[2] Prior to *Entre Nous*, only one female-directed film had received this degree of formal acclaim: in 1976, *The Seven Beauties*, a Holocaust retro film directed by Lina Wertmüller, was nominated for both Beth Director and Best Foreign Language Film. To

date, only two female-directed films have actually received Academy Awards, and these have been in the Best Foreign Language Film category: *Antonia's Line* (Marleen Gorris, Belgium/Netherlands/U.K., 1995), and *Nowhere in Africa* [*Nirgendwo in Afrika*] (Caroline Link, Germany, 2002). Few women have been nominated for the Best Director award: e.g., Jane Campion for *The Piano* (Australia/France, 1993), which lost to Stephen Spielberg for *Schindler's List* (a major Holocaust film); Sofia Coppola for *Lost in Translation* (U.S.A., 2003), and Kay Pollack for *As in Heaven* (U.S.A., 2004). Not incidentally, *Antonia's Line* and *Nowhere in Africa* are self-consciously post–Holocaust films and, like *Entre Nous*, both they and *The Piano* concern gender and sexual politics (Shale, *Academy Awards Index*, 287; and Ronald Bergan et al., *Academy Award Winners* [London: Prion, 1994], 681).

[3] E.g., David Ansen, "More Than Good Friends," *Newsweek*, February 6, 1984: 81; Molly Haskell, "Women's Friendships: Two Films Move Beyond the Clichés," *Ms.*, December 1983: 23; David Hughes, "A Subtle Hymn to Women's Love," *London Sunday Times*, October 9, 1983: 39; David Sterritt, "Building Bonds of Friendship and a Filmmaker's Career," *Christian Science Monitor*, August 3, 1984: 21–22; David Denby, "Les Girls," *New York Magazine*, January 23, 1984: 57–59; Maureen Peterson, "'Coup' Strikes Blow for Female Friendship," *Montréal Gazette*, September 10, 1983: C–4; Patricia Bosworth, "Some Secret Worlds Revealed," *Working Woman*, October 1983; Andrea Weiss, "Passionate Friends," *New York Native*, February 13–26, 1984: 34–35; Peter Wilson, "What Exactly Is This Film Trying To Say?" *Vancouver Sun*, February 24, 1984: B1, Stanley Kauffmann, "All for Love," *The New Republic*, February 27, 1984: 22–24; John Simon, "Dishonesty Recompensed," *National Review*, May 4, 1984: 54–56; John Gillett, rev. of *Entre Nous*, *Monthly Film Bulletin*, November 1983: 301; Leo Seligsohn, rev. of *Entre Nous*, *Newsday*, January 25, 1984: 51; Rex Reed, rev. of *Entre Nous*, *New York Post*, January 25, 1984: 19; Richard Corliss, rev. of *Entre Nous*, *Time*, January 30, 1984: 78; Vincent Canby, rev. of *Entre Nous*, *New York Times*, January 25, 1984: C17, and *New York Times*, February 4, 1993; Gary Arnold, "Notions of Love: 'Entre Nous'; Men and Women Apart," *Washington Post*, February 24, 1984: B1–2; and Rev. of *Entre Nous*, *Playboy*, February 1984: 28.

[4] At most, popular press engagement with the Holocaust-oriented aspects of *Entre Nous* was limited to providing abbreviated background information about the film's plot. Only French reviewer, Marie Cardinal, hinted at specific questions of antisemitism and the "Jewish" ("La chambre des dames," *Le Nouvel Observateur*, April 22, 1983: 96).

[5] Barbara Koenig Quart, *Women Directors: The Emergence of a New Cinema* (New York: Praeger, 1988), 3; Susan Hayward, *French National Cinema* (London: Routledge, 1993), 5; Chris Straayer, "The Hypothetical Lesbian Heroine in Narrative Feature Film," in *Deviant Eyes, Deviant Bodies: Sexual Re-orientation in Film and Video* (New York: Columbia University Press, 1996), 4; Hervé Wattelier, "*Entre Nous*: Gender Analyzed," *Jump Cut* 32 (1986): 8, 32, 37; and Christine Scollen-Jimack, "Diane Kurys: From *Diabolo Menthe* to *La Folie*: Whatever Happened to Sisterhood?" *Forum for Modern Language Studies* 35, no. 3 (1999): 322–30.

[6] Andrea Weiss, *Vampires and Violets: Lesbians in Film* (New York: Penguin, 1993), 123–24, 172 n.27–28; and Straayer, "Hypothetical Lesbian Heroine," 1–22. See also Guy

Austin, *Contemporary French Cinema: An Introduction* (Manchester and New York: Manchester University Press, 1996), 88.

[7] Minor exceptions include Insdorf, *Indelible Shadows*, which recognizes *Entre Nous'* depiction of the Holocaust while bluntly denying its categorizability as a "Holocaust film" (86); and Colombat, *The Holocaust in French Film*, 95. By contrast, *Entre Nous* is not mentioned at all in Naomi Green, *Landscapes of Loss: The National Past in Postwar French Cinema* (Princeton, NJ: Princeton University Press, 1999).

[8] Carrie Tarr, *Diane Kurys* (Manchester and New York: Manchester University Press, 1999).

[9] See Claudia Schoppmann, *Days of Masquerade: Life Stories of Lesbians During the Third Reich*, trans. Allison Brown (New York: Columbia University Press, 1996); Erica Fischer, *Aimée and Jaguar*, trans. Edna McCown (New York: HarperCollins, 1995); and Günter Grau, *Hidden Holocaust? Gay and Lesbian Persecution in Germany, 1933–45* (London: Cassell, 1995).

[10] Weiss, "Passionate Friends," 34.

[11] Peterson, "'Coup' Strikes Blow."

[12] Barbara Quart, rev. of *Entre Nous*, *Cinéaste* 13, no. 3 (1984): 45–47.

[13] Seligsohn, rev. of *Entre Nous*.

[14] Kurys quoted in Marcia Pally, "World of Our Mothers," *Film Comment* 20 no. 2 (1984): 17.

[15] Cohen, *Myth*; Silk, "Notes on the Judeo-Christian Tradition"; and Boston, *Why the Religious Right Is Wrong*.

[16] Hyam Maccoby, "Wandering Jew as Sacred Executioner."

[17] See John Dominic Crossan, *Who Killed Jesus? Exposing the Roots of Anti–Semitism in the Gospel Story of the Death of Jesus* (San Francisco: HarperSanFrancisco, 1995).

[18] Isaiah views post–kingdom Jews as "'the Servant(s) of God,' scorned and condemned by all nations, bearing their sins, until the time that God shall reward him for his faith and make him a cornerstone of his edifice" (Evron, *Jewish State*, 14). This reference to "suffering servant" is the textual source of the Wandering Jew myth propagated during the medieval crisis of the imperial Church. Renewed interest in the myth for its ostensible promise of Jewish imperial restoration was invoked by Zionists at the turn of the twentieth century.

[19] See Jacqueline Rose, *The Question of Zion* (Princeton, NJ: Princeton University Press, 2005).

[20] Qumsiyeh, *Sharing the Land of Canaan*, 59.

[21] See Elias Chacour, *Blood Brothers* (Tarrytown, NY: Chosen Books, 1984), 31–32; and Ateek, *Justice*, 50–52)

[22] As exemplified by Courtenay, *Judeo-Christian Heritage*; Hexter, *Judaeo-Christian Tradition*; and North, *Judeo-Christian Tradition*. For further critique, see Evron, *Jewish State*, 33–38.

[23] As recounted in Shohat, "Sephardim in Israel."

[24] See Churchill, *Little Matter of Genocide*; William K. Blum, *Killing Hope: U.S. Military and CIA Interventions Since World War II* (Washington, D.C.: Common Courage, 1995); Frank Chalk and Kurt Jonassohn, *The History and Sociology of Genocide: Analyses and Case Studies* (New Haven: Yale University Press, 1990); Adam

Jones, ed., *Gendercide and Genocide* (Nashville, TN: Vanderbilt University Press, 1994); and Pappe, *Ethnic Cleansing of Palestine.*

[25] See Gordon, *Hitler, Germans, and the "Jewish Question"*; and Noam Chomsky, *The Fateful Triangle: The U.S., Israel, and the Palestinians*, rev. ed. (1983; London: Pluto, 1999).

[26] As demonstrated by Eugene Kaelin, "Poesis as Parabolic Expression: Heidegger on How a Poem Means," *Art and Experience: A Phenomenological Aesthetics* (Lewisburg, PA: Bucknell University Press, 1970), 234–80.

[27] See Daniel Boyarin, "Dual Signs, Ambiguity, and the Dialectic of Intertextual Readings," *Intertextuality and the Reading of Midrash* (Bloomington and Indianapolis: Indiana University Press, 1990), 57–78; and Edmund Jabès, *The Little Book of Unsuspected Subversion* (Stanford, CA and London: Stanford University Press, 1996).

[28] Halevi, *History of the Jews.*

[29] Cf. Neusner, *Judaism in the Matrix*; and idem., *Judaism in the Beginning.*

[30] Neusner, *Talmudic Thinking.*

[31] Boyarin, "Dual Signs"; and Baruch Micah Bokser, "Talmudic Form Criticism," in *Essential Papers on Talmud*, ed. Michael Chernick (New York: New York University Press, 1994), 161–78.

[32] Irvine H. Anderson, *Biblical Interpretations and Middle East Policy: The Promised Land, America, and Israel, 1917–2002* (Gainesville: University of Florida Press, 2005), 7–15; and Whitelam, *Invention of Ancient Israel.*

[33] Handelman, *Slayer of Moses*, 74.

[34] Whitelam, *Invention of Ancient Israel*, 28, 62, 92. Examples of this tendency include: Alter, *Art of Biblical Narrative*; Crossan, *Who Killed Jesus?*; Geza Vermès, *Jesus the Jew: A Historian's Reading of the Gospel* (London: William Collins, 1973); Gerard Loughlin, *Telling God's Story: Bible, Church and Narrative Theology* (Cambridge and New York: Cambridge University Press, 1996); and Northrop Frye, *The Great Code: The Bible and Literature* (San Diego: Harvest/HBJ, 1982). Cf. Jesse M. Gellrich, *The Idea of the Book in the Middle Ages: Language, Theory, Mythology* (New York and London: Cornell University Press, 1995), 96–98.

[35] Reconstruction and Jewish liberation theology (Prophetic Judaism) are exceptions, while even progressive analyses such as Whitelam, *Invention of Ancient Israel*, and Shahak, *Jewish History, Jewish Religion*, have polemicized against textualism's mystificatory tendencies to the point of condemning the practice outright, which is ironic in view of these analyses' albeit differently positioned critiques of fundamentalism.

[36] Boer refers to "a colonizing fashion [...] of Christian [theological] discipline—mistakenly applied to religious traditions other than Christianity" ("Bowels of History," 371). Indeed for all his insight into the orientalism of Bible Studies, Whitelam fails to acknowledge, for instance, that the books of *tanakh* are arranged differently than those of the Christian Bible, nor does he cite any Jewish Bible scholars in the context of critiquing the field's Eurocentrism (while Anderson cites only Spinoza, a Jewish "heretic"). One might recall that the New Testament is interpretable as Judaically inflected (Heschel, "Revolt of the Colonized").

[37] Lynn Higgins, "Two Women Filmmakers Remember the Dark Years," *Modern and Contemporary France* 7, no. 1 (1999): 59–69.

[38] See Scott Gunther, "*Alors*, Are We 'Queer' Yet?" *The Gay and Lesbian Review* 12, no. 3 (2005): 23–25.

[39] Klonaris and Thomadaki quoted in Gunther, "*Alors*," 24–25.

[40] Lacanian psychoanalysis is not the only French (post)structuralist theory to position Woman along these romanticist lines. Derrida's literary deconstruction, for instance, figures Woman as matrix of (female-feminine) desire, an existential-erotic supplement to sheer ontological plenitude ("*jeu*"), posited as a quasi-gnostic, sublime compulsion: "becoming woman" (Derrida, *Of Grammatology*, trans. Gayatri Chakravorty Spivak [Baltimore: Johns Hopkins University Press, 1976], 141–64). Deleuze relocates *jeu/jouissance to* the corporeal body, designates Woman as its desiring matrix, and, pace Freud, pathologizes, as "masochism," the compulsion to satisfy that desire (*Masochism*, 9–138). Anglo-American cultural studies, including feminism and lesbian theory, often adopts this positioning (e.g., Annemarie Jagose, "Playing with the Closet: *Jeux d'occultation* and *Love, Death, and the Changing of the Seasons*," in *Lesbian Utopics* [London: Routledge, 1994], 69–96). For a connection of *jouissance* to the rhetoric of death and mourning, see Diana Knight, *Barthes and Utopia: Space, Travel, Writing* (London and New York: Oxford University Press, 1997).

[41] Luce Irigaray, *This Sex Which Is Not One*, trans. Catherine Porter with Carolyn Burke (Ithaca, NY: Cornell University Press, 1985), 113–14.

[42] Hughes, "A Subtle Hymn"; and David Robinson, "Richness of Moral Speculation," *London Times*, October 14, 1983: 11. These hail, not incidentally, from outside the U.S.

[43] Jacques Lacan, "God and the *Jouissance* of The Woman," *Feminine Sexuality: Jacques Lacan and the école freudienne*, trans. Jacqueline Rose (1975; repr., New York, Norton / London: Pantheon, 1982), 135–49; Irigaray, *This Sex*, 67, 97, 108–11, 117, 330–39; and Julia Kristeva, *Desire in Language: A Semiotic Approach to Literature and Art*, trans. Thomas Gora et al., ed. Leon S. Roudiez (New York: Columbia University Press, 1980), 210–70. Feminist poststructuralist Alice A. Jardine rationalizes this practice: "[M]odernity is a rethinking not only of sexual boundaries, but of sacred boundaries as well—in an attempt to both reconceptualize and control the archaic spaces that, hidden in the shade of the Big Dichotomies, finally emerged in all of their force in the nineteenth century" (Jardine, *Gynesis: Configurations of Women and Modernity* [Ithaca, NY and London: Cornell University Press, 1985], 80). Contemporary queer theory shifts the terms of this discussion onto the ideas of androgyny and hermaphrodism, thus recalling Paul's description of christic divinity as "neither male nor female" (Galatians 3:23–9 [NAB]) and Romanticism's iconization of that description into the phallic woman (Rebecca L. Bell-Metereau, *Hollywood Androgyny*, 2nd ed. [New York: Columbia University Press], 1993; Bruce Brasell, "A Seed for Change: The Engenderment of *A Florida Enchantment*," *Cinema Journal* 36, no. 4 [1997]: 3–21; Ruth Vanita, "Sapphic Virgins: Mythmaking Around Love Between Women in Meredith, Forster, Hope Mirrlees," in *Sappho and the Virgin Mary: Same-Sex Love and the English Literary Imagination* [New York: Columbia University Press, 1996], 136–64; Kirsten Moana Thompson, "The Allegorical Androgyne: Asta Nielsen and the Pathos of Mourning," paper presented at the annual meeting of the Society for Cinema Studies, Pittsburgh, PA, May 1992; and Julie Clague, "Divine Transgressions: The Female Christ-form in Art," *Critical Quarterly* 47, no. 3 [2005]: 47–63). See Buckley for a contemporary Christian

rearticulation. For critiques, see Benjamin, *Arcades Project*, 816; Jean-Luc Nancy and Pierre Lacoue-Labarthe, *The Title of the Letter: A Reading of Lacan*, trans. François Raffoul and David Pettigrew (Albany: State University of New York Press, 1992); David H. Fisher, "Introduction: Framing Lacan?" in *Lacan and Theological Discourse*, eds. Edith Wyschogrod et al. (Albany: State University of New York Press, 1989), 1–25; Jacob Neusner, *Androgynous Judaism: Masculine and Feminine in the Dual Torah* (Macon GA: Mercer University Press, 1993); Susannah Heschel, "Jesus as Theological Transvestite," in *Judaism Since Gender*, eds. Miriam Peskowitz and Laura Levitt (London: Routledge, 1997), 188–99; Rebecca Alpert, "Challenging Male/Female Complementarity: Jewish Lesbians and the Jewish Tradition," in Eilberg-Schwartz, *People of the Body*, 361–77; Charles Mopsik, "The Body of Engenderment in the Hebrew Bible, the Rabbinical Tradition and the Kabbalah," in *Zone: Fragments for a History of the Human Body*, vol. 1, eds. Michael Feher et al. (New York: Urzone, 1989), 48–73; Boyarin, *Carnal Israel* 35–36; Elliott R. Wolfson, "Woman—Feminine as Other in Theosophic Kabbalah: Some Philosophical Observations on the Divine Androgyne," in Silberstein and Cohn, *The Other in Jewish Thought and History*, 168–69, 193 n.13, 197; and Kibbey, *Theory of the Image*, 34–38.

[44] Hence the phonetic likeness often foregrounded between *"jouissance"* and "Jewishness," *"jeu,"* and "Jew." Feminist theorist Hélène Cixous literalizes this phonetic slippage with her pun, *juifemme*, meaning "I am a Jewish woman" (*La fiancée juive: de la tentation* [Paris: Des Femmes/Antoinette Fouque, 1995]). For a discussion of *"juifemme,"* see Elaine Marks, *Marrano as Metaphor: The Jewish Presence in Writing* (New York: Columbia University Press, 1996); and idem., *"Cendres juives*: Jews Writing in French 'after Auschwitz',"* in Kritzman, *Auschwitz and After*, 35–46.

[45] Fisher, "Framing Lacan."

[46] See Sandy Flitterman-Lewis, *To Desire Differently: Feminism and the French Cinema* (Urbana: University of Illinois Press, 1990); Patricia Mellencamp, *Indiscretions: Avant-Garde Film, Video, and Feminism* (Bloomington and Indianapolis: Indiana University Press, 1990); Susan Rubin Suleiman, *Subversive Intent: Gender, Politics, and the Avant-Garde* (Cambridge, MA and London: Harvard University Press, 1990); and Joreen, "The Tyranny of Structuralessness," in *Radical Feminism*, eds. Ann Koedt et al. (New York: Quadrangle), 285–99.

[47] Regarding Jewish masculinism, see Boyarin, *Unheroic Conduct*; Heschel, *Jewish Feminist*, xi–xviii; Irena Klepfisz, *Dreams of an Insomniac: Jewish Feminist Essays, Speeches and Diatribes* (Portland, OR: Eighth Mountain, 1990); and Jon Stratton, *Coming Out Jewish: Constructing Ambivalent Identities* (London: Routledge, 2000).

[48] See Wendy Brown, "Tolerance and/or Equality? The 'Jewish Question' and the 'Woman Question',"* *differences* 15, no. 2 (2004): 1–31; and Amos Morris-Reich, "The Beautiful Jew Is a Moneylender: Money and Individuality in Simmel's Rehabilitation of the 'Jew',"* *Theory, Culture and Society* 20, no. 4 (2003): 127–42.

[49] See Judith Butler, "No, It's Not Anti–Semitic," in *Reframing Anti–Semitism*, 33–35; and Alexander Cockburn and Jeremy St. Clair, *The Politics of Anti–Semitism* (Petrolia, CA: CounterPunch / Oakland, CA: AK Press, 2003).

[50] Joseph Leon Blau, *Christian Interpretation of the Kabbalah*, 15.

[51] Jansen, *Zionism, Israel and Asian Nationalism*, 133–41.

---

[52] This elision of naming also diverts attention from the pertinent intertextual significance of numerous appellations throughout the film in addition to that of "Sarah." E.g., "Madeleine" recalls the New Testament prostitute, Mary *Magdalena*, as well as Louis *Madelin*, chair of the Committee of Honor formed in 1948 by Pétain's attorneys in order to facilitate his release from prison. "Tito," Costa's dog, is a direct reference to President Joseph Tito of Yugoslavia, an anti–Stalinist but nonetheless socialist state, and George Guingouin a.k.a. "The Limousine *Tito*," a legendary French communist abandoned by the French Communist Party upon his 1953 arrest, as the Party was opportunistically siding with the Right against the *épuration* ["purge" of Nazi collaborators] ("Guingouin" itself evokes *gouine*, the French term for "dyke" deployed against Léna by Michel, and the *Gouine* Commission [1903–28], appointed in Québec to decide whether the Jewish community there would, like the Catholic and Protestant communities, receive government funding for parochial education). "Raymond" evokes *Raymond* Poincaré, a Second Republic (interwar) leader for whom many French still bear nostalgia (Marrus and Paxton); "René"/"Raymond" recalls *René Rémond*, an historian critical of Gaullism during the *épuration* and ensuing Cold War (Henry Rousso, *The Vichy Syndrome: History and Memory in France Since 1984*, trans. Arthur Goldhammer [Cambridge, MA and London: Harvard University Press, 1991]); "Roland" recalls Judge *Rolland*, whose 1975 ruling on the Touvier case set a French precedent for suspending the statute of limitations on prosecuting crimes against humanity; as well as *Roland* von Krug von Nidda, the German consul-general to Vichy, and Bernard *Rolland*, the Vichy consul-general to Spain, who was instrumental in securing passports to Spain for Jews and even helped prevent their possessions from being confiscated at the French–Spanish border. "Segara" evokes *Sejara*, a town in the Galilee where acute Jewish–Palestinian labor struggles have occurred, and *Zagora*, a Turkish tribe reputedly descended from Noah's third son, Japheth, and related ethnically to the Jewish Khazars, also descended from Japheth via his grandson, Togarma (Halevi, *History of the Jews*, 99) (hence the theory that most Ashkenazim are of Caucasian, not Israelite descent [Kevin Alan Brook, *The Jews of Khazaria* [Lanham, MD: Jason Aronson, 2002]); interestingly, "Segara" means "closed" in Hebrew. "Hélène Weber" is the precise name of respected German teacher and statesperson, *Helen Weber*, who taught French and philosophy at Bochum and Cologne, founded a Catholic school for women, worked for the Christian Democratic Union, and was a feminist committed to *Müttergenesungswerk* ["helping mothers and children during postwar reconstruction"] (Michael Schneider *Biographisches Lexikon zur Weimarer Republik* [Frankfurt am Main: C. H. Beck, 1988], 357). "Léna" is the name of the protagonist, *Lene*, in a German feminist film concerning the travails of a woman with children during Second World War, *Germany Pale Mother* [*Deutschland, Bleiche Mutter*] (Helma Sanders-Brahms, 1980), which has been accused of backgrounding the Holocaust (Barbara Hyams, "Is the Apolitical Woman at Peace? A Reading of the Fairy Tale in *Germany, Pale Mother*," in Ginsberg and Thompson, *Perspectives on German Cinema*, 346–60); it also became the title of a U.S. Holocaust tele-film, *Lena* (Ed Sherin, 1987), and recalls the title of an Israeli film, *Léna* (Eitan Green, 1981), concerning a Russian immigrant who campaigns to bring her dissident husband to Israel and is aided by her Hebrew teacher, with whom she has an affair. "*Coup de foudre*" recalls *Coup pour coup* (Marin Karmitz, France, 1972), a film about a Jewish-Romanian ex-patriot and

Holocaust survivor active in the postwar French labor movement; *Coup de torchon* ["Clean Slate"] (Bertrand Tavernier, France, 1981), which starred Huppert (and featured Marchand in the role of a sexist, conservative nationalist *legionnaire*) and concerned the genocidal exploitation of West Africans in French Bourkassa; and *Le Coup de grace* (Jean Cayrol and Claude Duvand, France, 1965), about corruption in the *Résistance* (Cayrol was the scriptwriter of *Night and Fog*). "Watteau," the pseudonym Léna uses in exile, is also the name of a famous Jewish painter whose works were used by Adolf Eichmann to trick the Hungarian Jewish authorities regarding his malicious intentions (Nora Levin, *The Holocaust: The Destruction of European Jewry, 1933–45* [New York: Thomas Y. Cromwell], 613; and Gita Rajan, "*Oeuvres* Intertwined: Walter Pater and Antoine Watteau," in *Textual Bodies: Changing Boundaries of Literary Representation*, ed. Lori H. Lefkowitz [Albany: State University of New York Press, 1997], 185–205). "*Entre Nous*" rhymes with *contrafeux*, which literally means "lighting small fires to save the entire forest," and which referred during the *épuration* to Vichy antisemitic policy; it is also the title of a book by Levinas and comprises part of a significant phrase in the French national anthem [*Marseillaise*]: "*...entre nous la tyrannie...*" ["between us, tyranny"] (my translation).

[53] Carrie Tarr refers to this aspect somewhat superficially as the "messiness of realistically represented interpersonal relationships" that on her view the film "refus[es] to sacrifice" (*Diane Kurys*, 62).

[54] Rousso, *The Vichy Syndrome*. His discourse also resonates with that of heterosexual paternalism (Molly Haskell, *From Reverence to Rape: The Treatment of Women in the Movies*, 2nd ed. [Chicago: University of Chicago Press, 1987]) and of incest (see Walker, *Trauma Cinema*), which were insinuated by Chevalier's roles in Hollywood films such as *Gigi* (Vincente Minnelli, U.S.A., 1957) and *Love in the Afternoon* [a.k.a. *Ariane*] (Billy Wilder, U.S.A., 1956), and which compounded his transgressive persona by foregrounding its taboo, even primordial character—both of which have been associated with Nazism and Holocaust film, not to mention the tragic mode itself that is undermined by *Entre Nous'* elliptical, undecidable trajectory. Chevalier was himself famous for his extraordinary love affairs, not least of which was with that international icon of androgyny, Marlene Dietrich (Maria Riva, *Marlene Dietrich, by Her Daughter* [New York: Ballantine, 1992], 183–84). His persona came to resonate intertextually with internationally successful French vocalists, including Yves Montand, known best in the U.S. for co-starring beside a gender-bending Barbra Streisand in *On a Clear Day You Can See Forever* (Vincente Minnelli, U.S.A., 1969), and Patachou, a campy nightclub performer known for her risqué lyrics and English ditties (e.g., "Only for Americans").

One might also note that "Ma Pomme" was the theme-song of a satirical French film of the same title (Marc-Gilberg Sauvajon, 1950), in which Chevalier played a tramp who inherits a large fortune. "Pomme" is also the nickname of Huppert's character in her feature debut, *The Lacemaker* [*La Dentelliere*] (Claude Goretta, France/Switzerland/West Germany, 1977), in which she plays a factory worker who becomes mentally ill and is institutionalized after being socially and sexually abused.

[55] Francis Jennings, *The Invasion of America: Indians, Colonialism, and the Cant of Conquest* (Chapel Hill: University of North Carolina Press, 1975); Stannard, *American Holocaust*; Slotkin, *Fatal Environment*; Hans Konig, *The Conquest of America: How the*

Indian Nations Lost their Continent (New York: Monthly Review Press, 1993); Howard Zinn, *A People's History of the United States: 1492–Present*, reprint edition (New York: Harper Perennial, 2003); Ward Churchill, *Fantasies of the Master Race: Literature, Cinema, and the Colonization of American Indians*, rev. ed. (San Francisco: City Lights, 1998); and Wolfgang Schivelbusch, *The Railway Journey: The Industrialization of Time and Space in the 19th Century* (Berkeley and Los Angeles: University of California Press, 1986).

Lest this reading seem far-fetched, one might refer to the moment's intertextual topos as it references the Huppert and Miou-Miou performance *oeuvres*. As Jefferson T. Kline notes citing Lacanian theorist Ellie-Ragland Sullivan, French cinema is a "cinema without walls" compelling "self-reflexivity of meaning" (*Screening the Text: Intertextuality in New Wave French Cinema* [Baltimore and London: Johns Hopkins University Press, 1992], 6). Only six years prior to *Entre Nous*, Huppert starred in *Les Indiens sont encour loin* ["The Indians Are Still Far Away"] (Patricia Moraz, France/Switzerland, 1977), an adolescent suicide tale also starring Christine Pascal, who plays Léna's concentrationary friend, Sarah, in *Entre Nous* and herself starred in a Holocaust film, *Black Thursday* [*Les gouichets du Louvre*] (Michael Mitrani, France, 1974), that raised the question of Jewish passivity during the Second World War. Three years later, Huppert was featured in *The Heiress* [*Örökség*] (Márta Mézáros, Hungary, 1980) playing a Jewish artist who conceives a child for a Gentile Hungarian woman so that the latter may inherit her father's estate, only to face betrayal when Nazi deportations begin. That same year, Huppert played the female lead in *Heaven's Gate* [a.k.a. *Johnson County Wars*] (Michael Cimino, U.S.A., 1980), in which a correlation is drawn between the effects of monopoly capitalism on Native Americans and Southern rural Blacks, with Huppert's character serving as the comparison's allegorical shifter. Eleven years after *Entre Nous*, Miou-Miou would star in *Indien dans la Ville* (*L'Indien*) (Hervé Palud, France, 1994), in which she plays a woman who abandons her husband in order to live with their son amongst a native tribe in a remote Venezuelan village. Incidentally, while Huppert was co-starring in *Heaven's Gate*, Miou-Miou was playing a French "foreigner" in *Au Revoir...À Lundi* (Maurice Dugowson, France, 1979–80), which combined issues of divorce and female friendship with those of emigration and multinationality (Pallister, *Cinema of Quebec*, 277).

[56] An intertextual reference is also salient here to *Umbrellas of Cherbourg* [*Les Parapluies de Cherbourg*] (Jacques Demy, France/West Germany, 1964), in which a story of French postwar embourgeoisement ends with the male lead and his wife, Madeleine, owning a gasoline station (in which, not coincidentally, their young son is portrayed wearing a chief's headdress on Christmas Eve).

[57] Simpson, *Romanticism*, 16; Patrick Kay Bidelman, *Pariahs Stand Up! The Foundations of the Liberal Feminist Movement in France, 1858–89* (Westport, CT: Greenwood, 1982); Marks, "*Cendres juives*"; and Brendan Murphy, *The Butcher of Lyon: The Story of Infamous Nazi Klaus Barbie* (New York: Empire, 1983). Lyon ratified a divorce law in 1792, upon which two-thirds of all French divorces were filed there and in Rouen until 1803. The city was also a center of Sephardi struggles for emancipation from French citizenship restrictions. During the Second World War, Lyon was both the capitol of the *Résistance* and the site of some of the most ruthless atrocities to have been

committed by the Vichy regime. E.g., the city's Hotel Terminus was headquarters of local Nazi S.D. (*Sicherheitsdienst*) leader, Klaus Barbie, a.k.a. "the Butcher of Lyon"; similarly, Paul Touvier, a Vichy functionary, headed the Lyon-based *Milice* in 1943, which would have been responsible for the murder of Madeleine's husband, Raymond, and the arrest of her teacher/lover, Roland. A tele-film about the postwar arrest and trial in Lyon of Klaus Barbie is entitled, *Nazi Hunter: The Beate Klarsfeld Story* (Michael Lindsay-Hogg, U.S.A., 1986); a renowned documentary was also made about the subject entitled, *Hotel Terminus: The Life and Times of Klaus Barbie* (Marcel Ophuls, U.S.A./France, 1998). (Lanzmann's *Shoah* was broadcast on French television during the Barbie trial.) The release of these films coincided with the French "Quarrel," which revolved around the verifiability and rationale of Vichy collaboration and was highlighted by the Lyon-based trials of Barbie and Touvier as well as by cases involving former Vichy police chief, René Bousquet, Vichy budget minister, Maurice Papon, and Holocaust denier, Paul Rassinier, who was disbarred from his teaching post at the University of Lyon Department of History for denying that the Nazis used Zyklon B to murder prisoners in gas chambers. See Rousso, *The Vichy Syndrome*; R. J. Golsan et al., eds., *Memory, the Holocaust, and French Justice: The Bousquet and Touvier Affairs*, trans. Lucy Golsan and Richard J. Golsan (Hanover, VT and London: University Press of New England, 1996); Marrus and Paxton, *Vichy France and the Jews*; and Alain Finkielkraut, *Remembering in Vain: The Klaus Barbie Trial and Crimes against Humanity*, trans. Roxanne Lapidus with Sima Godfrey (New York: Columbia University Press, 1992).

[58] Higgins, "Two Women Filmmakers," 63; and Phil Powrie, "*Coup de foudre*: Nostalgia and Lesbian," in *French Cinema in the 1980s: Nostalgia and the Crisis of Masculinity* (Oxford: Clarendon, 1997), 62–74.

[59] E.g., Dan Yakir, "Mlle. Kurys," *Film Comment* 19, no. 4 (1983): 66. See also Carrie Tarr with Brigitte Rollet, *Cinema and the Second Sex: Women Filmmaking in France in the 1980s and 1990s* (New York: Continuum, 2001).

[60] Straayer, "Hypothetical Lesbian Heroine," 21.

[61] Boer, "Bowels of History," 377.

[62] Seligsohn, rev. of *Entre Nous*.

[63] Barbara Koenig Quart, *Women Directors*, 29.

[64] Denby, "Les Girls," 59.

[65] Yakir, "Mlle. Kurys," 69.

CHAPTER FIVE

HOLOCAUST "IDENTITY" AND THE ISRAELI/PALESTINIAN *BALAGAN*

> Phenomenological reduction is a scene, a theater stage.
> —Derrida, "The Voice That Keeps Silence,"
> *Speech and Phenomenon*

During an interview with *Balagan*'s German director, Andres Veiel, Israeli actress Smadar "Madi" Ma'ayan exclaims, "The Holocaust is the new religion. It is the opium of the masses in Israel." Madi's ostensibly Marxist exclamation occurs at the beginning, and is repeated toward the conclusion, of *Balagan* ["Chaos" or "A Big Mess"], an acclaimed but obscure 1993 German documentary covering the controversial 1991 Israeli theatrical production, *Arbeit Macht Frei M' Toitland Europa* ["Work Liberates from the Deathland/Deutschland Europe"]. *Arbeit Macht Frei* is a station play, a mobile production spanning the Palestinian-Israeli town of Akko [Acre] and the nearby Ghetto Fighters Museum at Kibbutz Lohamai Hagetaot, which dramatizes the relationship of the Judeocide to the conflict in Israel/Palestine in a forceful and unusual way. Reminiscent of Polish stage director Jerzy Grotowski's Total Theater and of the Living Theater "happenings" of the 1960s and 1970s,[1] *Arbeit Macht Frei* features onstage performances in which actors play reflexive Israeli/Palestinian character types in the conventional context of a theater, along with offstage performances in which the same actors play "real" museum dozents, tour guides, and bus drivers who lead a participatory audience on a figurative journey through the land of Israel and the "holocaustal" social imaginary that has come to characterize it. *Balagan* not only documents this theatricalized journey but supplements it with actor interviews at various key locations in and around Akko, an ancient fortress city traditionally a site of strong anti–colonial and anti–Zionist resistance,[2] thereby coming itself to perform cinematically, as I shall elaborate, its own very particular interpretation of the experimental Holocaust play it takes as a critical documentary occasion. As the play's political problematics are played out cinematically, furthermore, they transfigure the conflict in Israel/Palestine aesthetically into a techno-ideological mise-en-abyme that serves finally to dissimulate Marxism's radical hope for emancipation from ideological obscurantism and its attendant holocaustal effects. This hope is one to which I shall demonstrate *Balagan* can only allude "obscenely," through a figurative parody of German fascism; it is a hope shared nonetheless by both Palestinians and Israelis as well as by contemporary Germans vis-à-vis a pervasively belligerent U.S.—a hope which *Balagan* literally allegorizes by its peculiarly unstable, unsettled history.

During her first interview with Veiel, which is also the first interview in *Balagan*, Madi, the child of a Jewish-Czech Holocaust survivor, then married to *Arbeit Macht Frei*'s director, David "Dudi" Ma'ayan, describes her apparently Marxist exclamation and the performance associated with it as a "provocation," a "blasphemy," a "doing the anti–" vis-à-vis the sacralized memory of the Holocaust in Israel. In so doing, Madi underscores the critical, ostensibly radical function of her theatrical work. Indeed, Madi's proverbial quotation from the famous introduction to Marx's "A Contribution to Hegel's Philosophy of Right"[3] would seem to suggest that the Holocaust has come to signify an ideological concept, "Holocaust," in the post–Holocaust state of Israel. On that suggestion, the Holocaust has been historicized, memorialized, and institutionalized by the Israeli culture and knowledge industries apropos of the commodity-form. The Israeli re-packaged "Holocaust" has come, in other words, to comprise an ideational fetish bearing transhistorical, often mystical, connotations that dissimulate the global social rupture marked by the actual Holocaust. Inscribed as irreparable trauma, this fetish in turn obscures possible critical theoretical re-understandings of "Holocaust" as a structurally overdetermined meaning-effect readily exploitable, both psychologically and economically, in the interests of ethnic chauvinism and transnational (under)development.[4]

Balagan's provocative approach to German/Jewish/Israeli history garnered it commercial screenings and numerous awards in Germany (first Prize from the International Federation of Film Societies; Honorable Mention at the 1993 Leipzig International Documentary Festival; the Peace Film Prize at the 1994 Berlin International Film Festival; the 1994 German Film Prize; the 1994 Otto Sprenger Prize; and a nomination for Film of the Month by the Evangelical Filmworks). The film was denounced, however, for its iconoclasty and apparent radicalism by print media critics in the U.S., where its exhibition was limited to film festivals and where it is now largely unavailable.[5] In what follows, I shall argue that the critical perspective offered on "Holocaust" by *Balagan* is neither original nor radical to either the German or Western European context, and that, in turn, the negative reviews *Balagan* received upon its release have strongly misrecognized the film's ideological orientation. Ignoring the way in which *Balagan*'s formal structures intersect with those of the theatrical *Arbeit Macht Frei*, these reviews overlooked the crucial aesthetic-effects presented by *Balagan* as *cinematic performance*, thereby obscuring the way in which those effects function in relation to prevailing discourse on the role of "Holocaust" in the formation of an Israeli/Palestinian "identity."

* * * * *

In considering *Balagan*'s European production and distribution contexts, one need only recall New German Cinema's explicit call for a national "coming to terms with the past,"[6] which played no small part during the 1970s and 1980s in an increasingly international series of public debates over the history and contemporary significance of the Nazi era, not least for the Middle East. These debates included the German *Historikerstreit* and the earlier French "Quarrel," both of which attracted global attention and have since come to inform the direction of European art cinema. In view of this cultural-discursive history, it is hardly surprising that Veil, speaking of *Balagan*, would describe himself as a "second-generation perpetrator," or that he would include interview footage of Madi describing *Arbeit Macht Frei*'s Israeli performers as "second-generation victims" who have "created a monster"—a description which Veil rehearses contentiously in a contemporary print-media interview as "the self-infecting wound Israel."[7]

The scholarly writing which has emerged around this critical perspective, and which draws analogies and certain comparisons between the politics of German fascism and the Israeli occupation of Palestine, has likewise garnered international attention and in recent years begun to receive a modicum of academic legitimacy in North America, primarily through the publications of Israeli New Historians and sympathetic scholars on the U.S., Canadian, and British Left.[8] Similar work, however, on *Balagan*'s relationship to this critical historiographic discourse is noticeably scant. The only extant article on the film, published in the conservative Jewish studies journal, *Prooftexts*, re-articulates *Balagan*'s implicit engagement of the Israeli New History through a depoliticized appropriation of Marianne Hirsch's theory of postmemory, whereupon an effective analysis of what I shall describe as *Balagan*'s deep-structural, *cinematic* performance of *Israel*'s decidedly incomplete coming to terms with the past is thoroughly elided.[9]

It is in fact my contention that the unfavorable print media reception and ongoing marginalization/suppression of *Balagan* and its scholarly analysis outside of Germany are due only superficially to the film's explicit critique of Zionism, and still less are reactions to its German provenance, both of which possibilities entail facile assumptions that *Balagan* is a blatant and unmitigated example of right-revisionism. Not only have German art films always been produced with an eye to international markets, in which they have circulated successfully;[10] numerous films of the New German Cinema, for example the noted films directed by Schlöndorff and von Trotta, have received wide discussion and acclaim and remained consistently available while inscribing anti–Zionist perspectives to varying degrees.

Instead of subscribing to facile assumptions, I argue more seriously that *Balagan* projects a postmodern vision of the Judeocide by which the film at once performs that event's global commoditization and supplies its critique through means that are neither simply reactionary nor exclusively "German" but, on the larger vision, profoundly christological. On these grounds, *Balagan* is at once uncannily threatening to non-German, especially U.S. audiences, for whom the envisaging of "Holocaust" as Christ-like "existent universal"[11] hits uncomfortably close to ideological—Judeo-Christian, capitalist-ethical—home, while the film also continues to serve post–unification German audiences with the sort of self-edifying, moral-psychological instruction that was widespread in Germany throughout the postwar era. This kind of instruction has often been considered less conducive to historical mourning-work than to the marshaling of a conservative *ressentiment*.[12]

My usage of *christological* in this chapter refers to a universalizing frame of intelligibility for which history is the reality-effect of an irremediably fallible human telos which plays out repeatedly as the blood sacrifice of "holy incarnate" beings and is exemplified by periodic instances of salvific—primarily, if sometimes only symbolically, Jewish—social catastrophe. This teleological narrative, the blood-sacrificial aspect of which has been compellingly elaborated in terms of its incipient racialism in the work of German cultural historian, Christina von Braun,[13] may be understood as part of a larger, sacramental framework for which the nature of "holy incarnate" beings comprises a hypostatic collocation of asymmetrically positioned "human" and "divine" qualities, the analogic paradigm of which is the transcendent figure of Jesus Christ. In the context of Holocaust studies, christology entails belief in the christic exemplarity of the Judeocide: scholars as theoretically disparate as theologian Franklin Littell and philosopher James Watson have insisted, for example, that the Holocaust "proves" the moral logic of christic sacrifice and potentiates religious conversion to Christianity.[14] Whereas a traditional christology will profess an ideologico-historical supersession of Judaism by Christianity, modern and contemporary reinscriptions articulate secularized versions of this myth to posthistorical, even post–trinitarian theories of communitarian dialogue and ethics, themselves derived from a Protestant ecumenical tradition that draws strongly upon, while significantly reducing the significance of, Judaism.[15] Indeed christology is originally a rearticulation of Jewish messianism, itself a rearticulation of biblical, pre-Judaic pan- and polytheistic eschatologies which became properly "Christian" only in the wake of Judeo-Christianity's Roman co-optation, reduction, and institutionalization. In the contemporary public sphere, where Christian theology is only a secondary co-efficient of modern, including Nazi, antisemitism, for which race, not religion, marks the rungs of social hierarchy and Jew-hatred, posthistorical theories have become powerful ideological tools for ostensibly humanitarian interests actually to encourage a missionary application of christology to non-Jewish genocides and ethnic cleansings and to non-Jewish victims of the Holocaust.[16] Among other things, this practice serves to obscure other, more far-reaching models for understanding and comparing those genocides for which, as I shall demonstrate, the christological framework remains nonetheless relevant.[17]

Madi's first utterance of the proverbial Marxist dictum would appear at first to counter an ascription of christology to *Balagan*. It is well-known that Marx was critical of Christianity, having seen it as the theological discourse most effective for underwriting the expansionist logic of capitalism, even and especially as Christian theology—unlike Judaism—ultimately espouses merely a submissive, distinctly resigned hope for emancipation therefrom:

> [F]or a society based upon the production of commodities, in which the producers in general enter into social relations with one another by treating their products as commodities and values, whereby they reduce their individual private labor to the standard of homogeneous human labor—for such a society, Christianity with its *cultus* of abstract man, more especially in its bourgeois developments, Protestantism, Deism, etcetera, is the most fitting form of religion. (Marx, *Capital*, 83)[18]

Israeli and Anglo-American New Historians have nonetheless re-understood Marx's claim in complementary, if slightly altered, terms, as facilitating an elucidation of ideological structures by which subjugated Palestinians are positioned, much like European Jews before them, as geopolitical agents and barter-balls in the Western capitalist struggle for global domination. As I shall elucidate, *Balagan*'s sympathetic portrayal of Khaled Abu-Ali, a Muslim-Palestinian Israeli and one of *Arbeit Macht Frei*'s central characters, places the film into partial consonance with this New Historiographic perspective. Khaled vociferously opposes the Israeli occupation of Palestine while working closely with Dudi Ma'ayan's primarily Jewish-Israeli experimental theater ensemble and articulating albeit ambivalent "belief" that the Holocaust "exists." The example of Khaled illustrates clearly the view of many New Historians that Israeli-defined "Holocaust" interpellates Palestinian as well as Jewish subjectivities, positioning them not as "terroristic" antagonists but as prisoners of what Derrida has called an "unhappy consciousness"[19] who are searching desperately to extricate themselves from a struggle often perceived as endless and irreconcilable. For Palestinians, that struggle is one which decries and rejects colonialist expropriation of their lands; for Jewish Israelis, by contrast, it is one which rehearses the holocaustal antisemitism that, at least in the Jewish-Israeli imaginary, persists in Israel/Palestine despite the abstract, asymmetrical logic such a cross-historical transposition entails. The positioning of Khaled as a geopolitical agent and barter-ball imprisoned in an unhappy consciousness certainly satisfies criteria not only for identifying but also, as I shall illustrate, for acknowledging key christological elements in *Balagan*.

* * * * *

On the one hand, *Balagan* explicitly invokes Marx, to whom christology would appear distasteful. Nevertheless, the film carries out its own form of christological narrative. This *dissimulative* tendency of *Balagan* recalls the Nazi retro film phenomenon, which Holocaust cultural critic Saul Friedländer has castigated as obscene kitsch, but which German film critics Reimer and Reimer have lauded as albeit incomplete instances of cultural mourning-work. In either respect, *Balagan* participates in what Peter Michelson defines as "obscenity" ("the Greek sense of bringing onstage what is customarily kept offstage in western culture," a practice which entails a presumably necessary aestheticization of the so-called un[re]presentable, "a perceptual alteration whereby the obscene, a species of the ugly, is reconstituted to a function akin to that of the beautiful" [xi]).[20] On this definition, it is possible to understand *Balagan*'s obscenity—its christological reformulation of a Marxist critique of Israeli "Holocaust"—as parodic, as referencing ironically an abject, carnivalesque condition that adopts qualities simultaneously of the culturally offensive, perversely pleasurable, and socially threatening. Put another way, it is possible to say that "obscene" *Balagan* plays *épater le bourgeois*.

Explicit examples of this "obscene" strategy include sequences in *Balagan* which depict onstage *ménages* of *Arbeit Macht Frei*'s actors engaged in various extreme activities, including: a topless woman spinning naked in an old, metal washtub while ingesting and expelling mush; another, similarly clad woman flailing wildly while enclosed within a glass cage stuffed with suffocating layers of shredded paper (fig. 5-1); a practically naked Madi clinging to a wire mesh fence, arms extended in christic formation and lower bodily stratum draped in diaper-like rags; the same actress, in the same state of indispose, swinging inverted from a hanging rope and later blaring incoherently, tongue depressed and teeth blackened, into a microphone; and a third central character, Moni Yosef, a Jewish-Iraqi (Mizrachi) Israeli who must reconcile his theatrical career with his observant religious background, performing gymnastics while wearing a Nazi S.S. uniform. Perhaps the most "obscene" of these activities is one that features a frontally nude Khaled beating himself with a rubber truncheon: in Holocaust cinema, male frontal nudity is generally confined to the depiction of corpses.[21]

Possibly more remarkable, though, are *Balagan*'s editorial alternations between these extreme corporeal representations and moments filmed in post–theatrical settings both backstage and offstage, which together form a veritable montage by which the sanctity of Israel as a Jewish nation-state, already implicitly referenced through the political intertexts of the onstage *ménages*, is itself, in Madi's words, overtly "blasphemed." A vivid example of this critical effect involves an extended shot of the perpetually naked Madi lying prone onstage apparently extracting hidden food from her vagina, cross-cut with shots of her and Veiel listening pleasurably at Madi's home to the *Hörstwessellied*, a notorious Nazi anthem which Madi compares favorably, if somewhat facetiously, to the "roaring animal noise" of Zionist hymns. A related example involves shots of the frontally nude, self-flagellating Khaled cross-cut with a backstage scene of physical contact between himself and Moni that may be read as homoerotic.

Fig. 5-1 – Theatrical "obscenity" in *Balagan*

Their shocking qualities notwithstanding, these on-/offstage montage sequences distinguish *Balagan* from earlier Nazi retro films, vis-à-vis which "obscenity" is usually explained as a textual-effect of what Lyotard has called "libidinal economy."[22] According to the Freudo-Marxist paradigm through which that concept was initially theorized, textual-effects may be understood as literal, potentially emancipatory enactments of otherwise sublimated psycho-sexual drives.[23] Because of their purported liberatory character, however, such effects are also considered vulnerable to containment, and the drives they manifest subject to repression.[24] *Balagan* is certainly replete with aspects of this psycho-sexual dynamic, which at its worst has been used to attribute the rise of fascism to a perceived increase in the social incidence of sexual perversion seen heterocentrically as a homosexual phenomenon. But as a postmodern instance furthermore documenting a theatrical occasion, the "obscenity" *Balagan* projects is more correctly defined as an *ostensive performance* rather than as a textualized representation of the libidinal function. Following performance theorist Keir Elam, "ostensivity" refers to a theatrical condition in which the formal structures and dramatological field of a performance become so nearly indistinguishable that the performance itself comes to take epistemological priority over what would be considered, in a conventional theatrical context, its distinct actional and referential (mimetic) content.[25] Whereas libidinal economy may be understood in light of the modern "repressive hypothesis," for which desublimation of psycho-sexual energies is at once attractive for its emancipatory promise and repulsive for the dashed hopes—including especially fascist developments—it presumably also prefigures, the performatics of ostensivity assume, by albeit related contrast, the reconfiguration of "repression" into an antifoundational, "virtual" condition of perpetual psychodramatic "flux."[26]

Balagan establishes its ostensivity by documenting a theatrical occasion that is both non-original and epic in quality. Indeed *Arbeit Macht Frei* is based upon and references intertextually another theatrical production, *Cherli Ka Cherli* (Danny Horowitz, Jerusalem Khan Theater, 1978), itself a parody of a culturally entrenched Israeli practice, *massachet*, a kibbutznik ritual comprising a communal meal and lively series of non-linear, highly theatricalized performances "revolving around [...] a mind drama [or] conceptual confrontation between personified notions."[27] *Arbeit Macht Frei* supplements *Cherli Ka Cherli*'s psychodramaticality with the Brechtian notion that characterological conflict refracts, and may be marshaled to engage, ideological problematics of audience reality.[28] Hence *Arbeit Macht Frei* disassociates its characters from realist conventions that invite audience identification and catharsis, and instead recasts them as "sociopsychic archetypes," reified figures who recall Brecht's theory of epic distanciation [*verfremdungsmachen*] for their transferential redirection of the spectatorial will to identify back onto the post–theatrical world. In fact, these figures are literal allegories, typological ciphers which problematize the security of the traditional "fourth wall." *Arbeit Macht Frei*'s audience is brought physically into the performance space, seated amidst set properties, addressed directly, and compelled to *move with* the performance, to enter its spatio-temporality, to *encounter* it, to *enliven* it, to make *it happen*.[29] By this technique, the play is hyperrealized, its post–theatrical scene destabilized and unsettled yet supplied with a revised symbolic logic by which its post–Holocaust inhabitants may renegotiate the terms of contemporary social crisis.

Indeed as Elam notes, the political grounding of *Arbeit Macht Frei*'s epic construction diverges from that of Brecht, an avowed Marxist, in its appropriation of Jerzy Grotowski's concept of Total Theater, with its explicit christological proselytic of self-sacrifice through liberatory-salvific exploration and display of extreme bodily experience, which it positions instead of the material relations of labor and exchange at the core of social crisis.[30] In addition to enacting extreme corporeality, Madi describes her performative "blasphemy" of "Holocaust" in the phenomenological spirit of Grotowski, as a haptic allegory of everyday life in Israel/Palestine, which she compares to being engulfed in a "well," a "big hole," a "wound," a *schwarze loch* [black hole]. Setting aside for a moment the problem such a description holds out for feminism,[31] these comparisons all suggest a life of profound existential disorientation, *balagan*, which, in Madi's words, can be "tasted" and "touched" but never managed or contained by reigning social institutions. To achieve a modicum of peace in the face of *balagan*, says Madi, she "will have to go to India"—an especially ironic statement considering the oft-compared histories of the Indian–Pakistani and Israeli–Palestinian partitions and the contemporary geopolitical alliance of India, Israel, and the U.S.[32] *Balagan* incorporates this mystical, orientalist phenomenology, otherwise intended as an avenue for Holocaust mourning-work, by giving it narratological centrality and establishing Madi at its apogee. Contrasting a contemporary Israeli film on the same play, *Al Tigu Li B'Shoah* ["Don't Touch My Holocaust"] (Asher Tlalim, 1994), to which difference from the German film I shall return, *Balagan*'s emphasis upon Madi's visceral extremity and haptic significance positions her as the apotheosis of a *superprotagonal triad*, a tripartite reflexive figuration oriented toward superseding and disambiguating identitarian borders between the film's central Mizrachi-Israeli and Muslim-Palestinian characters, Moni and Khaled, even and especially as those borders demarcate, or limn, the (post–)theatrical space ostensively.

According to Gad Kaynar, who has analyzed the phenomenon in some detail with respect to *Arbeit Macht Frei*, the "superprotagonist" may be defined as a theatrical figure who is at once spectator and actor as well as neither of these.[33] Superprotagonality, as distinct from mere ostensivity, subverts the standard Brechtian praxis of distanciation, insofar as its post–theatrical effectuality is indiscriminate, nay ecumenical: anyone is fair game for its proselytic, anyone an audience for its hyperreal transference, anyone an exemplar of its social lesson, which is thusly transhistorical and aesthetically based. In this respect, superprotagonality may be seen as a mythical, quasi-Jungian function describable in terms of Hannah Arendt's "biological superhuman personality," a form of subjectivity "perhaps not unlike [that of] the Puritan society of New England," which Zionism is known to have conferred upon Jews globally in order to lend Israel [...] an extra-territorial jurisdiction over Jews wherever they may be."[34] I shall now elaborate how, at the expense of critiquing the divisiveness and asymmetricality which actually comprise Israeli/Palestinian reality, it is precisely *Balagan*'s viscerally ostensive, hypersecular superprotagonality which dissimulates those social conditions aesthetically, and which, in turn, cagily distinguishes the film's ideology critique of "Holocaust" from that of a properly Marxist analysis.

An overriding example of this dissimulative tendency is the way in which *Balagan*'s superprotagonal structure, recalling nineteenth-century racialist discourse, will finally congeal into a "post–semitic" icon, a tropic figure which allegorizes christologically the uneven division and ideological overdeterminacy of the triadic relationship between the film's three central characters. In order that this may occur, an ethical and political differentiation is first established between Khaled and Moni, the film's two ethnic Arabs, whose relationship in turn becomes one of an asymmetrical dyad that rehearses the unequal positioning of Palestinians and Jewish Arabs in Israel/Palestine itself.

Khaled and Moni's uneven differentiation is structured largely through intellectual montage but also through parallel editing. In regard to ethical unevenness, Khaled, a secular Muslim, is shown briefly, via a fragmented shot sequence, dancing naked onstage, whereby his transgression of the Islamic proscription against public male nudity is rendered evident and only later, cursorily explained by Khaled himself as a counter to perceived Palestinian "backwardness." In a subsequent scene, by contrast, Moni, an observant Jew, is allotted steady and significant screen time in which to explain his choice to uphold similar Judaic law by refusing to perform without clothes. A similarly structured instance politically reorients this contrast between the ostensibly ethical Jew, Moni, and the ostensibly unethical Muslim, Khaled. Scenes comprising shots of Khaled's impoverished, primarily Palestinian home town of Sakhnin in the Galilee, site of the notorious 1976 Land Day Massacre in which six Palestinians were killed by Israelis, now depicted under constant IDF surveillance, are juxtaposed with scenes comprising shots of Moni's comfortable and well-protected home in Akko and that of his brother, a recalcitrant settler, in the Israeli-occupied Golan Heights. While ostensibly opening the film onto a critique of the Israeli economic underdevelopment of Palestine, a concomitant layer of the juxtaposition tends to undercut any such possibility. In this concomitant regard, Khaled is portrayed coming to experience alienation from darker-skinned Palestinian friends who themselves have undergone Israeli military arrest and imprisonment during the first Intifada, and who refer to Khaled as a collaborator after he admits giving Israeli soldiers rides to and from Akko. By contrast, Moni is portrayed coming to experience empathy for the plight of his right-wing brother after visiting his family's underground bunker, a veritable military stronghold reminiscent of Holocaust-era resistance fighting and located in an illegal Jewish settlement near the Syrian border. The effect of this twofold structuring is to render Khaled's membership in Dudi Ma'ayan's theater company an understandable effect of his overt disdain for and desire to distance himself from purportedly entrenched Palestinian violence and cultural stagnation, while Moni's participation in the same company is shown rooted in a socially respectable, albeit ambivalent love and concern for his post–Holocaust Jewish-Israeli brethren.

At the film's narrative-tropological register, where the ethical and political nearly converge, this uneven, differential construction is never ironized but instead reaffirmed. Khaled, a Palestinian citizen of Israel, comes to figure as a shifter,[35] an unstable signifier who oscillates stereotypically between expressions of belief in the "existence" of the Holocaust and Holocaust denial, and, by political extension, between hope for the largely disparaged possibility of transforming Israel/Palestine into a secular, regionally integrated, multicultural entity and resignation to the increasingly less feasible idea of dividing the Occupied Palestinian Territories into separate-but-equal cantons surrounded and traversed by Israel proper. By contrast, Moni, a Jewish Israeli, figures as a comparatively stable, if not monumental, signifier; although Mizrachi, he remains a convinced Zionist who expresses the generally unfounded but nonetheless widely acknowledged post–Holocaust Jewish-Israeli fear of being "pushed into the sea" by erstwhile Palestinian enemies, even as he voices sympathy for their subjugated plight.[36]

Despite their uneven differentiation, however, and because of the montage structure facilitating it, *Balagan*'s two Arab characters, Moni and Khaled, are likewise brought into identification, but in terms of (an anthropologically disproved) discourse of organic kinship rather than their demonstrably shared social history as Arabs. When they are portrayed embracing during a backstage rehearsal, for instance, their mutually balding heads are highlighted, giving each a decidedly phallic, almost homoerotic appearance. Less implicit is the visual reminder provided by Khaled's onstage frontal nudity of the circumcision ritual common to Islam and Judaism, which, notwithstanding real theological differences between the Muslim and Judaic observation and interpretation of that ancient ritual,[37] associates Khaled and Moni ethno-corporeally, that is, racially. These examples are but two in the film which illustrate how *Balagan* refigures *ethnicity*, a national-cultural, often diasporic category subject to political and economic determination, into a *racial* category,[38] and how it thereby mutually "identifies" these ethnic Arabs by positioning them ahistorically, as biological males capable of reproducing "semitic" bodies, whereupon their asymmetrical differentiation appears resolvable organically rather than politically, through the implementation of racialist ideologies originating in Christian Europe, rather than through real, social-structural change of the kind proffered within certain historical configurations of both Islam and Judaism that have since found secular and hybrid rearticulations in the Middle East and beyond.[39]

* * * * *

Balagan's racialist construction of Palestinians and Mizrachi Jews as "semites," eerily reminiscent of Nazi ideology, subsequently consolidates within the context of the film's christologic, as the "semitic" is fetishistically hypostatized through the Ashkenazi Madi's iconic troping of its Arab matrix. This iconic function is cultivated on two registers, the first of which becomes evident during a remarkable scene in which Madi is filmed at home preparing for the role of "Zelma," an elderly, physically decrepit Eastern-European Holocaust survivor who is featured as a museum dozent during the Ghetto Fighters Museum section of *Arbeit Macht Frei*.

In this scene, Madi is portrayed donning her Zelma costume before a mirror in a shadowy, candle-lit room. Because both Madi and her reflection are visible, an initial impression is given that the scene is framed in two-shot, and that Zelma is Madi's alter-ego. Yet Madi's transformation into Zelma entails a drastic alteration in the former's appearance and deportment, especially where age and stature are concerned, indicating something more and other than ego alterity. While gazing into the mirror at her gradually altering image, Madi describes Zelma using words with which Nazi concentration camp prisoners have often been described: as ghostlike, representative of "the living dead," a "two thousand year-old woman [...] neither dead nor alive" who subsists "in the twilight zone" and "comes and goes" randomly. Here again the scene invokes Brechtian theory, in this instance that for which a mere costume change can signify a radical character transformation subject to auto-critique by the very performer enacting the change. But the scene's mirror-effect also invokes the Lacanian Althusser, a structuralist Marxist philosopher for whom "ideology represents the imaginary relationship of individuals to their real conditions of existence."[40] Thus while the young, vivacious Madi transforms into the decrepit, funereal Zelma, a prototypically romantic, Christo-European ideology of eternal feminine hell may be seen to qualify the imaginary condition of Jewish decrepitude represented within the scene,[41] nearly overshadowing any attendant, pre-European sense of that suffering as described so frequently in the *tanakh* and as allegorized explicitly by Agamben's figure of the *Muselmann*.[42] Indeed the cinematic framing of Madi and her reflection in two-shot, the very matrix of auto-critique in the scene, literalizes a subjective cleavage between the Israeli and European layers of her characterological persona, under the refractional purview of which the "hell" that has come thusly under scrutiny is re-articulated to a European social imaginary that is certainly represented by the holocaustal Zelma, but that also must be seen ostensively, as an ideological site hailing a third figure, Madi/Zelma, the Ashkenazi-Israeli actress' very legacy as a tortured, haunted, "wandering" Jew. The scene elevates Madi as such into a self-reflexive Israeli type, a congealed, corporeal, almost christic image of eternal Jewish suffering that at one and the same time allegorizes a particularly European Zionist envisaging of the Israeli/Palestinian real. In effect the transformation of Madi into the "hellish"-holocaustal signifier, Madi/Zelma, comes to position her as a performative matrix of split Ashkenazi-Israeli subjectivity vis-à-vis which the post–theatrical Madi may come to expose and "blaspheme" the reputed persistence of Jewish suffering in Israel/Palestine through her own subsequent actions beyond the mirror, including ongoing and ensuing interviews with the post–Nazi German Veiel.

At a second register, however, the scene's potential function as global self-criticism is subverted, as Madi/Zelma is herself repositioned as an aesthetic supplement to the asymmetrical, racialized Arab dyad, Moni/Khaled. Paradigmatic of this ludic switch is a late sequence in which shots of Madi reminiscing about a visit to her father's prewar home in Czechoslovakia are juxtaposed with shots of Khaled visiting his family in the besieged Palestinian-Israeli town of Sakhnin, and with shots of Moni visiting his brother in the Israeli-occupied Golan. These juxtapositions are in one sense thematically unified, insofar as the familial "return" depicted in each instance proves dramatically unsatisfying. In contrast to prior visits and notwithstanding his explicit anti–occupation politics, for example, Khaled displays confusion over his assumed ethno-political alliances and affinities after receiving sharp rebukes from family and friends to whom he reveals his participation in *Arbeit Macht Frei*. By comparison, Moni, who had previously criticized the Israeli occupation of Palestine, reverses his politics after touring his brother's underground armed bunker, henceforth reaffirming his support for Zionist colonization of the region on what can best be interpreted as nostalgic, sentimental grounds. Similarly Madi, who initially evinces enthusiasm over her recounted visit to Czechoslovakia, subsequently expresses disappointment over having discovered her father's childhood home occupied and inhabited by non-Jews.

Although these unfulfilling, ambivalent "returns" clearly evoke salient political ironies, not least insofar as the repeated dissatisfactions they represent parallel discursively the modality of capitalist desire vis-à-vis the commodity-form, their structural supplementation by/under Madi/Zelma precludes a serious critique of either that modality or its political manifestation as colonialism, whether in the form of the Israeli occupation of Palestine or, previously, the Nazi occupation of Europe.[43] This is because the sequence in question never finally grounds Madi/Zelma's positioning as mythological "wanderer" in the material conditions which are known to have given rise historically to that myth and its abiding, colonialist rationale. As Michael Selzer reminds, even Zionist founder, Theodor Herzl, politicized the Jewish idea of homelessness long before his famous conversion to Jewish nationalism. Although he would later draw upon Christo-European antisemitism as its primary justification, Herzl initially believed, pre-dating Sartre, that Jewish "homelessness"—the fact that Jewish communities are *historically* diasporic—mitigated *against* the idea of a Jewish State: "And if the Jews really 'returned home' one day, they would discover on the next that they do not belong together. For centuries they have been rooted in diverse nationalisms; they differ from each other group by group; the only thing they have in common is the pressure which holds them together."[44] Instead recalling Heidegger, Madi/Zelma figures across this particular montage sequence as *essentially* homeless.[45]

In context of its various juxtapositions, for example, the sequence offers a depiction of Moni's and Khaled's respective familial locations, whereas Madi's paternal home in Eastern Europe is never shown. No archival footage of a comparable location is inserted for illustrative purposes during Madi's recollection, as would be customary in a conventional Holocaust documentary, nor, instead, is footage of the Holocaust inserted to explain the exclusion of any such material. In lieu of either option, a shot is inserted of a present-day IDF road sign demarcating a border between Israeli and Palestinian (Israeli-occupied) territory (fig. 5-2). Not only does this road sign's particular referent, a dividing line between would-be ethnic homelands that are each basically European colonies inhabited by a variety of "ethnicities," contradict the very notion of "home"; it allegorizes the antifoundational, peregrine quality of Madi/Zelma's mythological homelessness, even as it indexes, literally, the asymmetrical, racialized dyad, Moni/Khaled.

Fig. 5-2 – Signpost at Israeli–Palestinian border in *Balagan*

In other words, taken in context of the visual absence of Madi's paternal, Eastern European home, the Israeli/Palestinian road sign serves as a rhetorical means by which to collapse the christo-romantic ideology of eternal wandering associated with Madi/Zelma and, by extension, the Holocaust into an imaginary non-place of familial memory, and to further conflate the genealogical vacuum— the *schwarze loch*—thereby attributable to Madi's oedipal pursuit with the global political history by which force, and through which ensuing conflict, the borders riving Israel and Palestine—dividing Jews from Palestinians, and rendering the latter *actually* homeless—have historically been determined.[46] Put another way, Madi/Zelma's ideological function is as a supranational signifier of christological irresolution traceable "eternally" both to the German–Israeli nexus contextualizing *Balagan*'s very production, not to mention its historical conditions of possibility,[47] and to the U.S.-dominated global film industry actually enabling and facilitating both of these. Through this function, *Balagan* not only represents, but *itself performs* the racialist, (a)symmetrical relationship allegorized aesthetically by Madi/Zelma vis-à-vis Moni/Khaled, at once unveiling and obscuring the ideological determinants of the conflict in Israel/Palestine which Madi/Zelma at once "obscenely" embodies and reflexively transcends; and, in so doing, it transcribes *Arbeit Macht Frei*'s mobile-theatrical ostensivity into a *global cinematic* fetish.

A key figure in this transcription is, not unpredictably, Andres Veiel himself. As a veritable "outsider," a German in Israel, and a filmmaker documenting a theatrical production, Veiel easily mirrors Madi/Zelma's iconic function as world-weary wanderer; and, as a relatively well-funded European director, he is able literally to ensure the global dissemination of this iconic function—in the commodity-form of *Balagan*. The example of Veiel's peculiar mode of interviewing Moni and Khaled underscores this exploitative function. Several times throughout the film, Veiel is shown accompanying Moni and Khaled on their respective visits home, where, despite the latters' impressive multilingualism, Veiel conducts his interviews with them, as with the polyglossic Madi/Zelma, in English, the linguistic vehicle of contemporary U.S.-dominated international trade, commerce, and missionary expansion.[48] During these interviews, Veiel remains safely offscreen, his questions and comments excluded from the soundtrack. When his voice is finally heard (this occurs only once in the film), it is not in the context of speaking with these "semitic" men, from whom he will remain effectively disassociated for the film's duration, but in the company of the "eternal feminine" Madi, during her "obscene" rehearsal of the *Hörstwessellied*, which is not only a Nazi anthem but a commodified musical recording for which Madi says she "will pay" Veiel an exorbitant sum in order to own it in its entirety.

The "outsider" Veiel in this way would seem to allegorize Madi's iconic function to the global cultural register. His film, *Balagan*, however, would seem likewise to subvert any imputation of a profit motive—at least initially. In the scene just described, for example, Madi becomes the German Veiel's Jewish feminine prototype, their roles confounding through a process that recalls the rhetorical construction of Madi/Zelma. On the one hand, Madi veritably seduces Veiel, via the *Hörstwessellied*, into appearing in his own film, whereupon he becomes vulnerable to albeit critical reification and an eventual grafting alongside Moni and Khaled onto the superprotagonal configuration. On the other hand, Veiel's self-proclaimed status as "child-of-perpetrators" easily parallels the "eternal suffering" already attributed to Madi/Zelma in her status as (child of) a Holocaust survivor with all its racialized, aestheticized baggage. Hence, as Veiel is drawn thusly into the *balagan*, *Balagan*, at once his representative and instrument, relinquishes any claim it may seem to have staked, as a documentary, to objectivity or coherence, qualities generally considered necessary to successful commodification. Through Veiel's "ostensive" positioning with/as Madi/Zelma, that is, *Balagan* becomes part and parcel of the superprotagonal project, effectively condemned, like the christo-mythology it projects, to holocaustal self-sacrifice in the name of baseless, perpetual—"Jewish"—suffering.

By the same token, and as an effect of Veiel's very subsumption into the superprotagonal configuration, the exploitative function which Veiel seems nonetheless to signify remains an instantiation-effect of Madi/Zelma: it is she and the conflict in Israel/Palestine she allegorizes through her aesthetic triangulation of the racialized Moni/Khaled dyad, not Veiel and his German provenance, which elevates *Balagan* to the status of that conflict's iconic exemplar and upholds it as an "eternal," commodificatory matrix of Middle East crisis. The paradigmatic instance of this aesthetic-effect involves the positioning of Madi's second utterance of Marx's famous dictum as an aside to a scene in which *Arbeit Macht Frei*'s ensemble cast and Jewish-Israeli audience are shown participating mutually in a hyper–reflexive group confession of "shared feeling" regarding the Holocaust. In this scene, video recordings of audience declarations about the Holocaust and *Arbeit Macht Frei* are broadcast live onstage. Moni and Khaled provoke these declarations by forcefully interviewing audience members, including a Holocaust survivor, from within Eichmannesque glass booths lining the stage. In the course of these veritable interrogations, Moni and Khaled's "semitic" relationality, thus far figured corporeally via the superprotagonal Madi/Zelma, broaches a *hermeneutic* register that will effectively clinch the politics of her, and by extension *Balagan*'s, christic iconicity. Facilitated by intercutting between their faces as reflected in the glass, Moni and Khaled's relationality undergoes a transcription from the plane of organic kinship to that of imaginary dialogics, whereupon the two reified characters are now identified intersubjectively, in *cognitive*, not merely biological, terms: they are no longer merely biological "semites," naturally identifiable by their respective circumcisions; they are cognitive "semites," likewise identifiable by their stereotypical Arab "wrath," their "despotic oriental" behavior, and, perhaps as importantly, their analogic positioning nonetheless—even thereby—as *ex post facto* Holocaust victims.[49] The cross-cutting during the scene back to Madi's Marxist exclamation serves both to underscore and ironize this transcription, suggesting implicitly that the cognitive function it signifies marks that ideological means by which hypermediated confessions may be garnered and "virtual" rituals may be conducted in Israel/Palestine which simulate the mass religiosity critiqued by Marx as well as literalize the global cinematicity allegorized by Veiel and performed by *Balagan*.

In effect, the racially triangulated conflict in Israel/Palestine is transposed onto the commoditized plane of global cinematic culture as secular christology writ large. With Madi/Zelma as its apotheosis ("Madi" is phonetically similar to the Arabic word for "messiah," *mahdi*, and identical to the Arabic word for "past," *madi*; and Smadar, Madi's full name, means "budding fruit" in Hebrew),[50] *Balagan* enacts a romanticized, post–Holocaust performance of Israeli/Palestinian "identity" as *fateful triangulation* of biologically fallible "semites" vis-à-vis European/American "crusaders."[51] The film in this way also manages a non-sacral, Eurocentric dissimulation of Zionism's secular messianic claim of Israel as a supranational, ethno-racial homeland for the "Jews."[52]

* * * * *

This troubling interpretation strongly contrasts the meaning and significance of the Israeli film, *Al Tigu Li B'Shoah*, which won best Israeli documentary at the 1994 Santa Barbara Film Festival,[53] a point affirmed, even within the Zionist and post–Zionist camps, by Yosefa Loshitzky, Régine-Mihal Friedman, and Omer Bartov, who otherwise utilize thematic, historicist, and trauma-theoretical analysis to avoid discussing the larger historical truths concerning the function of "Holocaust" in Israel/Palestine (indeed Bartov actually associates the pursuit of such truths with the right-revisionism of German historian and Nazi apologist, Ernst Nolte).[54] Like *Balagan*, *Al Tigu* follows *Arbeit Macht Frei*'s ostensive personification of characters whose discursive and perspectival conflictuality rather than psychodramatic analogics compel a series of "obscene" matrices which trope theatrical and post–theatrical contexts into global cinematic, allegorical nodes. Although by no means free of ideological contradictions,[55] *Al Tigu* nonetheless contrasts *Balagan*'s performance and philosophy of ostensivity. Indeed the Mizrachi-directed Israeli film problematizes the christological discourse of superprotagonality, as it deconstructs the notion of aesthetic telos while remaining structurally founded within an albeit differential sense of political-historical development. *Al Tigu* at once recalls and problematizes the European nascence of Zionism, the conception and implementation of the Holocaust, and the continuing role of postwar Germany, alongside the U.S., as an arms supplier and financier to Israel, which continues to use those arms to secure its occupation of the Palestinian Territories.[56] By articulating characterological conflict to an historical problematic, that is, *Al Tigu* does not merely expose, aesthetically, the ideology- (and reality-) effects of the conflict in Israel/Palestine but presents them in the context of locating conceptual tools for its political resolution.

Whereas *Balagan* undermines any sense of narrative progression, instead organizing a collage-like structure, for example, *Al Tigu* figures a more linear, while nonetheless complexly layered, narratology. The film traces the very idea of "progress" to an originary matrix of Jewish-Israeli history, then deconstructs that matrix's defining concepts—the biblical Exodus, Zionism, the Holocaust—via a series of perspectival redefinitions represented respectively by each of the film's central characters as well as by editorial insertions of material from other films. *Al Tigu* begins and ends, respectively, with film footage that appears archival but is actually fictional, and live theatrical shots from *Arbeit Macht Frei*'s 1992 original-cast performance in Germany. In the first instance, classic images are supplied of German boxcar trains transporting Jewish prisoners to death camps; in the second instance, some of the more viscerally shocking scenes from the play are reproduced. In effect, the received matrix of Jewish-Israeli history is revealed a construct linked but not limited to the Ashkenazi, holocaustal past. Furthermore by decentering certain keywords which have come to overdetermine the direction and significance of Jewish-Israeli narratives about that past, *Al Tigu* likewise problematizes their conceptual framing. In a preliminary sequence from *Arbeit Macht Frei* restaged outdoors and entitled "Lexicon," concepts such as "Holocaust" and "Zyklon B" are subject to analysis by Moni, Khaled, Madi and director Dudi, as all four stand amidst the ruins of a bombed-out building, possibly a destroyed Palestinian home. The post–theatrical setting and inclusion of Dudi in the scene lends it a meta-discursive quality that, within the film's established parameters, positions *Al Tigu* as an intellectual project for which the deconstruction of terms becomes a means to re-narrate history on politically reconstituted grounds.

Readings such as this are generally lost on *Al Tigu*'s critics, whose reliance on trauma-theoretical and related paradigms leads them to misrecognize the conflict in Israel/Palestine as a largely post–*Holocaust* condition: their focus on the psycho-historical dimensions of the issue renders the Holocaust itself a "ground zero" for that conflict—what Bartov calls, quoting Madi, the "'dark secrets' [of] inexpressible, unbearable trauma,"[57] as though the long history of European colonialism, which supplied the rationale, if not the actual impetus for nineteenth- and early twentieth-century Ashkenazi settlement in Palestine, were irrelevant. In the absence of such analysis, these critics are also unable to recognize how *Al Tigu*'s differences from *Balagan* foreground the latter's real distance from the radical politics implied by the film's repetition of Madi's proverbial referencing of Marx. It may be more befitting, therefore, to designate *Balagan* an ideologically "obscene" instantiation of the "opium of the masses" to which Madi's references actually refer. In this case, however, the question of *Balagan*'s marginalization and uneven reception may turn less on the strength than on the weakness of its christologicality, here referring specifically to the capacity of its ostensive performatics to stand in for a materialist analysis of the conflict in Israel/Palestine while nonetheless exposing and exhibiting its deeply pervasive sociopsychological effects. After all, inasmuch as Zionism has been designated a travesty or blasphemy of *Judaism* by many secular (including some Mizrachi) and religious (including some ultra-observant) Jews,[58] an aesthetic performance that allegorizes Zionism to the so-called Christian "heresy" and its self-fulfilling prophecy of holocaustal doom seems uncannily appropriate to an enlarged understanding of the conflict in Israel/Palestine. A case in point is the current global reaction to the near-genocidal extremity into which the Israeli occupation of Palestine has devolved,[59] evidenced not least in Germany by massive anti–globalization rallies that have drawn none-too explicit—and justifiable—connections between the U.S. invasions of Iraq and Afghanistan and the Israeli occupation of Palestine, but also by a likewise documented increase in right-wing anti–Jewish incidents alongside more flagrant and preponderant anti–Muslim violence throughout the European Union and North America.[60] On this reasoning alone, *Balagan* is worthy of sustained viewing and analysis and should, therefore, be made more widely available.

Yet, although it must be conceded that *Balagan* is a limit-text, going farther than most Holocaust films before or since in problematizing the conflict in Israel/Palestine, the film must also be criticized for itself becoming a self-sacrificial instance, a liminal cinematic occasion that sustains its "burden of guilt" on racialized, aestheticized grounds, ultimately presuming to explain the conflict in Israel/Palestine by literally performing the old antisemitic canard that Jews are a "composite" race who necessarily invite and perpetuate suffering and "chaos" for their "obscene" refusal to relinquish their "rigid" covenantal beliefs and "oriental" customs. This is not only a mythological gesture per se, it actually undermines the effectiveness of *Balagan*'s own ostensible anti–Zionism by serving to obfuscate the very fact of eschatological traditions *within Judaism itself* that have served ideologically throughout the modern period both to revise *halakhah* and rationalize a constitutionally illegitimate, ethnocratic Israeli state.[61] It is indeed vis-à-vis the monopolistic coercion and exclusivity practiced by Jewish messianic Zionists (e.g., Gush Emunim) and messianic Jewish Zionists (Jews for Jesus) that secular Jewish Israelis have often utilized Christian symbols and imagery to express abstract, transcendental, even "obscene" parodic ideas—ideas which many messianists have themselves ironically welcomed, even appropriated, in the interests of preserving a Jewish-Israeli hegemon.[62] Although such utilization is facilitated by the perceived absence of a Jewish visual aesthetic tradition, which *Al Tigu* certainly refutes, it does not necessarily translate into an adherence to Christian principles, as *Balagan* would seem to have it—which is by no means to deny the significant historical role of Christian theology in both the institution and continued support for a Jewish Israel and, apropos of Marx, for the related project of Western global imperialism. Henceforth, the question might become one of whether, in deference to *Al Tigu*, *Balagan*'s superprotagonal troping of "Holocaust" does not ironically reify the Israeli–Palestinian conflict's material history at the expense of at least proposing a relevant and applicable political means toward its equitable, worldly resolution. What, after all, does it mean to figure the conflict in Israel/Palestine as a Christian moral exemplar of the European/American social imaginary, especially from within the context of a reunified, Protestant Germany that has come quickly to dominate a post–Cold War Europe now itself unified economically for the first time since the Holy Roman Empire and poised to reap the financial benefits of an "endless," exceedingly brutal U.S.-led global war, the epicenter of which is the Middle East?[63] Surely we have not forgotten the last time "semitic" differentiation became a favored "tropic" instance.

---

[1] See Darko Suvin, "Reflections on Happenings," *The Drama Review* 14, no. 3 (1970): 125–44.

[2] Jiryis, *Arabs in Israel*, 29; Childers, "Wordless Wish," 192; and Masalha, *Expulsion of the Palestinians*, 98. It should also be noted that Kibbutz Lohamai Hagetaot is known to have established an electronics factory during the 1980s in the South African Bantustan of Kwazulu (Hilton Obenzinger, "South Africa: The Israeli Connection," *American-Arab Affairs* 18 [1988]: 125).

[3] The pertinent lines are, "*Religious* suffering is at one and the same time the *expression* of real suffering and a protest against real suffering. Religion is the sigh of the oppressed creature, the heart of a heartless world and the soul of soulless conditions. It is the *opium* of the people" (Marx, *Karl Marx: Early Writings*, trans. Rodney Livingstone and Gregor Benton, ed. Lucio Colletti [1843–44; repr., New York: Vintage 1975], 244).

[4] See Judd Ne'eman, "The Death Mask of the Moderns: A Genealogy of *New Sensibility* Cinema in Israel," *Israel Studies* 4, no. 1 (1999): 100–28; Zertal, *From Catastrophe to Power*, 269-74; Bresheeth, "Great Taboo Broken"; and Gad Kaynar, "The Holocaust Experience through Theatrical Presentation," in *Staging the Holocaust: The Shoah in Drama and Performance*, ed. Claude Schumacher (Cambridge and New York: Cambridge University Press, 1998), 53–69.

[5] Susan Gerhard, "Blasphemera," *San Francisco Bay Guardian*, July 20, 1994: 38; Leah Garchick, rev. of *Balagan*, *San Francisco Chronicle*, July 25, 1994: E6; Chris Vognar, "Jewish Films on the Edge," *The Daily Californian*, n.p.; Dennis Harvey, rev. of *Balagan* in *Variety*, December 19, 1994: 76–77. Cf. Ilsa Lund, rev. of *Balagan* in *Moving Pictures*, February 17, 1994; Hajo, rev. of *Balagan* in *Märkische Allgemeine Zeitung*, February 18, 1994; Sven Siebert and Evelyn Gratzfeld, rev. of *Balagan* in *Dok Festival Leipzig*, November 30, 1993; Margit Voss, rev. of *Balagan* in *Film-Echo/Filmwoche*, December 3, 1993; "Balagan-Premier," rev. of *Balagan* in *Film-Echo/Filmwoche*, April 29, 1994: 14; Martin Rabius, "Balagan," *EPD Film* 11, no. 5 (1994): 44; Ron Holloway, "Balagan" *Kino* 55 (August 1994): 12–13; and Herbert Seifer, rev. of *Balagan* in *Neue Zürische Zeitung*, December 9, 1993. The film's print media reception in Israel was lukewarm, and its exhibition there similarly restricted. I have no further information about additional screenings or reception of *Balagan* except for those in Italy, where print media criticism was likewise cool. Originally, distribution rights to *Balagan* were held by a German company, Arsenal Films. Until about 1996, international distribution rights were held by Pinnacle Pictures of London. Subsequently, all distribution rights reverted to Klaus Volkenborn,

Balagan's producer. *Balagan* continues nonetheless to be listed in most film catalogs and online databases as either "distributed by Arsenal Films" or "not available."

[6] As stated in the Oberhausen Manifesto of 1962. See Thomas Elsaesser, *New German Cinema: A History* (New Brunswick: Rutgers University Press, 1989). Seminal German texts of this critical tendency are Alexander Mitserlisch and Margarete Mitserlisch, *The Inability to Mourn: Principles of Collective Behavior*, trans. Beverly R. Placzek (New York: Grove, 1975); and its renowned predecessor, Karl Jaspers, *The Question of German Guilt*, trans. E. B. Ashton (New York: Capricorn, 1961).

[7] "Recent Films from Germany," in *Museum of Modern Art Members Calendar* (New York: The Museum of Modern Art, December 1996). Veiel's 1995 film, *Die Überlebenden* ["The Survivors"], focuses precisely on the subject of German "second-generation perpetrators." Prior West German films have drawn similar connections—if only to contain them through reaction to feminist and anti–colonialist struggles. E.g., *Die Bleierne Zeit* ["Marianne and Juliane"] (Margarethe von Trotta, 1981); and *Die Fälschung* ["Circle of Deceit"] (Volker Schlöndorff, 1980–81).

[8] E.g., the North American academic journal, *Israel Studies*, published since 1995 by Indiana University Press, and the more longstanding *Journal of Palestine Studies*; also, in chronological order: Simha Flapan, *The Birth of Israel: Myths and Realities* (London: Croon Helm, 1970); Chomsky, *Fateful Triangle*; Tom Segev, *1949: The First Israelis*, ed. Arlen Neal Weinstein (New York: Free Press, 1986); Cheryl A. Rubenberg, *Israel and the American National Interest: A Critical Examination* (Urbana and Chicago: University of Illinois Press, 1986); Benny Morris, *The Birth of the Palestinian Refugee Problem, 1947– 1949* (Cambridge: Cambridge University Press, 1987); Ibrahim Abu-Lughod, *Transformation of Palestine*; Ilan Pappe, *Britain and the Arab–Israeli Conflict, 1948–1951* (London: Macmillan, 1988); Avi Shlaim, *Collusion Across the Jordan: King Abdullah, the Zionist Movement, and the Partition of Palestine* (Oxford: Clarendon, 1988); Harkabi, *Israel's Fateful Hour*; Muhammad Y. Muslih, *The Origins of Palestinian Nationalism* (New York: Columbia University Press, 1988); Tekiner, *Anti–Zionism*; Benny Morris, *1948 and After: Israel and the Palestinians* (1990; repr., Oxford: Oxford University Press, 1994); Segev, *The Seventh Million*; Akiva Orr, *Israel: Politics, Myths and Identity Crisis* (London: Pluto, 1994); Shahak, *Jewish History, Jewish Religion*; Camille Mansour, *Beyond Alliance: Israel in U.S. Foreign Policy*, trans. James A. Cohen (New York: Columbia University Press, 1994); Norman G. Finkelstein, *Image and Reality of the Israeli–Palestinian Conflict* (London: Verso, 1995); Naseer H. Aruri, *The Obstruction of Peace: The United States, Israel and the Palestinians* (Monroe, ME: Common Courage, 1995); Rashid Khalidi, *Palestinian Identity: The Construction of Modern National Consciousness* (New York: Columbia University Press, 1997); Zev Sternhell, *The Founding Myths of Israel: Nationalism, Socialism, and the Making of the Jewish State*, trans. David Maisel (Princeton, NJ: Princeton University Press, 1998); Zertal, *From Catastrophe to Power*; Shahak and Mezvinsky, *Jewish Fundamentalism in Israel*; Shlaim, *The Iron Wall: Israel and the Arab World* (New York: Norton, 2000); Pappe, *The Making of the Arab/Israeli Conflict, 1947– 1951* (London: I. B. Tauris, 2001); Tanya Reinhart, *Israel/Palestine: How to End the War of 1948* (New York: Seven Stories, 2002); Zertal, *Israel and the Politics of Nationhood*; and Pappe, *Ethnic Cleansing of Palestine*. These articulations of historical revisionism should be

distinguished from the reactionary Holocaust revisionism that gained international notoriety in Europe and Canada during the 1980s.

[9] Régine-Mihal Friedman, "The Double Legacy of *Arbeit Macht Frei*," *Prooftexts* 22 (2002): 204.

[10] Heidi Fehrenbach, *Cinema in Democratizing Germany* (Chapel Hill and London: University of North Carolina Press, 1995), 12–50.

[11] As deployed by John Rosenthal, *The Myth of the Dialectic: Reinterpreting the Marx–Hegel Relation*, (New York: St Martin's, 1988), x, quoted in Manfred B. Steger, rev. of Rosenthal, *Myth*, in *New Political Science* 22, no. 1 (2000): 125.

[12] See the essays collected under "Constellation C: The Jewish Question: Politics of Subjectivity," in Ginsberg and Thompson, *Perspectives on German Cinema*, 161–250; Vidal-Naquêt, *Assassins of Memory*; and Norman Finkelstein and Ruth Bettina Birn, *A Nation on Trial: The Goldhagen Thesis and Historical Truth* (New York: Holt, 1998).

[13] Braun, "*Blutschande.*"

[14] Franklin Littell, *The Crucifixion of the Jews* (Macon, GA: Mercer University Press 1986); and James R. Watson, *Between Auschwitz and perdition: Postmodern Reflections on the Task of Thinking* (Amsterdam: Editions Rodopi, 1994).

[15] E.g., Paul Ricoeur, *Interpretation Theory: Discourse and the Surplus of Meaning* (Fort Worth, TX: Texas Christian University, 1976); and Maurice Merleau-Ponty, *Sense and Nonsense*, trans. Hubert J. Dreyfus and Patricia Allen Dreyfus (Evanston, IL: Northwestern University Press, 1964).

[16] Traverso, *Origins of Nazi Violence*.

[17] A recent cinematic example of this tendency is the otherwise interesting and important *Lumumba* (Raoul Peck, France/Belgium/Germany/Haiti, 2000), the North American premier of which was held in New York City at the 2001 Human Rights Watch International Film Festival. Human Rights Watch is a non-profit humanitarian watchdog organization that receives funding and direction from, inter alia, the neoliberal Soros Foundation.

[18] For an important qualification of Marx's formulation as it misrecognizes the role of Judaism in this context, see Halevi, *History of the Jews*, 130–32; and for a pertinent critique of the limits of Marx's formulation which clarifies the ideological connection it makes possible between Christian theology and the "mysterious" properties of the commodity—the capitalist semiotics of equivalent exchange—see Kibbey, *Theory of the Image*, 17–20.

[19] The concept is deployed famously, critically, by Derrida in his *Writing and Difference*, 93.

[20] Michelson, *Speaking the Unspeakable*, xi.

[21] It is because of such depictions and, more frequently, those of female nakedness, and not because of the proverbial, oft-misunderstood Judaic proscription against fideistic imagery, that Jewish orthodoxy has so consistently repudiated visual documentation of the Holocaust (not to mention sexually explicit Holocaust narrative films depicting both male and female nakedness [corpses] *and* nudity [living beings]).

[22] The seminal text is Jean-François Lyotard, *Libidinal Economy*, trans. Iain Hamilton Grant (1973; repr., Bloomington and Indianapolis: Indiana University Press, 1993).

[23] See Wilhelm Reich, *The Mass Psychology of Fascism*, trans. Vincent R. Carfagno (1946; repr., New York: Farrar, 1970).

---

[24] See Herbert Marcuse, *An Essay on Liberation* (Boston: Beacon, 1969).

[25] Quoted in Isser, *Stages of Annihilation*, 20.

[26] As discussed in Ravetto, *Unmaking of Fascist Aesthetics*, 81–87. Indeed in the contemporary postmodern context, ostensivity is commensurate with the anti-representational functioning of the hyperrealist simulacrum, a reflexive significatory field devoid of referential models, whether real or ideal; and in the context of Holocaust cultural studies, ostensivity may be compared to the phenomenological discourse of reception aesthetics, for which cultural occasions are rhetorically overdeterminant. See Umberto Eco, *Travels in Hyperreality*, trans. William Weaver (San Diego: Harcourt, 1986); Jean Baudrillard, *Simulations*, trans. Paul Foss et al. (New York: Semiotext[e], 1983); Gilles Deleuze, "Plato and the Simulacrum," trans. Rosalind Krauss, *October* 27 (1983): 45–56; and Hans Robert Jauss, *Toward an Aesthetic of Reception*, trans. Timothy Bahti (Minneapolis: University of Minnesota Press, 1982).

[27] Gad Kaynar , "'Get Out of the Picture, Kid in a Cap': On the Interaction of the Israeli Drama and Reality Convention," in *Theater in Israel* , ed. Linda Ben-Zvi (Ann Arbor, MI: University of Michigan Press, 1996), 288–90. Ritual meals such as the *massachet* (what Freud might have referred to as a "totemic ritual") have served a particular, ideological function in official Israeli Holocaust education (see Avner Ben-Amos and Ilana Bet-El, "Holocaust Day and Memorial Day in Israeli Schools: Ceremonies, Education and History," *Israel Studies* 4, no. 1 [1999]: 258–84). It is not irrelevant to note that the word, *massachet*, is related etymologically to another Hebrew word, *massach*, which refers to the cinematic screen.

[28] John Willett, *The Theatre of Bertolt Brecht: A Study in Eight Aspects* (New York: New Directions, 1959), 167; and Darko Suvin, "The Mirror and the Dynamo: On Brecht's Aesthetic Point of View," *The Drama Review* 12, no. 1 (1967): 59–61.

[29] See Neil Turnbull, "Making 'It' Happen: Philosophy, Hermeneutics and the Truth of Art," *Theory, Culture and Society* 21, no. 6 (2004): 171–78.

[30] Grotowski is known, inter alia, for his Christian existentialist mystery plays, *Apocalypse cum figuris* and *Akropolis*, each of which was subject to cinematic documentation, and the latter of which is set in Auschwitz. See Zbigniew Osiński, *Grotowski and His Laboratory*, trans. and ed. Lillian Vallee and Robert Findlay (New York: PAJ, 1986); Tadeusz Burzyński and Zbigniew Osiński, *Grotowski's Laboratory* (Warsaw: Interpress, 1979); and Jennifer Kumiega, *The Theatre of Grotowski* (London: Methuen, 1985).

[31] Cf. Dinora Pines, "The Impact of the Holocaust on the Second Generation," *A Woman's Unconscious Use of Her Body* (London: Virago, 1993), 205–25; Ronit Lantin, "Re-occupying the Territories of Silence: Israeli Daughters of Shoah Survivors between Language and Silence," in *Women in the Holocaust: Narrative and Representation*, ed. Esther Fuchs (Lanham, MD, New York, Oxford: University Presses of America, 1999), 47–62; and Linda Kintz, "Gendering the Critique of Representation: Fascism, the Purified Body, and Theater in Adorno, Artaud, and Maria Irene Fornes," *Rethinking Marxism* 4, no. 3 (1991): 83–100.

[32] See, respectively, Masalha, *Expulsion of the Palestinians*, 43 n.50; and Michael Collins Piper, "New Bill in Congress Targets Teachers Who Dare to Question U.S. Support for Israel," *American Free Press*, April 12, 2004,

http://www.AmericanFreePress.net/03_19_04/New_Bill_html.

[33] Kaynar, "'Get Out of the Picture,'" and "'What's Wrong with the Usual Description of the Extermination?!' National Socialism and the Holocaust as a Self-image Metaphor in Israeli Drama: Aesthetic Conversion of a National Tragedy into Reality-Convention," *Theatron* 17 (1996): 202–3.

[34] Aruri, "Anti–Zionism," 43, 52. Aruri is speaking here in regard to the foundational Law of Jewish Return, the aestheticized rationale for which—model Jewish isolationism—dissimulates the internationally mandated Palestinian Right of Return. See also Aruri, ed., *Palestinian Refugees: The Right of Return* (London: Pluto, 2001).

[35] Cinema Studies usage of this concept is associated with Christian Metz, *The Imaginary Signifier: Psychoanalysis and the Cinema*, trans. Celia Britton et al. (Bloomington: Indiana University Press, 1982). Metz draws from Jacques Lacan, "The Mirror Stage as Formative Function of the 'I'," in *Ecrits: A Selection*, trans. Alan Sheridan (1966; repr. New York: Norton, 1977), 1–7; and Emile Benveniste, "The Nature of Pronouns," in *Problems in General Linguistics*, trans. Mary Elizabeth Meek (Coral Gables, FL: University of Miami Press, 1971).

[36] For a classic analysis of the Mizrachi relationship to Zionism, see Shohat, "Zionism from the Standpoint of Its Jewish Victims." For an elaborated historical background, see Jiladi, *Discord in Zion*. For a critical polemic, see Selzer, *Aryanization of the Jewish State*. For a situation of that background in the larger context of Jewish history, see Halevi, *History of the Jews*.

[37] See, respectively, Abdelwahab Bouhdiba and Abdu Khal, "Festivities of Violence: Circumcision and the Making of Men," and Yoram Bilu, "Circumcision, the First Haircut and the Torah: Ritual and Male Identity Among the Ultraorthodox Community of Israel," in *Imagined Masculinities: Male Identity and Culture in the Modern Middle East*, eds. Mai Ghoussoub and Emma Sinclair-Webb (London: Saqi, 2000), 19–32; 33–64. See also Bouhdiba, *Sexuality in Islam*, trans. Alan Sheridan (London: Routledge, 1985), 174–87; Hoffman, *Covenant of Blood*; and Shaye J. D. Cohen, *Why Aren't Jewish Women Circumcised? Gender and Covenant in Judaism* (Berkeley: University of California Press, 2005). A useful Christian interpretation of the ritual is Julia Reinhard Lipton, "*Ethnos* and Circumcision in Pauline Tradition: A Psychoanalytic Exegesis," in *The Psychoanalysis of Race*, ed. Christopher Lane (New York: Columbia University Press, 1998), 193–210.

[38] For an extended analysis of the "ethnic" dissimulation of race and racism, see Stephen Steinberg, *The Ethnic Myth: Race, Ethnicity, and Class in America*, 2nd ed. (Boston: Beacon, 1989). For a critique of the Western designation of the conflict in Israel/Palestine as "ethnic conflict," see Lina Khatib, *Filming the Modern Middle East: Politics in the Cinemas of Hollywood and the Arab World* (London: I. B. Tauris, 2006), 106–7.

[39] I employ "semitic" in full recognition of the twofold fact that, as Middle-Eastern indigenes, both Moni and Khaled are ethno-cultural Arabs, and that the designation of Arab culture as "semitic" invokes a racialist paradigm appropriated from prevailing linguistic theory by French pseudo-scientist, Ernst Renan, and deployed perniciously against European Jewry during the last third of nineteenth century. See Renan, *Etudes d'histoire religieuse* (Paris: Michel Lévy, 1862).

For contemporary rearticulations of Islam, see *Progressive Muslims: On Justice,*

Gender and Pluralism, ed. Omid Safi (Oxford: Oneworld, 2003); and Farid Esack, *Qur'ān, Liberation and Pluralism: An Islamic Perspective of Interreligious Solidarity against Oppression* (Oxford: Oneworld, 1997). For rearticulations of Judaism, see Marc H. Ellis, *Toward a Jewish Theology of Liberation: Into the 21st Century*, 3rd ed. (Waco, TX: Baylor University Press, 2004); and Tony Kushner and Alisa Solomon, eds., *Wrestling with Zion: Progressive Jewish-American Responses to the Israeli–Palestinian Conflict* (New York: Grove, 2003).

[40] Louis Althusser, "Ideology and Ideological State Apparatuses (Notes towards an Investigation)," in *Lenin and Philosophy and Other Essays*, trans. Ben Brewster (New York: Monthly Review Press, 1971), 162. See also Cornelius Castoriadis, *The Imaginary Institution of Society*, trans. Kathleen McLaughlin (1975; repr., Cambridge, MA: Polity, 1989).

[41] Regarding the morbid function of Woman in Romanticism, especially its political connotations, see Beth Ann Bassein, *Women and Death: Linkages in Western Thought and Literature* (Westport, CT: Greenwood, 1984); Stephen Bann, *Romanticism and the Rise of History* (New York: Twayne / Toronto: Maxwell Macmillan Canada, 1995); and Nancy L. Rosenblum, *Another Liberalism: Romanticism and the Reconstruction of Liberal Thought* (Cambridge, MA and London: Harvard University Press, 1987).

[42] Agamben, *Remnants of Auschwitz*.

[43] See, respectively, Maxime Rodinson, *Israel: A Colonial-Settler State?* trans. David Thorstad (New York: Pathfinder, 1973); and Traverso, *Origins of Nazi Violence*, 47–75.

[44] Quoted in Selzer, *Aryanization of the Jewish State*, 53–54. Sartre would pick up on this controversial thesis years later in his *Anti–Semite and Jew*. See *October* 87 (1999), special issue "Jean-Paul Sartre's *Anti–Semite and Jew*"; and Traverso, *Understanding Nazi Genocide*, 26–41. For a discussion of the "wandering" character of the ancient Habirus [Hebrews] themselves, see Qumsiyeh, *Sharing the Land of Canaan*, 12–22.

[45] Heidegger, *Being*, 1962.

[46] See Sizer, *Christian Zionism*, 210. As Shapiro and Sica note, the Heideggerian "home" is one that immerses in aesthetic-subliminal "unsafety" (*Hermeneutics*, 134 n.43). Regarding the Palestinian situation, Taylor actually refers to a "'Vichyization' of the occupied territories" (*Zionist Mind*, 135).

[47] Cf. Martin Kloke, *Israel und die deutsche linke: Zur Geschichte eines schwierigen Verhältnisses*, 2nd ed. (Frankfurt am Main: Haag und Herchen, 1994); Inge Deutschkron, *Bonn und Jerusalem: The Strange Coalition* (London: Chilton, 1970); Lily Gardner Feldman, *The Special Relationship between West Germany and Israel* (Boston: Allen and Unwin, 1984); and Angelika Timm, "The Burdened Relationship between the GDR and Israel," *Israel Studies* 2, no. 1 (1997): 22–49.

[48] As discussed in Sha'ban, *For Zion's Sake*, 87.

[49] For elaborations of the Zionist positioning of Palestinians and Mizrachim as post– Holocaust "victims," even as "new" Ashkenazim, see Massad, "Persistence of the Palestinian Question"; and Shohat, "Zionism from the Standpoint of Its Jewish Victims." On this view, the "original" Ashkenazim are positioned by Zionism as Gentiles, even as antisemites. See also Selzer, *Aryanization of the Jewish State*; and Beit-Hallahmi, *Original Sins*. In this light one might consider the significance of the opening by a Muslim

Palestinian of a Judeocide museum in Nazareth, birthplace of Jesus, in the interests of fostering reparational Israeli–Palestinian dialogue. http://www.washingtontimes.com/world/20050612-123836-6201r.htm.

[50] "Madi" also refers to a mostly Christian, Sudanese ethnic group that at one time believed prayer was most effective when channeled via the spirits of dead relatives. The term signifies "purity" for South Indian Brahmins.

[51] Surely not unrelated to this structural politics is the fact that *Arbeit Macht Frei* was performed in Germany following its initial run in Akko, whereupon Veiel, a former cognitive-behaviorist psychologist, student of Andrzej Wajda, and occasional instructor at Berlin's Künstlerhaus Bethanien (an Evangelical ["Confessional"] Church-sponsored cultural institute), saw the play when it traveled to Germany and became interested in transcribing it cinematically. As Loshitzky has indicated, Veiel managed successfully to solicit ample funding for *Balagan* from both the German and Israeli governments, but at the expense of like funding for the Israeli-produced *Al Tigu*, also at that time in pre-production ("Hybrid Victims: Second-Generation Israelis Screen the Holocaust," in Zelizer, *Remembering to Forget*, 36–46, 187 n.5).

[52] Regarding this claim, see Roselle Tekiner, "The 'Who Is a Jew?' Controversy in Israel: A Product of Political Zionism," in Tekiner, *Anti–Zionism*, 77, 87 n.3.

[53] Suzanne Weiss, "Innovative Documentary Probes Holocaust Myths and Truths," *Jewish Bulletin of Northern California*, July 21, 1994.

[54] Omer Bartov, *The Jew in Cinema: From* The Golem *to* Don't Touch My Holocaust (Bloomington and Indianapolis: Indiana University Press, 2005), 282–309; Loshitzky, *Identity Politics*; and Friedman, "Double Legacy."

[55] Examples are its proclivities 1) to displace, while seeming merely to analogize, the conflict in Israel/Palestine on/to the Jewish–German axis; 2) to limit analytic scope to Europe and the Middle East, thereby eliding the U.S. role in the conflict; 3) to downplay the function of "Holocaust" in Palestinian identity formation; and 3) to neglect any reference whatsoever to Marxist critiques of "Holocaust."

[56] See Segev, *The Seventh Million*, 189–252; also Benjamin Beit-Hallahmi, *The Israeli Connection: Who Arms Israel and Why?* (New York: Pantheon, 1987); Obenzinger, "South Africa"; Bishara Bahbah, *Israel and Latin America: The Military Connection* (New York: St. Martin's / Washington, D.C.: Institute for Palestine Studies, 1986); and Ian Black and Benny Morris, *Israel's Secret Wars: A History of Israel's Intelligence Services* (New York: Grove, 1991).

[57] Bartov, *Jew in Cinema*, 301.

[58] See Farber, *Radicals, Rabbis and Peacemakers*, 194–212; Taylor, *Zionist Mind*; Elmer Berger, *Memoirs of an Anti–Zionist Jew* (Beirut: Institute for Palestine Studies, 1978); Tekiner, *Anti–Zionism*; Weinstock, *Zionism: False Messiah*; and Ebie Weizfeld, ed., *The End of Zionism and the Liberation of the Jewish People* (Atlanta: Clarity, 1989).

[59] Sam Bahour and Michael Dahan, "Genocide by Public Policy," *News from Within* 20, no. 3 (2004): 4–5; and Pappe, *Ethnic Cleansing of Palestine*.

[60] See *Response* 26, no. 1 (2005), special issue on "60 Years after Europe's Liberation, Why Is Antisemitism on the Rise?" It should be noted that this magazine's publisher, the Simon Wiesenthal Center, is a Jewish-Zionist organization that deploys information it gathers

concerning antisemitic incidents and the persistence of global right-wing extremism toward pro-Zionist ends which more often than not involves the dissemination of anti–Arab rhetoric.

[61] Rose, *Question of Zion*; also Aviezer Ravitsky, *Messianism, Zionism, and Jewish Religious Radicalism*, trans. Michael Swirsky and Jonathan Chipman (Chicago and London: University of Chicago Press, 1993), 79–144.

[62] See David C. Jacobson, "The Ma'ale School: Catalyst for the Entrance of Religious Zionists into the World of Media Production," *Israel Studies* 9, no. 1 (2004): 36. Interestingly, the Christian imagery and symbolism utilized by secular Jewish Israelis marks what could be postulated as a visual rapprochement with their *haredi* counterparts that serves well the secular–religious rapprochement currently being renegotiated in Israel, the aim of which is a "New Zionist Hegemony," or preservation of Jewish ethnocracy in the context of Israel attempting finally to draw up an official state constitution (Jonathan Cook, "Israeli Constitutional Committee Faces Double Bind," *Middle East Report* 231 [2004]: 16–21). One might here recall Selzer's point that, in Israel, traditional Jewishness "recedes into the background as a factor for social cohesion" (*Aryanization of the Jewish State*, 54). See also Beit-Hallahmi, *Original Sins*, 119–36.

[63] One need only consider former German Prime Minister Joschka Fischer's Greater Middle East Initiative, which positions Germany as a "neutral" negotiator between Israel, Washington, and the Arab/Muslim world, as well as the support offered by a majority of the United Nations General Assembly for Germany to be granted a permanent seat on the U.N. Security Council (Paul Hockenos, "German Greens and Pax Europa: Joschka Fischer Envisions a European Alternative to American Hegemony," *The Nation*, July 12–26, 2004: 27).

CHAPTER SIX

HOLOCAUST Y2K:
A POLEMICAL CONCLUSION

> It is good to give materialist investigations a truncated ending.
> —Walter Benjamin

Since the release of *Balagan* thirteen years ago, Holocaust cinema studies has reached a peak of banality. Scholarly analysis of Holocaust film is still confined to phenomenological horizons; ideology critique based within political and economic considerations of aesthetic structuring remains a barely acknowledged taboo. This is true despite a contemporary proliferation of industry-produced Holocaust films that have come to comprise a global sub-genre I venture to dub *Holocaust Y2K* after the popular acronym for conceiving the turn of the twenty-first century in hyperreal, millenarian terms. Holocaust Y2K films have emerged alongside a wave of independent, often oppositional films that stand to confront the long history of Holocaust film's ideological colonization by U.S. imperial interests and their international nodes of collaboration.

While projecting the Judeo-Christian principle of manifest destiny familiar within Holocaust cultural theory and many Holocaust films, Holocaust Y2K films are aesthetically and intellectually more conservative than their predecessors, especially when compared with Holocaust films produced during the decade prior to the Reagan presidency. Throughout that earlier period, political onslaughts against organized labor and uncertain rates of profit articulated across the cinema in ways understood to contest and challenge an array of commonsense assumptions about the Holocaust and its legacy. Popular Hollywood productions such as *Julia* (Fred Zinnemann, U.S.A., 1977) and *Playing for Time*, and lesser known art films such as *Jakob der Lügner* and *Salò, or the 120 Days of Sodom* [*Salò, o le 120 giornate de Sodoma*] (Pier Paolo Pasolini, Italy, 1976) risked debilitating public controversy and outright condemnation in their efforts to convey political messages with creativity and emotional poignancy. It is indeed questionable whether these decidedly critical Holocaust films, the efforts of which are hardly implicit to connect the politics surrounding the Judeocide to those of Western capitalist expansion and the

Israeli occupation of Palestine, could have been produced and distributed in today's authoritarian populist milieu, in which plutocracy is linked to a horizontally rather than vertically integrated, globally extensive "New Hollywood" to form today's seemingly all-encompassing media-industrial complex. Among other things, the corporate permissibility during that prior era of promoting and disseminating radical star intertexts, for example those associated with celebrated actors Vanessa Redgrave, a PLO supporter, and Jane Fonda, an anti–Vietnam War activist, has diminished significantly since the end of the Cold War. *Julia*, in which Fonda and Redgrave co-starred, is to date the only Hollywood theatrical release ever to have offered a sustained feminist perspective on the Holocaust and to have done so in the politicized generic context of *film noir* (fig. 6-1). By contrast, Holocaust Y2K films, even those of

Fig. 6-1 – Jane Fonda and Vanessa Redgrave in *Julia*

non-U.S. origin, stand commensurate with those of the hyper–masculinist international adventure/intrigue genre in their rehearsal of a mythical belief that Western expansion and annexation of largely non-Christian, non-white, "oriental" territories is a self-evident, prophetic mission of "civilized" and "enlightened" nations.[1] Following in the footsteps of *Schindler's List*, Holocaust Y2K films refine and repackage classical European art cinema and new wave techniques—after all, what Hollywoodian film has yet approached the searing critique of fascism staged by Pasolini's masterful cinematic assault, *Salò*?—into simplified, post–Hollywoodian formats that rearticulate decontextualized narratives of human suffering and fallibility to melodramatic occasions for personal-psychological introspection and rumination on individual guilt and salvation. Holocaust Y2K films thus join the ranks of the new globalized film industry in whose homogenizing mainstream purview the aesthetic likes of *Korczak* and *Entre Nous* are now considered as disorienting and esoteric (read: intellectually challenging) as the admittedly difficult and voluminous cult classic, *The Saragossa Manuscript* [*Rekopis znaleziony w Saragossie*] (Wojiech Has, Poland, 1965).

Holocaust Y2K films hail from across North America and Europe. Many are directed by Eastern Europeans or emerge from former Soviet bloc countries fostering bids for influence and entry into the politically and economically still unstable European Union. The timely proliferation and discursive patterning of films such as *Fateless* [*Sorstalanság*] (Lajos Koltai, Hungary/Germany/U.K., 2005), *Sophie Scholl–Die Letzten Tage*, *The Pianist*, *The Grey Zone*, and *Sunshine* [*A Napfény íze*] (Istvan Szábo, Hungary/Germany/Austria/Canada, 1999) may lead to suppositions that many Holocaust Y2K films are little more than vehicles of confession to national implication in the Holocaust, the industrial cultivation of which has become an unspoken prerequisite for the E.U. membership of countries producing these films. On the other hand, the implication of Poland, Hungary, and other European as well as North American countries in genocidal crimes perpetrated or provoked *since* the Second World War remains a glaring absence in Holocaust Y2K films, the phenomenological horizons of which delineate tacit acceptance of horrors past and present. As I have indicated throughout the preceding chapters, the preponderance and persistent critical misrecognition of cinematic tendencies such as these symptomatize a large-scale conceptual incapacity, perhaps even a refusal, to transform the prevailing social structures that warp genuine efforts to work through collective remorse into the service of political and economic interests which exacerbate rather than eliminate holocaustal conditions worldwide.[2] Despite its contemporary irrelevance to many actual Jews and Christians, the Judeo-Christian sacrificialism projected across these films figures a powerful, cross-cultural, often trans-ideological trope for justifying neoconservative policies which continue to wreak global havoc and squelch sustained public criticism in the name of combating "terrorism" and "antisemitism."

By contrast, critical Holocaust films such as *Still Life*, *Route 181: Fragments of a Journey in Palestine/Israel*, and *Hiding and Seeking: Faith and Tolerance after the Holocaust* (Menachem Daum and Oren Rudavsky, U.S.A., 2004) rarely find mainstream distribution. In distinct ways, these independent films refuse to be silent about globalization and the conflict in Israel/Palestine, issues which a critical analysis reveals are ineluctably inscribed across the range of Holocaust films and much Holocaust film criticism. For critical Holocaust films, the Judeocide and the Palestinian *Nakba*, rather than standing in comparative, analogous relation, are literally continuous variations on a destructive Western theme: *Al-Nakba* is a geopolitical extension, both historically and ideologically, of the Judeocide, the widely accepted mystification of which into "Holocaust" has served to rationalize the ethnic cleansing of Palestine. As political scientist Norman Finkelstein has argued convincingly, minimal scholarly controversy exists over the factuality of *Al-Nakba* in this and other respects, and arguments to the contrary are largely contrived.[3] Holocaust films intent upon acknowledging *Al-Nakba* and its ramifications demonstrate a practiced aesthetic sophistication and command worthy of serious scholarly analysis. Unlike the propagandistic screed, *Columbia Unbecoming* (David Project, U.S.A., 2004), however, which received extensive U.S. media coverage despite its aesthetic and intellectual paucity,[4] contemporary critical and oppositional Holocaust films have been denied deserved focus and attention from scholars and critics alike. In fact the allure of controversy repeatedly legitimating more conservative cinematic efforts is decidedly absent from these films as they are quietly relegated to cultural oblivion.

It is increasingly fashionable in Cinema Studies to ignore critical and oppositional Holocaust films and the committed analyses they proffer in favor of the apolitical, decontextualized approaches forwarded by Holocaust Y2K films and their disciplinary analogue, the new film philosophy. Briefly referenced at the end of Chapter One and critiqued throughout Robert Stam's encyclopedic *Film Theory: An Introduction*, this recent, anti–theoretical turn in Cinema Studies pervades numerous contemporary texts that cull selectively the later writings of Wittgenstein in the interests of contributing an interpretive methodology to film studies that will bypass the perceived pitfalls of semiotics and structuralism while correcting purported errors of cognitivist and realist aesthetics through the practice of applied logic.[5] Reminiscent of Hirsch's *Afterimage* and *The Quarrel*'s *hilukim*, the new film philosophy claims to offer an alternative model for analyzing cinematic semiosis and spectatorship but fails to break epistemologically from the formalism which it attributes to its opposition, but which is actually traceable to the turn's predecessor, David Bordwell, famous long before "Freedom Fries" for having derogated and rejected contemporary film theory, much of it originating in France and carrying a decided left-orientation, with the dismissive acronym "SLAB theory," and for subsequently having spearheaded the anti–theoretical offensive in Cinema Studies during the global watershed years of the early 1990s.[6] The neo-Wittgensteinian development within this reactionary turn articulates variously in the U.K., U.S., Canada, and the E.U. and extends Bordwell's criticisms to the Frankfurt School and related models of aesthetic critique.[7] The turn's common denominator is an ideological stake in Eurocentric notions of gender, sexuality, ethnicity, race, and class, which texts of the new film philosophy baldly claim are normal and universal as against critical and oppositional reconceptualizations now de rigueur across the humanities. Whereas such reconceptualizations resist conformity with all unqualified universalisms, the new film philosophy dismisses their critical effects as "logically uncertain" or "mistaken" and therefore "useless." The question of who decides what counts as "certain," "correct," and "useful," much less what may be designated normal and universally applicable, is never broached within this series: the new film philosophy explicitly rejects theoretical interrogation as speculative, overly subjective, counter-intuitive—in short, ridiculous—in favor of sweeping, pseudo-scientific claims about the physiology of human perception and the mental cognition of cinematic forms. As a perceived corrective to critical theory, the new film philosophy propagates an unproblematized modality of rhetorical transparency—"clarity"—the *politics* of which it neglects to acknowledge, much less admit, despite the fact that the matter (recalling discourse on *Al-Nakba*) is no longer subject to serious debate in academic circles.

Contemporary Holocaust film studies has yet to extricate itself from the dangerous implications of this reactionary turn. True to its institutional history, which entails close ties to military-industrial Hollywood,[8] Cinema Studies has been reluctant to address the political aesthetics of Holocaust film, just as Holocaust films themselves have become overtly polemical in the context of the Bush/Blair "War on Terror"—the first military confrontation to have been declared endless since Hitler rabidly foretold a Thousand Year Reich more than half a century ago.[9] The Holocaust establishment-funded writing of Hanno Loewy is a case in point. Composed under the auspices of the United States Holocaust Memorial Museum's Center for Advanced Holocaust Studies, and supported by the Department of German and the Bildner Center for the Study of Jewish Life at Rutgers University, Loewy's 2003 Craig-Kade Lecture on Holocaust "movies and TV" echoes new film philosopher Colin McGinn[10] as it culls superficially from the longstanding, long problematized cinematic spectatorship theories of Balázs, Metz, and Baudry to forward a theoretically truncated, politically ambiguous argument about Holocaust film thematics and reception so riven by disciplinary gaps and foundational misreadings that it can hardly be considered of scholarly utility. Loewy's basic claim that cinema is a site of "illusory wish fulfillment" repositions Holocaust film naively, as a medium of mind, even as it pays lip-service to "strategies of deconstructing ideology" offered by films such as *Al Tigu Li B'Shoah* and *Made in Israel* (Ari

Fulman, Israel, 2001). Dismissing Avisar, Doneson, and Insdorf with the sweeping, unsubstantiated—incorrect—claim that those Holocaust film scholars "all agree on interpreting films in comparison to standards set by documentaries like Lanzmann's *Shoah* or Alain Resnais' *Night and Fog*,"[11] Loewy supplies a disjointed series of speculations on popular Holocaust film subgenres that is devoid not only of consistent theoretical grounding but of concrete textual and historiographical analysis. Instead recapitulating prevailing Holocaust film studies tendencies, Loewy evades the serious critique required for such grounding and analysis, in this instance generalizing about presumed Holocaust spectatorial submission to "superpower" imagery that he suggests, pace Jung, projects an illusion of "mobility and conscious control of perception" that manifests a "magical power" rooted atavistically and of necessity in the collective human psyche.

The expressed aim and intent of the present book has been to break this reactionary, mystificatory trend by offering the field of Cinema Studies a springboard for sustained reevaluation and critique of this regrettably still most troubling and misunderstood issue, the dominant formulations of which continue to obstruct the sorely needed repositioning of cultural thought within theoretical frameworks conducive to conceiving and representing a feasible, just, and lasting Middle East peace. The fact that Holocaust film and film studies are still so deeply mired in the ideological politics of world conflagration is certainly not surprising to anyone familiar with the facts; these show academia engaged in an ironic rehearsal of the Judeo-Christian tradition, which, in the name of Christian Zionism, and to the ostensible advantage of Jewish Zionism, renders the Judeocide an exemplary matrix of apocalypse and directs critical discourse about it into willful execution of the destructive means ostensibly refused and resisted within the field.[12]

In this light I shall close the present book with a call for Cinema Studies, now merging into Media Studies and undergoing rapid international expansion, to rethink its philosophical relegation of Holocaust film to the far reaches of a phenomenological sublimity in relation which, to borrow from Loewy recalling Loshitzky, they may be conceived to "play with virtuality" in order merely "to develop more and more ambivalent and open endings that pose questions but give no answers."[13] Reclaiming Holocaust film as a site of politically transformative contestation, as this book has done by in fact *respecting* the modality's phenomenological moments—themselves most saliently represented by Holocaust art films made neither in the U.S. nor by Hollywood—would be a welcome first step in reorienting the discipline away from the reactionary collusion of scholarship and mysticism characteristic of the new film philosophy and the authoritarian populism it tacitly supports, toward a veritable hearing of Marx's religious "sigh" as it expresses a dire social need for reconceiving the violent messianism against which Benjamin warned so desperately into a nominal global vehicle for mending, equality, and enduring peace.

---

[1] See Sha'ban, *For Zion's Sake*, 11–18; also Noble, *Beyond the Promised Land*; and Douglas Little, *American Orientalism: The United States and the Middle East since 1945* (Chapel Hill and London: University of North Carolina Press, 2002).

[2] See Bronner, *Blood in the Sand*, 119–39.

[3] Finkelstein, *Beyond Chutzpah*, 6, 18.

[4] Terri Ginsberg, "Academic Integrity Travestied at Columbia Middle East Studies Conference," *ZNet*, March, 2005, http://www.zmag.org/content/showarticle.cfm?SectionID=107&ItemID=7435.

[5] E.g., Richard Allen, *Projecting Illusion: Film Spectatorship and the Impression of Reality* (Cambridge and New York: Cambridge University Press, 1995); Allen and Murray Smith, eds., *Film Theory and Philosophy* (Oxford and New York: Oxford University Press, 1997); and Allen and Malcolm Turvey, eds., *Wittgenstein, Theory and the Arts* (London: Routledge, 2001).

[6] "SLAB" stands for "Saussure/Lacan/Althusser/Barthes." See Bordwell, *Making Meaning*.

[7] See Patrick McGee, *Cinema, Theory, and Political Responsibility in Contemporary Culture* (Cambridge and New York: Cambridge University Press, 1997).

[8] Ginsberg, "'Dumbing Down'," 21–23.

[9] See Carl Boggs, *Imperial Delusions: American Militarism and Endless War* (Lanham, MD: Rowman and Littlefield, 2005).

[10] See Gilberto Perez, "The Dream Life," rev. of *The Power of Movies: How Screen and Mind Interact*, by Colin McGinn (New York: Pantheon, 2005), *The Nation*, March 27, 2006: 34-40.

[11] Hanno Loewy, "Tales of Mass Destruction and Survival: Holocaust, Genre and Fiction in the Movies and TV," The 2003 Craig-Kade Lecture, *Rutgers German Studies Occasional Papers* 4 (New Brunswick, NJ: Rutgers German Studies, 2005), 13.

[12] Compare Joel Beinin, "The New McCarthyism: Policing Thought about the Middle East," in *Academic Freedom after September 11*, ed. Beshara Doumani (New York: Zone, 2006), 237–66. See also Rima Abdelkader and Terri Ginsberg, "Academic Freedom Declines across the United States," *Arabisto.com*, November 25, 2006, http://www.arabisto.com/p_blogEntry.cfm?blogEntryID=201.

[13] Ibid., 28.

SELECTED BIBLIOGRAPHY

HOLOCAUST FILM/TV STUDIES SOURCES

Avisar, Ilan. *Screening the Holocaust: Cinema's Images of the Unimaginable.* Bloomington and Indianapolis: Indiana University Press, 1988.

Avni, Ora. "Narrative Subject, Historic Subject: *Shoah* and *La Place de l'Etoile*," trans. Katherine Aschheim and Rhonda Garelick. *Poetics Today* 12, no. 3 (1991): 495–516.

Baron, Lawrence. *Projecting the Holocaust into the Present: The Changing Focus of Contemporary Holocaust Cinema.* New York: Roman & Littlefield, 2005.

Barta, Tony "Consuming the Holocaust: Memory Production and Popular Film." *Contention* 5, no. 2 (1996): 161–75.

Bathrick, David. "Rescreening 'The Holocaust': The Children's Stories," *New German Critique* 80 (2000): 41–58.

Bejski, Moshe "Oskar Schindler and *Schindler's List*," *Yad Vashem Studies* 24 (1995): 317–48.

Ben-Ghiat, Ruth. "The Secret Histories of Roberto Benigni's *Life Is Beautiful.*" *Yale Journal of Criticism* 14, no. 1 (2001): 253–66.

Bernard-Donals, Michael F. and Richard Glejzer. "Film and the Shoah: The Limits of Seeing." In *Between Witness and Testimony: The Holocaust and the Limits of Representation*, 103–29. Albany: State University of New York Press, 2001.

Brinkley, Robert, and Steven Youra. "Tracing *Shoah*." *PMLA* 111, no. 1 (1996): 108–27.

Bülent, Diken, and Carsten Bagge Lausten. "The Ghost of Auschwitz." *Journal for Cultural Research* 8, no. 3 (2004): 69–85.

Carr, Steven Alan. "The Holocaust in the Text: Victor Hugo's *Les Misérables* and the Allegorical Film Adaptation." *Film Criticism* 27, no. 1 (2002): 50–65.

Colombat, André Pierre. *The Holocaust in French Film.* Metuchen, NJ: Scarecrow, 1993.

Davies, Fred. *Film, History and the Holocaust.* Portland, OR: Vallentine-Mitchell, 2000.

Doneson, Judith E. *The Holocaust in American Film*. 1987. Reprint, Syracuse, NY: Syracuse University Press, 2002. Page references are to the 1987 edition.

Eisenstein, Paul. "Obsession and the Meaning of Jewish Rescue: Oskar Schindler as Spirit." In *Traumatic Encounters: Holocaust Representation and the Hegelian Subject*, 73–93. Albany: State University of New York Press, 2003.

Elsaesser, Thomas. "Subject Positions, Speaking Positions: From *Holocaust*, *Our Hitler*, and *Heimat* to *Shoah* and *Schindler's List*." In *The Persistence of History: Cinema, Television, and the Modern Event*, edited by Vivian Sobchak, 145–83. London: Routledge, 1996.

Ezrahi, Sidra DeKoven. "After Such Knowledge, What Laughter?" *Yale Journal of Criticism* 14, no. 1 (2001): 287–313.

Farrell, Kirby. "The Economies of *Schindler's List*." *Arizona Quarterly* 52, no. 1 (1996): 163–88.

Felman, Shoshana. "The Return of the Voice: Claude Lanzmann's *Shoah*." In *Testimony: Crisis of Witnessing in Literature, Psychoanalysis, and History*, by Shoshana Felman and Dori Laub, 204–83. London: Routledge, 1992.

Flanzbaum, Helene. "'But Wasn't It Terrific?' A Defense of Liking *Life Is Beautiful*." *Yale Journal of Criticism* 14, no. 1 (2001): 273–86.

Flitterman-Lewis, Sandy. "Documenting the Ineffable: Terror and Memory in Alain Resnais' *Night and Fog*." In *Documenting the Documentary*, edited by Barry Keith Grant and Jeannette Sloniowski, 204–21. Detroit: Wayne State University Press, 1998.

Fogel, Daniel Mark. "'Schindler's List' in Novel and Film: Exponential Conversion." *Historical Journal of Film, Radio and Television* 14, no. 3 (1994): 315–20.

Friedländer, Saul. *Reflections of Nazism: An Essay on Kitsch and Death*. Trans. Thomas Weyr. New York: Harper, 1984.

Furman, Nelly. "Called to Witness: Viewing Lanzmann's *Shoah*." In *Shaping Losses: Cultural Memory and the Holocaust*, edited by Julia Epstein and Lori Hope Lefkovitz, 55–74. Urbana and Chicago: University of Illinois Press, 2001.

Gellately, Robert. "*Schindler's List*." *Central European History* 26, no. 4 (1994): 475–90.

Geuens, Jean-Pierre. "Pornography and the Holocaust: The Last Transgression." *Film Criticism* 20, nos. 1–2 (1995–96): 114–30.

Haggith, Toby and Joanna Newman, eds. *Holocaust and the Moving Image: Representations in Film and Television since 1933*. London: Wallflower, 2005.

Hansen, Miriam Bratu. "*Schindler's List* Is Not *Shoah*: Second Commandment, Popular Modernism, and Public Memory." *Critical Inquiry* 22, no. 2 (1995): 292–312. Reprinted in Loshitzky, *Spielberg's Holocaust*, 77–103. Page references are to the Loshitzky edition.

Hartman, Geoffrey. "The Cinema Animal: On Spielberg's *Schindler's List.*" *Salmagundi* 106-7 (1995): 127–45.

Higgins, Lynn A. "If Looks Could Kill: Louis Malle's Portraits of Collaboration." In *Fascism, Aesthetics, and Culture*, edited by Richard J. Golsan, 198–211. Hanover and London: University Press of New England, 1992.

—. "Two Women Filmmakers Remember the Dark Years." *Modern and Contemporary France* 7, no. 1 (1999): 59–69.

Hirsch, Joshua F. *Afterimage: Film, Trauma, and the Holocaust*. Philadelphia: Temple University Press, 2004.

"The Holocaust on Film." Special double issue, *Film and History* 32, nos. 1–2 (2002).

Hornstein, Shelley and Florence Jacobowitz, eds. *Image and Remembrance: Representation and the Holocaust*. Bloomington and Indianapolis: Indiana University Press, 2003.

Insdorf, Annette. *Indelible Shadows: Film and the Holocaust*. 1983, 1989. Reprint, Cambridge, MA and New York: Cambridge University Press, 2003. Page references are to the 1989 edition.

Jacobowitz, Florence, "*Shoah* as Cinema." In Hornstein and Jacobowitz, 7–21.

Jablon, Rachel Leah. "Witnessing as *Shivah*; Memoir as *Yizkor*: The Formulation of Holocaust Survivor Literature as *Gemilut Khasadim*." *The Journal of Popular Culture* 38, no. 2 (2004): 306–24.

Kertzer, Adrienne. "Like a Fable, Not a Pretty Picture: Holocaust Representation in Roberto Benigni and Anita Lobel." *Michigan Quarterly Review* 39, no. 2 (2000): 279–300.

Koch, Gertrud. "The Aesthetic Transformation of the Image of the Unimaginable: Notes on Claude Lanzmann's *Shoah*." Trans. Jamie Owen Daniel and Miriam Hansen. *October* 48 (1989): 15–24.

—. "The Angel of Forgetfulness and the Black Box of Facticity: Trauma and Memory in Claude Lanzmann's *Shoah*." Trans. Ora Wiskind. *History and Memory* 3, no. 1 (1991): 119–34.

—. "On the Disappearance of the Dead among the Living—The Holocaust and the Confusion of Identities in the Films of Konrad Wolf." Trans. Jeremy Gaines. *New German Critique* 60 (1993): 57–75.

LaCapra, Dominick. "Lanzmann's *Shoah*: 'Here There Is No Why'." *Critical Inquiry* 23 (1997): 231–69.

Langford, Barry. "'You Cannot Look At This': Holocaust Film on the Threshold of the Unrepresentable." *Holocaust Studies* 8, no. 3 (1999): 23–40.

Linville, Susan E. "Agnieszka Holland's *Europa, Europa*: Deconstructive Humor in a Holocaust Film," *Film Criticism* 19, no. 3 (1995): 44–53.

Listoe, Daniel B. "Seeing Nothing: Allegory and the Holocaust's Absent Dead." *SubStance* 35, no. 2 (2006): 51–70.

Loewy, Hanno. "Tales of Mass Destruction and Survival: Holocaust, Genre and Fiction in the Movies and TV." The 2003 Craig-Kade Lecture. *Rutgers German Studies Occasional Papers* 4. New Brunswick, NJ: Rutgers German Studies, 1995.

Loshitzky, Yosefa. "Hybrid Victims: Second-Generation Israelis Screen the Holocaust." In *Visual Culture and the Holocaust*, edited by Barbie Zelizer, 152–75. New Brunswick, NJ: Rutgers University Press, 2001.

—, ed. *Spielberg's Holocaust: Critical Perspectives on "Schindler's List"*. Bloomington and Indiana: Indiana University Press, 1997.

Losson, Nicolas. "Notes on the Images of the Camps." Trans. Annette Michelson. *October* 90 (1999): 25–35.

Manchel, Frank. "A Reel Witness: Steven Spielberg's Representation of the Holocaust in *Schindler's List*." *Journal of Modern History* 67, no. 1 (1995): 83–101.

Marcus, Millicent. "Ghost Stories: The Haunted History of the Italian Holocaust and the Case of Rosetta Loy." In Raphael, 63–73.

Margry, Karel. "'Theresienstadt' (1944–1945): The Nazi Propaganda Film Depicting the Concentration Camp as Paradise." *Historical Journal of Film, Radio and Television* 12, no. 2 (1992): 145–62.

McCrillis, Neal R. "*Shtetl* and *Hotel Terminus*: History and Memory of the Shoah." *Film and History* 16, nos. 1–4 (1996): 94–95.

"Memories of Germany." Special issue, *New German Critique* 71 (1997).

Metz, Walter. "A Very Notorious Ranch, Indeed: Fritz Lang, Allegory, and the Holocaust." *Journal of Contemporary Thought* 13 (2001): 71–86.

Mintz, Alan. *Popular Culture and the Shaping of Holocaust Memory in America*. Seattle and London: University of Washington Press, 2001.

Montgomery, Scott L. "What Kind of Memory? Reflections on Images of the Holocaust." *Contention* 5, no. 1 (1995): 79–103.

Niv, Kobi. *Life Is Beautiful, but Not for Jews: Another View of the Film by Benigni*. Lanham, MD: Scarecrow, 2003.

Niven, William J. "The Reception of Steven Spielberg's '"Schindler's List' in the German Media." *Journal of European Studies* 25, nos. 8–9 (1995): 165–80.

Ó Dochartaigh, Pól. "Americanizing the Holocaust: The Case of *Jakob the Liar*." *Modern Language Review* 101, no. 1 (2006): 456–71.

O'Sickey, Ingeborg Mayer and Annette Van. "*Europa Europa*: On the Borders of *Vergangenheitsverdrängung* and *Vergangenheitsbewältigung*." In *Perspectives on German Cinema*, edited by Terri Ginsberg and Kirsten Moana Thompson, 231–50. New York: G. K. Hall / London: Prentice Hall International, 1996.

Palowski, Franciszek. *The Making of* Schindler's List*: Behind the Scenes of an Epic Film*. Trans. Anna and Robert G. Ware. New York: Birch Lane, 1990.

Pauly, Rebecca M. "From Shoah to Holocaust: Image and Ideology in Alain Resnais' *Nuit et brouillard* and *Hiroshima mon amour*." *French Cultural Studies* 3, no. 9 (1992): 253–61.

Picart, Caroline Joan (Kay), and David A. Frank. *Frames of Evil: The Holocaust as Horror in American Film*. Foreword by Dominick LaCapra. Carbondale: Southern Illinois University Press, 2006.

Raphael, Marc Lee, ed. *The Representation of the Holocaust in Literature and Film*. Williamsburg, VA: Department of Religion, College of William and Mary, 2003.

Rappaport, Lynne. "Holocaust Pornography: Profaning the Sacred in *Ilsa, She-Wolf of the SS*." *Shofar* 22, no. 1 (2003): 53–79.

Rawlinson, Mark. "Adapting the Holocaust: *Schindler's List*, Intellectuals and Public Knowledge." In *Adaptations: From Text to Screen, Screen to Text*, edited by Deborah Cartmell and Imelda Whelehan, 113–27. London: Routledge, 1999.

Rice, Louisa. "The Voice of Silence: Alain Resnais' *Night and Fog* and Collective Memory in Post–Holocaust France, 1944–1974." *Film and History* 32, no. 1 (2002): 22–29.

Robinson, Benjamin. "*The Specialist* on the Eichmann Precedent: Morality, Law, and Military Sovereignty." *Critical Inquiry* 30 (2003): 63–97.

Rothberg, Michael "W. E. B. Dubois in Warsaw: Holocaust Memory and the Color Line, 1949–1952." *Yale Journal of Criticism* 14, no. 1 (2001): 169–89.

Scollen-Jimack, Christine. "Diane Kurys: From *Diabolo Menthe* to *La Folie*: Whatever Happened to Sisterhood?" *Forum for Modern Language Studies* 35, no. 3 (1999): 322–30.

Shandler, Jeffrey. *While America Watches: Televising the Holocaust*. New York: Oxford University Press, 1999.

Silverman, Max. "Horror and the Everyday in Post–Holocaust France: *Nuit et brouillard* and Concentrationary Art." *French Cultural Studies* 17, no. 1 (2006): 5–18.

Skoller, Jeffrey. "The Shadows of Catastrophe: Towards an Ethics of Representation in Films by Antin, Eisenberg, and Spielberg. "*Discourse* 19, no. 1 (1999): 131–59.

Stein, A. "Humor and Irony in Two Films about the Holocaust." *Bulletin trimestriel de la fondation Auschwitz* 42–43 (1994): 83–94.

Suleiman, Susan Rubin. "History, Memory, and Moral Judgment in Documentary Film: On Marcel Ophul's *Hotel Terminus: The Life and Times of Klaus Barbie.*" *Critical Inquiry* 28 (2002): 509–41.

—. "Jewish Assimilation in Hungary, the Holocaust, and Epic Film: Reflections on István Szabó's *Sunshine.*" *Yale Journal of Criticism* 14, no. 1 (2001): 233–52.

Thornton, William H. "After the Carnival: The Filmic Prosaics of *Schindler's List.*" *Canadian Review of Comparative Literature* 23, no. 3 (1996): 701–8.

Van der Knaap, Ewout, ed. *Uncovering the Holocaust: The International Reception of* Night and Fog. London: Wallflower, 2006.

Viano, Maurizio. "*Life Is Beautiful*: Reception, Allegory, and Holocaust Laughter." *Film Quarterly* 53, no. 1 (1999): 26–34.

Waller, Marguerite. "Signifying the Holocaust: Liliana Cavani's *Portiere di notte.*" In *Feminisms in the Cinema*, edited by Laura Pietropaolo and Ada Testaferri, 206–19. Bloomington and Indianapolis: Indiana University Press, 1995.

Wiedmer, Caroline. "*The Nasty Girl.*" In *The Claims of Memory: Representations of the Holocaust in Contemporary Germany and France*, 87–103. Ithaca, NY and London: Cornell University Press.

Wildt, Michael. "The Invented and the Real: Historiographical Notes on *Schindler's List.*" *History Workshop Journal* 41 (1996): 240–49.

Wilson, Emma "Material Remains: *Night and Fog.*" *October* 112 (2005): 89–110.

Wood, Robin. "Gays and the Holocaust: Two Documentaries." In Hornstein and Jacobowitz, 114–36.

Wright, Melanie J. "'Don't Touch My Holocaust': Responding to *Life Is Beautiful.*" *Holocaust Studies* 9, no. 1 (2000): n.p.

Zielinski, Siegfried. "History as Entertainment and Provocation: The TV Series *Holocaust* in West Germany." In *Germans and Jews since the Holocaust: The Changing Situation*, edited by Anson Rabinbach and Jack Zipes, 258–83. New York: Holmes and Meier, 1986.

Zierler, Wendy. "'My Holocaust Is Not Your Holocaust': 'Facing' Black and Jewish Experience in *The Pawnbroker, Higher Ground*, and *The Nature of Blood.*" *Holocaust and Genocide Studies* 18, no. 1 (2004): 46–68.

INDEX